Love Songs

Love Songs

The Hidden History

TED GIOIA

OXFORD
UNIVERSITY PRESS

OXFORD
UNIVERSITY PRESS

Oxford University Press is a department of the
University of Oxford. It furthers the University's objective
of excellence in research, scholarship, and education
by publishing worldwide.

Oxford   New York
Auckland   Cape Town   Dar es Salaam   Hong Kong   Karachi
Kuala Lumpur   Madrid   Melbourne   Mexico City   Nairobi
New Delhi   Shanghai   Taipei   Toronto

With offices in
Argentina   Austria   Brazil   Chile   Czech Republic   France   Greece
Guatemala   Hungary   Italy   Japan   Poland   Portugal   Singapore
South Korea   Switzerland   Thailand   Turkey   Ukraine   Vietnam

Oxford is a registered trade mark of Oxford University Press
in the UK and certain other countries.

Published in the United States of America by
Oxford University Press
198 Madison Avenue, New York, NY 10016

Library of Congress Cataloging-in-Publication Data
Gioia, Ted.
Love songs : The hidden history / Ted Gioia.
pages   cm
Includes bibliographical references and index.
ISBN 978-0-19-935757-4 (hardback : alk. paper)
1. Love songs—History and criticism.   I. Title.
ML2854.G56   2015
782.42—dc23   2014018842

9 8 7 6 5 4 3 2 1

Printed in the United States of America
on acid-free paper

For my wife, Tara

The book of love has music in it.
In fact that's where music comes from.
—Stephin Merritt from *69 Love Songs*

CONTENTS

INTRODUCTION AND ACKNOWLEDGMENTS

I can see, from handwritten notes in my journals, that the first stirrings of this project date back to 1991. The initial core idea arose from my growing interest in the role of music as a change agent and a source of enchantment in day-to-day life.

With the benefit of hindsight, I believe I can identify a turning point in my own conception of music—a seed planted by chance that made this work not only possible, but perhaps even inevitable. Many years ago, a passing comment from philosopher and art critic Arthur Danto caught my interest and, although I didn't realize it until later, set me on a new course. In one of his essays, Danto predicted that the future of art would be marked by a return to what had always been its fundamental purpose, namely enriching the lives of individuals, communities, and societies. He dismissed the pervasive view that art would "advance" as a quasi-science in pursuit of "progress"—a broken-down model that many music critics and historians still pay lip service to, even as it fails to explain many of the most influential developments in recent decades. "The time for next things is past," Danto insisted. "After that there is nothing to do but live happily ever after.... One must learn to live within the limits of the world. As I see it, this means returning art to the serving of largely human ends."

I probably read these words some time in the late 1980s, but several years elapsed before I realized that Danto had actually laid out a promising line of inquiry into the history of music that few had pursued. I began asking myself what this history would look like if it were written from the perspective of everyday life and human needs, and not as a litany of great composers and celebrated performers. How did we get to this "happily ever after"? Could I possibly write this history myself?

As my mission became clearer, I realized that I wanted to tell the hidden history of music, *not* the familiar and hyped accounts of a few famous artists strutting on the concert hall stage or working in a recording studio, but the real story of song as it has transformed the intimate lives of millions of people. This alternative view struck me as all the more essential in the current day, with the music world becoming ever more stratified and celebrity-driven, an enterprise in which a tiny number of individuals gain renown and riches as performers, and everyone else gets relegated to the audience or, even worse, to the faceless "metrics" that now drive the global entertainment business. Despite the relentless commoditization of the art form, I firmly believe that songs possess a force of magic, of enchantment, a metaphysical, quasi-spiritual dimension that gets lost in star-driven accounts of music-making. It is hardly a coincidence that the Latin word for singing, *cantare*, can also refer to an incantation, a magic spell. That magic of music belongs to all of us, always has, and I wanted to write a history of music that acknowledges its potency.

For a number of years, my researches into these issues were scattershot and without definition. I read and took notes, and increasingly focused on sources far beyond those usually consulted by music writers. I uncovered new perspectives on music in the least expected places: folklore, myths, works of anthropology and social history, travel literature, journals and memoirs, epic poetry, scientific studies, scriptures of various creeds and sects, ancient texts written in cuneiform or hieroglyphs, even paintings on the walls of caves, among other disparate sources. I found my studies exhilarating, but for a long time I despaired of ever bringing these bits and pieces together into any kind of coherent account. Yet gradually my efforts coalesced around a series of clearly defined projects. I eventually realized that I could tell this hidden history by isolating specific strands in the rich tapestry of human song. Almost a decade ago, I published the first results of this expansive project in two companion volumes, *Work Songs* and *Healing Songs*.

At that time, I promised that I would follow up these efforts with a third book, on the history of love songs. But even as I made that promise I felt enormous trepidation about embarking upon such a daunting task. After all, most of our music-making since the beginning of time has been about love. Even after years of research into the social history of music, I had doubts about my ability to circumscribe this subject. Adding to the difficulty, the history of love songs branches off into so many other related areas, each thorny and complex. I realized that to tell the full story, I would also need to trace the history of ritual and romance, courtship and marriage, morals and sexuality, and many other matters far beyond those typically dealt with by music scholars.

I had few guides to rely on. No one had ever written an adequate survey of the love song. At first that surprised me, because this subject looms so large in the history of music. But as I measured the full scope of the project, I was no longer puzzled by this striking omission in the literature. Who could really get their arms around such a huge, amorphous topic?

Despite my doubts, I persisted in my research and eventually gained traction and momentum from the surprises I began to encounter. As I probed more deeply, I discovered that the conventional accounts of the love song were filled with gaps, phony generalizations, blatant errors, and misleading theories. The real innovators in the history of the love song were, again and again, written out of the history books. The key turning points in the evolution of the love song not only got misinterpreted but sometimes were erased from the surviving accounts. In a very real sense, the history of the love song was, I discovered, a secret history.

For a long time I puzzled over the emerging pattern. I have never seen myself as a revisionist historian. I invariably feel scorn for researchers who come up with extravagant theories that sacrifice empirical evidence in favor of shock value. I don't like spin, hype, exaggeration, or political correctness masquerading as scholarship. Yet the story of the love song, as I pieced it together, made clear to me that the innovations in this music came mostly from the marginalized and bohemian, the outsider and the upstart, peasants, slaves, prostitutes, and others operating on the fringes of society. Women, in particular, played a much larger role in the evolution of this music than I had ever suspected—in fact, as the following pages will make clear, they have contributed many of the key components that have come to define the love song. The conventional histories usually downplayed or even eradicated the role of these innovators and in the process often gave undue credit to the rich and famous, the established and respected. I soon saw that, whether I wanted to or not, I would need to take on the role of the revisionist if I hoped to tell this story with any depth or honesty.

Even after the mounting evidence became irrefutable, I wondered why this should be true. How did historians get so much of this story wrong? A long time elapsed before I fully realized the larger import of what I was seeing. I didn't comprehend, until many years into my research, how radical and disruptive the love song has been during almost every period in history. The established powers resist innovations in love music because these emotionally charged songs inevitably give rise to a growing sense of individualism and personal autonomy. Over the centuries, the love song has repeatedly challenged authoritarian rule and patriarchal institutions. It has demanded not only freedom of artistic expression, but other freedoms in matters both intimate and public. Moreover, these songs usually came from the young and disenfranchised, arriving on the scene with a vigor and insistence that unsettled the old and entrenched. At first I thought it must be mere coincidence that new styles of romantic music always seemed to spur backlash and social upheaval. Finally I understood that the power brokers had reasons for combating this music, and for rewriting the history books later to hide their tracks.

In casting a light on this process, I also uncovered a peculiar dialectic at play in the evolution of the love song—one that further serves to obscure the real story behind this body of music. The love song, repeatedly over the course of centuries, *turns into its opposite.* When the unruly upstarts and outsiders create new ways of singing about love, they almost always encounter an intense backlash. They are branded as sinners and radicals, and frequently face punishment as threats to society and corrupters of youth. But when these songs survive the opposition and eventually get adopted by the power elites—whether the Confucian scholars of antiquity, the singing lords of the troubadour era, or the raised-on–rock 'n' roll rulers of our current day—the music that once inspired fear and trembling gets legitimized, even enshrined as a cherished part of the national or global culture. The earlier battles are often downplayed or even forgotten, and thus omitted from the historical record. But behind many of these now respected innovations in love songs, the careful researcher can frequently reconstruct a bloody sequence of events.

So you can imagine my amusement when I encounter people who, when I tell them I am writing about the history of love songs, respond with a dismissive smile. In their opinion, this is *wimpy* music. They would have more respect for me if I were writing about thrash metal or the twelve-tone row. But if you stay with me until the end of this volume, you will learn that the love song deserves respect as the toughest and most battle-hardened mode of artistic expression. It has survived heated repressions and suppressions, even violence and executions, and almost always in the name of expanding the orbit of freedom and human rights. Those who prize the outré and cutting edge take note: the love song has earned its avant-garde credentials again and again, trailblazing at the forefront of social change, and will likely play that same role again in the future.

But even as I made a case for the defiant force of the love song, I also found myself growing more deeply attuned to the paradoxical nature of its power—which, in its purest form, often resembles the renunciation of power. The love song is the quintessential music for those moments when we let down our guard, leave ourselves defenseless, and accept the experiential richness of our deepest emotional vulnerability. Even as this music has stirred anger and outrage from its opponents, its own embedded messages have been built on (almost by definition, I dare say) more tender emotions. I came to see this part of my story as just as important as its larger social dimension, and perhaps even more timely given the current forces at play in our society. During the course of writing this book, I couldn't help remembering a strange prediction made by the late David Foster Wallace in 1990. Noting that the pervasive irony and cynicism of late twentieth-century art and culture no longer seemed quite so edgy and perhaps had reached an irreversible point of fatigue, Wallace wondered whether the next wave of rebels might go in the opposite direction and "risk accusations of sentimentality.... Of overcredulity. Of softness." This book, which charts how such "soft rebellions" have taken place in the past—and how they might do so again in the future—perhaps embodies precisely that type of risk.

A work of this scope couldn't have been written without the help of numerous scholars with expertise in a wide range of disciplines. I could never mention all those who influenced and shaped my understanding of the love song over the more than two decades that this project has been simmering. But I can list those who saw parts of the completed manuscript and gave me invaluable feedback.

In particular, I would like to thank Gordon Braden of the University of Virginia; Mary Ellen Brown of Indiana University; Matilda Bruckner of Boston College; Jerrold S. Cooper of Johns Hopkins University; Anthony M. Cummings of Lafayette College; Peggy Day of the University of Winnipeg; Patricia Fumerton of University of California, Santa Barbara; Simon Gaunt of King's College London; Bryan Gillingham of Carleton University; Thomas Habinek of University of Southern California; Judith P. Hallett of University of Maryland; Edward O. Henry of San Diego State University; Martin Kern of Princeton University; Donald Kroodsma of University of Massachusetts, Amherst; Suzanne Lord of Southern Illinois University; Robert Magrath of the Australian National University; Donna L. Maney of Emory University; Susan McClary of Case Western Reserve University; Timothy J. Moore of the University of Texas at Austin; Stephen Parkinson of St. Peter's College, University of Oxford; Diane J. Rayor of Grand Valley State University, who also graciously gave me an advance look at her new translation of Sappho for Cambridge University Press; Edward L. Shaughnessy of University of Chicago; Theron Stimmel of Texas State University; Johanna Stuckey of York University; and Blake Wilson of Dickinson College. I must exempt them, and all others who assisted me in this project, from any failings or limitations of the finished work. Some of them would no doubt disagree with various interpretations and conclusions presented in this book, but in every instance I learned from their guidance and feedback.

I am especially indebted to my brothers, Dana Gioia and Greg Gioia—how blessed I am to have siblings who know so much about music!—both of whom offered comments on parts of the manuscript. I also want to offer thanks to Rez Abbasi, Sam Abel-Palmer, Scott Timberg, and Jesse Sheidlower for their input. And I must express the deepest gratitude to Suzanne Ryan and her colleagues at Oxford University Press for their guidance and support.

Finally I offer my most heartfelt thanks to my wife, Tara, and my sons, Michael and Thomas, who have been my joy and delight and constant support, both when I am working on a book and at all other times. All my personal love songs are devoted to them.

Love Songs

CHAPTER 1

Birds Do It!

Birds do it. Bees do it...
Let's do it. Let's fall in love!
—Cole Porter, "Let's Do It"

Birds do it. Bees do it.

Or do they?

Did the love song begin here, in nests and hives, on trees and in the air? Attempts to explain the appeal of the love song—and, in fact, all kinds of music—from an evolutionary perspective often start by looking at the courting activities of birds and other animals. Artists would have good reason to be rankled at this genealogy. The creation of art—the making of something new where there was nothing before—was once seen as analogous to the divine force itself. But if artists once claimed kinship to God, they now find themselves categorized as mere imitators of the birds and the bees.

Darwin was quite insistent on this matter. The birth of music, he claimed, was best understood by studying the melodic vocalizations of the animal kingdom, especially those of birds. In *The Descent of Man* (1871), Darwin devoted almost twice as much space to bird songs as to human music. He saw these melodies, which play an important part in courtship and mating, as the prototype for more advanced types of music. Just as birds sing to attract the opposite sex, "primeval man, or rather some early progenitor of man, probably first used his voice in producing true musical cadences.... This power would have been especially exerted during the courtship of the sexes,—would have expressed various emotions, such as love, jealousy, triumph,—and would have served as a challenge to rivals." Put simply, all songs were originally love songs.

In its long history, music has brought people together in many ways—in work and worship, ritual and recreation, and other settings where social cohesion can benefit from its aural glue, its ability to transform isolated individuals into a larger whole. The love song, the focus of our attention, brings people together on a more intimate level, but even here the diversity and range of its uses are remarkable, encompassing everything from purely procreative purposes to the most stylized forms of modern-day romance. All kinds of coupling, even those that involve more than just a couple, have found expression in song, but also the metaphysical yearnings for a higher love untarnished by the desires of the flesh. The love song sometimes comes to us embedded in ritual and ceremony, or broadcast over the airwaves and through cyberspace, but it can also flourish when hidden from view during a private moment or clandestine rendezvous. Each of these demands our attention as we explore the history of this multifaceted music.

Darwin, for his part, aimed to trace all these manifestations back to the same biological origins; and once he found this key, he decided that it unlocked many doors. Early human songs of courtship and mating also served, he surmised, as the foundation for language. Not just vocal music but, according to Darwin, even instrumental performances had their roots in the animal kingdom. He called attention to the "drumming to the snipe's tail, the tapping of the woodpecker's beak," perceiving them as the forerunners of our musical rhythms. He heard prototypes for human song in the croaks of frogs and the squeaks of mice, in the sounds of alligators and tortoises, even in the "pleasing" notes produced by the "beautifully constructed stridulating organs" of insects and spiders.

The music of modern times, he insisted, continues to bear the traces of these evolutionary origins. "Love is still the commonest theme of our songs," Darwin noted. Nor should this be surprising. "From the deeply-laid principle of inherited associations, musical tones in this case would be likely to call up vaguely and indefinitely the strong emotions of a long-past age." He pushed his premise to lengths few are willing to travel, asserting confidently that birds "have nearly the same taste for the beautiful as we do. This is shown by our enjoyment of the singing of birds, and by our women, both civilized and savage, decking their heads with borrowed plumes, and using gems which are hardly more brilliantly colored than the naked skin and wattles of certain birds." The many philosophers who have debated the nature of our aesthetic sense may be pleased or dismayed, as they see fit, by the apparent simplicity of this solution to the problem of music's origin. No longer need they, like Pythagoras, seek for the source of music in the harmony of the spheres, but in the precoital squeals and grunts, the chirps and croaks of mating season at the zoo.

Darwin's focus on bird songs may appear odd at first glance, given the apparently wide evolutionary and biological gap between humans and birds. Monkeys or gorillas, with closer kinship to us, might seem more appropriate test cases for his theories. But though Darwin briefly examined the connections between primate calls and human music, the evidence drawn from such examples, as we shall see later, is far less compelling. The vocalizing skills of birds, in contrast, provide a dazzling demonstration of melodic inventiveness and purposeful sound-making.

The sheer variety of some species rivals that of skilled human musicians. The nightingale knows hundreds of songs, and ornithologists Donald E. Kroodsma and Linda D. Parker have written about a brown thrasher who, based on analysis and recordings, appeared to have a repertoire of more than 1,800 different song units. Yet, other species, such as the European redwing and white-crowned sparrow, know only one song, and others offer no melodies when courting their mate. But is this all so different from human societies, where both the pop song crooner and the so-called "strong, silent type" can find true love?

Almost from the start, scholars from a range of disciplines attempted to rebut Darwin's views on music. "In my opinion the simple beating of a drum contains more 'music' than all the sounds uttered by birds," wrote music historian Richard Wallaschek in 1893. Three years earlier, sociologist Herbert Spencer had published his refutation of Darwin's theory of music, in which he noted the many instances of birds singing outside of mating season and the prevalence of animal calls unconnected with courtship:

> The howling of dogs has no relation to sexual excitements; nor has their barking, which is used to express emotion of almost any kind. Pigs grunt sometimes through pleasurable expectation, sometimes during the gratifications of eating, sometimes from a general content while seeking about for food. The bleating of sheep, again, occur under the promptings of various feelings, usually of no great intensity—social and maternal rather than sexual. The like holds with the lowing of cattle. Nor is it otherwise with poultry.

Speaking perhaps for many Victorians, the celebrated art critic John Ruskin went even further in his criticism, not only rejecting the attempt to ground aesthetics in mating behavior, but taking particular exception to Darwin's focus on "obscene processes and prurient apparitions." (Perhaps Ruskin's own sexual squeamishness came to the forefront here—according to some commentators, he never consummated his marriage because he was so distraught over the unexpected discovery, made on his honeymoon night, that women possess pubic hair.)

Yet even Darwin hedged his bets, noting that bird songs serve an additional purpose, allowing the mate to assert territorial claims as well as court the female. But he gave little emphasis to this more belligerent function of music. One might indeed argue that war songs, not love songs, inspired the vocalizing of our earliest singing ancestors. Could this hypothesis provide a more appropriate evolutionary explanation for the origin of music? Researchers Edward Hagen and Gregory Bryant have recently argued that the role of music and dance in human natural selection derives from its unsurpassed power in drawing people together into large groups, rather than merely pairing men and women into procreating couples. Its evolutionary purpose in human societies, under this hypothesis, was coalition formation for war and other collective projects. In traditional societies, they argue, humans sing and dance in groups, not in couples or alone. Also humans show a marked preference for singing in same-sex groups. And certainly communal war songs outnumber personal love songs in many preindustrial cultures. Hagen and Bryant's hypothesis is further supported by studies showing that men and women asked to rank the attributes that attract them to the opposite sex give low marks to vocal qualities. According to the skeptics, if Darwin were right in linking the birth of human song to mating practices, a resonant voice or perfect pitch would rank higher on the desirability scale.

Meanwhile a growing body of research has documented the aggressive qualities of bird song. In the 1970s, ornithologist Douglas Smith found that birds surgically deprived of their singing ability were far more susceptible to territorial intrusions by other males. In some instances, however, they apparently continued to mate with females. Around this same time, zoologist J. R. Krebs demonstrated that when recordings of a male's song are played on loudspeakers, the sound alone can dissuade rivals from entering his territory. Although birds do not sing in unison, the way a human choir might, they will cooperate with other members of their group in establishing territorial rights by means of song. Even the apparently romantic dueting practices of male and female songbirds may be, according to zoologist Wolfgang Wickler, as much signs of cooperative territory-claiming as they are protestations of undying love. From this perspective, bird songs didn't evolve into love songs, but they did anticipate Neighborhood Watch.

Darwin's case is hardly strengthened by a consideration of the singing behavior of primates. "In contrast to birds, singing behavior is rare in mammals," writes primatologist Thomas Geissmann, who notes that it can be found in only 11 percent of primate species. This comparative scarcity of singing primates does not prevent Geissmann from surmising that "loud calls in modern apes and music in modern humans are derived from a common ancestral form of loud call." Yet even granting this, one is hard-pressed to see this early vocalizing as linked to mating and courtship. "If this interpretation is correct," Geissmann continues, "early hominid music may also have served functions resembling those of ape loud calls. Loud calls are believed to serve a variety of functions, including territorial advertisement; intergroup intimidation and spacing; announcing the precise locality of specific individuals, food sources or danger; and strengthening intragroup cohesion."

What has love to do with all this? Apparently very little. Geissmann concludes by suggesting that the functional role of early hominid music was "to display and possibly reinforce the unity of a social group toward other groups." Musician

Leonard Williams, father of the renowned guitarist John Williams, spent many years living amid a community of monkeys and thus had the dubious privilege of hearing and watching them fornicate on a regular basis. He too concluded that their calls and cries were "in no way connected with mating behavior." They do make sounds when they copulate, but these are "sighs, sobs, grunts and squeaks, and are anything but musical."

But just when Darwin's proposed evolutionary connection between animal songs and human music courtship seems about to collapse for lack of evidence, genetic science rushes to his rescue. In just the past few years, researchers have uncovered a host of hitherto unsuspected biological connections between music and sexual behavior, as well as between bird song and human music-making. The hormone vasopressin and its avian counterpart, vasotocin, have emerged as the key "missing links" connecting these different spheres of behavior. The injection of just a tiny amount of vasotocin in a frog's brain immediately leads to the initiation of mating behavior, and stimulation of vasopressin receptors in certain brain regions can turn a promiscuous vole into a monogamous one. Some have even started calling vasopressin the "monogamy hormone." A 2001 study found that young chicks exhibited less social inhibition when exposed to oxytocin or vasotocin, or—in a surprising discovery—to recordings of Beethoven *Hammerklavier Sonata*. And what about humans? Researchers have found that vasopressin not only plays a key role in regulating our sexual behavior—men in a state of sexual arousal show markedly higher levels—but is also linked to musical aptitude in humans, and even to receptivity in listening to music. If song and sex share the same hormonal triggers, might they also possess an intertwined evolutionary history?

And the plot thickens! Research conducted by Sarah Earp and Donna L. Maney at Emory University in 2012 shows that the neural patterns in female songbirds when exposed to the mating songs of males of their species resemble neural responses in the mesolimbic reward pathway of humans enjoying a musical performance. Neuroscience strikes another blow for Darwin! And, coming back full circle to *The Descent of Man*, recent research tells us that the avian hormone vasotocin, which differs by only one amino acid from our "monogamy hormone" vasopressin, is connected to increased singing by male sparrows and the acquisition of stable stereotyped song patterns in songbirds. Certainly there are many missing evolutionary links between the white-throated sparrow and the *Homo sapiens* performing in a rock band, but the basic functionality seems the same. Survival of the fittest is, at least to some extent, survival of the most melodic.

But the best evidence linking music and human mating behavior requires no observation of birds or monkeys, or unraveling of DNA strands. Just listen to the radio. In a survey of thousands of commercial recordings, evolutionary psychologist Geoffrey Miller found that 90 percent were recorded by males, most of them made during their peak years of sexual activity. This finding matches results, drawn across a wide range of species, that mating display practices tend to be exaggerated in one sex. If we judge by the *Billboard* charts, males initiate most of the musical courtships in human society, just as with Darwin's birds. (This finding is all the more striking when we consider the evidence, presented in the following chapters, that women have played a decisive role in shaping many of the key characteristics of love songs—but, as we shall see, even when women serve as innovators, men often move to the forefront as performers.) "Music is what happens," Miller explains, "when a smart, group-living, anthropoid ape stumbles into the evolutionary wonderland of runaway sexual selection for complex acoustic displays." He sings a song or, even better, has a hit record on the charts.

Oddly enough, the age and gender profile of recording artists is also strikingly similar to that of murderers. Some have suggested that homicidal behavior is also a type of sexual competitiveness, albeit much more disruptive on the community than performing a love song. We have already noted a puzzling overlap, in our consideration of bird songs, between the music of mating and the music of aggression. This seemingly paradoxical correlation between love and violence will also recur at several later stages of our history.

If you are still skeptical about music's role in sexual selection, consider the topics of human songs. Almost every hit record is about love or, increasingly in recent years, sex. And, yes, male singers are much more likely to refer to copulation in their songs—reminding us again of the similarity between pop crooners and mating birds. Indeed, love has been a dominant theme of popular song for at least a thousand years. Almost everything else about our musical lives has changed during this period. We have moved from monophonic chant to polyphony (and back to monophonic chant again, on many rap records). We have plugged in electric instruments, and then abandoned them for software and samples. We have digitized, uploaded, downloaded, streamed, and done a bunch of other things to our tunes that Schubert or Gershwin would never have sanctioned or imagined. But still, when we sing, we sing about love and sex.

If this model of sexual selection is correct, we should be able to measure female preference for men who are most skilled at making songs. I have already noted that perfect pitch doesn't get a guy a date on Saturday night, but if we probe deeper, we uncover surprising correlations between vocal qualities and perceived sexiness. Recent research confirms that men find higher-pitched female voices more attractive. By the same token, females tend to rate men with lower voices as more appealing, and the level of attraction rises when the women surveyed are ovulating. These low male voices are correlated with higher levels of testosterone and thus plausibly linked with success in fathering children.

(A 2007 study of hunter-gatherers in Tanzania, selected for research because no birth control was practiced by the community and tribe members select their own spouses, showed that men with lower voices had more offspring, but the pitch of women's voices had no correlation with the number of their children.) Women also pay closer attention to men with lower voices, as measured by studies testing memory retention. But the most unexpected finding came in a 2002 study showing that both male and female subjects, presented with two photographs and a recording of a person's voice, could match the photo and voice—of a total stranger!—with 76.5 percent accuracy. So even if we don't put vocal quality at the top of our list of desirables when scanning the listings at matchmaking websites, we clearly pay close attention to the sound of potential mates, perhaps more than we consciously realize.

What about other signs of musical ability? Do women prefer musicians over nonmusicians? The evidence suggests that they do. A recent study in France found that a man who approached random women in a shopping district and asked for their phone number had far greater success if he was carrying a guitar case. The musician successfully got the phone number in 31 percent of instances. When the same man was empty-handed, only 14 percent of women complied with his request. A similar study conducted in Israel found that women who received an unsolicited Facebook friend request were almost three times more likely to accept if the sender was shown playing a guitar in his photo. Then again, we hardly need statisticians to tell us that women are attracted to musicians— just read the autobiographies of male pop stars for salacious firsthand confirmation, or stand outside the stage door at the local rock concert and observe this mating behavior for yourself.

The average male has seven female sex partners over the course of his life, according to the National Center for Health Statistics, but Mick Jagger has allegedly slept with more than four thousand women. So much for getting no satisfaction! I do not attribute Jagger's superior procreative odds to his good looks, but perhaps others will disagree. As for Gene Simmons, the bassist for the band KISS, fans can hardly tell what he looks like behind all the clown makeup, but he has provided an actual count of sex partners—a staggering 4,897 women. In an interview with NPR's Terry Gross, the rocker summed up his sexual success in simple, if crude, terms: "If you want to welcome me with open arms, I'm afraid you also have to welcome me with open legs." To which the typically nonjudgmental Gross responded, not without justification: "That's a really obnoxious thing to say."

Researchers have found a correlation between teenagers listening to these copulatory songs and trying out some of behavior patterns described in them. Are you surprised? Outraged parents, without the benefit of statistical research to back up their hunches, have long aimed to regulate the music choices of their children, sensing some inexorable connection between songs and promiscuity. Their worst fears were perhaps best summed up by the famous classicist and curmudgeon Allan Bloom, who announced that "rock has the beat of sexual intercourse," a verdict that spurred endless debate on the morals of our times. But Bloom ought to have pointed out that the tango and the turkey trot were both condemned by religious authorities in the early twentieth century for similar reasons, as was the waltz in the nineteenth century, and the sarabande back in the sixteenth century. And who dares doubt that the lute music of the medieval troubadours titillated young listeners of its time and spurred them on to bouts of tumultuous lovemaking? Or that the fertility songs and dances of ancients led to, at a minimum, some steps in the direction of fertilization?

But which is the cause, and which the effect? Do we engage in courting behavior because we are interested in these songs? Or do we favor these songs because we are ready for romance?

The persistence of the love song throughout human history testifies to its hold on us. More than a cultural meme, it appears to be some sort of quasi-biological necessity. This persistence is all the more impressive given the fierce opposition these songs have faced over the centuries—indeed continue to face in the modern day—from parents and teachers, religious and civic leaders, politicians and censors, and various other upholders of public virtue. The history of the love song is also the history of the repression of the love song. And it is certainly no coincidence that the most ardent opponents of this music are males and females *outside* their peak years of reproductive activity. These are the folks who hold most of the prerogatives of power in society—always have, always will. But in this matchup between opponents, the smart money is on the love song. For, as we shall see again and again in the coming pages, it inevitably wins out in the end.

CHAPTER 2

Procreative Music

Systems of European morality go back to the opposed temperaments of those who thought copulation was good for the crops, and the opposed faction who thought it was bad for the crops.—Ezra Pound

The love song is as old as human history. Or perhaps I should say, the *fertility* song is as old as human history.

Musical expressions of romantic love, without overt connection to procreation, are less easily found in early societies. "There are in fact very few songs about personal love among those primitive peoples who have not passed out of the stage of hunting and food-gathering," writes scholar Leonard Williams. Colin Turnbull reached a similar conclusion during his stay with the Ik tribe in the mountains of Uganda. Based on his experiences there, he concluded that amorous love and other tender feelings, "far from being basic human qualities," were merely "superficial luxuries we can afford in times of plenty." In environments of scarcity or uncertainty, personal sentiments give way to communal needs and survival. Love is not a primary concern, or at least not romantic love as defined by our current-day popular culture, although copulation and fertility must always be.

Even in these settings, love songs can be found, but they are very different from those familiar to us today. In his 1962 account of his life with the Alawa tribe of Australian Aborigines, Waipuldanya notes that men may sing magical love songs for help in securing a mate, but Western notions of courtship and romance play no part in this process. "There is no cuddling in the Alawa," he explains. "There were no endearments, no fondling, no sly caressing in the dark, and certainly no kissing." His own engagement for marriage took place without a single word passing between himself and his bride-to-be. "Most aboriginal partners," he adds, "do not kiss even after marriage." Historian Frank Linderman encountered a similar situation when researching Native American cultures in the 1920s. "Tell me of your marriage.... Did you fall in love?" he inquired of an elderly Crow woman. "No," she replied, "young women did not then fall in love."

In the Disneyfied version of Native American life, as presented in the animated film *Pocahontas* and other such excursions in poetic mythmaking, Western notions of flirtation and wooing are imposed on traditional cultures that gave them little scope in mating arrangements. The reality of early hunting societies is that the imperatives of sex and procreation, aided by the prodding of elders, served to bring couples together—ends that could be achieved without kissing, cuddling, and romantic music to seal the deal.

But we can't put these traditional societies behind us quite so quickly. The long stretch of time during which *Homo sapiens* survived as hunter-gatherers— a period that accounts for approximately 99 percent of our history as a species—must have exerted a profound impact both on our later love life and on the songs and imagery that still surround it. Many of the musical instruments we use today evolved from primitive hunting practices: the horns of animals were turned into musical horns, the hides into drums, the bones into flutes. Even in modern times, we have seen the bows and sticks that killed prey transformed into musical instruments, sometimes in ways that have an uncanny bearing on our history of the love song. During his time with an isolated Bushman hunting community in the Kalahari Desert in the mid-1950s, Sir Laurens van der Post learned that the chief hunter, Nxou, was also the leading musician of the tribe; the same bow served him in both capacities. In this setting, a tribal member who wished to court a woman would carve a miniature bow and use it to shoot a tiny arrow that had been dipped in a love potion into the buttocks of the desired lady. If she did not immediately extract the arrow from her rump, this indicated that she would accept his advances. The similarity between this practice and the Western myth of Cupid, with his bows and arrows of love, is uncanny.

As we explore various courtship practices in the pages ahead, we will do well to remember that the quest for a suitable mate is itself a type of hunting and that the music that accompanies it not just a passive soundtrack, rather a formidable tool that, in the hands of a skilled hunter, contributes to success in the chase. The connection is most obvious when relationships are dysfunctional; here even the language we use—terms such as *stalker* or *predator*—come from the terminology of the hunt. But our licit and consecrated mating routines also retain these primal overtones, and if they are hidden in public discourse, they often come to the forefront in our music.

The situation was the exact opposite among our earliest ancestors, where lovey-dovey notions of romance, if they existed, probably played a minor role in the sanctioning of relationships; rather, such sentiments may have been seen as obstacles to the pragmatic goals of family elders and communities. But, as noted above, these societies could hardly have existed without a frank assessment of the demands of sexuality and propagation—and not just for themselves but also for the animals and plant life on which they depended. Thus at the very beginning, before there were ten commandments, simply one mandate existed: "Be fruitful and multiply," is the oldest requirement of humanity in the Judeo-Christian tradition, the divine insistence on copulation preceding all other rules and regulations. It is specified in the very first chapter of Genesis, where the injunction is explicitly linked to the management of the food supply: "Be fruitful, and multiply, and replenish the earth, and subdue it: and have dominion over the fish of the sea, and over the fowl of the air, and over every living thing that moveth upon the earth."

I have written elsewhere about the musical life of hunting societies, where song and dance are closely integrated into the subsistence needs of the tribe. The rituals of music-making in these societies frequently involve what we would today call *sympathetic magic*—the belief that what we sing and dance about will come true in the external world. For example, A. W. Howitt has described the opossum dance practiced by the Aboriginal people of southeastern Australia in which the entire process of hunting, finding, and killing the animal was performed in pantomime. Geoffrey Gorer has documented a similar antelope-hunting dance performed by a fifteen-year-old boy in Yamoussoukro in the Ivory Coast. The Andaman Islanders of an earlier day mimicked the motions of the swimming turtle in their hunting dance, and the Wahehe of Tanganyika imitated the cries of the elephant in their hunting songs. The underlying philosophy was: If you imitate them, they will come.

Strange to say, hunting rituals are also part of our story of love songs and very much aligned with the mandate to be fruitful and multiply. These traditional hunters were not just cold predators; they also cared about the well-being and propagation of the animals they killed. Their hunting was not like modern warfare or our debased video game models of conflict in which winners kill and losers get killed. The early hunter and his prey were linked in a synergistic relationship, in which both needed to mate and prosper in order for the tribe to survive. In such environments, the line between human and animal blurs; sometimes hunters are so closely identified with the prey that they adopt its identity as their personal name or totem. This connectivity is invariably reflected in the musical lives of these traditional societies, where men and women often join in the magical mimicry of songs and dances performed to ensure the procreation of the animal population.

Folklorist Frank Hamel, writing in 1915, described a Mandan animal festival "at which a man, painted black to represent the evil one, enters a village from the prairie, chases and terrifies the women and acts the part of a buffalo in a dance which is intended to ensure a good supply of this valuable animal during the year to come." Other tribes perform "a similar masquerade, in which males, dressed in buffalo skins, take the part of male buffaloes and the females personify the female animals, with a view to bringing about an increase of the species." Heinrich Botho Scheube, a German physician, observed a similar bear ritual among the Ainu people of Sakhalin, where not only both men and women participated, but a young bear was suckled by one of the females of the community. An anonymous observer among the Wolof tribe in West Africa documented the "dance of the amorous mallard," in which a couple emulate the mating of ducks to the accompaniment of a song with explicit lyrics. T. G. H. Strehlow witnessed the "kangaroo increase" ritual of the Australian Aborigines at Alice Springs in 1933 and another seventeen years later at Jay Creek, a ceremony treated with such secrecy by the participants that Strehlow believed he was the first outsider to observe it.

Perhaps these were our first love songs, performed to ensure procreation, but not in the way Darwin envisioned. They aim to propagate the species, but not *our* species. They were passed on from generation to generation, not through DNA, but as a cultural meme. The persistence of these songs of sympathetic magic into recent times does not necessarily disprove Darwin's thesis, but does remind us that belief systems and ritual are also very much a part of our inquiry into the origins and nature of the love song, just as important as the dictates of biology and physiology. Certainly we will encounter them at every turn in the pages ahead, as they shape not only our songs of romance and courtship but even the nature of love itself, as it too follows a development path of its own over the course of centuries.

With the rise of agricultural societies, the songs and rituals associated with fertility take on even greater cultural significance. I suspect that this new fixation with propagation is due to the potentially devastating risks associated with a more settled form of life. Hunting tribes were often nomadic, and if prey in one area became scarce, they could move on to other, more promising territories. But in a farming community, crop failure could lead to famine and death before the tribe had the opportunity to cultivate other grounds. In such settings, not just physical labor but psychic energy must be applied tirelessly to maintain the fertility of the land. Inevitably these societies matched their own annual cycle to that of the soil, and virtually every facet of their culture—myths, songs, dances, beliefs, celebrations, work and play and, yes, lovemaking—dealt in some degree with the recurring death and rebirth of the crops.

Even their gods needed to adjust to this cycle. Christianity has no monopoly on a deity who dies and is resurrected. Wherever we look in early agricultural societies, we find comparable traditions connected with the annual reawakening of vegetative life. In Egyptian mythology, Osiris rises from the dead, his return associated with the fertile soils enriched by the flooding of the Nile. Ishtar, the Babylonian goddess, descends to the underworld, her departure signaling the death of the crops and the cessation of sexual activity—again the perceived linkage between vegetative and human fertility—while her return coincides with the regeneration of the fields. In ancient times, her cult allegedly involved ritualized prostitution, condemned by the Greek historian Herodotus as "the ugliest of the customs among the Babylonians." Every woman was required to participate "once in her lifetime," he explains in a passage that has spurred much scholarly debate. On her arrival at the temple, she takes a seat and "may not go home until one of the strangers throws a piece of silver into her lap and lies with her, outside the temple." Even earlier we encounter Inanna, the comparable deity in Sumerian mythology. She is depicted on the famous Uruk Vase, one of the oldest surviving works of relief sculpture, dating back before 3000 BC. The bottom tier depicts the cultivated vegetation of the Tigris and Euphrates, and above it a row of naked men carry offerings of fruit and grain to the goddess.

At first glance, the ancient Jewish religious tradition stands out as the notable exception here, and monotheism in general might seem an inhospitable belief system for fertility deities and their rites. But we shouldn't underestimate the effort spent by ancient Jewish leaders in battling against these practices. The female followers of Tammuz, consort of Ishtar and another fertility god who descended to the underworld, are mentioned in the Book of Ezekiel—where the prophet decries the abomination of women weeping for Tammuz at the very gate of the Temple in Jerusalem. The story of Moses's outrage when he found his followers worshipping the golden calf is merely another example of this conflict. The calf was often a symbol of fertility and in this instance may have represented the Canaanite deity Baal or Egyptian Apis, dying-and-rising fertility gods worshipped by the Hebrews' ancient neighbors. Note that Moses's anger—so extreme that he throws and shatters the tablets containing the Ten Commandments—is spurred not so much by the golden calf itself as by the sight of the children of Israel singing and dancing, with abandon and perhaps unclothed, around the idol. Few details are given, yet the story—especially the prominent role of music in this account and the implied link between the idolatry and sexual license—makes clear both the persistence of the fertility song even in monotheistic religions, and the zeal with which such practices were combated.

These pagan tendencies were never completely eradicated. Long after the rise of Christianity, aspects of fertility rites persisted. Indeed, the very name *Easter* probably comes from Eostre, the Anglo-Saxon goddess of spring, who some believe may have a connection to the same Ishtar whose beloved Tammuz was decried by the prophet Ezekiel—perhaps via intermediaries, such as the Greek Astarte or the "Lady Ashtarot" mentioned in the Etruscan Pyrgi tablets discovered in 1964. Other hints and survivals of pagan fertility rituals continue to find expression in the present day. Religious leaders have typically shared Moses's abhorrence and desire to extirpate them, but sometimes even the most devout have been blind to the sexual symbolism hidden in time-honored observances.

Almost every early religion had a sex fixation, marked by recurring rituals devoted to these dying deities. From Quetzalcoatl of the Aztecs to the Japanese
Izanami, this figure plays a role in many belief systems and cultures. A host of
musical traditions were influenced by the ceremonies and beliefs associated
with these myths, not just love songs but also festive dances, religious and ritual
music, even laments. The last were expressions of mourning for the dead god,
and represent the flip side of the fertility song. In the current day, the idea that
the music of sexualized love is inextricably linked to songs for the dead would
strike most as strange, perhaps even absurd, but that connection will recur in
later centuries. It is perhaps no coincidence that Christian leaders for a thousand
years lumped together love songs and musical lamentations as sinful, typically
blaming both on women, who the clerics believed were especially susceptible to
the pernicious influence of these melodies. Long after the pagan origins of these
songs had been forgotten, the upholders of Christian virtue sensed not only the
danger they posed to the established religion, but also that these two kinds of
music were closely related. Both were eventually assimilated into Christianity,
which found that it too could benefit from the musical incitement of fervor for a
dying-and-rising deity. But that is far ahead in my story.

Our understanding of the linkage between fertility rites and love songs was
greatly enriched by the discovery of a small, battered alabaster disk in the sands
of southern Iraq in 1927. Here Sir Leonard Woolley worked for more than a
decade, excavating the ancient Mesopotamian city of Ur, under conditions so
severe that even his makeshift residence required the assistance of a hundred
men laboring four days to remove the sand from the summer's excessive sand-
storms, while in the rainy season he and his colleagues were sometimes waist
deep in water. These experiences, combined with his discovery of a deep layer
of alluvial clay, led him to propose that the flood described in Genesis had taken
place here, where the waters had covered so much land survivors believed that
the whole world had been inundated—certainly *their* entire landscape had been
afflicted. Indeed "Ur of the Chaldees" is cited in Genesis as the birthplace of
the patriarch Abraham, and the city is mentioned four times in the Torah. But
the disk of Enheduanna, discovered by Woolley, refers to a period even before
that of Abraham, whose dates are typically placed by scholars at some point between 2000 and 1500 BC. Enheduanna, the high priestess and poetess of Ur,
precedes him by roughly a half millennium. Her story begins during the reign of
her father, King Sargon of Akkad, who conquered the Sumerian city-states in the
twenty-third century BC.

The disk discovered by Woolley was in fragments, and he eventually concluded that it had been deliberately defaced. But the image of a woman in a ritual
procession could be clearly seen, and an inscription identified her as Enheduanna, further explaining that she was depicted in the act of dedicating a dais

in the temple of Inanna. In the engraving, Enheduanna is dressed in ceremonial attire, but she and her two companions are led by a naked male priest.

When these fragments were unearthed, no one had heard of Enheduanna. Archaeologists eventually recovered more than one hundred clay tablets covered with hymns attributed to her. Here in the desert sands, they had found the oldest poet commemorated by name in the history of literature—not just the first female author but the earliest identifiable literary figure in human civilization, man or woman, whose works have survived. More than a millennium before Homer and some 1,700 years before Sappho, Enheduanna had been honored for her writings, which were carefully preserved by later generations. Yet her most important work was not translated until 1968, and even today her name is hardly known outside specialists in Assyriology.

Then again, the title of poet may be misleading. The Sumerian poetic tradition was dominated by musical considerations. Often the lyrics are specifically designated as songs, and even lengthy narratives that might seem part of a storytelling tradition are labeled as *sir-gida*, "long songs." In many instances, a musical instrument is specified, as with *balag* songs, *tigi* songs, and *adab* songs, which refer to the string or percussion instrument that accompanied the pieces. In other words, this ancient tradition was more performance than literature, more song than poem, although many scholars, mesmerized by the cuneiform inscribed on clay tablets, have emphasized the text over the context.

We will encounter this bias again and again in the course of our survey of love songs. To some extent music scholars are themselves to blame for this distortion. The subject of love songs—or indeed of any vernacular song embedded in the day-to-day life of ordinary people—rarely gets their attention, and they are perhaps even less interested in musical traditions that haven't been preserved in notation, and thus involve nonmusicological skills in interpretation. As a result, the study of the Greek lyric or the troubadour song and numerous other musical traditions are often defined and codified by scholars without specific musical training. Song is described in the terminology of literary criticism, and an oral/ aural tradition is dealt with as if it were merely a series of texts. Any researcher probing into the early history of the love song needs to compensate for this distortion at almost every turn.

If the surviving texts ought to be understood as parts of songs, the songs in turn must be understood in the context of rituals. And the study of Sumerian love songs leads us inevitably to one of the most intriguing and mysterious rituals of the ancient world, namely the so-called *sacred marriage*. We will almost certainly never know the origins of this practice, which must long predate even the distant day of the priestess Enheduanna. Neolithic carvings from Mesopotamia from before the year 5000 BC show copulating couples, and these perhaps represent an earlier version of this ritual, but we can do little more than speculate about its nature at that distant point in time. Nor can we be certain when the ritual came to an end; long after the decline of the Sumerian civilization we encounter it in Greece, where it is known as *hieros gamos* (or "holy marriage"), and it may have survived in Rome too, although the question of whether these later traditions encompassed an actual sexual union, or were merely a matter of myth and symbol, is open to debate.

The concept of the sacred marriage is a simple one. In the Sumerian version, a king makes love to a goddess, and the society is rewarded with prosperity, perhaps abundant crops or, at a minimum, stability in the political order. After all, who would question the legitimacy of a ruler so honored by a deity? In ancient Mesopotamia, many kings may have fulfilled this function, but the role of husband to Inanna was most closely associated with Dumuzi, the third king in the legendary first dynasty of Uruk, who was worshipped as a deity and served as a precursor to the Babylonian vegetation god Tammuz. The part of the goddess was almost certainly performed by a priestess or votary of Inanna.

Surviving texts describe the king traveling to the temple of the goddess in conjunction with the celebrations for the New Year. He wears a ritual garment with a headpiece and brings with him sacrificial animals. Inanna is bathed, and scented oils are sprinkled on the ground. A marriage bed of cedar and rushes has been prepared. The couple lie together and join in lovemaking. The following day a ritual banquet is celebrated.

Perhaps, as some suggest, this was all symbol and pretense. Scholars often try to explain away explicit references to sex in venerable lyrics—in fact, the fervor with which some experts attempt to purify old texts is almost puritanical in its intensity—and the Sumerian love songs are no exception to this tendency. Yet the vivid language of the surviving hymns would indicate otherwise. The proximity of her lover has filled Inanna with such passion that, as described by scholar Samuel Noah Kramer, "then and there she composes a song for her vulva in which she compares it to a horn, 'the boat of heaven,' to the new crescent moon, to fallow land, to a high field, to a hillock," and ends by demanding "Who will plow it for me?" How does her royal visitor respond? "Oh Lordly Lady, the king will plow it for you, Dumuzi, the king, will plow it for you." His ability matches his willingness. For, as the hymn notes: "At the king's lap stood the rising cedar."

Could this really be all talk, no action? Other evidence tends to confirm that the sacred marriage rite was a real encounter, not just a mythic tale. In his excavations of the Temple of the goddess Ningal, Woolley found a low platform, which he believed might serve as the base for a ceremonial bed, in a prominent room of the shrine. A surviving stele mentions a gold-encrusted bed of Ningal, and Woolley may well have discovered its site. Another document lists marriage gifts presented to the goddess in conjunction with the New Year festival, and these confirm the importance of the ritual as well as its likely recurrence in an annual cycle. Royal hymns and inscriptions repeatedly describe the king as husband of Inanna, and clearly not only the fertility of the land but the legitimacy of the ruler depended on this relationship. Given both the wealth of detail and the psychological imperatives associated with this union, I find it difficult to settle for a symbolic interpretation of the evidence.

Kramer believed that the Song of Songs, a cornerstone of Jewish and Christian scripture attributed to King Solomon, is simply a variant on these love songs associated with the sacred marriage rite. Drawing on the work of scholar Theophile Meek, Kramer argued that the *Song of Songs*, or at least a considerable part of it, "is a modified and conventionalized form of an ancient Hebrew liturgy celebrating the reunion and marriage of the sun-god with the mother-goddess, which had flourished in Mesopotamia from earliest days." Under this interpretation, the Hebrews borrowed the sacred marriage and its fertility cult from the Canaanites or another neighboring culture, which in turn had adopted them from Akkadians, who had inherited them from the Sumerians.

This proposed lineage is conjectural but could explain the puzzling presence of erotic poetry in Judeo-Christian scripture. In fact, the Song of Songs makes no direct reference to God and, despite the attribution to Solomon, is presented largely from a female perspective. Theologians, scholars, and church leaders have wrestled with these passages for centuries, and although a few have raised doubts about the work's canonical status, most have adopted a symbolic interpretation of the text. Sanitized in this manner, the Song of Songs is not really about sex but rather allegorizes God's love for his chosen people, the children of Israel. Or perhaps it symbolizes Christ's love for the Church, or the soul's love of God. Or maybe, as Martin Luther insisted, the Song of Songs is a political allegory. These and other interpretations may have disagreed about the specific nature of symbolism, but they almost always concurred that readers of scripture needed to look *beyond* its erotic content.

But even those who offered these comforting explanations often perceived the dangers of such frank expressions of lust in a holy book. The third-century theologian Origen, who played a key role in propagating a respectable Christian interpretation of the work, nonetheless recognized its connection to the pagan *epithalamium*, or wedding song—a tradition whose insistent eroticism is discussed in the pages ahead—and advised those who were not of a sober and mature state of mind to avoid reading this particular book of the Bible. The risk was less for Origen himself since he had already shown his spiritual devotion by castrating himself. But others, less equipped spiritually if better equipped physically, could easily be led astray.

Although they had no concept of the sacred marriage rite of the pagan Sumerians, these later upholders of Judeo-Christian respectability actually came close to matching the original impetus behind the ancient fertility rituals in their interpretations of the salacious scriptural text. If, as they suggest, the Song of

Songs is *really about* a bond or covenant between the divine and the human and not just a wallowing in the erotic, the same can be said for the pagan lyrics about a king making love to a goddess. In both instances, the song seeks to secure or commemorate the divine blessings on the true believers, and—as in any marriage—love and sex serve to cement the bond.

But are these Sumerian and other ancient lyrics really love songs? Yitzhak Sefati uses precisely that term in his influential 1998 collection *Love Songs in Sumerian Literature*. Scholar Steve Tinney, for his part, prefers the term *sexual lyric*. Certainly the frankness of some of the texts could make a rapper blush, and they would no doubt require a parental warning label if anyone ever put them on the shelf at Walmart. Yet many have been drawn to these lyrics all the more because of their explicit nature. "The very existence of an ancient body of religious literature that sang praises to a woman's vulva fascinated me," admits Betty De Shong Meador, who would later translate many of these texts into English. "I began to track down the original Sumerian texts. Did the Sumerian language version really say 'vulva'?" Many are inclined to say that these songs, and their attendant rituals, are no more about love than, say, *The Vagina Monologues* or a copy of *Playboy* magazine, yet it's hard to draw the line between love and sex, whether you're in a relationship or merely studying Sumerian texts. I tend to concur with scholar Gonzalo Rubio, who concludes that "in spite of all possible pitfalls and shortcomings of generic labels, the term 'love' does seem appropriate for the contents of most of these lyrics, whether this love is full of carnal passion, or as elusive as a mere hint of what may have perhaps been an ancient ritual." Certainly by the time we get to the text of the Song of Songs, probably written no earlier than the tenth century BC, a more pronounced element of personal love and romantic longing has clearly entered the picture, with expressions familiar to us from modern-day songs: "Your love is more delightful than wine.... How beautiful you are my darling.... How handsome you are my beloved," and so on.

This intimate and confessional tone is even more evident in the surviving love lyrics from ancient Egypt. These remarkable songs from the nineteenth and twentieth dynasties, dating back to between 1300 and 1100 BC, are surprisingly similar to modern-day love ballads in tone and intent, and represent a clear break with the fertility music of earlier Mesopotamian culture. Like our own songs, the Egyptian lyrics celebrate the union of man and woman for the delight it brings rather than for procreative purposes. Unlike their Sumerian precursors, the Egyptian songs have little concern for weddings, whether real or symbolic, and the lovers depicted are young and apparently unmarried, although far from chaste and virginal. The consummation of their relationship has no impact on the crops or the prosperity of the community, and if the couple were prevented from fornicating, the gods would not be angry, although the lovers themselves might be sorely disappointed.

Here is a typical lyric, as translated by Egyptologist John L. Foster:

I love you through the daytimes,
   in the dark,
Through all the long divisions of the night,
   those hours
I, spendthrift, waste away alone,
   and lie, and turn, awake till whitened dawn.

These lines were found on fragments of a large broken vase excavated by French archaeologists from a trash pit at Deir el-Medina, a village once inhabited by artisans who helped build the tombs of the pharaohs in the Valley of the Kings. Other love lyrics from this period have survived on papyri, and present a similar tone of longing and desire, as well as a psychological depth and emotional content that have hardly aged even though three millennia separate us from the singers who first gave them expression.

This tone of ardent longing for the absent beloved is a new ingredient in the love lyric. The fertility rituals that gave birth to the oldest recorded love songs dealt only with successful couplings, and for a very good reason. Unhappy love songs had no place in a society that depended on the exemplary coitus between king and goddess, whose union would grant a beneficent propagation throughout the community for the good of all. But the Egyptian love songs, unlike their Sumerian counterparts, reveal a fascination with romantic frustration, with thwarted desire and its impact on the emotions and imagination. For the first time, song serves as an expression of romantic and sexual fantasy and as solace for those without a love partner. Today fantasy stands out as a key element in our love songs—perhaps the most decisive quality they bring to our lives, enabling the listener to experience vicariously the passion and intense feelings only rarely granted by our quotidian routine. But the creators of these ancient songs understood that an imagined encounter could bring its own kind of satisfaction to the denied lover. In the song that scholar Michael V. Fox has dubbed "Seven Wishes," the male singer offers a series of fantasies about his beloved:

If only I were her Nubian maid,
   her attendant in secret....
If only I were the laundryman...
Then I'd rub my body
   with her cast-off garments....
If only I were her little seal-ring,
   the keeper of her finger.

The meaning of these lyrics seems clear, although some have sought for alternative explanations, finding a purpose and orientation in them different from our own love songs. Perhaps, according to one theory, these aren't fantasies but magical incantations. I have already noted that a belief in sympathetic magic—the notion that "like produces like"—served as the foundation for the fertility songs that launched us on this human endeavor of singing about love and desire. And certainly the ancient Egyptians put great faith in the value and efficacy of incantations in matters of love, death, and almost everything else of importance in their life. It is also worth recalling that sorcerers often require some item—a piece of clothing, a snippet of hair, a nail clipping—from the person who is to be charmed. Under this interpretation the lover in the lyric wants to rub his body with the discarded clothes of his beloved not for sexual arousal—or not *merely* for sexual arousal—but as part of this magical process of securing her affections. This is a *fetish* in the original sense of the term, namely an inanimate object that is believed to possess supernatural powers.

But the preponderance of evidence suggests that these Egyptian songs were performed for enjoyment, not magic or ritual. A few references to religious or cultic practices can be found in the texts, but the same would be true with the later love lyrics of ancient Greece or the troubadour songs of western Europe. The idea of a clear separation between secular and religious concerns may not have been easily grasped by the originators of this music, but from our vantage point, these songs come across as decidedly secular. The perspective presented is personal, even intimate, and I can easily imagine such songs performed at a banquet or to accompany dancers at a festive celebration. Portraits of female harpists or lutenists performing in such settings have survived, and though we cannot be certain that love songs were part of the repertoire on such occasions, objects mentioned in these lyrics that we still associate with romance, such as flowers or jewelry, are often depicted as well.

A few surviving Egyptian images indicate a close connection between music and sexual activity. An eighteenth-dynasty drawing on leather dating from around 1500 BC, found during excavations of a temple on the west bank of Thebes, depicts a woman playing the harp while a man with an oversized erection dances. In a Theban tomb from this same period we find the image of a female lutenist still holding her instrument while engaged in sexual intercourse. But a papyrus scroll now located in Turin provides an even more graphic enactment of Shakespeare's dictum that "music be the food of love." Found in Deir el-Medina in the nineteenth century, this depiction of a dozen erotic scenarios is commonly referred to as the Turin Erotic Papyrus, although some have joked that it deserves to be known as "the world's first men's mag." The copulatory acts shown here involve fairly unattractive fellows—ill-proportioned, balding, short of stature, but with massive genitalia—in a range of sexual positions with attractive and very limber young ladies. One of these women is shown letting go of her lyre, which she may have been using to entertain her companion a few moments before. Another has put aside a sistrum in order to engage in sex while sitting on a high stool. Perhaps some of these ancient images relate to fertility rites, but the specific scenarios chosen by the artist seem drawn from a brothel rather than a temple.

The Turin papyrus should have made clear that the ancient Egyptians, or at least some of them, looked to music as an erotic stimulant. Even so, many scholars have been shocked at the frank sexual content of the surviving love lyrics and have hesitated before sharing them in print. As noted an Egyptologist as Sir Alan Gardiner, whose *Egyptian Grammar* taught generations of scholars how to decipher hieroglyphs, second-guessed his own accurate translations of these love lyrics and agonized over their obscene and licentious content. This scholar, born and raised during the reign of Queen Victoria, found the sentiments in these texts so contrary to Victorian proprieties that he wrote a letter to Alfred Chester Beatty, owner of the papyrus that contained some of these indiscreet expressions, apologizing for his renderings in English. Scholar Erik Iversen of the Royal Library in Copenhagen was even more determined to eliminate the sexual references in these songs—so much so, that he embraced bizarre translations such as "He brings colour to my cheeks by vomiting persistently" where a reference to a phallus seems intended by the scribe. (Renata Landgráfová and Hana Navrátilová render these same lines, "He offered me the charm of his loins—It is longer than it is wide!")

Did women write these songs? Certainly many of the surviving lyrics present a female perspective. On the other hand, a theme of fantasizing and imaginative projection is prominent in these songs, as already noted, and thus the texts that apparently express a woman's viewpoint may simply represent what an Egyptian man *wished* his beloved would think, say, and do. That might also explain the appearance of musical instruments in the pornographic images from the Turin papyrus—pornography serving as the most extreme form of imaginative projection and thus plausibly associated with songs that filled a similar purpose.

Nonetheless the frequent appearance of female musicians in surviving artwork indicates that women played a significant role in the musical culture of the period. And the sentiments of the lyrics, for all their sexual references, tend more toward emotional release and self-expression than mere titillation. My belief—supported not just by the evidence here but also by similar patterns uncovered in the later history of love songs—is that women were the innovators and men the disseminators. In this instance, I suspect that the scribes who actually wrote down these songs were men, and much of the audience was male, but the original oral/aural tradition they took care to preserve originated with women, whose creative and expressive talents played the decisive role in the development of a new musical genre. To a certain extent, this is the story of the love song throughout history. In fact, a very similar dynamic occurs again in Egypt itself in the late Middle Ages, when a rich body of love songs was created by female slaves and imitated by their male owners—a development that anticipated the tone of romantic lyrics in Europe in ensuing centuries, and even in our own day.

Scholar Michael V. Fox believes that these Egyptian love lyrics, *not* the Sumerian fertility rituals, served as the primary role model and inspiration for the biblical Song of Songs. He notes that Egypt controlled Palestine during the period in which these songs were written down, and that the same scribes who handled official business may also have studied and disseminated literary works of this sort. He also identifies a dozen themes that appear in both the Egyptian and Jewish texts, including the "wishing" motif discussed above, which he sees reappearing in chapter 8 of the Song of Songs (which begins, "O that thou wert as my brother"), the traveling to a rendezvous, the invitation for the beloved to come away, the setting of the garden, and—perhaps the most characteristic image of the Egyptian songs—the lover at the door of the object of his or her affection. This last motif appears so frequently in later love lyrics and dramatic settings that it has even earned a technical name, the *paraklausithyron*, the lament outside the door, a timeless conceit that even survives in modern popular music, for example "Can't You Hear Me Knockin'" by the Rolling Stones, Bob Dylan's "Temporary Like Achilles," and Steve Earle's "More Than I Can Do."

But Fox is hard-pressed to explain how an erotic love song became a religious text. True, religious occasions in ancient Israel were not devoted solely to sacrifice and prayer, and the festivities may also have allowed for secular entertainments, but the idea that the Israelites would eventually forget the difference between the sacred and profane songs, when the lyrics made the contrast so obvious, is hardly credible. Even if the ancient Hebrews were familiar with Egyptian love songs, their willingness to incorporate similar expressions into their own scripture, as well as their later explanations and justifications for this unexpected intrusion of eroticism in religious texts, are far more reminiscent of the sacred Sumerian wedding ritual and its associated concept of an intersection between the human and the divine.

Any plausible genealogy of love songs, whether as biblical texts or in other settings, needs to acknowledge both these pathbreaking traditions. The Egyptians provide us with our first musical expressions of a personal, psychologically intimate love, enriched by imagery and emotional content that still ring the cash register for the music business today. From the Sumerian fertility rites comes a perhaps even more radical idea, that human love can partake of the transcendent, the notion of (if I can borrow the mantra of jazz icon John Coltrane) a *love supreme*. This latter view of love—and the love song—still survives today, although more on the outskirts of popular culture, yet it also has a prominent part to play as our story unfolds. Both these attitudes were necessary preconditions for the Song of Songs to achieve its significance and potency. From Egypt it took its lyricism and intimacy, and from Mesopotamia came the permission to view love and sexuality as connected to religious ritual and worship.

If the end result has struck later commentators as paradoxical or contradictory, the reason is clear enough. These two traditions in the love song do not mix easily and will continue to engage in battle over the next three thousand years. Time and again, visionary thinkers will try to reconcile their opposition, the same dialectical synthesis preserved in the Song of Songs reappearing two millennia later in the visionary efforts of Dante and Rumi, and more recently in the fervor, naïve and inspired at the same time, that gave expression to Woodstock and the Summer of Love. Even now, in our jaded secular culture, we harbor a yearning for a song of love that will take us higher and higher. We are attracted by the jolt of eroticism in our music, but crave the transcendent as well as the orgasmic. We want to bridge the gap between these two opposed views of love, and suspect that something intangible and almost metaphysical like a song might still be the means to do so.

CHAPTER 3

Sappho and Confucius

I must think maidenly thoughts. And utter them with my tongue.—Pindar

We now arrive at Sappho, the famous poet of Lesbos and (according to the usual accounts) the visionary whose example taught the rest of us how to express romantic sentiments in song form. Barbara Johnson, a longtime Harvard professor of literature, has lauded her as "the first love poet." Melissa Fran Zeiger makes an even bolder assertion, staking a claim for Sappho as the "originator of lyric poetry." Others have called attention to her importance as the earliest woman poet or the first to offer a female perspective in lyrical form.

As made clear in the previous chapter, none of these claims is strictly true. Other women anticipated Sappho's innovations, some of them appearing on the scene more than a millennium before the Greek poet's birth in the late seventh century BC. In addition to the Sumerian and Egyptian precedents already considered, other traditions from Asia predate her. Even within Greek culture, she may have been influenced by the Spartan slave poet Alcman or her contemporary (and alleged lover) Alcaeus of Mytilene.

Yet Sappho retains her importance despite these antecedents. Almost every key issue that will confront us during our study of the history of love songs comes to the forefront in our consideration of this seminal figure. Many of these questions already emerged in previous chapters. Can love songs partake of both the sacred and the erotic, or are these mutually exclusive paths? What contribution, if any, do love songs make to the flourishing of the surrounding community and society? Or do they pose a threat to the social order? How do these songs relate to rituals and ruling powers, or is their role private and intimate, sheltered from the conventions and expectations of others? Do women play a distinctive role in the history of the love song, or are their contributions largely interchangeable with men's? Has their role been deliberately marginalized by later commentators or exploited by more powerful parties in the cultural hierarchy? These questions have already entered our purview and we will need to deal with each of them again in the pages ahead, but Sappho also introduces new issues, forcing us to grapple with issues of gender roles and sexual preference and their impact on the music and the lyric. Indeed she is an important figure not just in the history of the love song, but in the history of love itself.

Yet how much do we really know about Sappho? Her name is resonant with meanings, but they are meanings mostly created by us, her readers, rather than coming from her. We know few facts about her life and the situations that inspired her works, except for what she reveals in her lyrics. And these are little more than scattered fragments. Ah, if only we had access to Chamaeleon's now lost study of the Sappho. Or to the equally missing exegesis by Callias of Mytilene. Or even to the once admired guide to Sappho's meters by Dracon of Stratonicea. But these commentaries, like much of Sappho's work itself, did not survive. And the sources that were preserved serve as much to mystify as to elucidate.

How do we make sense of these "facts"? A scholiast commenting on Lucian writes that Sappho was "very ugly, small and dark," but Socrates and others proclaimed her "beautiful"—Damocharis even compared the loveliness of her face to that of the goddess Aphrodite. Alas, none of the sources is reliable, all of them dating to a century or more after Sappho's death. We have less consistency in descriptions of her family life. One of our better sources offers no fewer than eight possible identities for Sappho's father: she is described as "daughter of Simon or of Eumenus or of Eerigyius or of Ecrytus or of Semus or of Camon or of Etarchus or of Scamandronymus." The rhetorician Aelian hardly helps when he tries to clear up the confusion by suggesting that two different Sapphos may have lived on the island of Lesbos, one a poet, the other a whore.

Scholars have adopted different strategies for dealing with these contradictions and open issues. My favorite: the entry on Sappho in *Lesbian Peoples: Material for a Dictionary*, published by Monique Wittig and Sande Zeig in 1976, takes up an entire page. I note that it is also a blank page. It thus provides what must certainly be the only error-free account of this celebrated ancient life. Indeed the room for confusion is so large that scholar Thomas McEvilley feels compelled to specify that "all external and internal evidence" about Sappho leads him to the conclusion that "she was a woman." Thank goodness for small favors!

Even the best-known fact about Sappho, her advocacy of same-sex love—amply documented by her surviving love lyrics and posthumous reputation—has stirred endless controversy and debate. The very term *lesbian* originated as a reference to Sappho's native Lesbos. Yet we are also told that she had a husband named Cercylas, with whom she raised a daughter named Cleïs, and that she composed songs to celebrate the weddings of other heterosexual couples. By more than one account she even committed suicide because of her unrequited love for a younger man, the boatman Phaon. These bits of evidence for the 'straight' Sappho are themselves open to doubt, perhaps offered for the purpose of sanitizing, scapegoating, or satirizing. Other sources suggest that, instead of killing herself for love of a sailor, Sappho lived to a ripe old age and, in the words of McEvilley, was "wrinkled and white-haired before she died." Even the name of her supposed husband, Cercylas, can be read as a punning reference to the Greek word *kerkos*, signifying "tail" or "penis." In other words, the 'straight' Sappho may be just a crude joke, just as the 'gay' Sappho, according to Victorian scholars who found such practices abhorrent, was a distortion and calumny. Aelian's report of two different Sapphos probably reflects an early attempt to 'purify' the poet's biography. Many others would try to do the same in later years.

In other words, Sappho's life story is as fragmented as her songs, which have come down to us in beguiling bits and pieces. But one fact is beyond dispute, namely the high regard in which Sappho's poetry was held by the ancients. "I know of no woman who even came close to rivaling her as a poet," writes Strabo in his *Geography*. In the *Palatine Anthology* we read the confident prediction: "No day will ever dawn that does not speak the name of Sappho, the lyric poetess." The lexicographer Pollux tells us that the ancient inhabitants of Mytilene on the isle of Lesbos even engraved Sappho's image on their coins. An epigram attributed to Plato hails Sappho as the "Tenth Muse."

Yet we can't help wishing that the ancients who so admired these lyrics had done a better job of preserving them. Only a few hundred lines of poetry have survived to document and validate this high-flung praise. Still, I'm hardly surprised. One of the takeaways of this book is that for a period of four thousand years, very few love lyrics by women survived except by chance or in mutilated form—or, on the rarest of occasions, in slightly better shape due to the intercession of an influential male, often a patron or slave owner, or perhaps a plagiarist. Sappho allegedly left behind at least nine volumes of poetry, yet you could read her extant work in less than an hour. Her most famous complete poem, her hymn to Aphrodite, was preserved in a work by a man, Dionysos of Halicarnasos, who relied on it as an example in his guide to literary composition. A handful of other poems have come to light in complete or mostly complete form; two new finds were announced as recently as January 2014, and the papyrus was in such good shape that not a single word was in doubt. But these are exceptions to the general rule: most of Sappho's oeuvre, as it has come down to us, is riddled with holes. Was this just shoddy record-keeping by the Greeks, or did other considerations enter into the process?

Although Sappho is typically referred to as a writer or poet, she was in fact what we would nowadays call a singer-songwriter. Her music was performed to the accompaniment of a lyre, hence the origin of the term *lyric poetry*, a label that would later be applied to spoken poems but initially referred to songs. Scholars sometimes label these works *melic poetry*—the Greek word *melos* signifies a melody but also can refer to the limb of a body, suggesting an original connection between the expressions of a song and the movements of a dance. Perhaps Sappho performed some songs in the context of a dance or a ritual involving movement by participants, but the intimate, expressive quality of her lyrics suggests that many of them were presented in less ceremonial settings, probably in small gatherings of women.

What were these songs about? Many topics emerge in the surviving fragments, but one subject predominates: love in its various manifestations. "What did Sappho of Lesbos teach her girls except how to love?" writes the poet Ovid. But these lyrics may not match our stereotypical notions of love songs, especially those from the later Western tradition of romantic or sentimental music. Expressions of same-sex love predominate, and cover the full range of emotional responses from respectful affection to jealous eroticism.

We are perhaps better equipped to grapple with these lyrics than the classicists of earlier generations who preferred a sanitized Sappho, and the respectability of the ancient poet has certainly risen in tandem with a view that her concerns are aligned with the sensibilities of our own times. Yet there are few counterparts in our day to the ritualistic and religious overtones that also permeate Sappho's surviving lyrics. And just as strange to our modern minds is the pedagogical and admonitory tone to her songs. She was clearly trying to shape the young ladies in her charge into poised adults—so much so that some, with only slight exaggeration, have seen her as a type of schoolmistress. So, yes, if Sappho were resurrected today, she might very well turn in her lyre for a guitar and spread her message as a singer-songwriter akin to Patti Smith or Joni Mitchell. But I could also see her with a bare-the-heart TV talk show, spearheading a social movement, or fostering a spiritual revival. Intimations of all those callings can be found in her fragments. If you can combine the notion of a love song with all that, you have made a start in comprehending the complex artistry of Sappho.

The complexity—and sometimes the seeming contradictions—in these lyrics are due not just to Sappho, but also the tradition she inherited. Even the earliest Greek expressions of love in the form of intimate verse are filled with surprises for those unfamiliar with this tradition. Archilochus, probably born around a half-century before Sappho, is sometimes lauded as the first lyric poet—although the title may not be strictly accurate given unanswered questions about the role of the lyre in his work, and how much of it was sung versus recited. Yet the frankly erotic content of his poetry has shocked many classicists. When a new poem of his, found on the wrappings of a mummy, was published in 1974, one reviewer jokingly referred to it as "Last Tango in Paros," an allusion to the X-rated Bernardo Bertolucci film of the same period and Archilochus's native island Paros. Guy Davenport renders the conclusion of this fragment in vivid phrases:

Touched her hot breasts with light fingers,
Spraddled her neatly and pressed
Against her fine, hard, bared crotch.

I caressed the beauty of all her body
And came in a sudden white spurt
While I was stroking her hair.

No, not much is left to the imagination here, but the reviewer's punning reference to Paros may be even more revealing than he intended. This island in the Aegean was known in ancient times for cultic activity devoted to Dionysus and Demeter, both deities connected with sexuality, fertility, and the harvest. Archilochus's specialty, a peculiar kind of blaming-and-shaming poetry called *iambus* (not to be confused with iambic meter), may have connections with these rituals. We have already seen a similar linkage between explicit lyrics and fertility rites in our exploration of Sumerian and other ancient songs, and here again we find a similar dynamic at play in these personal expressions of love and sexual intent among the Greek poets.

But the question immediately arises, how personal were these expressions? While readers have long enjoyed Archilochus's intimate disclosures, they may be misinterpreting the surviving fragments. A large body of evidence suggests that Archilochus may have merely adopted a ritualized role familiar to his audience, notably in those passages where he seems most revealing of firsthand experiences. The best-known love story in his poetry relates his broken engagement with Neoboule, and his subsequent abusive denunciation of her father Lycambes and his two daughters—vituperations alleging the young ladies' participation in orgies and full of other tawdry details. But the noted scholar of ancient music Martin L. West has offered a different interpretation, suggesting that this incident may never have happened. "The possibility I am suggesting," he writes, "is that Lycambes and his libidinous daughters were not living contemporaries of Archilochus but stock characters in a traditional entertainment with some (perhaps forgotten) ritual basis." West points out that Aristotle offers an almost identical story about a wealthy man named Telestagoras and his two daughters on the island of Naxos, just twenty kilometers from Paros. "The insulting of an eminent citizen and of his two marriageable daughters seems a strange coincidence," West notes. "I suspect that there existed on Naxos a traditional entertainment similar to what existed on Paros."

At the beginning of the "Last Tango in Paros" fragment, Archilochus not only engages in precisely this kind of role-playing, but even takes on the part of a woman. The text is not clear enough to provide a detailed interpretation, but the significance of a male poet adopting a female voice should not be minimized. One of the most important conclusions to be drawn from this book is that the men who had the most impact in shaping the prevalent tone and attitude of the love song, bequeathing to us much of what we continue to admire in lyrics of romance and courtship today, often adopted a feminine perspective, either explicitly or implicitly, in their own works. Scholars have exercised endless ingenuity in explaining away this recurring tendency for men to *sing as though they were women*, but rather than representing an aberration, this gender shift appears to be constitutive of love songs as a genre, and after the rise of the troubadours will become such a common ingredient of the lyric that audiences will take it for granted.

At this early stage of our study, the connections between women and love songs are often revealed in an unambiguously female narrative voice. Indeed, the connection could hardly be clearer in the case of Alcman, the first and oldest of the nine great lyric poets canonized by the scholars of Alexandria and Sappho's most important predecessor. Alcman is known to us as a composer of *partheneia*, or maiden songs, which were performed by choruses of young girls. Even before considering the surviving texts, we must be struck by the apparent peculiarity of a celebrated male poet writing "maiden songs," but Alcman is by no means the only example of this cross-gender ventriloquism among the leading Greek poets. A fragment from Pindar, famous for his stately victory odes and songs of praise, offers the unexpected confession, "I must think maidenly thoughts. And utter them with my tongue." A surviving Greek water jar from around the time of Pindar depicts bearded men dancing in female attire, and though the intent here is comic, the amusement it generated may well have been due to the complicated gender roles enacted in real-life performances.

The adoption of a female voice is far from the only surprising ingredient here. A consideration of the lyrics raises several other vexing questions. On a papyrus of Alcman's work now housed at the Louvre, we can read phrases that inevitably remind us of love lyrics:

> And no longer coming to Ainesimbrota's house will you say:
> "if only Astaphis were mine,
> or Philylla would look my way,
> or Demareta, or lovely Vianthemis—
> but Hagesichora wears me out with desire."

But there are just too many female names here—Alcman refers to ten different individuals in just eight lines—and this alone should signal that we are dealing with a complex constellation of relationships different from those we would nowadays associate with the love lyric. Alcman may well have been, as a later Byzantine lexicon attests, the inventor of the love song, but the texts he has bequeathed to us suggest that he is either angling for a large-scale orgy or, more likely, operating out of a cultural milieu very different from our own. Perhaps as Eva Stehle has suggested, this song was directed at "young men of an age to marry and their families," many no doubt in the audience, and the praise of the various singers aimed at touting them as potential brides.

We envision a love song as the expression of one person's longing for another, but Alcman's music was decidedly a larger scale affair. His work is representative of the Greek tradition of choral lyrics performed by groups of young women. Singing was only one small part of these gatherings. "The songs came alive in performance," writes classicist Gloria Ferrari, "which included much else that is not in the text, namely, settings, costumes, props, and lighting." In other words, this was not a forum for the expression of intimacies, rather a public spectacle—although perhaps one with intentionally erotic overtones.

But even more than spectacle, these performances were embedded in ritual and religious observances. "The chorus does not act for itself," classicist Claude Calame explains in his seminal 1977 study *Choruses of Young Women in Ancient Greece*, "but always exists for a special occasion, most frequently a cult." We find female choruses participating, for example, in rituals devoted to Artemis, where the performers are unmarried adolescent girls. This festival may have served as a rite of passage, a milestone event signaling that these young ladies were leaving behind childhood and had reached an age at which they could receive suitors. On the island of Delos, choral performances were also part of the worship of Apollo, as well as Aphrodite, goddess of love and beauty. Aristophanes, in his *Frogs* from 405 BC, tells of females who celebrate a festival devoted to Demeter, goddess of the harvest, and Pausanias, more than three hundred years later, is still citing women who sing and dance in honor of this deity. Dionysus, the god of wine and intoxication, also had his groups of female singers; he is often depicted as surrounded by a chorus of women famed for their Bacchic frenzy. At the Anthesteria, an Athenian festival in his honor, the wife of the Archon Basileus was even given as a ceremonial bride to Dionysos, although whether this represented merely a symbolic union or resulted in actual intercourse is open to debate. Here, and in other instances, we can see similarities to the older fertility songs of Mesopotamia, but now procreation is just one part of a larger picture. These rituals and their music contributed to the stately and harmonious ordering of society—or, perhaps in the case of the cult of Dionysus, acknowledged (and channeled) forces that could disrupt it. Love plays a role here. Just as it serves as a kind of emotional glue or bonding agent holding couples together for the good of the family unit, it also contributes to the prosperity and stability of the broader community. The emotional content here is valuable, and thus deserved celebration, but only as part of this larger vision.

The rites of Dionysos present an especially puzzling intersection of the sacred and the transgressive—a conjunction in which, again, groups of music-making women played a significant role. In *The Bacchae* by Euripides, one of our best sources of information about the cult of this deity, every sort of outrage and violation of propriety is attributed to the *maenads* (which translates literally as "raving women") who honor Dionysos, including drunkenness, sexual license, and violent dismemberment of Pentheus, the Theban king who opposes them. Pentheus even dies at the hands of his own mother, who is so besotted with the Dionysian rites that she does not recognize her son. Certainly a dramatic work can't be taken as a literal history, but the tone and specifics of this tragedy make clear that this deity both demanded respect and legitimately inspired fear. Here, too, the musical associations of these rituals present a marked reversal of gender roles. The dithyramb, a hymn associated originally with the cult of Dionysos, somehow emerged as a performance piece for choruses of Athenian men or boys, and eventually evolves into a staid literary and musical genre (perhaps even serving as the source of Greek tragedy), albeit now mostly purged of its original significations. We lack the sources to trace this process with any precision, but it seems likely that here, as elsewhere in our story, a dangerous and disruptive musical tradition associated with women gains respectability, and turns into a source of social stability when men serve as its exponents and adjudicators.

We need to keep these various traditions in mind when envisioning the social context for Sappho's work. Sappho was surrounded by a group of women, often called her 'circle'. At first glance, this seems straightforward enough. Aren't we all too familiar with celebrated singers having their own entourage or posse? Fame does have its privileges. But as soon as we try to define the nature of this circle our job gets harder, and scholars have hotly debated the relationship between Sappho and her followers. As noted above, some have seen Sappho as a kind of schoolmistress, educating and training the ladies in her charge. This view of the lyric poet is emphasized in a surviving fragment, probably from Kallias of Mytilene in the third century BC, who notes of Sappho: "She lived a tranquil life, teaching young women of good families." In recent years, this view has been attacked by those who see it as a way, in the words of Holt Parker, "to explain away Sappho's passion for her 'girls'," and he mocks the image of the poet as "a friendly spinster teacher at a boarding school." A competing interpretation views Sappho's circle as a less formal and more intimate gathering, a kind of private songfest or poetry reading among friends, but charged with a large dose of sensuality. A third perspective sees Sappho as something akin to the musical director of a choral society, her role similar to Alcman's with regard to the young ladies who sang his maiden songs in ritual observances. This interpretation also has a revisionist angle—it represents a marked departure from the once dominant view of Sappho as a performer of monodic (or solo) lyric rather than choral (or group) lyric, and conceives of her 'circle' as much more than an audience for her creative impulses, instead serving as active participants.

Although fierce debate has raged among the proponents of these different views, it is worth noting that they are not mutually exclusive. In fact, ample evidence can be mounted for each. Sappho could very well have had close and intimate relationships with young ladies even while leading them in musical performances and offering teachings and guidance on their path to adulthood. Job descriptions weren't so narrowly defined in ancient Greece. Imagine trying to write a CV for Socrates—encompassing his role in the education of young men, his reputation as a gadfly in public matters, and his career objective of philosopher-king—and you get a sense of the dangers in squeezing the innovators of antiquity into contemporary job titles. No, Sappho wasn't a frumpy headmistress, but (like Socrates) she clearly took an interest in the development of the youths in her charge, and showed a deep concern for the rituals and responsibilities that shaped their roles in the larger community.

So even as we admire Sappho for her love songs, we must acknowledge that they were more than just love songs. This fact deserves our close attention, not just to help us understand Sappho, but also to shake us out of the complacent assumption, pervasive nowadays, that songs are best understood as entertainment. Much of my research and advocacy in recent years has focused on undermining this assumption, on exploring ways music is enriched when it is embedded in the day-to-day lives of individuals, communities, and societies. Our songs are not lessened by these quotidian connections, but gain power and meaning, and I have illustrated how this takes place in hundreds of different contexts. For this reason, I am perhaps especially sensitive to the damage done when we remove this contextualization from our considerations of Sappho.

My view is that Sappho sits at the intersection of different traditions, drawing on earlier conceptions of the love song even while giving voice to new ones. The personal and expressive qualities in her lyrics, her transformation of public music into intimate memoir, may be the most influential turning point in the history of Western song. But she also saw her music as expressing more than mere emotions and eroticism. Her songs encompassed her *circle* as well, and were often marked by a sharp admonitory tone—again and again we encounter phrases of entreaty and command, expressions that reveal a strong-willed woman whose songs aimed for more than mere self-expression. Yet Sappho's concern radiated out into larger *circles*—I now use the term as symbol and metaphor—expressing her focus on the proper observances and rituals that ensured the harmonious ordering of the universe.

In Sappho's time, this harmony and order came less from social and political institutions, and more from the conscious alignment of human activities with divine mandates. Yes, we justly praise ancient Greece for its invention of direct, participatory democracy, but this radical experiment by the Athenians would not take place until after Sappho's death—indeed, the word *dēmokratía* did not even exist during her lifetime. For Sappho and her circle, and those wider circles of community and society, the center of their orbit was not the public square or town hall meeting, but the ritualized practices inherited from the past. So we should not be surprised to find evocations of the older fertility rituals coexisting side by side with the new confessional tone in Sappho's surviving fragments. In one of them, we hear direct reference to the myth of the dying god, the essential motif of these cultic practices, and the commandment for her young ladies to participate in mourning for Adonis, the expiring deity of beauty and desire: "Delicate Adonis is dying, Cytherea; what are we to do? / Beat your breasts, girls, and tear your clothes." As noted earlier, we tend to see the lament for the dead as a fundamentally different kind of music from the love song, but a close inspection of historical sources reveals that they overlap in their origins, and will retain a peculiar, albeit usually hidden relationship long after the time of Sappho.

Sappho also echoes her Sumerian predecessors in the close attention she pays to wedding rituals, and though these marriages apparently no longer involve a god or goddess but a real human couple, her concern over the proper observances indicates that deities still hold sway over this aspect of human affairs. We will revisit Sappho's role in the Western tradition of the *epithalamium*, or wedding song, later in this book, and at that point will take account of the surprising persistence of pagan fertility symbols well into the Christian era. It is worth noting here that this song was performed literally at the door of the nuptial chamber, sometimes right before the sexual union of the couple, or on the following morning to awaken the newlyweds. The song delivered outside a closed door is already familiar to us from the previous chapter, and will also recur in many different guises in the later evolution of love lyrics.

This ceremonial Sappho, who is so concerned with the proprieties of public events, stands in stark contrast to the private Sappho, also well documented in the surviving texts. In her expressions of personal love, decorum and ritual are pushed aside by the jealousy of the rejected lover:

> To me it seems that man has the fortune
> of gods, whoever sits beside you
> and close...
> my tongue is broken. A delicate fire
> runs under my skin, my eyes
> see nothing.

Love's turbulence and its power to disrupt come to the fore in other surviving texts from Sappho, as in this almost haiku-like image: "Love shook my senses, / like wind crashing on the mountain oaks." But perhaps most characteristic of Sappho, she sees no paradox in combining these intensely personal emotions with her invocation of the deities:

On the throne of many hues, Immortal Aphrodite,
child of Zeus, weaving wiles: I beg you,
do not break my spirit, O Queen,
with pain or sorrow.

The Greeks had always recognized the dangers of love, and after Sappho the darker side of *eros*, their term for romantic or sexual attachment, would predominate in ancient artistic treatments of lovers. We see this clearly in the lyric poet Anacreon, born around the time of Sappho's death, whose love themes often take on the tone of a warning, even as he exults in the joys of a lover: "I love again, and do not love; / I am insane, and still I'm sane." Or: "The dice that Eros plays with / are raving madness and battle din." The same attitude is evident in his contemporary Ibycus, also canonized as one of the nine great lyric poets of ancient Greece, for whom "love is at rest in no season . . . rushing from Aphrodite with scorching fits of madness, dark and unrestrained."

Those who claim "all the world loves a lover" have not taken sufficient notice of Greek culture in the aftermath of Sappho. The ancients clearly believed it was far wiser to *fear* the lover. Following Sappho's death, the Greek dramatists who took the lead in reworking mythic and historic narratives for their generation (and posterity) often built their plays around love stories, but now invariably emphasized the destructive or, in the case of comedy, the ridiculous aspects of love. The most famous lovers of Greek drama include Oedipus, who marries his mother, Jocasta—she hangs herself, and he is forced into exile; Medea, who punishes her ex-husband Jason by murdering their children; Clytemnestra, who murders her husband Agamemnon on his return from the Trojan War; and Lysistrata, who teaches the women of Athens that love is a tool to be used in the manipulation of their husbands. The Greeks may have invented many narrative devices and themes, but, judging by the surviving texts, the romantic comedy with a happily-ever-after ending was not one of them—at least not at this early point in the evolution of Greek theater. We need to search long and hard to find happy and fulfilled couples presented on stage during this period. "Tragedy's only significant depiction of a loving relationship between husband and wife," writes classicist Sue Blundell, "is to be found in Euripides' *Alcestis*." But Blundell needs to add that "the heroine agrees to die in place of her husband Admetus." For the Greeks, even well-matched romantic partners were courting disaster, and the very love that brought them together might destroy them.

We should not be surprised that lyric poets showed less interest in singing about love after the rise of the great Greek dramatists. Instead of praising the beloved, they now preferred to enumerate the perfections of athletes, warriors, and politicians, or to emulate the narrative coherence of the playwrights in lyrics that related edifying stories. This tendency reaches its culmination in the work of

Pindar, who continues to present his poetry in the context of music and dance, much like his predecessors, but with a far different purpose than Sappho and Anacreon. "When Pindar speaks pridefully in the first person," warns classicist Elroy Bundy in his influential 1962 *Studia Pindarica*, "this is less likely to be the personal Pindar of Thebes than the Pindar privileged to praise the worthiest of men."

Later generations did a much better job of preserving Pindar's poetry. More of his work has survived than that of any of the other canonic lyric poets of ancient Greece. Sappho's, in contrast, has barely survived at all. The oldest papyrus containing her work was found in the wrapping of a mummy, and I suspect the intent was to preserve the mummy, not the poem. Is this just a matter of happenstance, or were the stately sentiments of Pindar, aligned with the values of civic order and prerogatives of the powerful, considered more worthy of preservation? Even what the ancients allowed to survive, later upholders of moral values stepped in to destroy: We hear accounts of Gregory of Nanzianus ordering the burning of Sappho's works in 380 AD, and Pope Gregory VII doing the same in 1073. Yet Sappho does triumph in the end. We have followed in her footsteps, not Pindar's. We can recognize ourselves in the deeply personal emotions of her lyrics. Our sense of what a song can and should do is still shaped by the example she gave us. In our music, we do not seek oratorical eloquence or "the praise of the worthiest of men." We seek passion and intimate expression, especially in matters of the heart.

There is probably a story hidden here, a conflict whose details are now lost to us but are reflected in the tension between the ardent feelings of Sappho and the eloquent propriety of Pindar. This conflict between matters of the heart and the dictates of cautious authorities accompanies every step in the history of the love song, whether we consider Charlemagne's prohibition of *winileodas* (literally "songs for a friend"), religious leaders' condemnation of the sarabande in the sixteenth century, or the CBS censors who forced the Rolling Stones to change the words to "Let's Spend the Night Together" before they would allow the song on *The Ed Sullivan Show*. Social institutions are built on orderliness and constraint, limits not recognized by love or those who sing its praises. Whether Sappho encountered official opposition or slanderous rumor during her life, we cannot say. But her later caricatured figure in Greek comedies—plays lost to us but, based on what we know, "coarse and scurrilous enough and filled with absurd stories," in the words of classicist William K. Prentice—and the surviving descriptions of Sappho of Lesbos as whore or suicide victim suggest that this innovative singer of love songs was not without her enemies during ancient times.

As if to reinforce this point, the historian of love songs encounters another awkward encounter between the music of love and the dictates of social order at almost the same time as Sappho's birth, but in a far distant part of the world.

According to Chinese tradition, an unusual musical project came to fruition around the midpoint of the Zhou Dynasty, in about the sixth century BC. Songs had been gathered from the different feudal states of the empire—a kind of taxation of musical expression unprecedented in human history. Around three thousand songs and poems were eventually collected, and the task of selecting the best of the best was, according to tradition, undertaken by Confucius. These lyrics from different regions, now referred to as the "Airs of the States," were preserved in the *Shijing* (known in English as the *Book of Songs* or *Book of Odes*), a collection of around three hundred airs, odes, and hymns. The *Shijing* is a defining work of Chinese literature and one of the "Five Classics," ancient texts that, along with the "Four Books" of philosophy, constitute the canonical works of Confucianism.

Was Confucius really the song competition judge of his day, the talent scout who evaluated musical offerings from different regions and picked the winners? Scholars have their doubts and point out that later generations often linked Confucius to various texts on the flimsiest of evidence. Many of the songs in the collection appear to predate Confucius, perhaps by several centuries—the consensus view places the origins of these lyrics in the period between 1000 and 600 BC—although that does not prove he didn't play a role in their compilation. Certainly the *Analects*, the core text of Confucius's teachings, includes specific praise of the *Shijing*: "The *Odes* number several hundred, and yet can be judged with a single phrase: 'Oh, they will not lead you astray.'"

Such praise, however, came at a cost. As these words from the *Analects* make clear, the purpose of the *Shijing* was neither to delight nor entertain but to provide moral instruction. Rulers and their advisers would memorize these lyrics and quote them on appropriate occasions, drawing lessons that guided behavior and corrected failings. Historians of the love song find much to interest them in these ancient works, especially in the singer's recurring reliance on scenes drawn from nature to establish a tone for a romantic situation—for example, in the well-known lyric "Guan Ju," the opening poem in the collection, in which the description of an osprey calling to its mate evokes an account of a man's longing for his beloved. Yet the extensive use of symbolic resonance in these songs made them susceptible to a wide range of interpretative stances, some leading to very surprising and bizarre endpoints. Here, as at other key junctures in the long history of the love song, powerful interests attempted to prove that lyrics seemingly focused on romantic love were *really* about something else. We will be forced to decide between two responses to these denials. Either romance is not quite so central to the evolution of the lyric as surface meanings might indicate; or (and this, I believe, is the far more frequent case) the love song has played such a catalytic role in advancing individualism and personal autonomy over the course of history, that various authorities have looked to defuse its power by channeling its emotions into meanings less threatening to the status quo, whether religious, political, or patriarchal. Recent archaeological findings now provide us with an insight into how these lyrics were interpreted as far back as circa 300 BC, and even at this early stage commentators sought to draw moral lessons from the *Book of Songs*. These canonized works contributed to a well-ordered society, and if we wish to draw a comparison with the Greek lyrics, the *Shijing* is closer in spirit to Pindar than Sappho.

The *Shijing* has survived in better condition than Sappho's works, but clearly the moral authority of Confucius played a key role in ensuring the survival of these songs. Even so, copies of the *Book of Songs* were destroyed during the purges of the Qin Dynasty, when Qin Shi Huang, the first emperor to rule over a unified China, decided that political and social stability would be improved by burning books—which, at the time, were texts written on bound bamboo strips. Between 213 and 210 BC, countless works of poetry, history, and philosophy were destroyed. The *Shijing* managed to survive despite the conflagrations; the burning of texts could not eradicate lyrics so well known and probably committed to memory by many individuals. But the scholars who studied the Confucian classics did not fare so well. Just discussing *The Book of Songs* could result in execution. We are told that in the second year of the prohibition some 460 scholars were buried alive in the capital city Xianyang.

This was hardly the last obstacle faced by the *Shijing*. Many authorities who stopped short of book burning found cause for alarm in the classic texts. The love songs in the collection inevitably stirred up controversy, especially those candid lyrics that express female desire. Today we would find most of these lyrics plaintive rather than erotic, but some texts hint at a longing that, in the context of Confucianism, crossed the lines of decency. Among the songs gathered from Zheng, in current-day Henan province, we find:

> A very handsome gentleman
> Waited for me in the lane;
> I am sorry I did not go with him.

In this lyric from the same region, the lady adopts a bolder stance:

> There was a man so lovely,
> Clear brow well rounded.
> By chance I came across him,
> And he let me have my will.

We would like to know more about the women who may have been the original source of these songs, but the *Shijing* offers little information on the composers of its canonic works. Of the more than three hundred songs in this collection, only three identify the singer by name. So we are left with the unfortunate result that a famous man, in this instance Confucius, becomes the official mouthpiece for the romantic sentiments apparently expressed by an unknown woman. We have already seen King Solomon and Pindar step forward as spokesmen for maidenly sentiments, and we will find many more male authority figures willing to do the same in the pages ahead.

We are also left guessing about the settings in which these songs were performed. Were these formal performances or happenstance events? Was this music an entertainment for elites, similar to the later love songs of European court society? Or were these songs exchanged by actual lovers in the heat of real romance? We have little firsthand evidence to draw on, but the twelfth-century Confucian scholar Zhu Xi tells us that many of the songs of the *Shijing* are "ditties of the villages and backways. They are what men and women sang to each other, each articulating their feelings." This commentary comes long after the fact, but others have exercised great ingenuity in their efforts to confirm the folkloric roots of these songs. For example, C. H. Wang, following in the footsteps of Albert Lord and Milman Parry's work in Eastern Europe, undertook a statistical analysis that aimed to link these texts to an oral/aural rather than literary tradition.

Marcel Granet has suggested that these songs originated in seasonal festivals, when "youths and girls, who at other times were kept apart, met with those of neighboring villages. On these unique occasions the girls saw men who were not related to them, and boys saw girls who were not their sisters or cousins, girls of the neighborhood whom they could marry, while the girls saw the men for whom they would leave behind parents and brothers." Granet continues:

> Then, in addition to other contests and competitions which must have taken place, groups of boys and girls vied with each other in contests of song and dance which brought poetry into being at the same time as love. While the groups dancing in procession to the sound of drums were crossing the river or climbing the hill, from one company to the other were flung rhythmical challenges and provocative songs. In antiphonal lines or songs a duel of impromptu verse was indulged in, often beginning with raillery, a fact which explains the mocking tone of many of the songs.

Perhaps this is true, but the songs themselves are quite unlike most pieces originating in ritualistic and communal settings. They are personal and often intimate. They dwell on emotions and psychological details. In short, they are surprisingly modern, speaking to us in words that we would understand from contemporary song and poetry about love:

My sad heart is consumed, I am harassed
By a host of small men.
I have borne vexations very many,
Received insults not few.
In the still of night I brood upon it;
In the waking hours I rend my breast.

Is this raillery? Or is it what a later generation would call *melancholy*? Is this a song for public edification? Or for private catharsis? Or is it possible that here in the *Shijing*, as with the lyrics of Sappho, we are offered a glimpse into a cultural tipping point, that juncture in the history of music when the ancient songs, with their emphasis on ritual observances and communal needs, morph into anthems of individuals, expressions of personal emotion and desire not much different from those heard on the radio in the current day?

In other instances, ancient Chinese love songs depart markedly from familiar attitudes to romance. This comes across with particular clarity in the *Chu Ci*, sometimes known as the *Songs of the South*, compiled after the *Shijing* and less esteemed by posterity than its Confucian counterpart, but more surprising in its contents. Here, for example, is a very different kind of love song, an address by a shaman to his tutelary spirit, but drawing on the language of romance. When she does not respond, he complains about her coyness:

The goddess comes not, she holds back shyly.
Who keeps her delaying within the island,
Lady of the lovely eyes and winning smile?...
I waft my magic and it does not reach her...
I am choked with longing for my lady.

In this song, attributed to Qu Yuan, born in the mid-fourth century BC, the attitude of servility to the beloved and the effusive terms of praise bear an uncanny resemblance to the sentiments of courtly love that will dominate the Western love lyric in the late Middle Ages—a European tradition that we will find has many non-Western precedents. Indeed we can detect other anticipations of later Western love songs in ancient Chinese lyrics, for example predecessors of the *alba*, or dawn song, that so charmed medieval listeners. But in this particular instance, the singer may have a hidden agenda, more practical and utilitarian than any found in a troubadour lyric: by calling attention to the shy reserve of his female spirit, he now has a ready-made excuse for any failures in his magic. The bashful lady, not the shaman, is at fault.

The love songs of the *Shijing* would have a strange afterlife. What apparently started out as folk music first became an officially sanctioned body of songs, codified and revered but still intended for performance. "Confucius," we are told, "put all three hundred and five compositions to the music of strings and voice." But with this canonical status, these songs gradually ossified into uplifting texts to be quoted, phrases that could be recycled to suit various nonmusical occasions. Detailed commentaries on the texts were written, and scholars took delight in offering elaborate exegeses of the edifying messages embedded in the lyrics. Even the most obvious passages were analyzed and interpreted at great length. In short, a song that may have started as a "ditty of the village" eventually turned into a kind of dogma-driven scripture.

And where, in this process, did our love go? Well, you can probably guess. When a love song becomes a revered text, scholars find a way of interpreting it as something other than a love song. Just as with the *Song of Songs*, *The Book of Songs* got this kind of treatment. Take, for example, this straightforward lyric:

> If along the highroad
> I caught hold of your hand,
> Do not be angry with me;
> Love takes time to overcome.

You might assume this song is about a rejected lover seeking out a scornful beloved. But later commentary clears up your misconception: "'Along the Highroad' describes thinking of one's noble lord; Duke Zhuang of Zheng neglected the proper way and the noble lords abandoned him." In other words, not just the erotic elements but even the romantic couple disappear in the hermeneutical fog. This zeal for removing romance from the songs of the *Shijing* prevailed for more than a thousand years, and still has its scholarly advocates in the present day. An alternative tradition, emphasizing love and desire in these lyrics, may have survived in some quarters, but only as a minority view in face of the relentlessly utilitarian quest to extract acceptable teachings from these texts. Not until the Song Dynasty (960–1279) would a more naturalistic interpretation of these lyrics come to the forefront. But finally, with striking candor, Zheng Qiao announced in the twelfth century, with regard to this same song, "These are the words of a licentious eloper; they have nothing to do with the business of Duke Zhuang."

Such an admission led to various complications. If scholars admitted that these songs had erotic content, how should they deal with them? Confucian scholar Zhu Xi (1130–1200) suggested that the "improper" lyrics be prohibited at "religious and ceremonial occasions." "When Confucius edited the *Shijing*," he surmised, "he included poems which were morally offensive in order to warn us, there being no reason why they ought to be suppressed when they could instruct." Thus even as the love content was reinserted into the old songs, the authorities were put on notice.

To some extent, the authorities are still on notice. The late ethnomusicologist Antoinet Schimmelpenninck, who studied love themes in Chinese folk music of recent decades, noted the "strong resistance among scholars and government officials in China" to sex and erotic metaphors in these songs, in striking contrast to the villagers, who "largely accept the erotic content as an inherent—rather than shocking or 'immoral' part of their song culture." It is worth noting that the rediscovery of Feng Menglong's collection *Shan'ge* (Mountain Songs) by a Shanghai bookseller in 1934, some three hundred years after the works were initially collected, generated a similar response. Folklorists praised the find as a major event, yet many still expressed shock at the frank description of sexual relations in the lyrics. Again females were condemned as the provocateurs, disturbing the social equilibrium with their unabashed expressions of desire. "Although women are often the main protagonists of the songs, little room is given to traditional female virtues like chastity and obedience," explains Sinologist Paolo Santangelo. Indeed many of these "mountain" songs were performed by courtesans, less focused on maintaining proprieties than on pleasing clientele. "The songs preserve a vast amount of tabooed materials that were marginalized by the mainstream culture," Santangelo notes, "and would have been lost had Feng Menglong not collected them." But he is quick to add: "From an ideological point of view, all the feelings expressed in the songs are subversive."

In tracing the history of such works, whether from Western or Eastern cultures, we see the legitimization of romantic longing as a proper subject for musical performance. But we can also trace the recurring forms of the backlash against these lyrics from those who feared their disruptive effect on the social order. We are still in the early stages of the history of love songs, but we have already encountered the full range of responses from the enemies of this music—responses that reappear with mind-numbing predictability. When you cut through all the rhetoric, they boil down to five tactics: reinterpretation, suppression, ridicule, destruction, and, the last resort of those no longer able to stop the rising tide, a wary and watchful tolerance.

CHAPTER 4

Love in Ancient Rome

He who falls in love meets a worse fate than he who leaps from a rock.
—Plautus

In his 1936 book *The Allegory of Love*, a study of medieval and Renaissance literature, the young scholar C. S. Lewis made a surprising claim, one that still shocks readers today. The ancients, Lewis contended, had no comprehension of romantic love. They would not have recognized the idea, so familiar to us, that happiness is derived from nurturing an intimate relationship with a soul mate. This idealized view of love, so central to our vision of the good life, is a more recent invention, or so Lewis claimed—a gift to us from Europeans of the late medieval period. In his broad survey of ancient literature, Lewis could detect no such attitude. The very word *romance* might derive from the name *Roman*, but the Romans themselves had no comparable concept. They lived in a romance-free world—as did the ancient Greeks and Hebrews, and even, in Lewis's view, the more recent inhabitants of Japan and India.

Of course, Lewis admitted, the ancients were quite familiar with the pleasures of sex and the advantages of marriage, and realized that these often brought deep emotional attachments. But these emotions, especially when they developed into intense passions, could be dangerous forces, hazardous to our personal happiness and the stability of our lives. To seek out such feelings willingly was to court disaster. Only a fool would go down that path.

At the heart of Lewis's claim is his evidence, convincing in its own way, that the most respected ancient authorities considered love a kind of madness or disease—in stark contrast to our own tendency to celebrate it not only as healthy, but as perhaps the key ingredient in a fulfilled, well-ordered life. A sensible Roman citizen, from Lewis's perspective, would point out that even our casual language betrays the dangers of romantic attachment. We speak of "falling" in love, not of "rising" to it. We acknowledge the existence of lovesickness but somehow find this illness worth catching. When we talk about someone deeply in love, we use language that emphasizes its pathology: "He is crazy about her!" "She is mad about him!" The implication seems clear: our attitude toward romantic love may have changed, but our words still bear the mark of an earlier age, when what we now praise was scorned.

How should we respond to Lewis? Those who have followed closely the preceding chapters will have a different interpretation of the facts he presents. First, as we have seen, the expression of romantic love, in a form almost identical to what we encounter in modern songs and poetry, did exist in ancient times. We find it in Egypt, in China, in Greece and in other settings—even in the pages of the Bible. But these songs were often perceived as posing a threat to the social order, and long before the late medieval period so lauded by Lewis, authorities had employed many strategies for dealing with them. Their tactics included censorship, reinterpretation, defacement, ridicule, and, in extreme cases, the actual burning of manuscripts and the execution of those who studied them. When Lewis looks in vain for praise of romantic love from the esteemed authorities of antiquity, he reaches the conclusion that its psychological and emotional basis was absent from these societies. But the very sources that he cites prove that romantic love not only existed, but was perceived as threatening enough to require extreme measures to combat its influence.

The very story of Rome's founding offers warnings against the dangers of romantic love. In the *Aeneid*, Virgil tells how the mythic prince Aeneas, whose successors went on to found the city of Rome, came to Italy after the fall of his native Troy. But Virgil makes sure to include a cautionary love story in his epic poem. Aeneas stops in Africa along the way, where he falls in love with Queen Dido of Carthage (although with some help from his mother Venus, the goddess of love, and Juno, goddess of marriage). Here Jupiter intervenes, and sends Mercury to remind Aeneas that he has a higher duty and must leave romance behind in order to fulfill his destiny in Italy. Aeneas agrees and sails away, while Dido, cursing her departed lover, kills herself.

We could hardly ask for a better story to illustrate that the ancients both knew and feared romantic love. It is also revealing that the advocates of romance in this case are the women (Dido, Venus, Juno), while the powerful men (Aeneas, Jupiter, Mercury) are the vigilant upholders of social order in the face of the disruptive force of love. There is also unintended symbolism in the geography presented here, with North Africa depicted as the breeding ground for this passion, and the city of Rome representing a higher order of discipline incompatible with romance. Virgil could hardly have known how the history of the love song would play out over the two thousand years after he wrote the *Aeneid*, but he could not have chosen settings for this conflict more resonant of the battles to come in its later evolution—marked by many conflicts between African and European musical traditions. (On the other hand, both Virgil and his audience would have been reminded of another example of a North African temptress leading a Roman hero from his call of duty, namely Cleopatra, whose fatal dalliance with Mark Antony occurred just a few months before Virgil began work on his epic.)

We can find many other instances—in myth, history, and literature—of Roman uneasiness about romantic love. Let's not forget that this society preserved and honored the story of the "rape of the Sabine women" as the official account of how the first Romans found wives. The civilization they established would later enact the most elaborate system of marriage laws in the ancient world. The relationship between husband and wife embodied a contract that served many purposes beyond romantic fulfillment, and the parents of eligible daughters often secured a match for a child as young as twelve, committing her before she was old enough to develop emotional ties that might run counter to family interests. Macrobius explains that females begin menstruating around age fourteen, and thus it was necessary to allow formal unions *two years before* the girl experienced the tumultuous feelings and desires of a young woman. In practice, even younger women were committed to husbands, as made clear by the Latin legal terminology (*in domum deducta, loco nuptiae*, etc.) to cover these instances—with their artful reference to the young woman who had been *brought into the house*. They needed to employ such terms because these girls weren't old enough to enter into a legal marriage but had still been sent off by their parents to live with successful suitors. Yes, the Romans knew romance quite well, and worked hard to circumscribe and restrain its disruptive influence on the social order.

The biggest obstacle in accepting Lewis's claim that Rome was a romance-free zone comes from the most famous Roman work on love, Ovid's *Ars Amatoria*. In this lively text, known in English as *The Art of Love*, Ovid not only recognizes the primacy of romantic passion—acknowledging that relationships between men and women were much more than a matter of contracts and economics—but even offers a guide to lovers. Indeed, much of what Ovid taught was adopted enthusiastically by the exponents of courtly love in the late medieval period, who played the key role in shaping notions of romance that still exert an influence on us today. How could ancient Romans be ignorant of romantic love if they gave us the most authoritative guide to the subject?

Lewis has a clever response to this question. Ovid, he claims, makes a joke out of the "art of love." "The joke consists in taking it seriously," Lewis claims, something no reasonable Roman would have done. "The conduct which Ovid recommends is felt to be shameful and absurd, and that is precisely why he recommends it." Lewis says we should not find this strange or surprising. The surprise came when the courtly lovers of the late medieval period actually took Ovid at his word. Put simply, they didn't get Ovid's joke. They believed that a man really should be at the lady's bidding, run errands for her, and serve at her beck and call—an attitude, Lewis grumbles, still prevalent in modern times. He notes, in passing, that any man who has gone shopping with a woman will recognize it in action.

I believe Lewis was correct in pointing out that irony and ridicule underpin Ovid's *Art of Love*. But he missed the larger point—namely that this humor wouldn't have entertained ancient Romans if they didn't know real lovers who actually behaved in this manner. A humorist does not parody something that doesn't exist, and certainly doesn't devote a lengthy work to ridiculing social customs that aren't commonly seen in the real world.

The same is true of Roman music, notably in the parodies of love songs found in the comic dramas of Plautus. The playwright is clearly poking fun at romantic love in passages such as this one, from the *Casina*:

> You can take it from me: not on land or at sea
> is there anything finer than love.
> Nothing half so entrancing, everyday life-enhancing
> not on earth nor heaven above.

> And I do think it odd, when a cook's at his job
> giving dishes the very best flavor,
> he can't use for a spice, what is *ever* so nice,
> just a sprinkling of *Love* to add savor!

Clearly some Romans of the period must have believed that romantic love was "entrancing" and "life-enhancing" or audiences would have been puzzled rather than amused by such songs.

I would go further and suggest that this attitude toward romantic love, and love songs, still lingers. Love songs may dominate our musical lives, but there is something shameful about them and the sentiments they express—at least judging by my personal experience. When I mention to people that I am writing a book on love songs, they often respond with a joke or dismissive rejoinder. They put on a mask, acting the part of someone who is immune to the allure of this music, although I know about all the albums they own filled with lovey-dovey music. As I noted in my introduction, even those who listen to love songs and know the words *by heart* (and who doesn't?) adopt a public posture that this is *wimpy* music, for emotional weaklings and sentimental fools—a view disproved again and again in these pages, but a pervasive attitude nonetheless. Love songs may dominate our popular culture, but music critics almost never call attention to this fact. Recalling his own puzzlement with this state of affairs, author Dave Hickey asks why "ninety percent of the pop songs ever written were love songs, while ninety percent of rock criticism was written about the other ten percent."

I can answer Hickey's question. The critics are embarrassed by this music, just as the ancient Romans were.

"Romance is frivolous and stupid, the argument goes," explains cultural critic Noah Berlatsky—and cites, among other examples, the outrage in Congress when the National Endowment for the Humanities recently funded "The Popular Romance Project," which explored the role of love in stories, songs, films, and comic books. But the scorn for love songs and other romance-infused popular culture cuts deeper than political ideology. Years ago, I played piano at a comedy club, where I provided musical interludes between the stand-up acts. I still recall one especially skilled comedian who had the audience in stitches at every performance with his long routine on dopey guys who listen to love songs. Even after I had heard the routine several times, I was still laughing at it. I could recognize myself in the joke (as did many of the men in the audience). Okay, the scene may have been a contemporary comedy club, but the sentiments were identical to those found in Plautus's work, and any gladiators in attendance that night would have laughed along with the rest of us. Another observation based on firsthand experience (at comedy clubs and elsewhere): men are especially ashamed to be caught listening to a dreamy romantic ballad. Women, less so— which may explain why they have so often been the innovators in this kind of music—but even they share a dose of the shame.

Why the embarrassment? I suspect that the answer is a simple one: emotions make us vulnerable. They may enhance the Darwinian survival of the *species*, but at the possible sacrifice of the *individual*—especially when the individual in question is a male. In July 2012, when James Holmes walked into a midnight showing of *The Dark Knight Rises* in Aurora, Colorado, and killed a dozen people with his cache of weapons, three of the victims were young men who used their bodies to shield their girlfriends—each of these women survived. I suspect the young men's response was immediate and instinctive, honed by thousands of years of evolutionary experience. When the *Titanic* sank, 72 percent of the women made it back to land but only 16 percent of the men. Even the men traveling first class had a lower survival rate than women traveling in second or third class. Darwin would have understood this, not because he was a Victorian gentlemen with courteous gentlemanly values, but because he knew that women are more important to species survival than men—one man on a desert island with ten women can produce ten times as many children as one woman on an island with ten men. From an evolutionary perspective, child-bearers are more valuable than inseminators.

Listening to a love song on the radio is, of course, a very different experience from dealing with one of these tragedies, but it too pulls on the same Darwinian emotional cues. We are enticed into vulnerability for the good of the species, even as our rational, practical side calculates the cost. Hence, we should hardly be surprised that the same ancient civilization that refined stoicism into one of the most plausible and practical philosophical systems ever devised should have an especially uneasy relationship with love and its attendant music. But you don't need to be a stoic, like Seneca and Marcus Aurelius, to be wary of the pain and suffering that comes from emotional attachments. Even as modern humans tend to prefer epicurean indulgence over stoic restraint, we hold on to the Roman scorn of romance—and for the simple reason that we recognize a dangerous susceptibility to it hardwired into our psyches.

Many warnings against the dangers of song and lyric poetry can be found in ancient Roman texts. Sober citizens, cognizant of their dignity, looked down upon such frivolities. "Cicero said that even if his lifetime were doubled he would still not have time to waste on reading the lyric poets," cites Seneca the Younger, who goes on to add his own words of approval for this sensible judgment. But far more despised by Romans who prized social order was "effeminate singing." Seneca the Elder complained that "the revolting pursuits of singing and dancing have these effeminates in their power; braiding their hair and thinning their voices to a feminine lilt.... *This* is the model our young men have!" Quintilian, born shortly after the dawn of the Roman Empire, laments the degraded music of his time in no uncertain terms: "Still I think I ought to be more emphatic than I have been in stating the music which I desire to see taught is not our modern music, which has been emasculated by the lascivious melodies of our effeminate stage and has to no small extent destroyed such manly vigour as we still possessed." Quintilian prefers the old songs, "employed to sing the praises of brave men," not the newer music, "unfit even for the use of a modest girl."

We would love to know more about these "lascivious melodies," but Quintilian provides few details. Yet the comparison he makes between dangerous "effeminate" performances and his preferred use of music to "sing praises of brave men" inevitably reminds us of the contrast between Sappho and Pindar or the conflicts over the love songs included in the Confucian canon. The social order is undermined by these *womanly* songs, the Roman rhetorician insists, yet he must acknowledge their popularity even as he decries their depravity.

Love songs must have flourished in many settings in ancient Roman culture, but theatrical productions and other public entertainments clearly played a key role in introducing and disseminating them. The Roman plays—which were more akin to musical theater than to the spoken dramas of our day—were initially performed in temporary wooden structures. But in 55 BC, the Theater of Pompey in Rome was completed, a huge structure that could accommodate thousands of spectators. In later years, many other permanent theaters were constructed in numerous cities throughout the Roman Empire, although the authorities continued to demonstrate, in various ways, their suspicion of theatrical entertainments and actors. As the size of the venues makes clear, the entertainments presented in such settings clearly drew a mass audience, not just the social elites and hangers-on of the ruling class. Hence, this must be the first place we turn in gauging the role of love songs and the artistic representation of romance in Roman times. Live performance, not literary texts, set the tone for the culture—perhaps only around 15 percent of the populace could read. But music and other forms of live entertainment were pervasive in everyday life.

Many of these theaters have endured, at least in part, but only a tiny percentage of the Roman plays have survived, and we know even less about the music that accompanied these works. For a glimpse of the stories presented on stage, we can turn to just a few texts by a handful of playwrights, notably Seneca, Plautus, and Terence. But even this meager evidence makes clear that both romantic love and sexual exploits were an important part of the proceedings. The comedies, in particular, relied heavily on stock characters and plot complications that reappear in the romantic comedies of today. We find eligible daughters, lovesick suitors, lusty old men, romantic rivals, interfering parents, and all the other ingredients necessary for a good love story. As C. S. Lewis noted, these figures are put on stage to be mocked, but the mockery implies that these same character types were recognizable to audiences from real life. And if we had any doubts, the playwright clears them up. In Plautus's *Miles Gloriosus*, the lover Pleusicles comes disguised as a sailor to rescue his girlfriend, who is being held captive in Ephesus. He is embarrassed to find himself resorting to such tactics, but justifies himself in the following words:

> If I didn't know that love had caused other men
> To act disgracefully, I'd be more ashamed
> To be parading here, for love, in this get-up.
> But I've been told that many men, for love,
> Have done many things dishonorable and unworthy.

The passage is revealing—both in indicating how common such behavior was and how much Romans scorned the weakness it represented.

These kinds of stories, filled with love triangles and other obstacles to romantic fulfillment, have not lost their allure two thousand years later. But where did they come from? Little has survived of the Greek "New Comedy" that emerged around the time of Alexander the Great's death in 323 BC, but the texts that have come down to us show a move away from mythological themes and a preference for stories of everyday life, especially love plots. The Romans clearly borrowed from these sources, often closely imitating their Greek predecessors. (Note that, in the scene from Plautus above, the Roman playwright gives his characters Greek names and sets the comedy in a Greek city.) But there must have been indigenous folk art traditions, now lost to us, that contributed to the love stories and songs presented on the stage. The Romans had little interest in preserving folk music, but classicist John G. Landels believes elements of these lost traditions were incorporated into theatrical productions. "It seems to me highly probable," he writes, "(though this is entirely speculative and without evidence) that Plautus' musicians would introduce elements of native Italian folk music." Various scholars have also called attention to the possible influence of Hellenistic music hall songs that were popular in southern Italy, as well as the improvised Atellan farces, a kind of rude popular theater that was eventually prohibited.

This leads inevitably to the question of who composed the love songs and other music featured in Roman comedies. Unlike the ancient Greeks, whose lyric poets were essentially songwriters, the Romans tended to separate their literary and musical cultures. The ruling class granted more status to the former and viewed the latter with some suspicion. We are told that a slave named Flaccus composed music for the comedies of Terence and would also accompany performers. Marcipor, a slave belonging to Oppius, served as accompanist to Plautus's *Stichus* and even played a role in the onstage comedy. Slaves probably took the lead in composing and performing music in other dramatic productions in ancient Rome, as well as at informal gatherings. We have good reason to believe that some of this slave music was erotic in content. Livy criticizes the army of Scipio Africanus for bringing female musicians back from their campaigns in the East for performances at banquets and amusements—and we have already seen, in our discussion of the Turin papyrus, what such "entertainments" might encompass.

Slavery and love songs? This will prove to be a recurring theme in our history of the love song, and it is worth stopping here to ask why slaves should have such a strong connection to the music of romance and sexuality. Were they superior musicians? Were they better lovers? Perhaps. But our inquiry into the love lyrics of Greece, China, and Rome suggests a different answer to this question. These societies struggled to reconcile two opposing views of the love song. On the one hand, this music appealed to audiences, who no doubt found it charming and titillating in the same way we do today. On the other hand, something about the emotional (and sometimes physical) surrender portrayed in the lyrics struck ancient authorities as shameful and undignified. This attitude is made explicit in the phrase *servitium amoris* (literally the "slavery of love"), frequently used by Latin poets of the first century BC. "Of all the figures used by the Roman elegists," scholar Frank Olin Copley has written in an influential essay, "probably none is quite so familiar as that of the lover as slave. It appears again and again in their poems, sometimes in simple form, sometimes considerably expanded." But the connection may have been even more marked in Roman music, where the slave lover is not a literary trope but an actual description of the performer. By assigning the task of performing this music to an outsider at the lowest rung in the social hierarchy, the ancients could enjoy their sexy music even while making clear its exclusion from respectable society.

This "solution" to the problem of the love song recurs throughout history, and explains why the evolution of the romantic lyric in the West emphasized attitudes of servility and deference on the part of the singing lover. Previous studies of music and literature have tended to explain these attitudes by reference to the spirit of courtly love that permeated western Europe in the late Middle Ages, but I will present a different lineage for this lyrical celebration of romantic enslavement—a cultural mindset that continues to influence how we think about love and love songs today. As will be made clear, lovers humbly serve the beloved in romantic music because the originators of these kinds of songs were literally slaves and servants. Even the ethos of courtly love, associated in the public's imagination with knights and fine ladies, shares this humble lineage.

I could cite many texts to demonstrate the scorn of Roman authorities for entertainers of any sort, but it's clear that they especially looked down on women performers. During the Imperial period, marriages between actresses and free-born males were declared invalid. Later laws regulating marriage and inheritance indicate both that Romans tried to get around these restrictions and that the lawmakers were determined to remove any wiggle room. Domitian took away the rights of inheritance from actresses, and Constantine later instituted punishments for any senator or dignitary who claimed as legitimate any child of an actress—or even any child of the daughter of an actress. The Theodosian Code went so far as to depict the aristocrats attracted to these women as victims, describing them as "profligates (*perditi*) whose mind's are corrupted by the women's poisons."

We would like to know more about the artistry and craft of female performers under the Roman Empire, but our sources prefer to emphasize the elements of scandal. Our best account of a woman entertainer comes from a late stage of the empire, after its shift to Constantinople, when Theodora (500–548) rose from the ranks of performers to marry Justinian I (the last emperor to speak Latin as his native tongue) and serve as empress over a huge part of the Western world. The scholar Procopius left us a gossipy, tell-all account of court life now known as *The Secret History*. When dealing with Theodora, this historian leaves little to the imagination—then again, neither did she. He writes: "Often in the theater, too, in full view of all the people she would throw off her clothes and stand naked in their midst, having only a girdle about her private parts and her loins—not, however, because she was ashamed to expose these also to the public, but because no one is allowed to appear there absolutely naked." I couldn't help but be reminded of this passage when pop star Madonna, around the time of her fifty-third birthday, pulled down her pants to show off her thong in the middle of a song. Clearly the spirit of Theodora lives on in the present age. Unfortunately

Procopius, who is so ready with salacious details, offers little information on the music involved in these ancient performances. However, he does mention that Theodora was "not a flautist or a harpist; she was not even qualified to join the corps of dancers," but merely "joined the women on stage." This implies that music typically played a role in these "entertainments,"—although this may have been more akin to the musical accompaniment at a strip club than to anything we might call a love song.

Long before the time of Theodora, however, many ancient authorities viewed female entertainers as a scandal and outrage against public decency. Mime, the performance style practiced by Theodora, owed much of its appeal to its erotic content, and over a period of centuries was subject to frequent condemnation and occasional prohibition. In surviving texts we find mimes listed alongside pimps and prostitutes in denunciations of rampant immorality. But mimes also had powerful patrons, who sometimes preferred the coarsest types of entertainment. Emperor Elagabulus allegedly demanded that the sex acts in these performances be real, not feigned. Yet even tamer versions of mime tended to emphasize the tawdry and sensationalistic. A papyrus from the first or second century AD preserves part of a script and gives us a sense of a typical female role in ancient mime. Here the "love triangle" involves a woman so filled with desire for a slave that she plots to poison her husband. Adultery was an especially popular theme—although Choricius, of Gaza, a sixth century Christian rhetorician, would later defend the morality of this subject, pointing out that adulterers in these mimes were usually punished for their indiscretions.

It is easy to lose sight of the music amid all this scandal, especially since none of it has survived. Yet the songs of female entertainers were often singled out in attacks. These were a kind of gateway drug, perhaps not as overtly shocking as live sex acts performed for a decadent emperor, but maybe even more dangerous as a lure into a life of dissipation for the innocent and unwary. Libanius warns against the "singing girls—man eaters...who have wrecked the career of many men." When Cicero wanted to attack an opponent, he compared his adversary to a "singing girl"—a reference that implied not only effeminacy but also immorality. After the rise of Christianity, these kinds of warnings against women's songs will be frequently repeated in sermons and theological writing, but this would merely be a continuation of pagan belief, which feared the weakness and disorder such music left in its wake.

As we look at the state of the love song under the Roman Empire, we inevitably ask what happened to the Greek tradition of romantic lyric and the even older fertility rituals, those twin pillars for the music of courtship and sexuality in ancient times. Had the Romans forgotten these? Blinded by their pursuit of entertainment, did they lose interest in the lyrical expression of deeply felt emotions or the sacred ceremonies of propagation and increase? Or did they continue these traditions, shaping their own musical and ritualistic practices, as they did with so many other aspects of their culture, on role models from older civilizations?

In fact, they probably did a little of both. They nurtured some aspects of this cultural legacy, even as they jettisoned elements that didn't fit their own values and priorities. The tradition of lyric love poetry did not disappear, but its connection to the lyre and musical performance was immeasurably weakened. This process is difficult to trace. Latin texts often employ words signifying "song" (*carmen, canto, cano,* etc.) to refer to anything that departed from the patterns of everyday speech; this might include chanting, magical incantations, ritual speech, theatrical monologues, legal precepts, orations, or poetry. But the overall trend is unmistakable: *musical* traditions inherited from the Greeks get turned into *literary* practices by the Romans. Virgil may declare, in the opening of the *Aeneid,* "I sing of arms and of a man" (*Arma virumque cano*), but he does nothing of the kind. He is writing, perhaps on some occasions reciting to an audience, but not singing. The epithalamium, or wedding song, flourishes in ancient Rome, but it is now primarily a literary genre rather than a ritual song. Horace may be lauded as the Roman heir of Sappho and the greatest master of Latin lyric in the Augustan Age, but, strictly speaking, he wrote poems, not lyrics. As far as we can tell, only one of his poems was designed for musical performance, his *Carmen Saeculare,* commissioned by Emperor Augustus for the Centennial Games in 17 BC. Horace, however, did not sing it himself; instead it was performed by a choir of twenty-seven boys and twenty-seven girls, to match the "chosen virgins and chaste boys" (*virgines lectas puerosque castos*) described in the text of the hymn.

Horace wrote this hymn in Sapphic meter, and those determined to find celebrations of love and fertility in its words will note references to Venus and Ceres, as well as an entreaty to the deities for an increase in crops and cattle. But the real higher power that needed to be placated in this setting was the emperor in the audience, and Horace accordingly devotes more verbiage to the expansion of imperial dominion and the preservation of civic order than to any subject that might interest a romantic couple. Yet Sappho's more intimate concerns were not entirely forgotten under the Roman Empire. Plutarch describes the singing of Sappho's poems of love for entertainment after dinner. Aulus Gellius relates a similar scene from the household of Antonius Julianus, a Spanish rhetor from the second century AD, where the Greek love songs of Sappho were part of the program. Catullus translated Sappho, and even assigned his beloved the pseudonym Lesbia in apparent homage to the Greek lyric poet. Despite these acknowledgments, poets writing in Latin did little to challenge Sappho's preeminence in matters of the heart, and if any lyrics from the Roman world surpassed her expressions of love and passion, the history books have preserved no trace of such works. As for female lyric poets from ancient Rome, complete poems of only one survive, Sulpicia, who probably lived during the late first century BC. And like Sappho, whose best-known poem was preserved in a work by a man, Sulpicia's lyrics survived only because they were included in a text attributed to Tibullus.

Love poetry as a *literary* genre is beyond the scope of this book, but I must dwell for a moment on this aspect of Roman culture because it gives us insights into the psychological basis of romance at a decisive juncture in Western history and sets the foundation for the later chapters in our story. Modern readers are often fascinated by the frank eroticism in poems from the late republic and early imperial times, seeing in them attitudes that would be familiar in our own day. Tom Stoppard, in his 1997 play *The Invention of Love*, even traces the birth of romantic love back to Propertius and the other poets of this period. Yet I must present a dissenting voice here. I find mostly dysfunctional love in the works of Ovid, Propertius, Catullus, and others. Their descriptions of love as a kind of disease or madness could be enumerated at length, but going beyond this trope, I am even more distressed at a kind of imperialistic attitude to eros that permeates the poetry of imperial Rome. Propertius summed it up best in a line from one of his poems: "You are conquered or you conquer, this is love's wheel."

The Roman poets preferred the role of conqueror, and when they found themselves on the other end of the transaction, they complained bitterly. It is hardly a coincidence that the ancients referred to a love verse as a *querella*, a "complaint" or "quarrel." The basic model for Roman love poetry, as refined by Catullus and Propertius, is for a captivating if untrustworthy woman to ensnare the starry-eyed poet, who may enjoy some of the fruits of love, but is ultimately left reeling and suffering. In the opening lines of his first love poem for Cynthia, Propertius declares:

> Cynthia's eyes ensnared me who'd never before been caught
> in desire's nets: then I bent my once proud head...in submission to Amor's
>   triumph.
> That villain forced me to do his vulgar dance.

This may be a love poem, but Eros is the enemy (or "villain"), demanding submission to one who would rather be calling the shots. The concept that vulnerability, and the openness to emotional intimacy that results from it, could be a pathway to a deeper love, is mostly foreign to poets of the late Roman Republic and Augustan Age. In other words, they missed the most essential part of romance (and the love song as we know it today). Their sexual candor may mislead us into thinking that the Roman poets were much like us. But it is far easier to drop the trousers (or toga) than to lay bare the heart. The ease with which one achieves the former often comes at the expense of the latter.

I think this is what scholar Peter Dronke is getting at when he labels Catullus, Propertius, and Tibullus "egocentric" and narrow in range. Reading these poems, I am inevitably reminded of David Foster Wallace's putdown of John Updike, Norman Mailer, and the other "Great American Male Novelists" who dominated the literary scene during the Cold War (another era dominated by imperialistic tendencies). Wallace called Updike the "chronicler of probably the most self-absorbed generation since Louis XIV," but he might as well have made the comparison to the era of Catullus and Propertius. Wallace goes on to describe what he calls a "peculiarly American loneliness," which he defines as "the prospect of dying without even once having loved something more than yourself." Some have taken Wallace to task for these words, but my only gripe is with his view that America invented this narcissistic tone. In fact, we inherited it from Rome, and if these Latin poets are, as Tom Stoppard suggests, the "inventors" of romance, it is only romance of the most shallow kind.

Yet the Romans did preserve and enhance one tradition of romantic lyric, namely the *paraklausithyron*, the "song outside the door," in which the unhappy lover finds himself barred from his beloved's home and delivers his passionate outbursts—filled with threats, pleadings, complaints, and praise—from the street. This song is a forerunner of the serenade, familiar to all later Romeos who need to deliver their love songs to a Juliet on her balcony or locked inside her abode, and early examples can be found among the ancient Egyptians. The *paraklausithyron* almost certainly originated as an actual song, but by the time of the ancient Greeks had blossomed into a rich literary genre, inspiring both poetry and scenes in staged dramas. Yet the Romans showed even greater enthusiasm for the song of the excluded lover, *exclusus amator*, developing countless variations on the theme. Their enthusiasm is so marked that scholar Frank Copley speculates that, long before Romans began imitating Greek role models, "Italians already had a native song at the *shut* door which played a significant part in their folk literature." Yet even in this emotionally charged genre, Roman authors did everything possible to undercut the romantic possibilities of the song at the door. Lucretius, in his tirade against love in book 4 of *De Rerum Natura*, specifically mocks the beseecher by the door, citing his abject state as an example of the follies of such wretched men. In Plautus, the barred lover is turned into a comic figure, his ridiculous song actually addressed to the door rather than to the woman inside. Catullus also sings to the door, spouting abusive and defamatory statements. Horace actually resorts to threatening the door itself. The singing fools in these lyrics are often depicted as intoxicated and are almost certain to fail in their entreaties—as the name of the genre makes clear, the man is an *excluded* lover, not a successful suitor, and an aura of ineptitude, often accompanied by shallow vulgarity, permeates these works. We learn much about Roman attitudes from these lyrics, but very little about romance.

Before leaving the pagan era, we must turn from love back to sex. Or, to be more specific, back to the question of fertility rituals and their music—that hybrid of eroticism, religious belief, and art that started us off on our history of the love song back with the Sumerians. Did these practices continue in ancient Rome? Do they still have relevance to our inquiry into the nature of the love song as we move ahead into the Middle Ages and the Christian era?

At first glance, this ritualized concern with the gods and goddesses of propagation seems pervasive in the Roman world, and the connection with human fertility is still strongly impressed on the mind of the populace. Numerous festivals and celebrations testify to the vitality of these traditions. For example, at the Lupercalia, held each year in the middle of February, the youth of Rome ran through the streets naked or nearly so. Women who wanted to conceive a child would deliberately get in the way of the runners, who would slap them with a goatskin thong—this, they believed, would lead to pregnancy and an easy childbirth. Plutarch tells us that even women of high status would participate in this ritual. After the rise of Christianity, when pagan rites of this sort had been outlawed, the Lupercalia persisted and, judging by an angry epistle by Pope Gelasius, was still celebrated at the end of the fifth century. Some believe that we still celebrate the Lupercalia today: our own Valentine's Day coincides with the Roman celebration, although the precise historical connection, if any, between the two traditions is much debated.

Yet the very mention of the Lupercalia in conjunction with Valentine's Day leads us to consider the process by which a sacred ritual becomes a secular practice. At some point, the fertility rites of antiquity lost their aura of divine sanction and turned into something else—perhaps merely an excuse for drinking and carousing. Shrove Tuesday changes into Mardi Gras. The Lupercalia disappears, and Valentine's Day shows up in its place. The sacred music for a divine fertility ritual gets transformed into a different kind of song, perhaps a love song or secular dance or the background accompaniment to anything from a wedding to a seduction. This is an important part of our history, but a very difficult process to trace, if only because it requires us to measure something impossible to measure: what people actually believed when they participated in these rituals at various points in history. The silence of our main historical sources adds to the challenge. Today scholars undertake meticulous studies of folklore and folk music, but ancient historians preferred to study rulers and elites, giving us only the most sparse accounts of everyday life. We know gossipy details about the love life of Mark Antony and Cleopatra, but very little about the romances of the shopkeepers, unskilled workers, and slaves of the Roman Empire.

Despite these obstacles, we can detect an inevitable secularizing tendency at work in Roman times. This is perhaps best seen in the so-called mystery religions, voluntary associations of initiates whose cults often had some lingering connection with fertility rites and dying-and-reborn deities. The details here are maddeningly difficult to uncover. Indeed *mystery cult* is a fitting title for organizations that imposed such vigilant secrecy on their practices. Even after centuries of research, scholars still struggle to answer the most basic questions about what these groups did and believed. Yet a few clear facts emerge from the evidence. First, these rituals were not for entire communities, but for a small subset of the population—and, even more to the point, a tiny community that kept tight controls on the information it shared with outsiders. This, on its own, implies marginalization and separation from the concerns of the society at large, especially when one considers the uneasy competition among many different mystery cults. There was no reason why one couldn't participate in the Eleusinian cult *and* the Mithraic mysteries *and* the cult of Dionysus, but the demands on the initiate were such that choices had to be made, and it seems inevitable that considerations of social status and fellowship became, at some point, more important than religious belief. The sketchy accounts of initiation (for example from Apuleius, whose comic description from the late second century, is our best firsthand description of the process) still emphasize some magical or transformative experience, but this is now an individual experience, without the emphasis on the prosperity of the broader society that is so central to the rituals we studied in earlier chapters. Personal inclination and a desire for sociability and enjoyment gradually take center stage; the deities retreat into a lesser role, as symbols or sources of superstition, no longer dominating the proceedings.

And of course there was music to accompany all this. We are told that "sacred sounds" and "sacred sights" were all part of this initiation into the mystery. Few specifics about this music have survived, and the facts we do possess are often peculiar. We hear, for example, of initiates eating from a tambourine and drinking from a cymbal. Perhaps our best path is to look at the surviving *public* rituals of Roman times and judge from those. But did the secret mystery rites really resemble the infamous Bacchanalia, which got so out-of-control that the Senate prohibited the festivities in 186 BC? The songs and cries of participants woke up law-abiding citizens in the middle of the night, and every kind of sexual outrage allegedly transpired at these gatherings of frenzied participants. Many like to think that mystery cults involved orgies, and perhaps they did. But maybe the *taurobolium* ritual practiced in the cult of the Great Mother and other settings is more typical. Here initiates would crouch in a pit and get splattered with huge quantities of hot blood from a freshly slaughtered bull. Priests in this cult were even known to castrate themselves in their devotion to the goddess. It takes a great leap of the imagination to move from such descriptions to a view of cultic practices as a kind of sexcapade.

One thing is clear, however. Over time, both the rituals and their music lost the respect of the authorities and cultural elites. Aristides Quintilianus, one of the few ancient experts on music to comment on these practices, specifies that only the ignorant got involved in them. "This is the purpose of the Bacchic initiation," he explains in the third century AD, "that the depressive anxiety [*ptoiesis*] of less educated people, produced by their state of life, or some misfortune, be cleared away through the melodies and dances of the ritual in a joyful and playful way."

If we can believe Quintilianus, we have now arrived at the moment when ritual music turns into entertainment. The trappings of ritual remain, but personal ecstasy is now the primary goal. So long temple, hello Woodstock! But this transformation comes at a high price. When the music of love was integrated into the sacred, it earned the respect and support of the ruling powers. But once it loses this connection with the divine, ecstatic music-making raises the suspicions of the people in power. *Especially* when the songs deal with love and sex. And *especially* when they are sung by women, slaves, or outcasts and the ruling elites are men. And *especially* when Christianity becomes the dominant belief system of the West, and has its own deeply held ideas about love and sex.

CHAPTER 5

Debauched Maidens and Lustful Harlots

Let the maid of God be, as it were, deaf toward instruments. Let her not know why the flute, the lyre, and the zither have been made.—St. Jerome

Few love songs have survived from late antiquity and the early medieval period. But we can be certain of their existence, if only by the vehemence with which the authorities condemned them. For a thousand years Christianity tried to eradicate the love song. Church leaders and theologians condemned its indecency and vulgarity, denouncing these songs from the pulpit and inside the confessional, and secular authorities often joined them in attempts to extirpate this blight from Christendom. But they had little success, if we can judge by the frequency with which the denunciations were repeated over the passing centuries.

Medievalist John Haines surmises that there must have been "thousands if not millions of vernacular love songs performed before AD 1200." Yet what has come down to us is little more than tantalizing scraps, supplemented by countless secondhand references. The historian of this music is thus forced to act like an investigator at a crime scene, where the body and murder weapon are missing, and only circumstantial evidence—accusations, denunciations, and the occasional culprit's confession—have survived to guide the inquiry.

Often a snippet of song survived only because it was hidden in an unexpected place. Bernhard Bischoff discovered two eleventh-century strophes in 1984, copied by a German scribe into a manuscript of the ancient Roman playwright Terence. The texts surprised scholars with their suggestion that even the earliest known troubadours were inspired by preexisting traditions of vernacular love lyrics. These expressions of melancholy desire for the kisses of the beloved made clear their Provençal and Old French influences, but with Germanized spellings that reveal how far the song had traveled before being set down in writing. And clearly this text was intended for singing: accompanying German neumes even provide a melody for the lyrics.

Scholars of love lyrics have grown accustomed to these surprising juxtapositions. In a monastery in Thuringia, in central Germany, a passionate Latin love lyric, circa 900, was discovered in a theological manuscript, hidden between a sermon by St. Augustine and an epistle from St. Jerome. Seven love songs of Portugal's King Denis were found by Harvey L. Sharrer on the parchment used as the cover for a sixteenth-century notarial register in Lisbon. A copy of the constitution of Frederick II, dated February 11, 1234, in Frankfurt, includes a Sicilian fragment of Giacomino Pugliese's "Isplendiente stella d'albore." Still other love songs must have survived, but with all the sinful elements replaced by more edifying lyrics. The story is told of Henry of Pisa hearing a love song on the lips of a servant girl, and complaining that "the Devil should not have all the best tunes"—a lament taken up in later ages by other churchmen—turned it into a Christian hymn. Who knows how many other sanitized songs of romance and eroticism found their way, by such paths, into the mouths of the pious?

Even after sorting through the evidence, the mystery remains. With only tiny scraps of songs at our disposal, we are still largely ignorant of what the earliest European vernacular love songs sounded like, or the range of sentiments they expressed. But the hostility they engendered is a matter of record. The Council of Auxerre (561–65) issued a prohibition of secular music, and in particular the "girl's songs," or *puellarum cantica*—a term that we encounter in other, similar proscriptions. The Council of Chalon-sur-Saône, almost a century later, denounced "obscene and shameful songs." An eighth-century ecclesiastic condemnation of festivities on the feast day of St. John the Baptist repudiates "wanton love songs," and expresses outrage that the same mouths that partake of the sacred wafer can sing these sinful melodies—a comparison that is repeated in other attacks on bawdy lyrics. In the tenth century, Atto of Vercelli is still fretting over these songs, warning the devout against "beguiling performances of titillating stories about debauched maidens and lustful harlots." Another tenth-century source demands that *cantica amatoria* (love songs) be prohibited during any church festival.

This mixture of erotic songs and religious observations may seem strange to the modern mind, but our own uninhibited revelry initiating Lent at Mardi Gras festivities reminds us that we still enjoy this piquant overlap of sacred and profane traditions. For the medieval Christian, this commingling of opposites represented a constant temptation, and warnings against impure songs at church celebrations are repeated again and again in medieval texts. "Do not allow women's songs and ring dances and playful games," Pope Eutychianus, who became pontiff in 274, warned with regard to Sundays and feast days. The sixth-century Merovingian king Childebert II condemned the songs and buffoonery that tainted the nightly vigils at "Easter, Christmas and other feast days." These transgressions were sometimes listed in medieval penitentials, guides to priests who heard confessions listing sins and what their perpetrators might do to gain absolution. Yet the performance of amorous songs and dances in the vicinity of a church during feasts could be a sin too grave for forgiveness. Three surviving continental penitentials call for the excommunication of those guilty of such indecencies.

Women were frequently singled out in ecclesiastical denunciations of inappropriate songs and dances. The tone of suspicion and distrust invariably reminds us of the long history of invective against females as purveyors of dangerous powers—whether through music, magical spells, or other disruptive arts. The Canons of Basil, probably dating from around the year 400, specifically denounce the "woman who dances in taverns and allures people by her beautiful singing." Caesarius, bishop of Arles in 542, offered a similar complaint: "How many peasants and how many women know by heart and recite out loud the Devil's songs, erotic and obscene?" In the mid-seventh century, the Council of Chalon-sur-Saône specified that the lewd songs it sought to extirpate were performed by "choruses of women." Councils in Rome issued similar condemnations in 826 and 853. Indeed, until the rise of the troubadours in the late medieval period, these attacks would continue, testifying both to the hostility of the Church and its inability to stop women from singing alluring songs.

When women weren't attacked for singing about love, they were accused of preparing love potions and aphrodisiacs. "A woman might mix [her spouse's] urine and excrement in his food," scholar Bernadette Filotas explains, citing an account of dark magic dating from the ninth or tenth century—noting that this concoction allegedly strengthened the amorous bonds between husband and wife. But she adds: "It is not clear which of them was expected to eat the preparation or who was supposed to be the more loved as a result; presumably it was she." Burchard of Worms, a bishop of this same period, apparently believed that such aberrant culinary practices were widespread. He called attention to women "who take a live fish and put it into their vagina and keep it there until it dies, then boil or roast the fish and hand it to their husbands to eat: and this they do so that they will burn the more with love for them." Burchard had many similar tales to tell—of women who mix menstrual blood with their husband's dinner or serve them bread that comes from dough kneaded on their bare buttocks, all with the intent of inspiring erotic desire. The skeptical modern reader is tempted to dismiss such accounts as the result of a cleric's overheated imagination, yet we need to remember that these same priests heard confessions on a regular basis as part of their ecclesiastical responsibilities, and thus based their knowledge of aberrant practices on firmer ground than any secular expert of the period could match.

Readers who have followed my account so far will hardly be surprised to learn that two Old English love lyrics preserved in the tenth century Exeter

Manuscript are presented from a female perspective. Yet scholars long tried to find some other interpretation of "The Wife's Lament" and "Wulf and Eadwacer." They ignored the feminine inflectional endings in the former in an attempt to make the speaker a man—perhaps the copyist inserted those inconvenient gender mistakes, no? Or offered up an allegorical reading in which the lamenting woman represented the Church as the bride of Christ awaiting the triumphant return of the Savior. Or suggested that the poem was not a love lyric at all, but rather a riddle, similar to others in the Exeter Manuscript. But even the riddles in this document tell us that Christian teaching had little influence on whoever compiled it—for example, the following teaser, which may or may not describe a house key:

> A strange thing hangs by a man's thigh,
> under its master's clothes. It is pierced in front,
> is stiff and hard....
> He wishes to visit
> with the head of this hanging instrument the familiar hole,
> which it, when of equal length, has often filled before.

Scholars took a similar approach to "Wulf and Eadwacer," another love lament from a woman's perspective. Perhaps it might also be a riddle, they suggested, albeit an incomprehensible one. Or the lady here was talking about her son—a much more respectable subject for a song than an absent lover. Nineteenth-century Anglo-Saxon scholar Benjamin Thorpe, the poem's first modern editor, even refused to translate "Wulf and Eadwacer," insisting that it made no sense. Yet viewed in the context of the long history of love lyrics, the simplest explanation is also the most plausible: a woman longs for her absent husband, and expresses her melancholy in a song.

What could be objectionable about a love song between husband and wife? Yet religious authorities showed considerable interest in love songs that people sang in their own homes. "Do not perform lewd and sensuous songs and those diabolical games either in the streets or in your houses," commands one ninth-century source. "Flee lewd and sensuous songs like the devil's arrows, either in churches or in your houses," stresses a seventh-century Church authority. Rarely do the documents provide much detail about these wicked domestic songs, but the most frequent terms of description are *luxuriosa* (sensuous), *turpia* (lewd), and *amatoria* (amatory).

These forbidden love songs performed in the home no doubt included the *epithalamia* sung at wedding feasts. In the late sixth century, Caesarius, bishop of Arles, condemned the "sensuous singers" at these banquets. This tradition, as we have already seen, dates back to antiquity, and although the *epithalamium* was primarily a song of praise, blessing the newlyweds and predicting their happy life together, it also could be quite bawdy. Even the oldest *epithalamia*, reconstructed from the fragments of Sappho, rely on this potent combination of religion and eroticism. How much of this contradictory tradition survived into the Christian era? Certainly the written *epithalamia* show a surprisingly large dose of pagan elements. For example, Dracontius, a deeply religious poet residing in Carthage and Italy during the fifth century, displayed great knowledge of the Bible in his works, but when he wrote his wedding hymns, he filled them with references to Pan, Bacchus, drunken Silenus riding an ass, and the retinue of Venus, goddess of love. We should hesitate before drawing too many conclusions from these stylized literary works, but actual wedding ceremonies in early Christian society were likely to show comparable carryovers from the pagan past.

As you may recall from our discussion of ancient Greek wedding songs, the culmination of the marriage ritual—and the performance of the *epithalamium*—took place at the door to the bridal chamber, immediately before the husband and wife consummated their union. Is it mere coincidence that so many medieval marriages were celebrated at the door to the church, rather than inside the building? Even when a wedding mass was conducted at the altar, the couple often first exchanged vows and the ring at the entrance—a clear continuation of pagan ritual. In Chaucer's *Canterbury Tales*, the Wife of Bath boasts that "husbands at church door have I had five," and the practice continued to flourish despite prohibitions—from, for example, Edward VI and the 1583 Council of Rheims. As late as the middle of the eighteenth century, ministers were advertising the "beautiful porches" of their churches.

Other elements of pagan wedding rituals persist to this day. The procession, accompanied by music, remains the most dramatic moment of the ceremony, although it now takes place down the aisle rather than to the conjugal bed. The jesting and joking directed at the groom persist, although now separated from the formal ceremony and relegated to the best man's speech or sometimes raunchy toasts, as do feasting and revelry with song and dance. Even our practice of throwing rice predates the Christian era, the grain representing the fertility we symbolically bestow upon the married couple. Other fertility symbols of pagan origin survived the conversion to Christianity, especially during the medieval era. The use of the sword in many medieval marriage ceremonies was sometimes described by Christian commentators as a warning of the harsh penalties awaiting an unfaithful wife, but anthropologists today would see the intrusion of the weapon into a wedding as a phallic symbol or an emblem of fertility—perhaps echoed nowadays in the thrust of the knife into the virginally white wedding cake. If we are still loyal to pagan custom and erotic symbol in our increasingly secular age, how much more so must have been newlyweds and wedding participants a thousand years ago?

Church authorities were not alone in their condemnation of wedding-day excesses. By the close of the Middle Ages, the view that peasant weddings celebrated crudeness and lewdness rather than more ennobling Christian virtues had become a familiar stereotype spread through poems, paintings, and satires. Literary works such as *Meier Betz*, Wernher der Gartenaere's *Meier Helmbrecht*, and Heinrich Wittenwiler's poem *The Ring* found inspiration in the excesses of these celebrations. The most famous visual depiction of the peasant wedding comes from Pieter Bruegel the Elder, whose 1567 painting shows pipers providing a musical accompaniment to guests more intent on drinking and eating. Other paintings of such festivities by Martin Van Cleve present even less decorous behavior, with guests intoxicated, engaged in uninhibited dances or sensuous embrace. But the peasant wedding as a cultural meme representing excess and dissipation, or held up as a target of mockery or outrage, was already several hundred years old by the time of these works.

The condemnation of the conjugal love songs of husband and wife accompanied an ongoing debate in the Church over whether all love between man and woman, even within the confines of marriage, incurred God's displeasure. When the monk Jovinian asserted in the late fourth century that God approved equally of married life and celibacy, a controversy ensued that drew in many leading Church teachers of the day. Both Ambrose and Jerome, doctors of the Church who were each later canonized, launched savage attacks on this dangerous doctrine, and the latter offered such a caustic diatribe against the fair sex that few have matched its venom in the ensuing centuries. A woman's love, Jerome warns, is insatiable: "Put it out, it bursts into flame; give it plenty, it is again in need. It enervates a man's mind and engrosses all thought except for the passion which it feeds." But even away from the marriage bed, the man's life is made miserable. The wife fills the husband's house "with her constant nagging and daily chatter, and ousts him from his own home, that is the Church." In summary, the Christian theologian quotes with approval the ancient Roman Varius Geminus, who "says well 'The man who does not quarrel is a bachelor.'"

But if love and its musical accompaniment within marriage drew criticism, how much more dangerous were the beguiling songs of whores? Nowadays we would scoff at the notion that a prostitute might benefit from musical talent or training, but a careful historian can uncover the connection between these two vocations in every part of the world and at virtually all stages of human history. Christian authorities were especially sensitive to this linkage. They frequently condemned musical entertainments as incitements to sin, and medieval references to erotic love songs sometimes explicitly describe the singers as prostitutes. "See, therefore, how the prostitutes of Venus sit at the northern door, sensuously weeping their loves and making up love songs," wrote Bruno, a twelfth-century bishop of Segni. A medieval municipal statute from Bagnols in the south of France asserts that "no public woman be so bold as to sing or chant by night in the streets"—an apparent prohibition on the solicitations of prostitutes. In the anonymous medieval romance *Libro de Apolonio*, the heroine Tarsiana makes clear that, although she sings in the marketplace, she has not adopted the livelihood associated with it, namely prostitution. "I am not one of the *juglaresas* who can be bought," she proclaims—using a word that, in a revealing overlap of meanings, denotes both *whore* and *minstrel*. We can hardly hope to trace the process by which these songs of solicitation influenced the broader streams of Western music, or vice versa, but such cross-fertilization must have been inevitable, especially after the love song found wider acceptability with the rise of the troubadours. By one account, the familiar song "Greensleeves" gained popularity as a melody used to solicit clients, and the title possibly alludes to the grass stains on the attire of women who had sex with customers outdoors. (Another interpretation holds that the woman is mistaken for a prostitute—which would explain her feeling wronged when she is "cast off discourteously.")

The Church might have been expected to condemn sex for hire. Yet, though frequent attempts were made to eradicate the vice from Christian society, more pragmatic voices within the hierarchy realized not only the difficulty but the negative repercussions of zero-tolerance policies. Augustine, famous for his own wayward youth in the fleshpots of Carthage, warned: "If you remove harlots from society you will disrupt everything because of lust." Thomas Aquinas later offered a comparison between prostitution and a sewer in a palace, noting that if you got rid of the sewer the whole palace would be contaminated. Given this perspective, the songs of prostitutes legitimately demanded more vigilant repression than the sex acts themselves. They announced in public what should remain hidden in private, and served to adorn with art a transaction that, even if necessary, should appear vile and shameful.

Yet the surviving denunciations rarely limit themselves to attacks on open purveyors of vice, and often express a fear that secular songs, even in chaste settings, could corrupt the innocent and undermine the pious. Church authorities were so afraid of the dangerous combination of women and music that their prohibitions extended beyond love songs and encompassed almost any emotionally charged vocalizing by a female. Women's laments at funerals, whether by relatives of the deceased or hired female mourners (*lamentatrices*), were a frequent source of irritation to Church authorities, and numerous condemnations of them have survived. At times even the very sound of a feminine voice was castigated—men, too, were criticized when they practiced effeminate singing. These condemnations of secular songs need to be understood in the context of a more general suspicion of the influence of music and dance on impressionable minds (and bodies). Church leaders saw the risk spelled out in Holy Scripture, where sacrilege and debauchery often arrived on the scene with musical accompaniment.

Religious authorities could cite, for example, the well-known account of Moses returning from Mount Sinai with the Ten Commandments, only to find the children of Israel singing and dancing around the golden calf—a transgression that even the execution of three thousand sinners could not completely absolve. Moses's plight stood as a warning to religious leaders that even a chosen people and devout flock could lapse into forbidden practices under the mesmerizing influence of music. Gregory of Tours explicitly references this biblical story when condemning the cultic practices of the medieval Franks, and Caesarius of Arles draws on the same passage in his sermons, adding the sweeping claim that "the custom of dancing is a left-over of the practice of the pagans." But the bishop leaps to an even bolder assertion about those who sing and dance: "After he has got drunk, he rises to dance [*ballare*] like a frenetic madman in a diabolical way, to dance [*saltare*], to sing shameful, amatory, indulgent [*luxuriosa*] words. This sort of man would not hesitate to commit theft or fear to engage in adultery, to give false evidence, to curse, to perjure." Here we see the whole process laid bare: you start with a drink and a song, and end up committing theft and perjury.

Even devotees of the sacred were sometimes susceptible to the allure of amatory music. In 789, Charlemagne issued a strict order to abbesses that they prevent those under their charge from composing *winileodas* (literally "songs for a friend") or sending them to acquaintances outside the convent. How this demand was enforced is not known, but the prohibition was severe enough to ensure that these songs were not preserved for the benefit of later scholars. Just how friendly, we wonder, were these holy ladies? Did their texting amount to medieval sexting? We will never know. But the surviving correspondence between nuns and priests from the period frequently refers to love, and though such expressions were expected to signify *amor spiritualis* rather than *amor carnalis*, the feelings in question and the words in which they were described occasionally strayed from their prescribed limits.

How, for example, should we interpret the following extract from medieval correspondence? "I avow the bond of your love; when I tasted it in my inmost being a fragrance as of honeyed sweetness entered into my veins. . . . Believe me, the tempest-tossed sailor does not long for his haven, the thirsty fields for their rain, the anxious mother waiting at the bend of the shore for her son, as much as I long to delight in seeing you." We would not hesitate to call this a love letter, or perhaps a come-on or seduction. But when Abbess Egburg sent this missive to St. Boniface in the early eighth century, such passionate declarations of longing were possible in a chaste relationship between celibates. Even so, such documents are part of our history of the love song. When romantic and erotic lyrics entered the mainstream of European culture during the late medieval period, they drew on the overheated language of transcendence and longing that had been disseminated among religious leaders and mystics for centuries. In a very real sense, our modern discourse of love, even at its most carnal, is constructed on a foundation of spiritual aspirations and metaphysical paradigms.

Romantic and erotic themes abound in many other medieval works by members of religious orders, such as the dramatic works by the tenth-century abbess Hrotsvitha, the Latin epic *Waltharius* by her contemporary the monk Ekkehard, and the romance *Ruodlieb* by an anonymous Bavarian monk, written a few decades later. If love stories held such appeal for religious leaders residing in cloisters and monasteries, one can only imagine the tales and songs that circulated in the towns and villages, where the context might justify less decorum and a bolder expression of affective ties.

Strange to say, when love songs finally came out of their hiding places in the late medieval period, many of the lyrics emerged from the ecclesiastical world itself—or at least a renegade branch of it. These songs are the legacy of the *clerici vagi*, sometimes known as wandering scholars or Goliards, who played a prominent role in disseminating secular songs, especially during the twelfth and thirteenth centuries. The etymology of the term *Goliard* is in dispute, but the various suggested origins make clear the poor reputation of these itinerant beggars who could charm an audience with Latin songs, both sacred and profane. Perhaps the name came from the Latin *gula*, or gluttony. Others trace a connection with Golias, the name for Goliath in the Vulgate Bible. If so, the insult is a clever one; Goliath was the blowhard opponent of the shepherd David, the most famous purveyor of praiseworthy religious songs, and any comparison between the two draws attention to the advantages of the psalmist, whether in battle or virtue or just plain music-making.

The Church had long struggled to impose discipline on its clerics, and as far back as the fifth century had lost control over many who had abandoned the cloisters in favor of life on the road. If Jack Kerouac had lived during the Middle Ages, this would have been the closest he could have gotten to a medieval beatnik lifestyle, traveling light and scrounging a living from edgy versifying and the kindness of strangers. With the rise of the European universities, the numbers of these wayfaring students, literate in Latin but untethered to any stable vocation or community, increased sharply. "The young scholars soon fell into a way of traveling from one school to another," writes George F. Whicher in his study *The Goliard Poets*, "as the contemporary saying went, seeking the liberal arts at Paris, law at Orleans, medicine at Salerno, magic at Toledo, and manners and morals nowhere."

Yet the conventional image of the Goliards as jolly students captures only part of the truth. Many of their songs may have come from respected teachers and craftsmen poets. Moreover the influential connections of some of the authors— for example, the anonymous Archpoet, who had close ties to the archbishop of Cologne—force us to adopt a more expansive notion of the origins of these lyrics.

The Church perhaps had good reasons to assign blame for some scurrilous songs on lowlifes and vagabonds, but the generalizations of religious leaders about musicians were probably no more accurate in the Middle Ages than they are today. The vice, such as it was, of bawdy versifying, almost certainly found adherents, or at least receptive audiences, in some corners of the Church's own hierarchy.

Even if a few Goliards managed to obtain official posts, they never quite threw off the taint of vulgarity lingering over their entertainments. Yet they may have prized this very reputation for rude jocularity. One suspects that their "service" to influential patrons must often have resembled Falstaff's companionship with Prince Hal. Sometimes the bawdiness and boldness may have been consciously exaggerated as a pleasing pose. Even the Archpoet may have simply been mimicking the dissipated tone of the vagabond for the entertainment of his elite audiences, a kind of medieval slumming for those who avoided settings where real "wandering students" offered up their coarse fare. In his most famous lyric, his Goliard's "confession," the Archpoet proclaims:

> Dull and dour sobriety
> Never takes my money,
> Give me loose society
> Where the jokes are funny....
> Shunning virtue, doing most
> Things that I ought not to....
> Since the soul is bound to roast
> Save the skin's my motto.

Perhaps our poet actually lived up to these claims, but the tone reminds me more of boasting teens presenting a faux dissipation meant to impress peers rather than describe actual exploits.

The best-known manuscript of Goliard texts, the *Carmina Burana*, came to light in the early nineteenth century and is one of our most important sources of medieval love songs. Baron Johann Christoph von Aretin discovered the manuscript in 1803—one of seven thousand items he seized from an eighth century Bavarian Benedictine monastery for the state libraries as part of the secularization movement in the aftermath of the French Revolution. So many works were confiscated from this single site that a local sawmill spent days cutting boards to make containers for them, and wagons collapsed under the weight of the accumulated learning, manuscripts and books spilling to the ground.

The *Carmina Burana*, a collection of lyrics compiled in the thirteenth century, containing more than a hundred love songs, was an especially rare and prized trophy, perhaps all the more so since it represented a different kind of secularizing rebellion against Church authorities of an earlier era—a symbolic resonance that (as subsequent events would make clear) could be turned to various ideological purposes. The manuscript was transferred to Munich, where it stands out, even today, as one of the choicest cultural treasures among the ten million items currently housed in the Bavarian State Library. Indeed the *Carmina Burana* may have suffered from becoming too great a German cultural treasure. It gained both fame and infamy in the twentieth century when composer Carl Orff set two dozen of its texts to music, and his *Carmina Burana*, despite some early reservations expressed by Goebbels, was adopted by Nazi propagandists as a signature work and emblem of the Aryan life force.

This taint is perhaps unfair to Orff, whose complicated relationship with Nazi authorities is beyond the scope of this book, and certainly to the medieval scribes who set down these songs that dealt with drinking, gambling, love, fate, and occasionally moral or religious topics. Despite some German stanzas in the collection, the frequency of Italian spellings and the appearance of songs from France, Spain, and northern Italy undercut any attempt to turn the *Carmina Burana* into an emblem of Teutonic exceptionalism. And the love lyrics that represent more than a third of the poems collected in the manuscript present sentiments beyond the dictates of national boundaries or political allegiances.

Sometimes the expressions are chaste, advocating a love untainted by physical union—and thus not incompatible with a successful career in the Church. "I am hot with flaming desire for an outstanding maiden," proclaims one of these lyrics, "and every day my love for her grows." Yet in this same song, the author admits, "I am virgin among virgins, and am repelled by shop-soiled women, I loathe the married no less than the harlots, for with such as these the pleasure is base." Elsewhere a rare reference to homosexual love is made, but in the context of a disavowal: "Why does my mistress hold me in suspicion?...I am content with natural love and have learned to take the active, not the passive role." But Goliard songs offer more confessions than denials, as in this frank (and frankly disturbing) lyric from the *Codex Buranus*, enumerating favors granted by the beloved, and those seized by the unsatisfied lover: "The maiden has allowed me the enjoyment of beholding, conversing, touching, kissing; but absent from my love was the final and best stage." Albeit not for long. The end of this song, which describes the "triumph" of the lover's "battle plan," makes a mockery of the romantic preamble. "With overboldness I use force. She rampages with her sharp nails, tears my hair.... She coils herself and entwines her knees to prevent the door of her maidenhead from being unbarred." Although the singer assures us that, after the act, "my lover grew gentler and reproached me less, bestowing honeyed kisses," the modern reader would hardly hesitate before classifying this encounter as date rape.

The *Carmina Burana* is a comparatively late source of Goliardic songs, the manuscript dating from a period after the rise of the troubadours. So we must search for other sources to unlock the mystery of love songs during that thousand-year period of repression following the rise of Christianity. We are fortunate that an unknown English traveler copied down close to a hundred lyrics on a series of parchment leaves at an unknown date before the Norman Conquest, and brought them back from a trip to the continent. We remain unsure of the purpose of the anthology. Did the compiler collect the songs for his personal enjoyment? Did the document serve as a songbook for an actual wandering entertainer? Perhaps the manuscript was intended as a guide to the writing of Latin verse—indeed, scraps of Horace and Virgil show up alongside the earthier fare. The inclusion of musical notation for some of the songs suggests that the intended audience might have included performers as well as readers, yet we can only guess at what uses they made of the document. Ten parchment leaves eventually found their way to the Abbey of St. Augustine in Canterbury and are now housed at Cambridge University. As a result, these boisterous and sometimes bawdy performance pieces, mostly in medieval Latin but a few in a dialect of Old High German, have been given the refined title of the *Cambridge Songs*.

Some of the contents were too scandalous for their Benedictine custodians, who erased or blotted out lyrics deemed too erotic to be housed under a monastery roof. But those that survive or have been reconstructed reveal how far these songs differ from the proclamations of courtly love that would soon emerge as the dominant influence on love songs on the continent. Here the Goliard makes clear what he wants from his mistress:

> Why not be brave and say that you
> Will do soon what you're bound to do?
> What sense is there in hesitating?
> Come precious—I'm not good at waiting.

And here:

> Nay, come and visit me, sweet friend,
> Heart of my heart, this prayer I send:
> Enter I beg, my little room
> So trimly decked—you know for whom.

Even so, the theme of love is hardly as dominant in this collection as it would soon become in vernacular songs. The *Cambridge Songs* also includes many religious lyrics, folktales in verse, and songs praising nature and the seasons. Scholar Peter Dronke, considering the *Cambridge Songs* in the context of its time, marvels that "already around the year 1000 practically all the basic types of medieval and Renaissance lyric had evolved."

Medieval authorities civil and ecclesiastical did not share these enthusiastic appraisals of the modern scholar. They greeted the arrival of the Goliard in their communities with caution or hostility. From their perspective, these wandering scholars were, at best, a nuisance; at worst, outlaws. Church authorities even grew suspicious of erudition and a knack for literary composition, seeing these now as warning signs increasingly linked to the most debased, carnal love. "Alas, how seldom in these days do virtue and learning come together," laments Hélinand of Froidmont, the minstrel who abandoned love songs to join the Cistercian order at the close of the twelfth century. "By some—I know not what—factious bond, lust and literature cling together, a union no less prodigious than pernicious." In time the hostility of these upholders of virtue—as well as the competition from popular performers in vernacular tongues—led to the decline and eventual disappearance of the Goliards. The name lived on, but by the fourteenth century it was more a term of abuse than an actual craft. Thus does Chaucer refer to his miller as a "janglere and a goliardeys" whose repertoire consists of "synne and harlotries."

Any discussion of Goliards inevitably brings us to the strange, tragic history of Peter Abelard, an individual who came to be considered as emblematic of the wanton scholar. After Abelard's fall from grace, St. Bernard referred to him as a "Golias," or Goliath, and the scandal surrounding this controversial theologian played no small role in the backlash against the Goliards and the growing perception that literary talent and licentious behavior often went hand in hand. Some have even suggested that Abelard's followers happily adopted this label of opprobrium as an emblem of their admiration for him—indeed that 'Goliard' was embraced by them because it blended together the names Golias and Abelard. For our purposes, Abelard warrants our attention not only as a scholar and composer of love songs, but as one of the protagonists, along with his beloved Heloise, in the most famous true-life romance story of its time.

Peter Abelard, born near Nantes in 1079, first gained renown as a logician and scholastic philosopher, and he would still be remembered today even if he had never met the future abbess Heloise, or bequeathed to us the famous narrative and correspondence of their relationship that serve as key documents in the history of love and sexuality. These frank texts so captivated later readers that Abelard's reputation as a great thinker, formidable in his time, would eventually be eclipsed by his renown as an unhappy lover. Abelard and Heloise achieved such notoriety that they were celebrated in the *Romance of the Rose*, acknowledged by Chaucer, and served as inspiration for novels, plays, and doubtless many other subsequent love affairs.

Heloise d'Argenteuil, like Abelard, deserves to known as more than just an unfortunate protagonist in a sex scandal. She was one of the most brilliant women of her day, a scholar of Latin, Greek, and Hebrew at a time when few women could pursue advanced studies of any sort. Abelard refers to her as *nominatissima* ("most renowned"), and a letter from Peter the Venerable notes that he had first heard her name because of her reputation for "knowledge of letters," "secular learning," and "virtuous and praiseworthy studies"—all this before the affair that forced Heloise into a religious life. Certainly her surviving writings reflect a woman whose mind was as penetrating as her spirit was passionate.

Modern readers can hardly comprehend the status and renown enjoyed by Abelard, even before his fall from grace. In the current day, theologians are hardly considered A-list celebrities. But in Paris during the Middle Ages, Abelard drew thousands of followers from all parts of France and as far away as Rome. "No distance over land, no mountain ranges, no deep gorges, no difficult road or danger from robbers, prevented students from rushing to you," reminisced the monk Fulk, who adds that, after Abelard's downfall, the women of Paris wept in sympathy as though for a stricken lover or husband. Heloise, for her part, declares in her recollection of the days of their romance: "What king or philosopher could match your fame? What district, town or village did not long to see you.... Every wife, every young girl desired you in absence and was on fire in your presence." Heloise's testimony is no doubt biased by her personal attachment, but by any measure, Abelard was a larger-than-life figure in his day.

While living in Paris with her uncle, the canon Fulbert, Heloise fell under the influence of the charming Abelard, first as his student and then as his lover. When Heloise became pregnant, Abelard took her away to his native Brittany, where she stayed with his sister until their son was born. He then brought Heloise back to Paris, where the couple was married in a secret ceremony, with Fulbert on hand. But the uncle grew incensed when Abelard refused to acknowledge the marriage in public, and Heloise joined her husband in these denials. When Abelard took the further step of placing Heloise in a convent in Argentueil, near Paris, the uncle interpreted this as a shameful repudiation of responsibility, tantamount to divorcing his niece after having already dishonored her. Fulbert decided to exact revenge. Aided by friends and relatives, he plotted an assault on Abelard in the middle of the night. The conspirators bribed a servant to gain access to the scholar's sleeping chamber, and then, in Abelard's words, "took cruel vengeance on me of such appalling barbarity as to shock the whole world; they cut off the parts of my body whereby I had committed the wrong of which they complained."

In the aftermath of this attack, Abelard retreated into monastic life and for a time subsisted as a hermit in a cabin of reeds and straw. But students continued to flock to him, even in this setting, and built their own huts near their teacher's. He later moved to the Abbey of Saint-Gildas-de-Rhuys in Brittany, where he served as abbot, and continued to write and play a prominent role in the intellectual debates of the Church. Following a comparable retreat into the religious life, Heloise eventually became an abbess at the Oratory of the Paraclete in Ferreux-Quincey. The couple's relationship continued via correspondence, but Abelard now adopted the stance of a spiritual director rather than a lover. Indeed as a castrated monk he hardly had a choice, although his letters show more resignation to this fate than does Heloise, who boldly proclaims: "Men call me chaste; they do not know the hypocrite I am," and admits to "lewd visions" of their past pleasures, even during the celebration of the Mass. Abelard, for his part, now sent Heloise religious songs for her nuns instead of the love lyrics he once composed.

In his autobiographical account of his tragic romance, Abelard makes passing reference to these musical expressions of his passion:

> Now the more I was taken up with these pleasures, the less time I could give to philosophy and the less attention I paid to my school....As my interest and concentration flagged, my lectures lacked all inspiration and were merely repetitive; I could do no more than repeat what had been said long ago, and when inspiration did come to me, it was for writing love-songs, not the secrets of philosophy. A lot of these songs, as you know, are still popular and sung in many places, particularly by those who enjoy the kind of life I led.

Is it possible that Abelard's love songs were better known during his lifetime than his celebrated scholastic writings? Heloise later recalled the fame these lyrics brought both to him and to her. "You left many love-songs and verses which won wide popularity for the charm of their words and tunes and kept your name continually on everyone's lips," she reminisced. "The beauty of the airs ensured that even the unlettered did not forget you....And as most of these songs told of our love, they soon made me widely known and roused the envy of many women against me."

Abelard probably wrote these lyrics in Latin, or perhaps in a combination of Latin and French, but none of these love songs has survived, despite these testimonials to their popularity. A few scholars have suggested that Abelard might be the author of some of the anonymous Latin love lyrics of the late medieval period, for example the "Hebet sidus" found in the *Carmina Burana* manuscript, compiled almost a hundred years after Abelard's death in 1142: "How many kisses from her lips did I steal through the impulse of opportunity by night....But she wastes away, lacking the hope of consolation. Her youthful bloom is withering. Would that our separation at this great distance could be expunged, so that the sundering we endure may bestow unchallenged rights on us when we are united." It would be pleasing to imagine Abelard singing these words to Heloise. Yet this attribution rests on little more than imaginative speculation.

The disappearance of such well-known songs from a famous public figure serves as a telling reminder of the ongoing Christian hostility to love lyrics during this period. Abelard's career coincides with the first stirrings of the troubadour movement in the south, and the love song would eventually find supporters and advocates throughout European society. But he could hardly expect to encounter the kind of acceptance for such lyrics that, a few years later, the Archpoet would achieve, or Dante and Petrarch would enjoy in a later age. True, other factors may have contributed to the disappearance of these songs, notably the shame and infamy that surrounded this chapter in Abelard's life, or perhaps just the fickle destiny that led to the haphazard destruction of so many other medieval texts. Yet I am tempted to put most of the blame on Abelard himself, who could have taken steps to preserve these poetic outpourings but did not even quote from them in the autobiographical narrative that recounts his notorious love story. In fact, in later life, Abelard appeared to accept the verdict of cautious Church authorities, and denounced poets alongside "jesters and other singers of filth." When contrasted with the longevity of his writing on other matters— roughly one million of Abelard's words have survived—the absence of his love songs can hardly be happenstance, and almost certainly reflects their author's own repugnance for his youthful outpourings.

But give both Abelard and Heloise their due. Under the influence of Jacob Burckhardt and other historians, we have come to identify the age of Dante as the moment of liberation and legitimization for the interior life in European societies, a turning point when emotional truths became as valid as scholastic dictums, when the outpourings of the heart found a channel in art, poetry, narrative, and music. Yet with Abelard and Heloise we find true medieval figures, espousing wisdom drawn from St. Jerome and Seneca, studying the rule of St. Benedict, yet also revealing an intense passion for love and song as modern as anything found in the later history of romance. The autobiographical and confessional elements so familiar to us nowadays, the blending of emotional expression and personal history that we perceive as the antithesis of the medieval sensibility, figure prominently in the tale of these two unhappy lovers. This intimate tone permeates their letters and narratives, and we would no doubt find it even more marked in their love songs, had they survived. Medievalist Etienne Gilson was so struck by this incongruous modern element that he felt it posed a challenge to the standard definitions of historical periods. "Before attempting to define the Middle Ages," he writes, "we should have first to define Heloise." But the problem here may not be with our sense of history, but with the limitations of our psychological theories, which betray a subtle bias in favor of the supposedly greater depth and complexity of our post-Freudian minds, accompanied by a stubborn unwillingness to allow that men and women of earlier ages might have possessed inner lives as rich as our own.

But if our sense of superiority in matters of the heart is challenged by Heloise and Abelard, it is toppled by the next stage in our story. Here the love song not only comes out in the open, after a thousand years of repression, but does so with an intensity and imagery that continue to haunt our own romantic ideals so many centuries later. Even our ways of speaking about love reveal the lasting legacy of the new sense of courtly love that will now spread throughout western Europe. We still describe the first advances in a romance as a "courtship," a term that has somehow managed to survive the sexual revolution and the age of hook-ups and online dating. Even in the virtual world of web relationships, managers of the eHarmony website—with more than 20 million registered users in 150 countries searching for a romantic connection via their Internet connection—wisely tag articles on dating advice with the word *courtship*, still resonant with overtones of courtly love and the fineries and flummeries of the ideal relationships of nobles. By the same token, the person who sings of love is still known as a troubadour, especially when the song is moody, emotionally charged, and personally revealing. Colloquial language continues to describe the woman seeking her "knight in shining armor" and the man putting his lady love "on a pedestal"—terms we immediately understand, even if the references bear little resemblance to what actually happens on our dates and flings.

These telling reminders of the late medieval period, however falsified by our imagination and historical distortions, make clear that we have now arrived at the moment when the key elements of our modern love songs were not just codified and disseminated. They also changed our hidden fantasies and secret dreams of what romance might be. For the love song not only was coming out into the open with the troubadours but arrived with a pageantry and stirring imagery, a confidence and aplomb, that have never been surpassed.

But before we arrive at this flowering of the love song in Europe, we must take a detour and a change of scenery, and instead look at extraordinary developments in North Africa and the Middle East. For here we will encounter precedents for the troubadour revolution still insufficiently understood and acknowledged by scholars. Even while the thousand-year repression of this music was under way in Christendom, the love song enlisted surprising champions in the Muslim world. Here, far from the native lands and cultures of Abelard and Dante, we find the stage set not only for the blossoming of the romantic lyric in the West, but even the first stirrings of the courtly love ethos. Indeed, as we shall now see, our idealized attitudes toward romance and the ways of giving them expression in music, first appeared in Africa long before they arrived on European shores.

CHAPTER 6

The North African and Middle Eastern Connection

The Christians of the Peninsula heard the Moors playing and singing for five or six hundred years. Although they made it a rule not to learn Moorish songs, how could they distinguish when half asleep at night, whether a serenade in the street outside were sung by Christians or Moors? Moreover the Moors sang ravishing love-songs.—Julian Ribera

How often has the forced interaction of African and European populations set off a musical revolution? The most recent took place during the late nineteenth and early twentieth century, when a variety of Africanized musical styles—jazz, blues, ragtime, the spiritual, and others—entered into mainstream American society. These foreign idioms fundamentally changed Western aural culture and continue to influence our songs and dances, as well as the global entertainment business at large. In fact, almost every aspect of modern life would be different had this revolution not taken place—from ways of worship at church to the winners of TV singing competitions. But were there earlier revolutions? Is it possible that the musical DNA introduced by an enslaved population into our songs reinforced a similar cultural mutation that took place a millennium before, only this time introduced by conquerors from Africa itself?

Indeed, exactly one thousand years before the first slaves were brought to New Orleans by the French in 1718, Islamic forces completed their conquest of Hispania, establishing North African supremacy over most of present-day Spain and Portugal, a region known by the new rulers as al-Andalus. In a reversal of the situation that would later set off a musical revolution in the Americas, the dominant power now came from Africa, and the Christian European culture was forced into subservience. Yet a comparable mixture of musical cultures inevitably ensued and had a decisive and still poorly understood impact on the later evolution of the Western love song. In truth, even the love songs we hear on the radio and stream over the web bear the lasting imprint of this now distant historical interlude.

In the nineteenth century, Belgian musicologist François-Joseph Fétis speculated on the possibility of Arabic influence on European music. "The songs of the troubadours," he noted, "repeat the same phrases found among the Arabs, and these phrases are embellished with similar appogaturas, turns and trills." But such observations merely spurred hostility and derision. "Our music has absorbed no influence from the Arabs," Spanish composer and musicologist Felipe Pedrell confidently responded. "Those who admit it are mistaken." Again in the 1920s, scholar Julian Ribera argued that many of the melodies of Spanish Christians were Arabic in origin, and "had grown popular in the [Iberian] Peninsula and had spread all over Europe." Spanish folk music obviously bore this stamp, Ribera argued, but even that masterpiece of medieval Christian music, the *Cantigas*—whose strange combination of religious music and love ballad will be studied later in this volume—was, in his opinion, "a splendid collection of Arabic music."

Spanish musicologists had previously emphasized the European roots of their musical traditions, sometimes tracing their origins back to the ancient Celts. Ribera challenged this image of Western music as an isolated, self-contained system, speculating on a path of influence that started in the Arab world and spread through the Iberian Peninsula and onward through Europe via the troubadours and other emissaries. This dependence on outside inspiration was, he insisted, no cause for shame. Rather, Spain could pride itself on serving as the nexus in what may have been the most important transformational shift in the history of music. "The artistic Spain of olden times," he declared, "thus becomes the central bond which ties ancient to modern."

In 1948, this theory got a new boost when an Oxford student named Samuel Stern showed that parts of Arabic poems from Muslim Spain previously dismissed as gibberish were actually written in a vernacular Romance language. Stern achieved this breakthrough by daring, in the words of María Rosa Menocal, "to read some poems from eleventh-century Spain as if eleventh-century Spain had been a multicultural, multilingual society"—a leap that previous scholars had perhaps been unwilling or unable, due to the extreme specialization of medieval studies, to make. Stern's revelation was stunning, and for several reasons. The appearance of any song lyrics in a European vernacular language from this medieval period would have been noteworthy, but their insertion in Arabic and Hebrew texts was particularly surprising. Above all, the subject matter of these lyrics, with their candid references to love affairs and sexual matters, inevitably grabbed the attention of scholars—and not just those focused on North African and Spanish literary traditions. As experts in other fields tried to make sense of these discoveries, they started pondering whether a whole host of

European artistic traditions—from the troubadour revolution to the rise of the love sonnet—didn't need to be reevaluated in the face of this hybrid song style from al-Andalus.

What were these songs? The *muwashshah*, a strophic song in classical Arabic or Hebrew, was concluded with a *kharja* (from the Arabic word for "exit"), lines in classical or vernacular Arabic, or Ibero-Romance interspersed with Arabic words. The *kharja*s are noteworthy both for their erotic frankness and the active role of their female protagonists. Unlike most troubadour lyrics, in which the woman is often restricted to a passive, on-a-pedestal role, in the *kharja* we find sentiments such as the following:

> My Lord Ibrahim,
> oh my sweet love,
> Come to me
> at night!
> If not, if you don't want to,
> I shall come to you.
> Tell me where
> to see you!

The women in these songs can be equally insistent when fending off a romantic advance: "Don't bite me my love; I don't want anything harmful! / The trousers are fragile; that's enough now! I refuse everything!" Again and again, the woman steps forth confidently in these Romance *kharja*s, in striking contrast to comparable works written entirely in Arabic, and reveals a degree of agency and forthrightness that we simply cannot find in lyrics from Christendom in this era.

The forcefulness of these closing lines is so striking that many scholars have wondered whether the *kharja* served as inspiration for the entire song, almost like those detective stories constructed by the author with the solution of the mystery dictating the essential elements of the preceding chapters. The shift in tone and language provides a contrast between the serious demeanor of the main body of the *muwashshah* and the less formal quality of the concluding *kharja*, a contrast that must have delighted the audience for these songs. The *kharja* would also sometime appear at the end of the *zajal*, a more colloquial lyric. Here the transition is less abrupt, but the whole song is enlivened by this appealingly intimate tone. Adding to the complexity of this cultural hybrid, Jewish poets in this milieu composed similar songs in Hebrew, and these might conclude with *kharja*s in Arabic or Spanish.

Why would singers change language at the end of a song? "No genuine lyrical poetry has ever to borrow from another tongue words like ... 'the beloved one' ... 'lover' ... 'absence' ... 'dark one' ... 'blonde' ... 'watcher,' etc.," points out scholar Federico Corriente. Yet such apparently unnecessary linguistic borrowings do have a psychological value that commentators may have missed. I would compare the *kharja* to similar shifts in the poetry of early modernists such as T. S. Eliot and Ezra Pound, whose readers are forced to deal with abrupt insertions of phrases in a foreign language. A careful appraisal of these lines reveals that these poets often presented their most intimate and revealing thoughts in such passages, almost as if the coded or quasi-hidden quality of the expression gave them license that would have been forbidden in their native tongue. Perhaps the singers in al-Andalus felt similar liberties when drawing on these phrases in the vernacular. As Corriente notes, they didn't lack the words in Arabic or Hebrew but probably felt less inhibited making these intimate disclosures in the language of the streets. Also, as we shall see later in this chapter, the Islamic culture had a long tradition of looking to foreigners and infidels to provide daring musical entertainment, in particular songs that dealt with love and sexuality. The nonbeliever was granted a freedom of expression not allowed to a Muslim, and this attitude may well have influenced the ruling class's perception of suitable topics for lyrics in Romance dialects.

In any event, the informality and use of vernacular in these works kept them out of most of the medieval anthologies. A thirteenth-century Maghribi chronicler apologizes for not including *muwashshahat* (plural of *muwashshah*) he admires because it "was not customary to do so in sizeable respectable works." Moses ibn Ezra, a Jewish philosopher and poet active in Muslim Spain, goes further, admitting he sinned by writing such lyrics during his youth. We have already encountered similar reservations in our study of the love songs of Christian Europe during this period, so we should hardly be surprised to hear them echoed by influential parties of other faiths. Perhaps the more intriguing question is why these songs were preserved, despite such opposition, in Muslim Spain, while they were still hidden from view elsewhere.

According to our sources, the *muwashshah* dates back to the ninth century, thus anticipating the earliest troubadour lyrics by some two centuries. Unfortunately the scholars who provide this information lived in the twelfth century or later, and no *muwashshahat* from this earlier stage of development have survived. We are likewise dependent on late sources for details on the colloquial *zajal*, which was first studied by the early fourteenth-century poet Safi ad-Din al-Hilli. He believed the *zajal* evolved from the *muwashshah*, but many modern scholars have suggested that the vernacular form has older roots in a popular song tradition, and achieved literary status only with the rise of the *muwashshah*. The brilliant Spanish Muslim philosopher and scientist Avempace (also known as Ibn Bajja), who flourished around the dawn of the troubadour revolution, is sometimes credited with this innovation, but we have good reason to trace the origins of the *zajal* to a period long before his birth.

Performances of *muwashshahat* did not maintain concert hall decorum, and were more akin to a modern-day rave than a recital. "The (wine) cups went round and round on its melody, while people tore their clothes (in ecstasy)," reports Ibn Sana' al-Mulk, although this late twelfth-century native of Cairo never had the opportunity to hear this music in its land of origin. He compensated for his lack of firsthand experience by his enthusiasm—he was an unabashed aficionado of the genre and is one of our most detailed early sources. He adds that the songs were performed by "men and women," "young and old," and were heard at wedding parties or could serve as "greetings among companions."

The very fact that we must consult an Egyptian source for basic information on these songs testifies to their dissemination not just in Spain but through North Africa and into the Middle East. By the thirteenth century, these areas surpassed Islamic Spain in their zeal for this style of performance. And the lyrics matched the fervor of their admirers, displaying a bawdy candor appropriate for settings where people tore off their clothes in paroxysms of joy. Indeed the graphic depictions of this vernacular popular song tradition would be striking even by our own R-rated standards. Safi ad-Din al-Hilli shares a lyric in the Egyptian style, a complaint by a man overcome with lustful desires: "How can I change my ways / when God created my penis with a hole in it." Clearly the popularity of these works drew on their brazen eroticism, which inspired imitation even in locales far removed from the genre's homeland.

Ibn Sana' al-Mulk also gives us more details on the *kharja*, the concluding section of these songs. He specifies that it must be in colloquial Arabic or a foreign non-Arabic language. The insistence on this requirement from an expert source in twelfth-century Egypt shows the flip side of the Muslim influence in European music—namely that the transformation worked in both directions. A Cairo admirer of secular songs could prize the foreign ingredients he found in them, just as European audiences took delight in "oriental" musical instruments brought back from the Crusades. Alas, Ibn Sana' al-Mulk admits that he does not know the Romance tongue of the Iberian Peninsula, so he must turn to Persian to give an exotic flavor to his *kharjas*—even though he acknowledges that the role models most worthy of emulation come from the poets of the West. Yet not only is a different language required in the close of these songs, but also a different perspective. The *kharja* represents a change to a different narrative voice, a shift to "he (or she) said"—thus a male singer can offer a female perspective. This juxtaposition is all the more striking given the apparent scarcity of *muwashshahat* composed by women. These cumulative ingredients create a moment of disjunction, perhaps even of shock, at the conclusion of the performance. Later sources tell us that the musical accompaniment also contributed to this abrupt transition in the song, and we are probably safe in assuming that the same was true of the early examples from al-Andalus.

Why would people in North Africa and the Middle East admire songs written in a language they hardly knew? Certainly the exoticism and newness of a musical style add to its allure. And I have already noted the tendency for poets to reveal intimacies when speaking in a language other than their own. But other factors probably played a significant role in the spread of this genre. I suspect that the music came equipped with "hooks" that drew Islamic listeners to embrace songs with pronounced European elements. We see a similar phenomenon today, when pop-rock megastars fill stadiums far from home, even in locales where few in the audience understand their lyrics. Al-Jahiz, a ninth-century scholar from Basra in modern-day Iraq, offers some clues to how this might have happened in the medieval period, explaining that Arabs "match their melodies to the meter of the poem," but foreigners "may expand or contract their words and phrases in order to fit the tune. Strict forms of poetry are superimposed on a fluid, musical base." Ibn Sana' al-Mulk makes a similar comment about the *kharja*, noting that the form permitted the addition of words such as "lā, lā, lā" to fit the meter or melody. Even the example here—la, la, la?—reminds us of modern pop music relying on throwaway words (the Beatles' famous "yeah, yeah, yeah") and nonsense syllables to impart an ineffable charm to the proceedings. If the music is strong enough, semantic meaning is optional.

The troubadour songs that would soon beguile Europe were often composed by members of the nobility, especially during the early period of their dissemination, but the lyrics of Muslim Iberia tend to have a less aristocratic lineage. Some of the authors are described as illiterate, others as blind. Many must have relied on their artistry to survive, literally singing for their supper. Ibn Quzman, who flourished in the early and middle decades of the twelfth century, brought his considerable talents to Seville, Granada, Málaga, Almería, Valencia, Jaén, and his native Córdoba, and his lyrics praising local potentates reflect his clear grasp of his state of dependency. A few poets or singers may have had more secure positions, either in a court or some other capacity; accounts tell of those who also gained distinction as a judge, landowner, or doctor. Nobles, even kings, sometimes certainly composed nonclassical poetry in al-Andalus. But the overall picture is more diverse and less elitist than in the south of France during the troubadour era. The vocations mentioned in the *kharjas* tend to confirm this view: a bricklayer, shop owner, barkeeper, glazier, and other such lowly occupations. "I shout in the streets: I am in love with a young tailor and what a tailor!" proclaims a *kharja* by Ibn al-Sabuni, a thirteenth-century Moorish poet of Seville. "He has a chin sprinkled with ink (as a consequence) of sewing so many carpets."

These vocational references and other urban details suggest that these songs flourished in the cities of Muslim Spain rather than in the countryside. These cities would also contain the largest number of bilingual residents, and this helps to explain the mixture of languages in these love songs. It is hardly a coincidence that the largest, most prosperous cities in western Europe at the close of the first millennium were located in present-day Spain. Córdoba boasted ten times the population of London or Rome in the year 1000. Seville may have had four times as many residents as Paris. The role of urbanization in the rise of the love song has not been adequately studied, but we will encounter this connection at many junctures in our history. In Europe, the love lyric came out of hiding during a period of migration from the country to the city, and the dense population of these growing urban centers would eventually prove more important than the patronage of nobles, and a host of other factors, in allowing these lyrics of romance and courtship to flourish and spread.

"Everybody, the elite and the common people, liked and knew these poems," wrote the fourteenth-century Muslim historian Ibn Khaldun, "because they were easy to grasp and understand." Despite this popularity, the ethos of love celebrated in the lyrics ran counter to prevailing values. Again and again, Hispano-Arabic love songs make reference to the enemies of love—and, by implication, of the music that celebrated it. Three adversaries appear most frequently in these songs: the censurer, the backbiter, and the spy. The spies are the most feared since they often include family members who will be quick to punish the offending lovers. But the delights of love are intensified by the satisfaction of outwitting these guardians of virtue. "How suspicious is the spy!" announces one lyric. "My lady, let us do what the spy suspects!" Sometimes the opponents of love are generalized as public opinion, at other times they take on specific identities. "Come, my love, come this night," proclaims a typical song, "my brothers are absent and they did not come back."

The tone and attitude of these lyrics anticipate the late medieval love songs of Europe, especially with their recurring emphasis on the anguish and suffering that come with affairs of the heart. "There is usually the mood of the unhappy lover," writes medievalist Vicente Cantarino, "his yearning and desires, his despair in his loneliness and rejection. The lover is endlessly submerged in love pains or he is aroused by memories of a sweet past and by hopes for a tender future." The theme of lovesickness appears again and again, and sometimes the beloved is described as the doctor who holds the only cure for this malady. Scholar Linda Fish Compton enumerates a few of the symptoms suffered by the unfortunate lovers in these songs: "insomnia, emaciation, madness, humiliation, loss of patience, despair, rivers of tears which can't extinguish flames of passion, a willingness to offer one's own father as ransom for the beloved, or even abjuring Islam to worship a willowy sweetheart."

But not all lovers in these songs are frustrated. Many songs contain explicit scenarios rarely matched by the lyrics of medieval Christendom—or at least not by the surviving lyrics. "Break my bracelet and loosen my belt, my lover Ahmad, climb with me into bed." Or: "Mess up my hair, rub my breast, frightened bird, drink my saliva and kiss my cheek." Occasionally the amorous advances in these lyrics are too aggressive—and incite a bitter or angry response from the beloved. "He assaulted me and kissed my mouth, I am going to tell my mother." Or: "Do you really want all this? Can't you be satisfied with a kiss?" Sometimes we hear a passing suggestion of restraint—requests not to rip the lover's trousers or bruise the lady's breasts with such rough handling. But just as often, these words of reproach seem aimed at slowing down the proceedings, not halting them. Even specific sexual postures might be specified: "Raise my anklets up to my earrings. My husband is busy." Or this emphatic variant: "I shall not kill you but on condition that you make my anklets reach my earrings." A lyric from the Hebrew texts proclaims: "Lady, come, come, kiss and embrace me, put yourself under me or on top of me."

In our studies of this song tradition we find again and again a hidden influence of female innovators lingering just below the surface of the surviving accounts. We hear of the contributions of Avempace, the Arab polymath born in Aragon in 1095, mentioned above with regard to the *zajal*, who "secluded himself for several years with skilled singing girls" and thus "combined the songs of the Christians with those of the East." If these love songs were the creation of men, why did he need to sequester himself with women? In further confirmation that men borrowed much of the musical language of love from women, we find *kharjas* attributed to a female voice that are echoed in later songs where identical sentiments are delivered from a male perspective.

Any theory about the *kharja* as a nexus in a process of cultural transmission from North Africa and the Middle East to Europe has a significant advantage in its favor from the outset—namely the bilingual nature of these songs. Yet the broader linguistic context in which these lyrics appeared has long been a matter of dispute. The arrival of the Visigoths in the early fifth century may have signaled the end of Roman rule in Spain, but apparently had little influence on local dialects. In contrast, the Arab invasion of 711 had more far-reaching effects. In a famous passage from the ninth century, Álvaro of Córdoba laments: "Alas! Christians do not know their own law, and Latins do not use their own tongue." Some scholars have concluded that Moorish Iberia was a monolingual Arabic-speaking country in regions under Arab control. At the other extreme, some believe that the vast majority of the populace spoke Romance dialects, and only a comparatively small group used Arabic. Still others have argued for widespread bilingualism, or separate monolingual cultures with only a few intermediaries moving with fluency from one group to another. The discovery of these bilingual lyrics has dealt a devastating blow to scholars who want to study these intermixed cultures as though they existed in isolation. The *kharjas* force us to accept a more dynamic model of cultural transmission, a creative interaction between Arabic and European traditions in the Iberian Peninsula that clearly had important repercussions beyond its borders.

Can we conclude that the erotic elements in these songs were European in origin? Certainly the fact that the most frank and sensual parts of these songs were often the closing expressions in a Romance vernacular might suggest this is case. Yet, if so, why did this kind of music only find acceptance in the portion of the continent under Islamic control? Perhaps the creative friction between two very different cultures ultimately served as the key catalyst. As we have already seen, the erotic love song had always existed in medieval Europe, but was forced into hiding by the Christian authorities. Once those authorities were displaced, the love songs came out in the open—especially because the now ascendant Arabic culture, which had long shown far more tolerance to eroticism and love lyrics, found them compatible with their own musical practices.

In recent years, scholars of European music have increasingly acknowledged, sometimes begrudgingly, the importance of the *kharja* and its potential influence on the troubadours, but they have ignored the long history of singing slave girls documented in Arabic medieval culture—a tradition that deserves close study from anyone concerned with the later rise of courtly love and its music. The *qayna*, the elite female singing slave of the early Abbasid era, deserves a prominent place in the history of the love song, but is virtually unknown to Western music scholars. She held a paradoxical position in society. In many ways, the *qayna* had more freedom than other women in Islamic society. She often had access to education and tutors who taught her music, reading, and etiquette and comportment. The *qiyan* (plural of *qayna*) also had more liberty in personal attire, wearing stylish clothing and not covering their faces, while the ostensibly free women of the era were hidden top to bottom in loose, unbecoming cloaks. The most prized slaves often conversed with powerful men and sometimes exerted influence through their lovers. On the other hand, they could be bought and sold like a piece of merchandise and might be treated with callousness or even physical violence. Like the Japanese geisha, the *qayna* strived to project an image of elegance and sophistication, but this would hardly prevent others from despising her as little more than a prostitute.

We have already witnessed at several junctures the close connection between prostitution and the musical arts—and this linkage will continue into the twenty-first century, albeit in a state of marked decline. As far back as we can delve, leading courtesans were expected to possess artistic skills. The *Kama Sutra* cites singing, dancing, and instrumental music among the sixty-four talents necessary for elite lovers, whether professional or aristocratic (alongside less obviously erotic practices, such as metallurgy, carpentry, and teaching parrots how to talk). In many cultural settings, music served as the key differentiator elevating more accomplished courtesans to the top ranks. We find this, for example, in the Tang Dynasty of China (AD 618–907), which coincides with many of the examples from Islamic culture presented in this chapter, or among the *hetaerae*, the elite courtesans of ancient Greece, or prostitutes of the Italian renaissance, or the *tawaif* of India during the Mughal Empire. Some cultures tried to separate prostitution and sensual entertainment. The Japanese geisha is perhaps the most notable example. Her craft, as it evolved, emphasized music and dance, not the sale of sex. "But the division was never clear cut," writes scholar Lesley Downer. "The fact that the geisha originated in the pleasure quarters inevitably colored the way in which they were perceived by the rest of society." In Korea, we encounter a similar profession, the *kiaseng*, but here the division between musical entertainment and prostitution proved even harder to enforce. During the course of the twentieth century, the *kiaseng* tradition was engulfed by the sex trade, although a few researchers and performers continue their efforts to preserve the artistic side of this cultural legacy. In most times and places, slaves and courtesans have filled this role of sensual singer. The melodies, movements, and rituals differ based on the setting and surrounding culture, but the universality of the connection between prostitution and performance warrants close attention, reminding us of the intimate connection between music and eros, and the many contributions to the evolution of the love song made by women from the margins of society.

Islam, like Christianity and Judaism during this period, tolerated the institution of slavery, although the Koran admonished masters to treat their slaves with kindness. Accounts tell of men who possessed a thousand or more females—or sometimes their wives took charge of the women slaves. Forcing a slave girl into prostitution was prohibited, but having sexual relations with her was deemed lawful. In practice, female slaves often worked in houses of pleasure that were essentially brothels, although wine and entertainment might also be provided to patrons in these retreats for revelry and carousing. The Muslim conquests swelled the ranks of these captive women, who become property of the soldiers, subject to a tax of one-fifth their value paid to the treasury. Others were given as tribute from non-Muslims. Every major city boasted its own slave market, and the international mix of the captives put up for sale—which included Persians, Europeans, Berbers, Nubians, Asians and others—ensured that the subjugated population was more cosmopolitan than much of the ruling class. Most of these female slaves worked as domestics in the households of their masters, but the more attractive and talented might be trained to serve as entertainers, and were prized for their performing skills and womanly charms. This instruction of slaves could be a luxury or an investment, depending on the master's intentions. An especially gifted *qayna* with proven skills as a singer and poet could sell for more than some free workers earned in a lifetime.

A surviving auction catalog of slaves outlines the pros and cons of different nationalities. Berbers are praised for their "obedience, fidelity and energy." Abyssinians are "slender and soft" but "useless for singing and dancing." The Turks have a "tendency to sullenness." Yemenis are noteworthy for their "pretty faces." Armenians "would be pleasing were it not for their monstrous legs." As such descriptions make clear, musical and performing skills were prized alongside physical beauty and desirable character traits. Indeed, the connection between the musical arts and slavery was deeply embedded in Abbasid culture—so much so that Ibrahim al-Mawsili (742–804) could gain renown as the leading singer and music teacher of his day and also as a celebrated slave trader. The business of 'improving' slaves was one of the most lucrative trades, and even elite performers felt no shame in engaging in it as a profitable sideline.

Many of these slaves must have brought musical skills with them from their native culture. We know little about African and Middle Eastern love songs from the early medieval period, but they must have existed, and perhaps in abundance. St. Valerius, who died in 695, mentions an Ethiopian priest who performed love songs that he accompanied on a lute. Valerius lived in Spain before the Muslim conquest, and his commentary indicates that love songs were already coming from Africa into Europe during the Visigoth era. Performers of this sort must have been even more common in the Arab world. In the early medieval era, Ethiopia was the single largest source of slaves for Arab traders, and those with musical talent must have often been encouraged to perform by their owners.

Unlike the later Atlantic slave trade, in which men represented the vast majority of captives, the Islamic markets demanded more females, who outnumbered males by a two-to-one margin. The most celebrated female slaves gained acclaim for their poetry and singing. These songs often dealt with amatory matters, ranging from the most refined sentiments to the coarsest erotic observations. The story is told of the famous slave 'Inan, renowned for her beauty and quick wit, who was left unsatisfied after five bouts of lovemaking, and sang the following to her spent partner: "O host of lovers how execrable is love / if there is flabbiness in the lover's prick." The surviving accounts include many anecdotes of celebrated female slaves who responded with mockery and ridicule to suitors, denouncing their appearance, lovemaking skills, or insufficient wealth. Yet these same women have also left us passionate love lyrics that prefigure many of the themes that would dominate the later songs of the troubadours and their followers. The famous ninth-century slave 'Arib, who boasted that she had slept with eight caliphs, composed the following song, seemingly so heartfelt but actually written for another woman to present to her lover:

Sire, you have burdened me with sleeplessness
and it is you who taught my love ecstasy and passion
But for you I would not have minded any illness ever
but it is that you so much filled my heart that it caught fire

Can we believe lyrics of this sort, coming from the mouth of a captive? The whole ugly institution of slavery requires us to approach the effusive expressions of love and devotion in these songs with caution and skepticism. On the other hand, surviving testimonies from slave singers make frank comparisons between men, distinguishing ones they truly loved from those they merely served. Certainly we must hesitate before dismissing all of these amorous songs as examples of false consciousness. And is this situation really so different from the current day, when the love songs we hear on the radio or in concert are performed for pay and not as a reward for our individual charms and lovemaking skills? Even so, the enduring connection between love songs and slavery—which, as documented in these pages, persisted from antiquity well into the modern era—is especially fraught with complex overtones and potential for distortion. In truth, we can hardly consider this subject without examining the long-standing linkage in the popular imagination, and in prevalent fantasies (of a *Fifty Shades of Grey* flavor), between love and enslavement. The whole succeeding history of the love song in particular, and of Western romance in general, is filled with celebrations of captivity. This enslavement can be taken literally—as the adherents of chains-and-handcuffs liaisons remind us—or merely as metaphor. But it is always present, at some level, in our conceptualization of romance. We are left to wonder whether this fixation is a carryover from a day when love songs were the specialty of actual slaves. Few would disagree with Moroccan feminist Fatima Mernissi, who, in a critique of this tradition of singing slave girls, complains: "Love, seduction and enslavement are forever linked in our imagination." Yet, as our subsequent history will show, this mindset has hardly been limited to women. If, as I contend, male singers of love songs have repeatedly drawn on the innovations of female role models, even these men must have found some erotic charge in an attitude of subservience to the beloved. As we shall see in the next chapter, this servile stance stands out as the dominant theme of courtly love, and ranks among the medieval world's most influential contributions to the Western psyche. But, by the time we arrive at the age of the troubadours, the innovations of women and slaves are forgotten—or at least written out of the histories; instead powerful men emerge as leading advocates of the bondage metaphor in Western romance.

Very few lyrics from free-born women in the Islamic societies of this period have survived. Yet the ones preserved show that even high-born ladies relied on the same language of servitude. Here ʿUlayya (777–825), the daughter of a caliph and sister to three others, announces her love in the same language as a *qayna*:

Neither happiness nor sadness takes my mind off you
how and how can one forget your beautiful face

Neither my heart nor my body is free from you
my whole is occupied by and in bondage to your whole.

'Ulayya goes on to announce that her "soul becomes a vassal" to her lover—a comparison all the more surprising when we learn that the object of this powerful lady's affection was a mere palace youth, possibly a eunuch. This hypothesis perhaps explain 'Ulayya's lament in a cryptic lyric that her beloved "has no way to enter."

We will continue to encounter, in later chapters, the sometimes puzzling situation of men writing love songs from a female perspective. In the early Abbasid era this gender shift was driven by many motives. Love songs were sometimes written by men with the intention that they be performed by a female slave or free woman—or they were dedicated to her, or she is mentioned by name in a lyric. In some instances the *qayna* or her owner may have commissioned these works. Yet, whether a man or woman is writing the words, the language of enslavement remains. Muti' ibn Ayas makes playful reference to this paradox in an ode dedicated to the slave who rules his heart:

Muti has become ardent in love
sad and seriously ill
Free as perceived by the beloved
but acknowledging his bondage.

Even the caliph found no incongruity in this imagery of the male lover in servitude. In a poem addressed to his three favorite slave girls, Harun al-Rashid declared that these "three ladies hold my reins." And if anyone doubts this peculiar claim, he emphasizes the point: "The whole of mankind obey me while I am ruled by them."

But when we turn our attention to the male professional singers of Islamic society, the influence of women is even more marked. Tuways, the first documented professional singer in Medina after the rise of Islam, was labeled a *mukhannath*—a term that designates an effeminate man, and in practice might encompass a wide range of individuals, from homosexuals to eunuchs or hermaphrodites. With regard to Tuways, who married and fathered children, this term might describe his high-pitched vocal delivery or what we would nowadays describe as his 'lifestyle', or both. The *mukhannathun* were often subjected to derision and punishment—the story is told of the prophet Muhammad banishing a *mukhannath* to an area outside of Medina, but refusing to sanction the murder of these outcasts. Other prominent musicians were similarly described as effeminate, among them the renowned singer Ibn Surayj, who made his reputation as a performer of laments—a type of song closely associated with women (and love songs) throughout history. One commentator ranked Ibn Surayj as the best of the *female* singers. The context makes it impossible to know whether he is making a wisecrack, offering a musical judgment on Ibn Surayj's vocal delivery, or referring to the singer's way of life. In a similar vein, the celebrated master of early Abbasid love lyrics Abbas Ibn al-Ahnaf, who composed ghazals that were set to music and performed in the caliph's court, is described as "delicate, attractive, tender and full of ideas"—and here the qualities emphasized are clearly personal ones. We are left with an almost inescapable conclusion: that both performers and audiences saw a link between feminine qualities and skill as a purveyor of musical entertainment, especially love songs.

How did patrons and audiences react to this 'effeminate' manner of singing? A noble singer of the old style was chastised by his son for changing his approach in his old age and adopting the popular vocal style of the *mukhannathun*. He replied, "Be quiet, ignorant boy!," and pointed out that he had lived in poverty for sixty years singing in the old style but now had "made more money than you'd ever seen before" by adapting to the new manner of performing.

The popularity of secular music grew in tandem with its connections to sensuality. During the early Abbasid era, a true music industry developed, with entertainment and festivities no longer restricted to celebratory events, but available at permanent establishments that aimed to gratify the desires of the audience...and not just for songs. We have already seen the close connection between love songs and prostitution, but the link between music-making and alcohol is even more evident during the reign of the early Abbasid caliphs—ninth century Baghdad prized wine songs to a degree that no other culture has ever surpassed. The courts and major cities of medieval Europe may have cherished their talented musicians and enjoyed their performances, but none of them could match the Arab world's celebration of music as a source of pleasure, and as such inevitably linked to eroticism and intoxication.

This licentious era would gradually come to end following the murder of Caliph al-Mutawakkil in the year 861 by the Turkish palace guard, and the ensuing rise to power of the military chiefs. At first, the impact on the institution of the slave girls and their love songs must have been insignificant—after all, these women did not hold official positions, and their allegiances (as well as ownership) could shift with the changing political currents. But the ensuing turbulence and violent succession of puppet caliphs eventually drained the treasury in the face of constant demands for money from the Turkish soldiers, who now served as the ultimate sources of authority and control. Private citizens also had their wealth seized, and even the appearance of prosperity might be sufficient to incite demands from the avaricious troops. In such an environment, lavish expenditure on wine, women, and song inevitably declined, as did ostentatious patronage of culture and the arts.

Many of the slave girls moved on to other settings, including Muslim Spain. We hear of Qamar, a Baghdad native, purchased by the emir of Seville, and of Fadl al-Madiniyya trained in Medina before coming to the Iberian Peninsula. Abd al-Rahman II, who became emir of Córdoba in 822, set aside a section of his palace for female singers, among whom pride of place was given to Fadl and the others trained in Medina. Sometimes talented women journeyed in the opposite direction for 'finishing', for example Qalam of Navarre, who was a slave in Muslim Spain but was sent to Medina for training. On her return, she gained renowned as a musician, as well as for her literary talents. But for every famous slave singer known to us, many others must have gained notoriety in their day, although their names have not survived. "There are expert old women who teach singing to slave girls they own," writes Arabic poet Ahmad al-Tifashi with regard to Seville, "as well as to salaried half-Arab female servants of theirs." He notes that these slaves could be sold for large sums of money, and would come with a register listing all the songs they had memorized.

Celebrated male singers also made the move to Muslim Spain, most notably the famous performer and teacher Ziryab, probably a freed slave of African or mixed African-Arab origins—his name translates as Blackbird—who served at the court of Harun al-Rashid in Baghdad. Ziryab was forced to leave Baghdad, possibly because he had surpassed his mentor in musical skill, and in 822 moved to Córdoba, where he served as court entertainer for Abd al-Rahman II. No one played a larger role in shaping the musical culture of Muslim Spain than this black slave from Baghdad. Ziryab set up a music school in Córdoba, and others in Seville, Granada, Valencia, and Toledo followed his example. His repertoire was said to encompass ten thousand songs, but his innovations extended beyond music. Accounts tell of Ziryab inventing formulas for deodorant and toothpaste, serving as an advocate for asparagus, and establishing various hair styles. He is also credited with the introduction of chess into Europe.

But even in this case, the renowned man had strong musical ties to female performers. His two daughters were also esteemed musicians, and his students included his slave girl Metaa. The story is told of Ziryab teaching his best songs to Metaa, who performed them for Abd-al-Rahman II. The sultan grew enamored with the young lady but hesitated to act on his passion, out of consideration for Ziryab. But Metaa took matters into her own hands. She expressed her longing in her songs, and chided the emir for his silence. When Ziryab learned of this, he released Metaa from his service and presented her to his patron. Afterwards she resided permanently at the palace.

These historical precedents are of vital importance when we try to measure the impact of the Islamic musical culture that entered European society via the Iberian Peninsula. The conquerors had long looked to enslaved and conquered populations for entertainment, and especially for love songs. In this regard, the similarity with American music during the nineteenth and twentieth centuries is striking, and we can perhaps imagine the situation in the medieval Islamic world by extrapolation. The master, who needs to maintain the values of the dominant society, with all its sanctions and proprieties, is nonetheless fascinated by the transgressive possibilities that can come only from the slave, the outsider, the infidel—individuals whose very exclusion from the established order makes them a source of innovation and creative energy.

Sociopolitical institutions and artistic currents present rival hierarchies, and the inevitable tensions can be repressed or resolved in a wide range of ways. One can only wonder what would have happened in the antebellum South if plantation owners had followed their Islamic predecessors and viewed the training in arts and literary matters of their most talented slaves as a profitable investment. As it stands, withholding education from the black population may have slowed down the Africanization of American entertainment, but could hardly stop it, and by the early twentieth century the main innovations in Western musical culture were coming primarily from the sons and grandsons of slaves. In many instances, the star performer might still be white—Paul Whiteman, Benny Goodman, Elvis Presley, the Rolling Stones—but the wellspring and specific sources of inspiration were black.

A similar process may have led to the blossoming of love songs in the West during the late medieval period. Nietzsche famously labeled Christianity a "slave morality" and saw its celebration of meekness and subservience as a source of lassitude, an emasculating tendency that allowed the weak to hold back the strong. Is it possible that the modern love lyric filled a similar function, and is by that token a slave song style, a poetic espousal of servitude to the beloved that reverses the conventional power structures? Certainly the whole Western discourse of courtly love, as it evolved over several hundred years, showed a remarkable—at times almost pathological—obsession with themes of subjugation and obedience. But when we cast our gaze at the Islamic culture that entered southern Europe before the rise of the troubadours we see more than a discourse of servitude. We encounter an actual musical culture and a large body of love songs composed by slaves, for slaves, or in imitation of slaves. Scholars of European music have paid almost no attention to this extraordinary state of affairs, but its importance can hardly be exaggerated. As we shall see, the North African and Middle Eastern connections will help us understand many otherwise puzzling developments in the subsequent history of the love song.

The medieval love lyric was "invented in bitter exile," writes Menocal, who notes that the love song often takes on the wistful tone of people removed from their land of origin. She focuses most of her attention on Dante, banished from his native Florence in 1302, but this bittersweet flavor that pervades the Western love song predates Dante by centuries, and can be traced to the slaves who established the basic formulas for our music of romance. These slaves were eternal exiles, and their sense of separation and loss made a lasting imprint on their lyrics, even when the subject at hand was personal, not political. (We will see the same phenomenon when we arrive at the blues in a later chapter.) Menocal gives little attention to this issue, and explores instead the love lyrics of cultural elites, yet we need to reverse this hierarchy, and praise instead the innovations of the oppressed and marginalized, individuals mostly ignored in works of literary and music history.

Our focus now must turn to the south of France, where the most important revolution in the history of the love song is about to take place. Only a little more than two hundred miles separate Toulouse, the capital of the former province of Languedoc, where this new style came to light, from Zaragoza in present-day Spain, under Muslim control at the dawn of the troubadour age. Now the Christian world will emerge as the epicenter of innovation in love songs. Even more, the whole ethos of romance and courtship will change in tandem with the music of love. Should we be surprised, or merely nod our heads with bemused understanding, when we see that the same fixation on servitude and bondage of the Arab slave girls is now espoused by the European nobility, rich and powerful men who will eventually get written into the history of books as the inventors of this piquant new way of singing about love?

CHAPTER 7

The Troubadours

The first who began to write as a poet of the common tongue was moved
to do so because he wished to make his words understandable by a lady to
whom verse in Latin was hard to understand. And this argues against those
who rhyme on other matters than love, because it is a fact that this mode of
speaking was first invented in order to speak of love.—Dante, *La Vita Nuova*

So many changes come at us at this juncture in our story. The love song, previously marginalized and repressed in Christian Europe, now takes center stage via
the troubadours, who rhapsodize on eros with a brashness and confidence that,
in many ways, anticipate the popular music of our own time. A hundred years
earlier, such songs would have been a mark of shame and sinfulness, condemned
from the pulpit and excised from the public record. But in the late medieval
period, they not only gain acceptance, but serve as a path to fame and acclaim.

In this new environment, composers of love songs are no longer content to
remain anonymous, but proudly attach their names to their works. Biographical details are preserved, sometimes with a breathless, gossipy tone not entirely different from what we find today. Perhaps the facts are exaggerated or
plain wrong—but is that any different from accounts of today's pop stars in
the tabloids? Nor is it mere coincidence that a modern-day singer-songwriter
is often called a troubadour. Indeed, the public's insatiable appetite for the im-
modest presentation of stylized autobiographical elements in song form, taken
for granted nowadays, first appeared in recognizable form with these celebrated
performers of the late Middle Ages.

Above all, the *attitude* of these songs will also be familiar to us, even in their
most idealized and unrealistic aspects. The very ingredients that might make
these lyrics seem hopelessly out of touch with our current romances—the chivalric grandiloquence and hyperbole, the extravagant gestures of devotion—
mesmerize us with a beguiling ideal that charms even as we recognize the
exaggerations. No, the world of the troubadours is not our world, and its exigencies and constraints would madden the modern mind; but the freshness and

youthful vigor with which the troubadours brought love into the forefront of the musical arts—close to half of the songs of the troubadours deal with romance; not much different than what you might encounter on a playlist today—set an example that, playfully or earnestly, we still recognize as part of our own conceptualization of love.

For a period of roughly 250 years, the art of the troubadours played a central role in the musical and emotional life of southern Europe. We know the names of close to five hundred troubadours—extraordinary given the anonymity of so many previous poets and musicians. Around 2,500 songs have survived. Melodies are more elusive. They were documented for around 10 percent of the songs, but even these few are imperfectly notated, with pitches indicated but neither their duration nor the aggregate rhythms.

The term *courtly love* appears again and again in scholarly studies of the troubadours, applied not only to the values embodied in the songs but even to the zeitgeist of the cultural milieu that produced them. The phrase evokes the peculiar combination of erotic intensity and spiritual devotion of these lyrics, and images of the noble, chivalric lovers who wrote them—although often singing the praises of women married to other men. Yet scholars have challenged and debated the usage and rightly point out that the term 'courtly love' was applied after the fact—its acceptance as a label traced back to Gaston Paris in 1883, who used it to describe the romances of northern France, not the troubadour songs of the south.

But the fiercest arguments have been about more than mere terminology. The most pressing debates focus on love itself. What did love mean to the people who made these songs? To what extent did amatory attitudes and practices change during the age of the troubadours? Should we believe C. S. Lewis, who confidently proclaimed that "French poets, in the eleventh century, discovered or invented or were the first to express, the romantic species of passion"? In his words, a revolution of love took place, and "compared with this revolution the Renaissance is a mere ripple on the surface of literature." Or do we trust scholar Peter Dronke, who asserts that courtly love always existed, "or is at least as old as Egypt of the second millennium B.C."?

Even stranger, for many scholars courtly love has nothing to do with romance, and "should be interpreted as a collective fantasy caused by an infantile mother fixation"—a view that Roger Boase assures us "has been accepted, in one form or another, by all those who have analyzed medieval love poetry." Or perhaps we should follow the lead of Denis de Rougemont, who argues that courtly love must be viewed as a vehicle for heretical Christian doctrine, and thus anticipated the Reformation. Under this interpretation, these earthy lyrics *appear* to celebrate carnal love but were actually focused on *sublimating* sexuality. And then we have the growing body of evidence, presented in the previous chapter, that the ethos of courtly love—especially its stylized deference to the beloved and emphasis on subjugation and servitude—came from those who were forced by necessity to defer and serve, namely the slaves of the Islamic world, whose songs and attitudes came to Europe via the Muslim conquest of Spain. The *qiyan*, or female singing slaves of the early Abbasid era, have been ignored in almost all of the scholarly literature on the troubadours, yet their songs clearly anticipated the tone and attitude of the new music now embraced by the nobility of southern France.

Great energy and scholastic ingenuity has been spent in attempting to prove that troubadour songs were about something other than love. Marxist theorists have labored to uncover economic and social desires hidden beneath the corporeal longings celebrated in troubadour lyrics. From such a perspective, singers may have celebrated the beloved's eyes, lips, voices...but were actually motivated by the ladies' dowries, inheritances, and property rights. Put simply, rich widows whose husbands died in the Crusades inspired courtly love—and it wasn't because of their physical charms. Other commentators, perhaps higher-minded and less cynical, have found in the troubadour art a secular displacement of the cult of the Virgin Mary, which was a powerful force in religious life during the Middle Ages—more than twenty feast days in honor of the mother of Christ were celebrated in medieval Europe. Another interpretation highlights the playful element in these songs and sees them as a formulaic game men played primarily to impress other men. Ezra Pound even insisted that a song by Bertran de Born, ostensibly about an ideal lady, whose beauty was assembled from different traits of various women, was actually a coded message about castles and related military intelligence.

Our focus here is on love songs, so I make no apologies for taking these troubadours at their word. I am confident that similarly reductionist approaches to modern love songs could affirm that the Beatles' "Can't Buy Me Love" is actually about class consciousness among Liverpool youth, and Sonny and Cher's "I Got You Babe" is a parable of Soviet-U.S. relations during the Cold War. Such is the richness of works of art that scholars are able to dig far below the surface and find inexhaustible riches...or perhaps just fool's gold. We do well to remember that gems and nuggets also sometimes appear on the surface. Certainly when dealing with the songs of the troubadours, we ignore the surface meanings at a heavy cost. And if our study of the history of love songs so far has taught us anything, it should be that the romantic and erotic imagination constantly seeks to express itself in music, and does not require external justification. A close inspection of the troubadours in the broader context of the *full* history of the love song suggests that a hidden musical tradition was now simply coming out into the open, no doubt modified by the different cultural imperatives of the time, but also fortified by a thousand-year buildup in which amatory lyrics had persisted despite the best efforts of civil and religious authorities to eliminate them.

Yet the tale of the troubadours is more than a simple matter of love set free, and a full accounting inevitably returns us to the economic and class considerations mentioned above. Romantic love has always had to confront the influence of money and power, and lovers throughout the ages have agonized over conflicts between dictates of the heart and worldly interests. This was true for the troubadours just as it is true for us today. Troubadours clearly understood the danger of pushing love's claims too assiduously—especially when singing the praises of women of noble birth, often married to powerful, jealous men. Such a balancing act required both ingenuity and caution. One solution was to pay homage to an *unnamed* lady, perhaps only in the final lines mentioning the noblewoman to whom the song was dedicated. In other instances, troubadours employed disclaimers not dissimilar to the small print on modern-day advertisements. Bernart de Ventadorn, for example, sings: "For her body is beautiful and pleasing and white beneath her clothes. I say this only on the basis of my imagination." Even so, troubadours might find themselves in trouble due to the fidelity with which their lives imitated their art. Bernart addressed love songs to Marguerite de Turenne, wife of his patron Viscount Ventadorn, but his amorous ambitions may have gone beyond the realm of musical performance—with the result that Marguerite was allegedly put under lock and key and the troubadour sent packing. Perhaps the viscount merely lacked a trained literary mind, and couldn't see beyond the surface meaning of the songs, which he interpreted as expressing real emotions and intentions. Then again, the same may be said of Bernart himself: he openly proclaims in "Be m'an perdut" that his success as a troubadour is based not on technical skill but on the intensity with which his heart was drawn to love.

Even as love serves as the primary motivating force in the art of the troubadour, its power is clearly augmented by other interests. The Christian faith, which had fought so vehemently against the purveyors of love songs in earlier days, increasingly found its imagery and metaphysics usurped by its longtime foe. A spirit of *devotion* now permeates the love lyric, a transference of prerogatives formerly assigned to the divine and sainted. In this regard, the legends associated with the troubadours are as revealing as the songs themselves. Jaufre Rudel, a troubadour of the early twelfth century, is best known today for celebrating the concept of "love from a distance"—he was said to have been so inspired by accounts of Countess Hodierna of Tripoli that he enlisted in the Crusades in hopes of seeing her in the flesh. He fell ill on his journey but, according to the traditional account, died happy in the lady's arms. Here love draws on notions of pilgrimages, knightly military exploits, and deathbed redemptions. Although Rudel may actually have traveled (and died) in service of the Church, the transformation of this devotion into a story about his love for a woman was very much aligned with the spirit of the age.

The Church itself was moving in response to these new secular forces, reex-amining what has always been the most fundamental issue of religious thought: the conflict between the physical and the spiritual. Charged with a new opti-mism, influential thinkers believed that a bridge between the two might be forged, using God-given wisdom and reason as tools in reconciling the passions of the body with the yearnings of the soul. William of St. Thierry, an intimate friend of St. Bernard and one of the fiercest critics of the famous lovelorn monk Abelard, elaborated on this approach in his *De Natura et Dignitate Amoris* (The Nature and Dignity of Love), written in the early twelfth century. "The art of arts is the art of love," William proclaims, in words that might have come from a troubadour. "Love is naturally implanted in the soul by the Author of nature," he continues, but then cautions that "foul, fleshly love once had teachers of foulness," dangerous instructors who must be avoided because they are "so skillful and effective in hav-ing been corrupted and corrupting others."

The reference here is to Ovid, whose guide to seduction, the *Ars Amatoria*, was surprisingly well-known among medieval monks—so much so that some have re-ferred to this period of the Middle Ages as the Ovidian Epoch. But these words also remind us of contemporaneous events: the scandal of Abelard and the notoriety of his love songs—publicized around the same time William wrote his theological work—as well as the lyrics of the troubadours and other vernacular love songs. Love was a dangerous force, yet William did not aim to extirpate it, but rather channel it, "so that it may be purified and the way purified.... The heart naturally has been placed by the Author of nature in the narrow and central part of the body where it may govern and regulate the fortress of the higher senses and [the commonwealth] of the lower body." Similar views were offered by other religious thinkers but, even more surprising, they also find expression in moralizing troubadour songs.

But if the Church's view of love was evolving, so was its attitude toward the performers who sang of it. "It seems that Thomas Aquinas," Dronke notes with astonishment, "was the first theologian to argue expressly that the entertainer's profession was not in itself sinful." The timing here is interesting—Aquinas wrote during the height of the troubadour era, a period in which love songs had come out into the open, and their singers, no longer anonymous, were celebrated as great artists. He operated, moreover, in France and Italy, where he must have had some contact with these singers and their works. Theology, in other words, was hardly leading the way, merely recognizing an attitudinal shift that had already permeated the courts and nobility of the period. The attacks that the Church had repeatedly launched against the love songs of village women and wandering scholars no longer met the needs of an era when the most famous lyrics of court-ship and romance came from the ruling class.

But the songs themselves also needed to adapt to this changed state of affairs. The music of love needed to impose limits on the bawdy and indecent, putting in their place rules of decorum and proper behavior that bore some resemblance, or at least paid lip service, to the reigning theology. Love songs no doubt led, on occasion, to steamy affairs between the troubadour and the beloved commemorated in the lyric. Yet this was probably the exception, a deviation from the highly idealized relationships that allowed this music to flourish and spread from court to court. And this idealization explains certain aspects of the troubadour art that otherwise remain inexplicable to the modern mind. How many modern love songs can you name that praise the moral character of the beloved? You're scratching your head, trying to think of even one. Yet this was a common theme of the day. Even more odd, to our way of thinking, was the standard troubadour practice of addressing songs to women who were already married. Very few troubadour lyrics sang the praises of single, eligible ladies, and the idea that the love song might be an opening gesture in an real courtship—implicit in the vast majority of modern-day tunes—ran counter to the actual role of these songs in court life. They might convey fantasy or flattery, foster the fame of a lady, or enhance the feudal splendor of a noble family, but these were not (with, of course, the occasional scandalous exception) songs of adulterous seduction.

Women also had to play this game by the same rules, perhaps enjoying the sensuality of the troubadour's songs and the frisson of courtly love, but also recognizing the pervasive moral code of the time. "Queen Eleanor was asked to decide which she would rather have as a lover—a young man of no virtue or an old man of much virtue," Diane Ackerman reminds us in *A Natural History of Love*. "She picked the old man, because in courtly love virtue was paramount." Yes, this sounds like a lesson straight out of a school abstinence training program, but that may not be an inapt comparison. Both spiritual and secular authorities, including the courts that hosted the troubadours, had come to realize that corporeal love could not be excluded from culture and art, let alone daily life; but like the abstinence teacher, the power brokers hoped it still might be chastened and channeled.

This was, however, a risky proposition. The troubadour's songs were a powder keg. The lyrics recognized the importance of individual choice in pair bonding, the validity of emotional chemistry, the possibility of self-directed love—in short, they anticipated the future of romance in Western life. The troubadours inherited a world in which the dictates of love were circumscribed by a host of vested interests. Especially in the court society that gave rise to this music, marriages were seen as a means of advancing family ambitions, obtaining or preserving wealth and property, solidifying or strengthening social position, adapting to political shifts, and achieving other practical ends. After the reforms instituted by Pope Gregory VII in the eleventh century, the Church attempted to exert more control over these practices—for example, denouncing the endogamous marriages that families used to keep property within their control, or divorce and remarriage as a tool in securing socioeconomic advantages. These limitations on the use of matrimonial alliances to achieve pragmatic ends helped strengthen the idea that marriage should involve the free consent of the individuals involved. To this extent, the troubadour songs advanced the policies of the established religion, even as they gave broader scope to expressions of love and desire.

Just as many have neglected the *love* in these love songs, others have put aside the element of *song*, treating the works as mere literary texts. Yet as scholar Simon Gaunt emphasizes: "One has to assume that the metrical sophistication and complexity of the versification was matched by equally complex musical forms." In fact, this degree of self-conscious complexity, musical and metrical, may signal the most important difference between the troubadour lyrics and the love songs in the vernacular languages, condemned, prohibited, and mostly lost to us, from the earlier medieval period. Those were probably more akin to what we nowadays call folk songs, but the troubadours saw their craft as the creation of art songs and strove not only to express their emotions in musical form, but also to impress audiences with the sophisticated ways they could do so.

Re-creating the love songs of the troubadours in the modern day is mostly an exercise in guesswork and artistic license. Performances and recordings strive to bring this music to life, but with what degree of accuracy? I'm hardly surprised that, given this uncertainty, many prefer to read the troubadour lyrics as literary texts—even if this gives only the most shadowy sense of their splendor. Yet the question remains: Should we view the troubadours as singers or as poets? Were they authors or entertainers? Did they create their works envisioning a posterity of readers, or merely the audience in front of them?

In truth, this very distinction is misleading. The gap between writer and performer was much narrower in medieval culture, and at times there was no gap at all. Scholar H. J. Chaytor explains this peculiarity of the troubadour's world: "If an author wished to know whether his work was good or bad, he tried it on an audience; if it was approved, he was soon followed by imitators. . . . Development proceeded by trial and error, the audience being the means of experiment." In short, the troubadour as poet cannot be separated from the troubadour as performer. Certainly the emotional power of the troubadour's songs drew from these artists' distinct advantages during this age: as frequent performers who faced a range of audiences in different settings they learned the hard way what touched their listeners' hearts. Like the pianist in a cocktail bar or the busker playing guitar in a subway station, the troubadour gauged the value of a lyric from the results it produced—sometimes measured in cold, hard cash. The tip jar tells no lies. Because they were so successful 'live', as we would describe it today, posterity has found it possible to celebrate them long after they are dead; but to do so, historians of culture first needed to transform these creative spirits into significant *authors*.

Much of the classification and codification of this body of work took place after the fact. Even the native tongue of the troubadours has been repeatedly renamed and reclassified. Dante called it the *lingua d'oc*—referring to the distinctive way of saying the word *yes* (*òc*) of this region and distinguishing it from the *oïl* favored in the north. François Raynouard, writing in the early nineteenth century, described the troubadour's language as *Roman*, thus highlighting its connection to the vernacular Latin spoken in the Roman Empire. In the second half of the nineteenth century Frédéric Mistral helped popularize the term *Provençal* in describing the language and literature of the troubadours. In more recent years, *Occitan* has been the preferred term, encompassing the culture and dialects of southern France, Monaco, the Val d'Aran in Spain, and the Occitan Valleys in Italy. Provençal is sometimes still used as a synonym, but is more commonly restricted in application to the specific dialect of Occitan spoken in Provence.

Troubadour culture neither began nor ended in Provence. Guilhèm de Peitieus (1071–1126), also known as Duke William IX of Aquitaine, is the earliest of the troubadours whose works have survived. He hardly fits our stereotypical image of a dreamy-eyed poet of love. At his father's death, the fifteen-year-old became duke and would later make his mark as a warlike leader, conquering Toulouse and eventually leading a Crusade, where his recklessness led to the eventual decimation of his army. After a defeat against the Turks at Heraclea in 1101, the noble troubadour barely escaped and returned to Antioch with only six soldiers left under his command.

Those seeking connections between the troubadour art and the Islamic musical culture of Spain will be more interested in William's military adventures as part of the *Reconquista* of the Iberian Peninsula. This effort came toward the close of his military career, and thus his poetic style must already have been formed. Yet I note with interest that William received the gift of a valuable rock crystal vase from a Muslim ally during this campaign, which he valued so much that he bequeathed it to Eleanor of Aquitaine, his granddaughter—it now sits in the Louvre. One inevitably wonders how close this first known troubadour's ties were with Muslim friends, and whether musical gifts may also have passed between the two cultures via this intermediary.

Duke William scarcely had better luck in religious affairs than in military matters, and enjoyed the rare distinction of twice finding himself excommunicated, a rare double damnation that few artists of any era could match. The first instance was over taxes, but the second reveals the romantic side of the aristocratic troubadour. William allegedly abducted the wife of a vassal—although apparently with her complicity. According to this account, the duke was so devoted to the lady, strikingly named the *Viscountess Dangereuse*, that he painted her image on his shield. While flatterers praised his physical beauty and military valor, critics paid more attention to his assaults on feminine virtue and chastity. In a surviving *vida*, the name given to the sometimes fanciful biographical sketches of the troubadours—which scholars both deride and copiously quote from—William is called "one of the greatest deceivers of women.... He wandered around the world in order to deceive the ladies." His more lasting fame comes from his eleven surviving lyrics—a small body of work, but of critical importance in signaling the birth of a new era of secular love songs in Europe.

Although many of the lyrics that have come down to us are the work of nobles, the era of the troubadours also witnessed the elevation of singers from the lower classes. Marcabru, whose patrons included William X—the son of our first troubadour—hinted at his illegitimate birth in one of his songs:

> Marcabru, the son of Lady Bruna
> was begotten under such a moon
> that he knows how love wreaks havoc.

The traditional account of Marcabru's life tells of his impoverished mother leaving the infant at the door of a rich man. His ill-starred origins may partly explain the acerbic tone to his troubadour lyrics, with their moralizing attitude, which spares no one—not even the powerful and mighty. The singer's death may have come at the hands of unhappy nobles who resented Marcabru's sharp tongue. In truth, Marcabru might seem a most unlikely singer of love songs, and it is testimony to the changes afoot in the south of France that this intransigent character feels compelled to address the subject of love again and again—but only to distinguish between healthy and aberrant manifestations of *amor*. Even while castigating the seducer, the adulterer, the deceiver, the lustful, he celebrates the constancy of true lovers, whose bonds are precious, pure, and dear.

The term *joglar*, often used to describe singers of lowly birth, could also refer to various types of nonmusical performers. In addition to singing love songs, their skills might include juggling, animal taming, contortionism, acrobatics, storytelling, and other forms of entertainment. The *joglars* are typically distinguished from the composers of songs—with the term *troubadour* ordinarily used solely in reference to the latter. But even here, barriers between high and low were blurring: the *joglar* sometimes served as the vehicle through which the songs of a noble were performed and taken on the road. Think of the relationship as akin to that between Tin Pan Alley tunesmiths and the performers who would bring their music to the broader public. Yet a talented individual, such as Marcabru, could graduate from the ranks of the *joglars* and gain a reputation for songs of his own composition.

Many troubadour lyrics present unhappy accounts of romance thwarted and love unreciprocated—little different from love songs of more recent vintage. All

the world loves a lover, but the despairing lover has invariably been the most popular. But at least one song type of the troubadour period, the *alba*, celebrated the
joys of love's consummation during a clandestine night together. Yet even here a
tinge of melancholy pervades the poetry: the word *alba* translates as 'dawn', and
the setting of these songs is the morning after, when the lovers must part. The
warning of the watchman or guard alerts them that their time together has come
to a close. The recurring image of the sentry calling from a tower might indicate
the influence of Islamic antecedents on the form, and in other settings would
have represented the Muslim's morning call to prayer. We have already seen the
alba anticipated in ancient Chinese love lyrics, and echoes of this song continue
to haunt later artistic traditions—scholars have detected its reverberations everywhere from Shakespeare's *Romeo and Juliet* to Act 2 of Wagner's *Tristan*. The
latter is an "extended alba," according to scholar Gale Sigal, who notes extensions
of this genre in many surprising nooks and crannies of Western culture . . . all the
way to the Everly Brothers' chart-topping single "Wake Up Little Susie" from
1957 and the 1981 Juice Newton hit record "Angel of the Morning."

In the *pastorela*, another popular lyric genre among the troubadours, a knight
encounters a shepherdess, perhaps with the intent to seduce her—and the tone
here is usually more playful than pensive. The *tenso*, a stylized debate in song
form, did not always address love, but it was a favorite topic. The *descort*, which
translates as "discord," draws its name from the irregularity of its stanzas and
the lack of harmony in its sentiments. "If you want to compose a *descort*, you
should speak of love as one who is deprived of it," writes the author of *De la doctrina de compondré dictatz* (On the Art of Composing Poems), often attributed
to the thirteenth-century troubadour Jofre de Foixà. The *retroncha*, a song form
of four stanzas, also deals with love, but from a more psychological angle. "If
you want to compose a *retroncha*," writes this same author, "know that you must
speak of love, according to the state to which it has reduced you, be it joyful or
troubled, and you should not mix into it any other subject." In contrast, "if you
want to compose a *danca*, you should speak of love well and agreeably, no matter
what the state in which it has placed you." The *canso*, a love song of five or six
stanzas, is the best known and most characteristic of troubadour lyrics. "A canso
must speak agreeably of love," explains the author of *De la doctrina de compondré dictatz*. "You may include some sample of another topic in your discourse,
but without speaking ill of anything and without praising anything but love." He
adds that, while other songs might borrow a familiar tune, the *canso* requires that
the composer "give the song a new melody, as best you can."

Love was not always the source of inspiration for troubadour songs. Other
types include the *balada*, or "dance song"; the *planh*, a musical lament com-
memorating the death of a member of the nobility, a poet, or other significant
person; and *sirventes*, songs of praise or censure that could take a political or

religious tone. In short, secular song in the vernacular tongue was blossoming on a wide range of fronts. But love predominated, both as the most characteristic topic of these songs, and as the key determinant of how later generations would look back on this historical interlude—a time of war that posterity prefers to remember as an era of deeply felt romantic sentiment.

No, the troubadours did not create this tradition out of thin air. As we have seen, the Arab world had its secular love songs, and these no doubt spread into Europe via Muslim Spain at least as far back as the ninth century. Europe also had its own indigenous tradition of love songs, very few of them preserved but clearly indicated in a handful of surviving texts. If we trace these traditions to ancient times, we encounter the *joculatores*, performers who entertained the Roman conquerors of Gaul. These performers, clear antecedents of the later *joglars* of Provence, were known for their clowning, miming, acting, tumbling, and singing. Even so, the troubadours who arrived on the scene in the eleventh century delivered something markedly different from the idle entertainments of the *joculatores* or the folk songs of the streets, creating instead a paradoxical hybrid, an evocation of love that was earthy and corporeal, yet also idealized and metaphysical.

Perhaps the most telling proof of their success can be found in the simple fact that these songs have survived. As we have seen, the amorous lyrics of Abelard and of so many others who sang of love in the centuries leading up to the troubadours were fiercely repressed and ultimately destroyed. But the troubadours found a formula that placated the vested interests of the late medieval period—at least sufficiently to be granted documentation and dissemination. Of course, the troubadours offered something in return. Their love was chivalrous; it showed deference to a host of institutional forces—religious, military, political, feudal. It was decorous and hierarchical. No, not all the time—the physical chemistry sometimes overwhelmed the tidier Platonic elements—but enough to legitimize the love song to a degree unknown previously in Christian society.

And what role did women play in this revolution of poetry and song? Was the lady merely the *beloved*, obliged to receive praise and devotion, or did she have a more direct, creative impact on these extraordinary changes in European musical and literary culture? Although traditional accounts tend to assign most of the credit for the troubadour revolution to men, I agree with social historian Arnold Hauser, who sees a markedly "feminine character" dominating the court culture of the period. "It is feminine," he explains, "not merely in that the women take part in the intellectual life of the court and influence the line of poetic creation, but also in that the thought and feeling of the men is in many respects feminine." Our speculations on this front are aided immeasurably by the survival of a small body of work by women troubadours—or *trobairitz*, as they are often called. Around twenty have been identified by name, and no doubt many more were active during this period whose work was not preserved. In addition, more than a dozen dialogues have survived, presenting a named male troubadour in discussion with an unnamed lady—which suggests that real, albeit anonymous women may have been involved in the creation of these works. In other instances, the name of a *trobairitz* has survived in a document, but without any lyrics representative of her art.

Nowadays the works of these female troubadours are often assessed as a whole, almost as if they were a separate group, distinct from their male counterparts. Yet both men and women clearly saw themselves as part of the same tradition, sharing similar views of love and its place in society—indeed many of the troubadour and *trobairitz* lyrics are presented as collaborative efforts between the two sexes. Even so, the women's lyrics reveal some subtle differences from those of their male counterparts. They are less dependent on flashy wordplay, more direct, and—to the extent that we can judge these matters at such a distance—more sincere and straightforward. Sometimes the women can be surprisingly blunt. "One night I'd like to take my swain to bed and hug him, wearing no clothes," sings the Comtessa de Dia. "I'd give him reason to suppose he was in heaven." No, there is not much need to read between the lines there. This straightforward tone also leads Alaisina Yselda and Carenza, in their *tenso*, to address some consequences of love left unmentioned by their male counterparts:

> Lady Carenza, taking a husband suits me,
> but I think that making babies is harsh penance,
> for the breasts droop way down,
> the belly stretches and gets ugly.

Certainly male troubadours were known to turn a skeptical eye to the institution of marriage, but here we encounter a distinctively female perspective—one that addresses a familiar subject of love lyrics but adds a new angle even while adopting a pragmatic, everyday tone.

The women also allow for more give-and-take. Around half of the surviving lyrics by women are in the *tenso* form—as noted above, a stylized dialogue presenting different views. By comparison, the *tenso* represents less than 10 percent of the surviving troubadour output as a whole. This sense of seeking alignment with the other is highlighted in other ways in the *trobairitz* lyrics. A study of word choices finds that the women are more likely to emphasize trust and fidelity and other collaborative virtues. In comparison with their male counterparts, they are more likely to sing of an existing relationship interrupted than effuse over an idealized love that flourishes only in the imagination. The women, in short, seem more grounded and realistic.

Under any circumstances, we would prize these lyrics, which offer us a rare glimpse into a view of courtly love that is not filtered through the dominant male gaze. But I suspect that the contributions of the *trobairitz* may be far more significant than most commentators suspect; in fact, they may help us understand the broader sweep of vernacular love songs as they changed the shape of European music during the late Middle Ages. As we have already seen, very few vernacular love lyrics from the earlier medieval period have survived, and most of what we know about them comes from the denunciations and prohibitions of the clergy. These attacks frequently link love songs specifically to women—so much so that a modern scholar sifting through the available evidence might assume that women had some special relationship or sympathy with this type of music. When we keep this in mind, the marvel of the troubadour era is *not* that women sang love songs—that had long been the case—but rather that the men had finally caught up with the ladies. From this perspective, troubadour songs reflect men borrowing much of their new worldview from a preexisting tradition established by women, and maintained by them, despite repeated attempts to eradicate it over a period of centuries.

This interpretation of courtly love finds support in a revealing manuscript —described by Dronke as "one of the strangest in the entire Middle Ages" —found in the monastery of St. Denis at Shäftlarn in Bavaria. Here, amid bits and pieces from various Christian and classical sources, as well as verses, proverbs, and other materials sacred and profane, we find around fifty love letters, some written by men but most from young women. The scribe who compiled this portion of the manuscript, probably in the early twelfth century, seems to have copied down the contents of the surviving papers of a scholar, apparently with no attempt at organizing, prioritizing, or censoring their contents. The letters cast light on the relationship between a scholar from Liège and his female students at a convent—well-born young ladies, several of whom seem to have fallen in love with their teacher. The verses included in their correspondence may have been justified as composition assignments, but the affections of the women, and their rivalry with each other in their attempts to win the teacher's favor, give us insight into various female responses to the language and ideology of love at a time when the troubadour ethos was in ascendancy.

And what do we learn from these letters? The intimate conversational tone draws our attention, but the confidence and assertiveness of these young ladies are even more striking. The students boldly impose the values of courtly love on their teacher, undeterred by their respective roles as master and pupil. The ladies set themselves up as judges of the proper decorum required in matters of the heart. Even the teacher must recognize that in his pupils he confronts a higher authority, although not an entirely unyielding one: "A lady's grace will grant whatever is reasonable," one of female correspondents declares. "This she will give to one who always asks with due deference." Again and again, this correspondence reveals women dictating the terms we now associate with courtly love. They demand service and politesse from the man, and accept as their due the resulting reversal of gender power relationships that prevailed in other sectors of society.

We encounter a similar tone in other surviving documents from the period. In a revealing love letter from the late twelfth century, the woman admits that her limited education makes her reluctant to respond in her "uncultivated language" to the scholar who has sought her favor, but she shows no hesitation in the demands she makes on him—even insisting that love is supposed to be an arduous affair for the man. "It seems a troubling, difficult thing you are trying to win from me—my complete trust, which I have never yet promised to any man." But she does allow a path by which he can gain her approbation: "Yet if I know I shall be loved by you in a pure love, and my pledge of innocence is not to be violated, I do not refuse you the hardship, or the love." Then, to make sure he understands, she elaborates on this point. "If it exists without pain, it cannot be called love, to which the greatest hardship belongs." Finally the woman concludes: "Take care that no one sees this letter—it was not written with permission." Clearly the woman is not mistress of her own fate—she can't even send this letter without fearing the consequences—but she knows that in her relationship with the scholar she is in the position of power and can dictate terms.

The surviving literature shows, again and again, women playing a decisive role in determining the values and predilections that would shape this new conception of love. In the late twelfth century, Andreas Capellanus describes Eleanor of Aquitaine and her daughter Marie de Champagne deciding on issues relating to lovers' quarrels in a manner akin to judge and jury in a court of law. Other references to courts of love presided over by women have survived, but even if we lacked this evidence, we merely need to consult the male troubadour lyrics themselves, with their constant pressing of the man's "suit"—a word that, even today, has both legal and romantic connotations, hence our term *suitor*—with hopes of a favorable verdict from the woman, who is viewed as the arbiter of his fate. In fact, the deference and ritualistic respect shown to the beloved ladies in these songs is strikingly similar to one's expected behavior in front of a magistrate.

Such examples don't prove conclusively that the ethos of the troubadour era represented the ascendancy of a female perspective on love and its adoption by a large number of men. But they make clear that, at a minimum, young women were quite ready to play by these rules, even if they did not create them. They certainly felt empowered to insist on them if the men veered from their proper course. Here, as elsewhere in our history, the flourishing of a new kind of love song is inextricably linked to an expansion in human rights and an enlargement of the sphere of individual choice.

Perhaps this idea—that women would dictate cultural conventions and men would oblige by adopting them—surprises you. Yet my research into the social history of music tells me that such a path of influence has emerged repeatedly over the centuries, although it is rarely given its due in our textbooks and survey courses. For example, it seems likely that the tradition of shamanic music started with women, whose role was later usurped by male shamans and priests. Even in more recent times, the anthropological record is filled with accounts of male shamans who dress like women and take on stereotypical female roles—accounts that make perfect sense when one see the women as establishing the tradition in the first place. The same may be true with the music of ecstatic cults, where women played a significant role, according to the oldest surviving accounts. As already noted, women are closely linked to the development of the lament, the lullaby, and other song types.

And with love songs? In an earlier chapter, we encountered ancient Chinese love songs from a woman's perspective included in a work linked to Confucius—the lady's name is lost forever, but the famous man ensured the survival of the text. The role of Sappho in establishing the tradition of the Western lyric is better documented, yet the works of many men who followed her example have survived in much better shape than her fragmented texts. Even earlier in our story, we find the defaced disk of Enheduanna, hinting at another story of a female innovator and her problematic legacy. Just as in the early Middle Ages, women were acknowledged (or rather denounced) as the main propagators of European love songs; and, once more, the lyrics themselves are mostly lost to us. During this same period, female slaves played the key role in shaping the love songs of the Islamic world, and again men of power and distinction followed their example. Do we see a pattern here? If men finally come to the forefront after the rise of the troubadours, we rightly give them credit for their contributions in legitimizing the love song. Yet, taking a longer view, we are not amiss in seeing this as one more example of men assuming a dominant position in a musical field after women had made the visionary—and often transgressive—first steps.

At the same time, the history of the troubadours also testifies to the power of secular ideals to confront—and at times transform—the institutional and cultural power of the Church. The exultation of the poet, for a brief spell, could counter exhortations from the pulpit. Yet the risk of sin was ever present: a surviving illustration from the edifying writings of Abbess Herrad von Landsberg, from the late twelfth century, depicts the seven liberal arts encircling the grand discipline of *Philosophia*, attended by Socrates and Plato, but the poets are shown laboring with pens in hand and little devils whispering advice in their ears. This illustration could serve as a symbol for the new love song of the era. It was now on the map, a recognized part of the shared culture, yet its exponents were only a step away from wickedness and perdition.

We should hardly be surprised, then, that the end of the troubadour era came amid rumblings from Rome, where papal directives served to curtail the new songs—although not in a direct assault. Pope Innocent III, true to his name, paid little attention to the love songs and their inroads on the Church's dominion over souls. But the pontiff was intent on extirpating theological dissent from the south of France, where proponents of the so-called Albigensian heresy had found a stronghold. The troubadours were caught in the crossfire of this larger conflict—one that eventually contributed to the rise of the Inquisition and the unification of France.

A complete assessment of the theological complexities of this clash would take us far afield from the subject of love songs. Suffice it to say that the heretics resurrected a controversy that had plagued Christianity at least as far back as the third century. The Albigensians saw good and evil as two opposed divine forces, with the corrupt physical world standing in sharp contrast to the perfection of pure spirit—a perspective that easily lent itself to a harsh critique of the worldly aspirations of the Catholic hierarchy. Pope Innocent III's initial attempts to quell the dissent proved unsuccessful, and the murder of his emissary Pierre de Castelnau in 1208 caused a furor and led to a large-scale military response. The pope called for a crusade—seeing no irony in using that term to describe a war against fellow Christians on European soil—and in 1209 ten thousand soldiers swept into southern France, setting off two decades of conflict that effectively eliminated the distinct culture and court life that had given rise to the troubadours.

The tumult of the period is epitomized in the strange figure of Folquet of Marseilles. This Genoese son of a merchant family first came to prominence as a troubadour—singing about noblewomen with whom he was rumored to have affairs. Yet he made an unexpected career change in the final years of the twelfth century, joining the Cistercian order and rising through the Church hierarchy to become bishop of Toulouse in 1205. In this new role, the one-time singer of love songs emerged as a strident opponent of heresy and, in the words of one critic, "such a fire was spread throughout the land that never for any water will it be quenched; for there did he bring destruction of life and body and soul upon more than fifteen hundred of high and low." This erstwhile purveyor of amorous lyrics was later responsible for introducing the Inquisition into the land of the troubadours. His songs continued to find imitators even after his death, but legend tells of Folquet exacting a penance on himself after hearing one of his lyrics sung by a Parisian minstrel. Folquet has the distinction of being the only troubadour placed by Dante in Paradise, but for the aficionados of love songs his arrival on the scene announced the end of a golden era.

That said, not even a Crusade and Inquisition could prevent the example of the troubadours from spreading, and finding adherents in later times and other places. Their ethos finds expression in northern France via the works of the *trouvères*, in the Arthurian narratives of Chrétien de Troyes, in the *Roman de la Rose*, and other works. We hear it in the *dolce stil novo*, the "sweet new style" of Dante, and the poetry of Petrarch. The themes of the troubadours would be taken up by Spanish and Catalan poets, and influence others in Germany, Sicily, England, and elsewhere.

Even today, the language of our love songs is permeated with the spirit of the troubadours: their metaphors, their attitudes, their transference of a reverential and quasi-spiritual tone of worship to the beloved are our inheritance, if only as a subconscious stratum or unrealized ideals wedged into our cerebral cortex. Anachronistic? Impracticable? Naïve? Guilty on all counts! Yet the patently obvious fact that our modern romances bear so little resemblance to the traditions of courtly love merely heightens their allure. What could be sweeter than a love that avoids the messiness of our own affairs, a love that plays by actual rules, that mixes the transcendent with the merely carnal, that heightens romance and embeds it in pageantry and sweet music? Perhaps we could grow up and forget all that, but would we really want to?

CHAPTER 8

The Triumph of Romance

Love has commanded that I should sing.—Count Rudolf of
Fenis-Neuenburg

The rise of the troubadours signals the end of a thousand years of Christian outrage and repression directed at love songs. An uneasy truce has now put an end
to hostilities, although skirmishes and pockets of resistance will continue to
reflect the instability of this rapprochement. Some stragglers may still fear the
influence of this too sensual music, but these opponents are now fighting a rear-
guard action. Under the protection of powerful advocates, the love song is now
legitimized, and over the next four hundred years will be in the ascendancy. In
later stages of our story, the eventual emergence of the madrigal, popular ballad,
and opera as dominant forces in Western song will confirm this state of affairs.
Whether the art is highbrow or lowbrow, the audience educated or unlettered,
wealthy or impoverished, their chosen songs will increasingly gravitate, with
very few exceptions, to matters of the heart. We are still at the early stages of this
process, but its inevitability was already recognized in the late medieval period,
even by the religious institutions that had previously proved such hostile foes of
love songs.

But if spiritual leaders needed to make concessions, so did the singers. The
troubadours needed to control and sometimes eliminate the eroticism and carnality of their lyrics—never with complete success, since these qualities lurk
beneath the surface of all romance and often insist on their prerogatives. But
in most instances, concupiscence deferred to an uneasy restraint, reflecting a
sufficient allegiance to what modern jurists describe as "prevailing community
standards." This tension results in the paradoxical quality at the heart of these
songs. Those of us raised on saucier fare puzzle over a lover who declares his passionate desire for his beloved, but then asserts, "Of course, I don't want to sleep
with her." And even when this comment is not made overtly in these lyrics, it is
implicit in the countless songs addressed to women who simply could not be
seduced—the wife of another man or a noble lady who presided over the court.

Many are tempted to interpret such songs as a celebration of frustrated adulterous impulses, but I believe they tell us a different story—reminding us of the pervasive institutionalized morality of the period, so severe in matters of sexual intent that singers willingly directed their love songs at unobtainable ladies. A host of nonreligious factors, both cultural and economic, also conspired to direct their attention at irreproachable women of power, wealth, and influence. Under these constraints, the love song is allowed out into the open, like a criminal on parole who must still be closely supervised—and, yes, as with all parolees, we find violators of the terms of the agreement, but not so many that the innovations of the troubadours are prevented from spreading elsewhere in Europe.

In this guarded manner, the love song is given space to move, confident in its emotional appeal and sure of its reception. As a result, our sources from this point on are less vague, our ability to trace the evolution of this music more precise. Even so, there is still much we don't know, especially as we struggle to frame the context in which this détente took place. Was this solely a musical or poetic phenomenon, or did the nature of love itself change during the course of these years? Even if we grant the influence of courtly love and stylized notions of romance on the real-life behavior of couples, we are left wondering whether these attitudes were restricted to the ruling classes. Did commoners also fall under the spell of new ways of envisioning relationships? Are the inner workings of the heart really so malleable as to adjust to these larger cultural movements? Or did the change in love and romance happen first, and the songs reflect this new state of affairs only after the fact?

Certainly something new is taking place in the love life of the Western world. In the waning years of the Middle Ages, different attitudes to marriage and courtship take root. In particular, the notion that marriage rests primarily on the consent of husband and wife gains widespread support throughout the Christian world. Gratian's *Decretum* from the middle of the twelfth century asserts that without consent no valid marriage can occur. The mere presence of a bride and groom at the wedding ceremony fails to provide a sufficient basis for holy matrimony. Parents may continue to haggle over terms and prospects, but can no longer ignore the opinions of the two main bargaining chips in their negotiation, the prospective husband and wife. Later papal decrees from Alexander III and Gregory IX give further support to the Church's advocacy of consensual marriages. Courts and civic authorities, for their part, align local laws and legal decisions with the now prevalent theology. Perhaps this falls short of an official embrace of courtly love, but clearly the concept of *courtship* gains in influence as mere coercion loses its moral legitimacy.

Demographic trends contribute to new attitudes toward love. Europe at the time of Gratian's *Decretum* had fundamentally changed in the century and a half since the end of the first millennium. In the year 1000, no large urban centers existed in the Christian West. The most populous western European cities were in Muslim Spain, notably Córdoba and Seville—and we have already seen how these settings gave rise to love songs even before the emergence of the troubadours—but even these were small by current standards of urban density. Rome may have boasted thirty thousand inhabitants; London in the late eleventh century was a city of perhaps eight thousand. Most of the continent's scattered inhabitants supported themselves with agriculture, herding, and other solitary tasks. In such settings, communal values and ways of life were dictated by family elders, tradition, and Church teaching.

The latter had long viewed even conjugal relationships between husband and wife with a heavy dose of suspicion. Following in the steps of Paul's praise of chastity and reluctant approval of marriage in his Epistle to the Corinthians—taking a spouse was granted only to those who lacked the self-control for sexual abstinence—early Church fathers could hardly offer encouragement to erotic notions of love. Tertullian, an influential theologian born in the second century, had confidently told believers that the resurrected body would still possess genitals, but they would be nonfunctional. Augustine, who documented his own struggles with lust in his *Confessions*, lamented the "shame of nuptial pleasures," and argued that the depraved state of human nature after the Original Sin of Adam and Eve had infected the organs of procreation, making them immune to reason.

But the rapid growth of Europe's population around the time of the early troubadours, the migration to cities and villages, and the accompanying loosening of feudal dependency inevitably changed how men and women dealt with matters of love, sexuality, and marriage. With the rise of densely populated cities, the intimate affairs of friends and neighbors were now subject to scrutiny and discussion, perhaps even more so than in our own day. In the court case of *Alice contra John the Blacksmith*, circa 1200, the woman needed to prove that a marriage existed, and drew on testimony of her landlady and fellow tenants who asserted that they had frequently seen the couple in bed together. In the trial of the prostitute Salvaza, held in Florence in the late medieval period, a witness admitted that "she had frequently looked through a window of Salvaza's house and had seen her nude in bed with men, engaging in those indecent acts which are practiced by prostitutes." We find many such stories of voyeurism and brazen sexuality in popular tales—check out Boccaccio's *Decameron* for numerous examples. They tell us not only about the moral values people applied to their own lives but also their deep familiarity with those practiced by their neighbors. In the crowded urban centers, individuals learned the ground rules about relationships between men and women through firsthand observation rather than from the pulpit.

In such an environment, even Church teachings were forced to adapt to prevalent public mores. By the close of the Middle Ages, doctrine and dogma have started to move into alignment with the love celebrated in stories and song. Nicholas of Lyra, the head of the Franciscans in France and a doctor at the Sorbonne, acknowledges that sex between husband and wife creates bonds of attraction that strengthen the marriage, and Albert the Great, the leading German theologian of the era, determines that the conjugal union is good in itself—and even discusses five different positions for the sex act, stating his preference for the missionary but stopping short of forbidding the others. Indeed, he sees sex as potentially meritorious from a spiritual perspective, provided that it is ruled by love, not lust, and pursued with openness to procreation. Love thus gains unprecedented legitimacy, reinforced by firsthand examples and the highest authorities, in the private moments of couples just as in the music and entertainments of the public sphere.

Some religious leaders continued to condemn love songs and warn their more devout followers of the dangers of this seductive music, especially when enticing lyrics came from the mouths of females. "The worldly woman is the organ of Satan," proclaimed Bernard de Clairvaux in the twelfth century. "She sings to you that which stirs up the enticements of this world and points to the narrow paths of Satan....Below she is like a Siren of the sea, and from the navel up like the most beautiful and shapely virgin....And through her many sweet silly songs she has deceived many sailors and led them into danger." The renowned Torah scholar Moses Maimonides, writing a short while later, cautioned against music that "arouses and praises the instinct of lust," and especially attacks these lyrics when sung in Hebrew as "the most reprehensible thing one can do in the eyes of the Holy Law." But these diatribes, for all their fervor, could hardly reverse the obvious trend. Numerous accounts from the period mention people of all ranks dancing the *carole*, a circular dance popular at festive occasions typically accompanied by love lyrics in the courtly tradition. Scholar Robert Mullally finds references to the *carole* in "prose romances, chronicles, collections of anecdotes, moral treatises, a treatise on poetry, the life of a saint, and even in a treatise on astronomy!" The music of love is now welcomed, indeed fostered and cherished, in the highest circles. We find the king and his court dancing to the *carole*, but also shepherds and servants.

The music of love would have eventually prevailed even without noble sponsors, but its splendors and successes no doubt benefited from the support of these influential patrons, notably that of the most eligible heiress of the twelfth century. Eleanor of Aquitaine made her mark in many ways—not least by managing to serve as consort to the kings of both England and France—and her prominent role in any chronicle of the history of love is assured if only by her own high-profile romances. But her cultural legacy also includes the propagation of the troubadour love song, a fitting achievement given that her grandfather William IX, Duke of Aquitaine, is the earliest known troubadour.

In the decades following Eleanor's marriage to Louis VII in 1137, the courtly love song emerges as a dominant style of secular music in the north of France. Some 1,500 examples in Old French from the mid-twelfth through thirteenth century have survived, along with their melodies. The exponents of this music were known as *trouvères*, distinguished from the troubadours by their use of different dialects. But like their southern counterparts, the *trouvères* turn again and again to the subject of love, which now rivals, and perhaps surpasses, religious themes as a source of inspiration for song throughout the king's domain.

Even after Eleanor moved on to England, as wife of King Henry II, her daughters by Louis, Marie and Alix, carried on in her stead, supporting the *trouvères'* art in particular and the culture of courtly love in general. Chrétien de Troyes, who served at the court of Marie in Champagne, is best known for his Arthurian narratives, and is the likely originator of the famous story of the adulterous affair between the knight Lancelot and Arthur's Queen Guinevere. His stories played a key role in popularizing a romanticized and idealized version of courtly love that still lingers in the collective unconscious of suitors and sweethearts today. We take for granted that romantic entanglements will form the centerpiece of any beguiling tale, but that was hardly the case during most of the Middle Ages. "Their favorite stories were not, like ours, stories of how a man married, or failed to marry, a woman," C. S. Lewis writes. "They preferred to hear how a holy man went to heaven or how a brave man went to battle." But Chrétien understood the new temperament of his age, which demanded that even a story of valor and bravery needed a love interest—some have gone so far as to laud him as the originator of the modern novel. Yet this author's commitment to romance went beyond storytelling: he is also acclaimed as the earliest of the *trouvères*, penning at least two love songs that testify to his advocacy of the new musical style in the north of France.

Many others soon followed his lead. Around the time of Chrétien's death, Gace Brulé, the most illustrious of the early *trouvères*, composed more than seventy songs of courtly love in Old French and performed at Eleanor's court, as well as at the court of Count Geoffrey II of Brittany. His favorite theme was his despairing love for a lady of nobler birth, yet Gace must have been a member of the ruling class himself—he is depicted as a knight on horseback, and we know that he was a landowner in Groslière. During this early period, the art of the *trouvère* may have flourished primarily as a pastime practiced by the nobility entertaining each other in their homes; Thibaut de Champagne, the most famous *trouvère* to write love songs in Old French during the next generation, even became king of Navarre in 1234 and led a crusading army. But the cultural elites could hardly prevent commoners from imitating their musical practices, and inevitably the *trouvère* song spread to all classes of society.

A more fluid and diverse musical scene emerges with particular intensity in the vicinity of Arras on the Scarpe River, near France's present-day border with Belgium. We know of some two hundred *trouvères* from this area. Their collective efforts produced more than half of the lyric poetry composed in Old French—an especially remarkable turn of events when one considers that the population could not have been much more than twenty thousand. Here the taste for courtly love songs was cultivated among the wealthy bourgeoisie, these parvenus embracing love songs the way later upwardly mobile groups might feel inclined to support the local symphony or art museum. Yet this studied emulation of the nobility represented more than mere social climbing. Just as a royal wedding even nowadays excites the imagination and stirs the passions of onlookers, the love songs of the nobles must have served as a piquant ingredient in the fantasy life of commoners, who probably viewed Eleanor of Aquitaine in the same dreamy light that a modern shop clerk or schoolteacher frets over the slings and arrows of outrageous fortune suffered by the Princess of Wales or Duchess of Cambridge or some other royal bride. Such vivid imaginings are made explicit in the following lyric from the *Carmina Burana*, which Helen Waddell suggests "is surely the work of a German student, haunted by a passing glimpse" of Queen Eleanor:

> Were the world all mine
> From the sea to the Rhine,
> I'd give it all
> If so be the Queen of England
> Lay in my arms.

The music of courtly love thus served a double purpose as it spread, not just geographically but through the socioeconomic hierarchies of the age. The songs were an imitation of court society meant to set the right public image for those rising in the social hierarchy, as well as a spur to the erotic imagination that filled a purely private function.

A different type of love song emerges around this same time, or perhaps even earlier. The *chansons de toile* were probably sung by women while weaving and sewing, and thus may, at first glance, represent a less elitist, working-class alternative to the court-centered love songs of the *trouvères*. Yet the songs themselves depict the daughters of nobility and were probably sung by them, although most likely by commoners as well. The words often reference the handwork of the laborer, but these quotidian chores are merely a springboard for the romantic story that is the main focus of the lyrics. We know little about the composers of these songs, although surviving texts attributed to Audefroi le Bastart, a *trouvère* of the early thirteenth century, make clear that these works were not necessarily written by women, despite the feminine perspective of the lyrics. Yet the stylized literary outpourings of Audefroi and others almost certainly drew on a more vibrant tradition of actual work songs performed by ladies laboring over thread and cloth.

These songs mark the continuation of a musical tradition that dates back to the earliest recorded times. An ancient Egyptian lyric mentions women singing as they turned flax into linen, and I have elsewhere documented comparable examples from other traditional cultures—China, Africa, India, the Hebrides, the Balkans, Vietnam, and other settings. The congruence of these far-flung practices indicates an almost universal use of music by women laboring in the production of clothing. "Women who are weaving, or disentangling the thread on their spindle, often sing," wrote St. John Chrysostom in the early Middle Ages. "Sometimes each of them sings for herself, at other times they all harmonize a melody together." And the same was no doubt true a thousand years before and after this passage was written. The appearance of Germanic names in *chansons de toile* reinforces our sense that these songs have older roots and different paths of dissemination than those *trouvère* lyrics that clearly imitate the troubadours of the south.

In Portugal during this same period, we encounter *cantigas de amor*—love songs that follow closely the role models set by French troubadours. But far more interesting is the *cantiga de amigo*, literally a song about a boyfriend. Our best source of these texts is a songbook now housed at the Portuguese National Library in Lisbon and a related volume owned by the Vatican Library. Around five hundred examples from the thirteenth century have survived, and they represent the single largest body of love lyrics, medieval or ancient, presented from a female perspective. The named authors, however, are uniformly male, and range from the highest noble—King Denis of Portugal, the so-called Farmer King and grandson of King Alfonso X, is responsible for more than fifty lyrics—all the way down to squires and the humble *jograls*, paid performers of low standing.

The decision by male singers to adopt a female persona has puzzled many scholars, but here again the most likely explanation is found in the vibrant, and frequently suppressed, pre-troubadour tradition of female love songs. Rather than representing a radical break with the past, such lyrics harken back to the *puellarum cantica*, or "songs of girls," condemned by the early Church councils, the *winileodas* that Charlemagne tried to extirpate from the convents in 789, the *kharjas* of Arabic origin—which were especially influential in the Iberian Peninsula—and many other comparable traditions, most of them probably lost to posterity.

Certainly the tone here departs markedly from the typical troubadour model. Many of these songs present a girl confiding to another female—a friend, a sister, or her mother. Needless to say, moms do not make frequent appearances in medieval amorous lyrics; songs directed to her are perhaps not quite as rare as the male singer addressing the mother-in-law, but still an anomaly that, when we encounter it in these texts, must remind us of the prominent role of the virgin mother of Christ, who was now also influencing European love songs. Yet the figure of the mother also appears in the Romance *kharjas* of the Hispano-Arabic tradition, so perhaps a North African lineage is just as important as any Christian precedent here. Certainly the *cantiga de amigo* adopts a heartfelt, sometimes even chatty tone that has little in common with Christian worship. And the mother in these songs, unlike the Virgin Mary, often prefers to meddle and interrogate rather than offer help:

> "Daughter, I'd like, if you please, to know
> about you and your friend one thing:
> how is it with you and how does it go?"

> "Mother, I'm willing to tell you that
> I love him well as he does me,
> and I tell you truly, there's nothing more."

Here the conflict between the dictates of love and the moral constraints of Christian society, implicit in so many other songs, turns into an actual dialogue between bickering parties.

A frequent theme of the *cantiga de amigo* is the longing of the woman for the absent 'friend', sometimes with the song set in an emotionally charged location, for example, the shore where the singer awaits her beloved's return from the sea. But in these lyrics, even the smallest objects can take on talismanic significance if they carry a reminder of the lover. This depth of feeling and heartfelt quality set these songs apart from the more stylized representations of courtly love, and in some degree anticipate the greater psychological intensity that would characterize the love song with the rise of the madrigal. If the troubadour established an ideal of love that still inhabits our romantic dreams, the composers of the *cantigas de amigo* have left us a more penetrating account of human relationships grounded in the obstacles and uncertainties of the real world, an evocation perhaps less glamorous than the imagery and pageantry of knights and their ladies, but all the more plausible for their very absence.

As such examples make clear, innovations in love songs in the Western world during the late medieval period tended to originate in the sunnier climes of the south. But eventually the new ethos of courtly love and the music that proclaimed it were destined to spread northward. In Germany, love songs found a receptive audience among the nobility, as they had elsewhere. But the marriage of Friedrich I, German monarch and Holy Roman emperor, to Princess Beatrice of Burgundy in 1156 brought Provence, the homeland of troubadour song, under his control and forced German culture into closer contact with that of France.

We know that the *trouvère* Guiot de Provins was a member of the bride's retinue and his work served as a notable influence on the nascent German love song tradition. But a host of other French musical imports soon followed this same path of dissemination. Under Friedrich and his successors, music and festivities flourished in the courts of Germany, in sharp contrast to the more austere practices of a former day, and performers and poets thrived in this receptive setting.

In Germany, the love song benefited from the advocacy of the minnesingers—indeed, their very name derives from the Middle High German term *minne*, signifying 'love'. These performers first come to our attention in the middle of the twelfth century, and in the earliest examples of their work the influence of troubadour and *trouvère* models is marked; sometimes the German text follows so closely the line form of French works that we can assume they were sung to the same melody. Yet over the course of the thirteenth century, the art of the minnesinger gradually takes on a more distinctly Germanic character, most likely due to the assimilation of homegrown musical traditions.

The *Spielmann*, or wandering entertainer, for example, was a frequent sight in German towns and villages during the medieval period, and served as a living repository of poems, songs, and minidramas. These performers might also play the role of the clown, acrobat, mime, juggler, and dancer, or show their mastery of various other stunts or skills. Both men and women found employment in this manner. They traveled as individuals and jointly in troupes, and their services were much in demand despite the condemnation of Church leaders and sporadic badgering from secular authorities. Charlemagne ordered monasteries to turn them away if they sought shelter, yet members of the nobility were hardly immune to the charms of such skilled entertainers. Some *Spielleute* (plural of *Spielmann*) were granted fiefs by a patron, and thus became aristocrats in their own right. Female performers who found favor with a member of the nobility might enjoy the prerogatives of power themselves, much as Theodora had with the Byzantine emperor Justinian in the early Middle Ages, rising from entertainer to empress. The poet Ottacker tells us, for example, of a dancer named Agnes who achieved considerable influence as mistress of King Wenceslaus II of Bohemia, and was suspected of foul play when the monarch died at the age of thirty-four in 1305. We know little of the love songs that must have been part of the *Spielmann* repertoire before the rise of the minnesingers—none of this music has survived. Yet this body of work probably had more impact on the minnesingers than the Latin versifying of the Goliards, and clearly was better known among the towns and villages than the lyrics of performers singing in Occitan or the northern Old French dialects of the *trouvères*.

Although minnesingers dealt with topics other than love—taking up religious, didactic, or autobiographical themes, as well as addressing political issues and current events—these were overshadowed by the performer's stylized evocations of courtship and romance. The *Weschel* was a dialogue between lovers, sometimes in each other's presence, in other instances relying on a messenger or intermediary. The *Tagelied*, a dawn song conveying the sadness of lovers parting at sunrise, presents a context familiar to us from the albas of southern France. The crusading songs of the French troubadours had their German equivalent in the *Kreuzlied*, which might also refer to love and the sorrows of a separation. The *Liebesgruss* is a man's salutation praising his beloved. The *Frauenlied*, popular with the early minnesingers, presented the lament of a woman who complains about her absent or disdainful lover. The fact that the latter songs, like the *cantiga de amigo*, were composed by men has posed problems for many commentators, who have struggled to explain the seemingly autobiographical tone of the lyrics. Some have preferred to interpret them as coded attempts to express emotions that might seem too sentimental coming from a knight, or have hypothesized that the poet possessed a *feminine soul* beneath a tough masculine exterior. Yet here, as in the case of the Portuguese-Galician lyrics, we merely need to point to the dominance of women in preserving vernacular love songs during the preceding thousand years of Church repression. If the earliest minnesingers adopted a female perspective in their songs, this may have simply been due to the fact that these were the preexisting role models available to them in their native tongue— but neglected by later scholars because they were not preserved for posterity.

The preferred instruments of the minnesinger were bowed string instruments, notably the pear-shaped *gige*, known elsewhere as the *rebec*, and the oval *fidel*, with its similarities and etymological connection to our modern-day fiddle, although harps, lutes, recorders, percussion, and other accompaniment could also be employed as the situation warranted. A surviving illustration of the minnesinger Heinrich Frauenlob shows him playing a *fidel*, while other musicians hold recorder, shawm, bagpipe, and a second, smaller *fidel*. One participant appears to be clapping hands, and the image inevitably reminds us of a modern-day fiddler playing at a hoedown or informal dance. Dance songs were clearly an important part of the repertoire, and surviving lyrics that refer to specific times of the year suggest that these entertainments were featured at seasonal folk festivals. Neidhart von Reuental, one of the most influential thirteenth-century minnesingers, gained particular renown for such works, with his *Sommerlieder* (summer songs for outdoor dances), distinguished from the *Winderlieder* (winter songs for indoor dances); but though his lyrics dealt with courting and wooing, the style of expression is less elegant, and sometimes far coarser, than in the traditional courtly love song.

Walther von der Vogelweide stands out today as the most famous of the minnesingers, but surviving documents from his lifetime are mostly silent about this seminal figure. A rare exception comes from the expense accounting of a bishop, who gave the singer money to buy a winter coat on November 12, 1203. But even this brief notice is revealing, indicating that the vernacular love song, associated with the nobility and the prerogatives of power during its rise to prominence in Provence, now requires the assistance of Christian charity. With each passing generation, the rank of the minnesingers declined, with propertied aristocrats giving way to down-and-out nobles who worked as professional performers, and finally commoners and artisans whose only claim to status came from their skills as entertainers.

Walther sings of his travels, and by his description they brought him a considerable distance from his native land:

> I have traveled far and wide,
> have traversed the best of lands indeed;
> may misfortune be my guide,
> should I make my erring heart concede
> that it was impressed by their foreign ways.

In this work, which has been called the "first patriotic song of German literature," Walther adopts the political tone that distinguishes much of his surviving lyrics. Elsewhere he takes aim at religious institutions—with a daring that has earned him a reputation for anticipating Martin Luther. But even when expressing national pride, the theme of love is never far from the singer's mind, and his patriotism seems due, in large part, to his appreciation of the local ladies:

> He who understands
> lovely forms as well
> as I, would swear, by God, our peasant girls excel
> fine ladies in all other lands.

The music itself inevitably changed as the German courtly tradition of singing nobles was transformed into a less elitist art form and the privileges of feudalism were eroded by the emergence of new institutions and socioeconomic forces. In Germany this shift is marked by the rise of the *Meistersinger*, or 'master singer', a musical artisan whose professional status was conferred by membership in a guild, a common form of vocational organization that dominated urban economic life in Germany and other parts of Europe from the late Middle Ages until early modern times. At the high point of guild influence, some cities contained a hundred or more of these organizations, embracing a wide range of crafts and trades. The Meistersingers were especially influential in southern Germany, where they played a dominant role in shaping the musical culture during the fifteenth and sixteenth centuries.

In such environments, the purveyors of song organized their activities and codified their practices in the same manner as blacksmiths, shoemakers and other vocations. Even after the rise of these organizations, the older tradition of independent minstrels must have lingered on to some degree, and the Meistersingers themselves emphasized their connections to their predecessors. Their pride in their vocation was built, in no small part, on their sense of maintaining venerable traditions—Meistersingers boasted of connections to the tenth century or, in some instances, all the way back to Celtic bards and the time of Abraham. Yet this institutionalization of the singer's craft was hardly conducive to the expression of passionate sentiments in song, and the Meistersinger's insistence on imposing a standardized code of practice often threatened to turn the singer's craft into a stodgy bureaucracy.

Can you write songs according to a rule book? Certainly the Meistersingers must have believed so. Perhaps preeminently in the history of popular song, they favored form over content but with a formalism so severe that it went beyond matters of aesthetic judgment and became a kind of micromanagement of trade practices, imposed with the same zeal that countries apply tariffs and restrictions on manufactured goods. Among the regulations for the singers' guild, rules existed for all exigencies, from permissible rhymes to the placement of breaths, and the famous Meistersinger competitions judged contestants on the basis of an elaborate system of infractions and their penalties. The victor was the singer who made the fewest mistakes. The subjects of songs were now primarily drawn from the Bible rather than the precepts of courtly love, although, over time, romance and other secular themes entered the Meistersinger repertoire. Here again, love—or at least its musical expression—conquered all, finding a place even in this rigid systemization of song, just as it had overcome institutional obstacles in so many earlier periods.

But no dominant cultural movement is completely immune from backlashes and countermovements, least of all the love song. Even so, the scope of this response is stunning in its ambition, and the next chapter in our story presents one of the most unexpected twists in the long and dramatic history of this music. Did religious leaders attempt to force love songs back into hiding? Hardly! That would have proven beyond the powers of even the most fervent moralists. Instead religion now aimed to co-opt the music of romance, to claim it as its own and force it into subservience to a higher power and the dominant theology. The goal was nothing less than a transcendent purification, an alchemy of desire in which simmering passions were turned into what John Coltrane would later call a *love supreme*. Perhaps most surprising of all, the leading advocates for this new response were no longer angry clerics and dogmatic theologians, neither inquisitioners nor civil leaders, but the two greatest poets of the late medieval period, Dante and Rumi.

CHAPTER 9

A Love Supreme

Good lady, I think I see God when I gaze upon your delicate body.
—Peire Vidal

The pursuit of a higher love, freed from bondage to fierce passions and carnal desire, is usually connected in Western thought with Plato, who left us the single most important philosophical work on love in the Western canon. His Symposium is ostensibly the account of a dinner party held in 416 BC, during which Socrates and a half-dozen other participants each offer a speech in praise of Eros. A variety of perspectives are presented and debated over the course of the evening, but Socrates takes center stage with his provocative assertion that the "beauties of the body are as nothing to the beauties of the soul" and that the true lover must aspire to seeing "heavenly beauty face to face." This view has proven so influential that even today we speak of "platonic love" when referring to emotional bonds that operate outside of the gravitational pull of erotic impulses.

Socrates claims to have consulted Diotima of Mantinea in shaping his conception of love. We know nothing about this woman beyond the reference to her in the Symposium. She must have been a kind of seer or priestess. Socrates claims that she "brought about a ten years' postponement of the great plague of Athens on the occasion of a certain sacrifice, and it was she who taught me the philosophy of Love." Some have suggested that this woman is a fictional character, an invention by Plato to add color to his account, but so many personages in these dialogues are based on historical figures that we must hesitate before dismissing Diotima as a myth or invention. In any event, the acknowledgement of an all-but-unknown woman as the source of Plato's influential theory of love will come as no surprise to readers who have accompanied me this far in our study. As we have seen again and again, from the age of Sappho until the late medieval period, women often played the decisive, if sometimes hidden role in shaping our conceptualization of love and its outpouring in song.

Yet Christians might have reason to dispute the prominence of Plato (not to mention Socrates and Diotima) in accounts of a purified, spiritual love.

They can rightly contend that Christ placed this higher love at the center of his teachings. Christians call this form of love *agape*, adapting a Greek word that in its initial signification meant the love for a spouse or family member but now denotes the transcendent love that chastely binds God to his creation, and individuals to each other, in ties of fellowship. In chapter 22 of the Gospel of Matthew in the New Testament, Jesus leaves no doubt about his priorities, responding to a tricky question "Master, which is the great commandment in the law?" with a nod in the direction of Athens: "Thou shalt love the Lord thy God with all thy heart, and with all thy soul, and with all thy mind. This is the first and great commandment. And the second is like unto it, Thou shalt love thy neighbor as thyself." With such a clear and unambiguous tenet at the core of their religion, medieval Christians rightly felt that they need defer to no one—whether Platonist or troubadour—when asserting their authority on matters of the heart.

Of course, the question is far more complex than a simple choice between Plato and Christ. The Church itself was shaped by Platonic and Neoplatonic ideals, and the Christian teachings on love and other matters, as they evolved during the Middle Ages, frequently acknowledged the precedents of pagan philosophy. Indeed the convergence, rather than the disagreement, of these two traditions, and the authority of a philosophy of love that could draw on both these powerful and influential currents, come to the forefront in the next stage of the history of the love song. The troubadours may have brought this music out from hiding, but they still faced a powerful adversary that had one more strategy to play, and here the Church could call on philosophy as a potent ally in the task at hand.

This sense that love is at the core of the Christian worldview—and not just any love, but the *highest degree and fulfillment of human love*—explains why a dramatically spiritualized attitude toward the love lyric emerges soon after the troubadours and their followers set in motion a new personalized style of musical expression in the West. The Church sagaciously realized that it no longer possessed sufficient power and influence to suppress these songs of courtly love, but that hardly mattered anymore. The dominant religion didn't need to prohibit the love song, because it felt it had all the tools necessary to *take it over*.

Strange signs of this response appeared in various places in Europe, but perhaps none more striking than in Assisi, a small city in Italy where Francis, the son of a wealthy merchant who had taken a vow of poverty, found himself at the forefront of an early thirteenth-century populist movement to revitalize Christianity's commitment to love and charity. Francis would have more influence on European religious life than any other figure of his era, and was eventually canonized by the Church he worked so hard to reform. Yet he also sought to reform the love song, and in the process left us the first major work of lyrical poetry in the Italian vernacular. The saint who inspired so many others may himself have been inspired by the troubadours to write his famous "Canticle of the Sun," which borrows on the same natural imagery of the Provençal singers as well as their impassioned language of love and adoration. "Praised be You, my Lord, through Sister Moon and the stars," Francis proclaimed, "in heaven You formed them clear and precious and beautiful." The beloved here may be the Lord, but the rhetorical flourishes and attitude of humbling and pledged service are familiar to any reader of troubadour lyrics.

We know that Francis's father, Pietro, a successful cloth merchant, made business trips to France, and it is likely that his son joined him in visits to locales where they would have encountered performances of the fashionable songs of romance and courtship. He "loved to sing his Provençal songs," biographer Walter Nigg tells us, and another authority on the saint, Sophie Jewett, went so far as to give the title *God's Troubadour* to her book on Francis. Certainly Francis's decision to compose his lyric in the vernacular Umbrian dialect of Italian, rather than the formal Latin of religious writing, reminds us of the same informality of expression found in the love songs of the period. Perhaps most revealing of all: Francis invited ridicule by referring to his followers as *joculatores Dei*—minstrels of God, drawing on the same term used to describe the lowliest of street singers.

Religious teachings and the troubadour tradition did not always mix with such grace and simplicity. The most unusual love songs of the late medieval period may be those that emerged in conjunction with the cult of the Virgin Mary, which impacted ritual and worship with particular force during the waning of the Middle Ages. All of the artistic disciplines were transformed by this new theme in Christian belief. Although painted images of the Madonna and infant Jesus date back to the earliest days of the Church—they can be found in the Roman catacombs—this visual representation of the maternal and the divine came to rival the crucifixion as the preferred subject for religious art during the late medieval period. When Parisians rebuilt their cathedral in the mid-twelfth century they dedicated it to Notre Dame, "Our Lady," and when the city of Chartres undertook a similarly ambitious project a few decades later, the towering High Gothic edifice was also named for the Virgin Mary. From Siena to Luxembourg, numerous other communities pledged their centers of worship to the Madonna, and where large churches already stood, chapels dedicated to Mary were added—as, for example, Henry III did at Westminster Abbey in 1220. In music, hymns such as the "Salve Regina" and "Ave Maris Stella" testify to this intense devotion to the mother of Christ. Beginning in the eleventh century Marian antiphons, anthems to the mother of Christ, emerged as a prominent part of Christian worship, and in time they entered the monasteries, where they were sung to conclude the liturgical day—and continue to do so in modern-day monastic communities. The Cistercian order instituted the daily singing of "Salve Regina" in 1218, and the Dominicans did the same, first the monks in Bologna after a miracle in 1230 and then the whole order in 1250. In 1249, the Franciscans prescribed four Marian antiphons for regular use, and not long afterward the Franciscan Jacopone da Todi wrote the "Stabat Mater," later set to music by dozens of well-known composers, from Palestrina to Arvo Pärt. Private donors in various parts of Europe contributed funds to endow the singing of Marian antiphons and the celebration of Marian masses *in perpetuity*—a bold ambition, no doubt, but some of these endowments have lasted to the present day.

Can we properly classify these as love songs? Certainly the language of the hymns to Mary bears an uncanny resemblance to the love lyrics of the era. We encounter the same supplicatory attitude, the same praise of the lady—"our life, our sweetness and our hope," in the words of the "Salve Regina"—and even a similar enumeration of physical charms. In the "Ave Regina Caelorum," Mary is distinguished as "lovely beyond all others" and a "most beautiful maiden." Yet the most pronounced overlap between love song and Marian worship emerges in the Iberian Peninsula. Here, under the reign of King Alfonso X of Castile, a massive musical tribute to the Virgin Mary came to life—a work encompassing 420 poems with musical notation, every one of them making reference to the Virgin Mary. These *Cantigas de Santa Maria*, or "Songs of Holy Mary," are composed in the vernacular language, much like the troubadour songs, in this instance Galician-Portuguese. Also, as with the first love lyrics in Occitan, the *Cantigas* are attributed to a noble author, namely King Alfonso himself, although most scholars now believe that others played a significant role in creating this body of work. (The king, for his part, had wide-ranging literary aspirations and, in addition to his contributions to this project, also left behind some bawdy and amatory secular verses.)

The Virgin Mary in these songs exhibits jealousy, anger, and a taste for vengeance more appropriate for a jilted lover than the mother of Christ. Even more surprising, these lyrics often describe erotic situations in vivid detail, especially in the story songs relating the miracles of the Blessed Virgin. Rape, prostitution, incest, indeed the full range of sexual sins and satisfactions are held up for display. The illustrations that accompanied these songs match the tone of the lyrics, and sometimes seem designed to titillate rather than edify—for example, a depiction of groom and bride shows them in bed together, nude from the waist up, the husband fondling his wife's breast. Another song tells of a husband stabbing his wife because she refuses to have sex with him—but, in a moment of chaste reserve, the author adds that modesty forbids describing the specific location of the wound. The accompanying image of a spread-eagled woman receiving medical treatment is not quite so modest. In still another illustration, an abbess strips and stands half-naked before a bishop and his retinue, as well as the assembled nuns, ostensibly to prove that she is not pregnant. She convinces the onlookers, but only because Mary has sent angels to deliver the baby and remove it to a hiding place. The abbess, we are told, had slept with a man from Bologna who provided supplies to the convent, but is saved from public embarrassment (although not public display) by the good graces of the Madonna. The melody supporting this lurid tale is drawn from a Church chant. Perhaps such songs inspired the devotion of listeners, but not necessarily a devotion to chastity and the spiritual life.

Writing in the 1920s, Julian Ribera tried to unlock the mystery of this music by showing its strong connections to Islamic musical practices that gained prominence in the Iberian Peninsula during the Muslim conquest. As we have already seen, a number of musicologists attacked this hypothesis, but we now need to return to it in assessing the significance of the *Cantigas*, and again Ribera's insights help us understand the otherwise peculiar aspects of this seminal work. He may have pushed his speculations too far—for example in his dubious assertions on the Moorish chord changes to these songs—yet his 'big picture' contention of the influence of Islamic traditions on Spanish music in general and the *Cantigas* in particular is convincing. Even skeptics find it hard to explain away the illustration in one of the manuscript sources of the *Cantigas*. It shows a dark-skinned musician, of obvious African origins, performing on a stringed instrument beside a Christian playing a similar lute-like chordophone, who seems to be taking his cues from his Moorish companion. The dark-skinned performer is to the viewer's left, and accordingly to the right of the other player. "In all of the miniatures the principal musician is thus placed," Ribera points out. "Thus the Moor is in the position of honor, rather than the Christian." This cultural intersection would go a long way toward explaining the unexpected eroticism of the *Cantigas*, so alien to Christian religious music but characteristic of the North African and Middle Eastern currents that flowed into al-Andalus before the rise of the troubadours.

These peculiar precedents merely set the stage for the most ambitious attempt to merge the ethos of courtly love with the scholasticism of the Church fathers. It would take the genius of Dante to create a lasting union of two such disparate worldviews without lapsing into the awkwardness and incongruities that are so jarring in the *Cantigas*. Strange to say, Italy at first reacted cautiously to the innovations of the troubadours. With the advent of the Renaissance, Italy would emerge as the epicenter of the sophisticated love song, initiating an emotionally robust tradition, with the *canzone*, the *ballata*, the *frottola*, the madrigal, and finally the opera setting the tone for love songs elsewhere in Europe. But in the thirteenth century, Italian courts preferred to hear troubadours from the south of France, who sang in their own native tongue. These performers from afar, many of them refugees from the Albigensian Crusade, found receptive audiences and patrons throughout Italy, from the feudal courts of the north to Sicily far to the south. Their reputation stood so high that even Dante pondered whether love lyrics ought to be written in the Occitan language rather than his native Tuscan vernacular. Yet even as the Italian poet took up the challenge of infusing his own language with the spirit of courtly love, he also set himself on a path that would drastically reconfigure the worldview he had inherited from France.

More than a half century had elapsed since St. Francis composed his canticle, and only now was the vernacular love lyric ready to take center stage in Italian literary life. Dante's pathbreaking work *La Vita Nuova* (The New Life), with its intensely personal combination of memoir and lyric poetry, must have been a revelation to its first readers at the close of the thirteenth century. Here Dante not only left us one of the most beguiling love stories in history, but even dared to play the starring role himself. The object of his adoration, Beatrice Portinari, had died at twenty-four just five years earlier, and by his own account, Dante had only enjoyed two brief encounters with her and no romantic connection—she married banker Simone dei Bardi in 1287. But her presence hovered over his entire oeuvre. In the highest compliment he could pay his departed love, Dante installed her in Paradiso in his *Divine Comedy*, where she serves as his guide in heaven—perhaps the most daring literary conflation of spirituality and romance since the emergence of the Orpheus myth at the dawn of Western civilization. In time, other famous couples have come to eclipse Dante and Beatrice in our collective imagination, but none of them can match these medieval role models in exemplifying Plato's vision of a love that could grow from the corporeal to the spiritual, even while retaining all the passion and intensity of feeling we long for in our stories of romance and courtship.

But can we rely on Dante and his contemporaries for an accurate account of love and ways of the heart in the late medieval epoch? Do we dare fall under the spell they cast, embracing the idealization of romance presented in their surviving works? After all, Dante may have written about Beatrice, but he married Gemma Donati, a woman who is never mentioned by name in his literary works—an extraordinary state of affairs when one considers how much this poet relied on autobiographical elements for literary inspiration. A few decades later, Petrarch gained renown for his love sonnets about his beloved Laura, the wife of another man, but showed no interest in singing the praises of the real-life mistress who bore him two illegitimate children. Mere poetic license? Or do these discrepancies between the real love lives of the poets and their idealized recrafting in verse point to a deeper dishonesty, a false ideology of love that masked the baser truths of intimate human relationships during the late medieval period? In short, was their advocacy of a higher love merely a literary conceit, incapable of realization in day-to-day life?

As we look at the full scale of love's assault on Western culture during this period, crossing conventional boundaries between the secular and the spiritual, we can't help seeing it as a kind of ideology, the centerpiece of an insurgent worldview that now demands obeisance from those who, in other times and places, would have been its fiercest foes. Scholar F. Alberto Gallo marvels over the fact that virtually all of the fourteenth-century Florentine composers were "priests or members of religious orders and spent their lives performing their duties in the religious institutions of the city," yet the texts they set to music "were almost entirely on the theme of love." Even when love songs were attacked, the nature of the assault acknowledged their popularity and power. Franco Sacchetti, an Italian poet of the fourteenth century, complained that "clever things can scarcely be turned into song: music is always kept to be at the service of amorous verses." Sacchetti himself, it is worth noting, wrote love lyrics. He may have felt scorn for "amorous verses," yet his own practice indicates his inability to resist the zeitgeist.

The ascendancy of love as a dominant cultural value increasingly caused a creative tension in late medieval society—a tension that may have been theological in its origins but artistic in its results. For all his admiration for the troubadours and their followers, Dante is reluctant to admit them to Paradise in *The Divine Comedy*. Arnaut Daniel and Guido Guinizzelli atone in Purgatory for sins of lust, and Bertran de Born languishes in the eighth circle of Dante's Inferno, where he carries his severed head in punishment for sowing dissent. The Church itself laid the groundwork for this conflict, even wrote it into its doctrines. Scholar R. Howard Bloch summarizes the Church's paradoxical attitude to women: "You are at one and the same time the 'Bride of Christ' and the 'Devil's gateway,' seducer and redeemer, but nothing in between." This conflict, internalized in the medieval mind, inevitably played itself out in poetry and music. Thus we encounter peculiar songs, in which the beloved is held up as the object of desire, yet the singer begs her never to allow him to satisfy his sexual longing. Here we arrive at the foundation of a love that felt most confident when attached to another man's wife, not because it aimed at adultery but due instead to the strange solace of a passion that did not run the risk of a tainted consummation. We can hardly blame the poets and singers for not resolving this tension—it could not be resolved given the prevalent value system of the day.

A psychologist of our own time might smile fondly at these figures from the past, seeing their literary works as monuments to the creative power of repression and transference. From such a perspective, Dante and Petrarch—and many of the other purveyors of love lyrics from the late medieval period—took the building blocks of neuroses and transformed them into charming, if unrealistic, poems and songs. But a more sympathetic interpretation, and one truer to the actual belief systems of that age, might acknowledge this attempted reconciliation of carnal and spiritual love as one of the great heroic projects of Western history. So many later conundrums and controversies, from Cartesian dualism to the expanding claims of our own neuroscientists, inevitably arrive at the same chasm between soul and body that singers of love tried to bridge in the thirteenth century. And if that divide could not be crossed—at least not by the masses of humanity; perhaps Dante himself and a few other enlightened souls could succeed in finding that love supreme—the ideal remains. Perhaps it haunts our imagination today just as deeply as does the imagery of knights and courtly ladies from the troubadours, although more ethereally and in a way hard for us to articulate in the cold, empirical formulas of current-day scholarship. Those who sang about love during the late medieval period wanted it both ways. They wanted love that was sensual and earthy in the extreme, but they also wanted it to take them, in the words of the pop song, "higher and higher." And what about us? In our age, so tilted toward carnality in the body-soul debate, we tend to ignore this higher love, even as we feel the pain of its absence. Maybe Dante gets the last laugh on the psychologists, no?

Although he acknowledged the interdependence of music and poetry, Dante was not a musician himself, and his influence on the love song would be modest in comparison to those who followed in his wake. In contrast, Francesco Petrarca, from the next generation of Tuscan writers, easily surpassed Dante in this regard. Petrarch, as he is commonly known to us, began writing the love poetry that would constitute his *Canzoniere*, or "song book," less than a decade after Dante's death, and his beloved Laura would fill the same role in his oeuvre that Beatrice served in Dante's work. Petrarch's *Canzoniere* would eventually inspire more composers and lead to more musical settings than any other collection of lyrical poetry in the Italian language. But, as we shall see, more than 150 years would elapse before this effusive lover and lyricist would exert his greatest influence on the musical landscape.

This later popularity makes the paucity of musical settings from Dante's and Petrarch's own day all the more puzzling. Only a few contemporaries recognized the potential for turning these literary lyrics into true songs. Jacopo da Bologna provided a melody for Petrarch's "Non al suo amante" when the poet was still alive, but this is the only setting that has survived from that era. Dante, for his part, memorializes his friend Casella in the *Divine Comedy*, placing him on the shores of Purgatory, where the Tuscan musician sings Dante's canzone "Amor che nella mente mi ragiona" ("Love that within my mind discourses"). Dante tries three times to embrace his dead friend, each time grasping only empty air, but even this vain attempt testifies to the deep bond that must have existed in life between poet and musician.

Fame was not handed out equally to these two vocations, at least not in Dante's day. The composers who set Italian poetry to music during this period are hardly known to us when compared to those who provided the texts. Even as a distinctive Italian style of composition came to the fore, and the use of polyphony grew more assured, the pioneers responsible for these advances are little more than names to us—and sometimes not even that. The Rossi Codex, the most important manuscript documenting Italian vernacular music from the early fourteenth century, does not identify any of its composers (although some have been discovered through other sources). Over the course of the century, biographical information on the leading composers becomes more detailed and secure, but the process is gradual and frustratingly incomplete. In the early and middle decades, these artists are of so little consequence that either their last name is completely forgotten (as with the great Maestro Piero, the first major figure of Italian vernacular song of the thirteenth century) or, more commonly, presents a mere geographical designation. Thus we encounter Jacopo da Bologna, Vincenzo da Rimini, Giovanni da Cascia, Gherardello da Firenze, Bartolino da Padova, and other figures of Trecento vernacular music. In some instances, a few facts have survived about these individuals, in other cases we know next to nothing beyond the place of origin or residence indicated in their name. Some evidence suggests that composers of Italian love songs during this period may have been associated with universities. Jacopo da Bologna, the most illustrious of this group, wrote a treatise on music that may have been used as textbook; Bologna, the city designated in the composer's name, served as home to the oldest university in Italy. In any event, we can safely assume that these purveyors of song must have traveled widely—you don't get known as "Vincent from Rimini" or "Jacob from Bologna" if you stay in Rimini or Bologna—but the extent of their journeys and the true scope of their musical efforts are mostly a matter of conjecture.

And the ladies they sang about present a mystery just as enticing as the composers themselves. In particular, we encounter hidden references to a woman named Anna, whose name is slyly incorporated into lyrics by Giovanni, Jacopo, and Piero. Do we surmise that she coyly flirted with the leading songwriters of her day? Perhaps a more likely explanation is that these composers had been engaged to compete with each other—not for the affection of a woman but in a display of musical acumen, as part of a contest to show their cleverness and please an influential patron of the arts. But even the seemingly obvious words and phrases of fourteenth-century songs may hold hidden significations. The references to lovely birds or animals may well be hidden allusions to specific women, and descriptions of the hunt symbolize a more amorous pursuit. The age delighted in coded messages, and the practice of hiding someone's identity in the lyrics—similar to the code name, or *senhal*, employed by the troubadours—and the popularity of acrostics, in which the opening letters of each line spells out a name or message, make clear both the playful spirit of this music, as well as the need for care in interpreting even seemingly straightforward songs.

We are on firmer ground in discussing the formal qualities of this music. A new style of secular song emerges in the works of these Italian composers of the early fourteenth century, and is named the *madrigal*—probably from the Latin *matricale*, referring to the choice of the mother tongue, the vernacular Italian, rather than the Latin of the ecclesiastical music of the day. Antonio da Tempo, a Paduan judge and poet who was a contemporary of these composers, offered a different etymology, typically derided by later scholars, from the Italian *mandria*, or "flock," and suggested that the style of singing originated with shepherds. And perhaps there is a connection here, if not with actual herders, at least with the idealization of rustic pastoral life that is evident in so many songs and lyric poems of this period. In any event, the Trecento madrigal needs to be distinguished from the far more influential madrigal that would come to dominate European secular music two hundred years later—the name may be the same, but the style of the music, as we shall see, is different. Tuscan poet Francesco da Barberino, a contemporary of Dante, dismissed the earlier madrigal as "disorganized singing of unpolished people." This scorn seems hardly warranted by the surviving works. These songs displayed their composers' skill in polyphony, usually for two voices, and consisted of one or more tercets, or three-line stanzas, sung to the same music, followed by a concluding one- or two-line send-off known as the *ritornello*. The structure bears some stylistic similarities with the sonnet form that inspired the finest expressions of love from Petrarch, Shakespeare, and so many later poets—although with a quatrain instead of a tercet serving as the sonnet's basic building block. Moreover, the shift in tone of the *ritornello* also reminds us of the *kharja*, and the pervasive reliance on these striking concluding passages in both the love songs and poetry of the late medieval period. In a modern love song, we would call this the 'hook', and even in these much older lyrics these sprightly turnabouts are often the most memorable parts of the surviving works.

Despite these significant developments in Italy, the real musical superstars of this era, for both liturgical and secular music, still came from the north. Dante and Petrarch may have inspired a poetic revolution, fueled in no small part by their ardent love for a special lady, but French dialects remained the preferred language of love in song form, and the most celebrated composers and performers at the close of the medieval period hailed from present-day France, Belgium, and the Netherlands. During the early and middle decades of the thirteenth century, European music took on new depth and light under the influence of their *ars nova*, a more expressive polyphonic approach to composition that originated in France and the Burgundian Low Countries. Guillaume de Machaut, born around the year 1300 in the area around Reims (perhaps in the tiny village of Machault, near the current border with Belgium), stands out as the chief instigator and advocate for the new sound. And not just due to his skill in melody and counterpoint: Machaut's fame as a poet matched and, in his own day, perhaps even surpassed his impact as a maker of music. A whole generation of authors, including Geoffrey Chaucer, were influenced by his writings. Today, however, we remember Machaut mostly for his musical daring. He wrote both polyphonic and monophonic, sacred and secular compositions, and continued the tradition of the *trouvères*, even as he embraced new techniques that would contribute to the demise of this earlier style of love song.

Indeed, the ease with which Machaut and other composers from this period moved from religious works to love songs tells us much about the growing cross-hybridization taking place in these once stridently opposed camps. As Machaut's biography shows, the composer demonstrated a similar facility in moving between the demands of God and Cupid in his personal life. Although he took holy orders and served as a canon in various French parishes, Machaut commemorated his affection for a specific lady in his artistic oeuvre, much like Dante and Petrarch. In Machaut's case, this passion was kindled late in life for nineteen-year-old Péronne d'Armentières—at least if we can believe the semi-autobiographical account in *Le Voir Dit*, probably written when the poet-composer was in his sixties.

Like many a Frenchman before and after him, Machaut's poetic sensibility found frequent inspiration in the traditions of courtly love, but with a piquant new twist. Suitors in the late medieval period, including those depicted in Machaut's songs, are a sorry lot. Again and again we encounter the beleaguered, suffering lover, a pitiable figure who has replaced the more self-assured knightly troubadours of an earlier day.

> Love makes my heart languish
> and when it is against me,
> neither does she deign to cure me
> nor am I able to be pleasing
> to the beautiful one whom I love and desire,
> who at her pleasure
> is able to make and destroy me.

Such complaints were even more pronounced in Machaut's contemporary Petrarch, who worked endless variations on this theme, and would later exert unparalleled influence on the lyrics of European love songs. Machaut and Petrarch, and many others of their generation, turn love into a disease, a physical affliction, to be lamented even as it is enjoyed. Hints of this tone can be traced back to the troubadours and, even earlier, the view of love as illness was a pervasive theme among the ancient Roman lyricists, but not to the extent that we witness at the close of the medieval period. A diagnostics and pathology of romantic love will now dominate Western poetry. Again a theological or philosophical underpinning can be detected beneath the quasi-medical attitude of the singers. With the poets' growing allegiance to a spiritualized conception of eros comes a comparable awareness of the path by which love turns into lovesickness, a malaise of the spirit but with acute physical symptoms. Above all, the suitor or singer who takes seriously Christian teachings on sexuality is consigned to this never-ending suffering whenever the beloved is someone other than a lawfully wedded spouse—unless the lover rises to the higher, quasi-Platonic devotion Dante depicts in *Paradiso*. Given the difficulties of achieving this transcendent stage, who can be surprised at the proliferation of love songs filled with unhappy laments and an enumeration of unhealthy symptoms?

In Italy, the leading exponent of *ars nova*, Francesco Landini, focused almost entirely on secular songs, with love as their predominant theme—at least if we can judge his output by the works that have survived. Indeed, in Landini, we finally encounter a composer of Italian love songs whose talent and work were so revered that contemporaries took care to preserve both his music and some details of his life. A memorial to Landini can still be seen at the Basilica of San Lorenzo in Florence, and it is telling that all of the most illustrious members of the Medici family are buried in this same edifice. The inscription reads: "Francesco, deprived of sight, but with a mind skilled in instrumental music, whom alone Music has set above all others, has left his ashes here, his soul above the stars. Taken from mankind on 2, September, 1397." The son of an artisan painter, Landini rose to such a level of renown that he was crowned with the laurel by the king of Cyprus, just as Petrarch had become a 'laureate' a quarter of a century earlier in a famous ceremony on Rome's Capitoline Hill in 1341, with King Robert of Naples presiding.

While still a child, Landini survived a case of smallpox but, as his epitaph indicates, was left blind. As with so many who have lost their eyesight, the youngster found compensation in the gifts of his ear. He began composing at an early age, first melodies for singing, and later works for strings and organ. His dexterity and expressiveness on the latter "surpassed any organist in living memory," asserts his biographer Filippo Villani, but Landini also earned praise for his skill with the lute, the fiddle and "every other sort of instrument," some of which he invented. In time, admirers would refer to him as "il divino"—the same term of praise applied to Dante and later to Michelangelo.

Landini appears as a character in *Il Paradiso degli Alberti*, a work in the style of the *Decameron* written by Giovanni di Gherardo da Prato in the late fourteenth century. Here the composer's music is described in rapturous terms: "Francesco, who was in high spirits, took his little organ and began to play so sweetly his songs of love that there was no-one present who did not feel, through the sweetness of this sweetest harmony, as if overflowing joy would make their hearts burst from their breasts." (The instrument described here is the small handheld organ common in the period, sometimes called the *portative organ*—think of it as a kind of accordion equipped with pipes. Landini's tombstone depicts him playing one.) Two young maidens then sang Landini's "Orsù, gentili spirti": "Rise up, gentle souls, eager for love. / Would you like to see 'Paradise'?" Their performance was delivered "in such pleasing tones and with such angelic voices" that even the birds in the cypress trees, we are assured, listened to the music and began to sing their own songs more sweetly.

Despite the precedent of Landini, the epicenter of the Western love song was still not ready to move from France to Italy. Around the time of Landini's death, the court of the Duke of Burgundy was coming into ascendancy as a major source of musical innovation in Europe, and the cities of Brussels, Bruges, Lille, and Arras would now play a central role in European cultural life that they would never again match. Unlike Landini, the leading Franco-Flemish composers did not focus on love songs—the towering figures from the north, such as Guillaume Dufay, Johannes Ockeghem, and Josquin des Prez, are remembered today primarily for their sacred music. But, as we have already seen with Machaut, church composers often wrote chansons as well, although the texts of the love songs from the north were hardly as innovative as their music, and often reiterated the same, now hackneyed sentiments of courtly love or Petrarchan pathological love. Perhaps more interesting, the melodies of love songs could serve as the basis for solemn ecclesiastical works. Thus Dufay incorporates his chanson "Se La Face Ay Pale" ("If my face is pale, love is to blame") into one of his most famous masses. Similarly "De plus en plus" from Gille Binchois, the leading Burgundian composer of secular songs and one of the great melodists of the fifteenth century, is drawn on by Ockeghem for one of his early masses. If, as I have suggested, the main attitude of the Church toward love songs during this period was a strategy of assimilation and co-optation, one could hardly ask for more symbolically resonant examples than these sacred works that forced the music of romance to pay homage to the divine.

But what happened outside of western Europe during this period? What role did love songs have in other communities and societies, in the public and private lives of individuals? If European sources are scanty for much of the medieval period, they are even more elusive as we cast our gaze over a wider terrain. Our queries are further complicated by larger questions about the nature of love and romance, and how these vary across cultural boundaries and historical eras. Is romantic love a universal concept, a Darwinian bond assisting in the survival of the race and thus likely to be found, with minor variations, in every nook and cranny of the globe? Or is it, as some contend, a new idea that spread through Europe in the eleventh century, and then outward to other ports of call, less a psychological universal, more a popular export?

When we encounter Byzantine love songs of the late medieval period espousing the sentiments of courtly love, we can probably draw a connecting line back

to influences from the West. Here we find the same fatalistic love and sweet subservience in a lyric, translated from the Greek, that dates back at least to the
twelfth century: "Give me a kiss, sweet kiss, light of my eyes, / Or let me die by
you my love." But how do we explain the marked similarity between Asad Gor-
gani's eleventh-century Persian epic about lovers Vis and Rāmin and the Celtic
tale of Tristan and Iseult, which inspired French authors of the twelfth century?
Is this a mere coincidence, a sign of direct influence, or was a new idealized
image of love rising up spontaneously in far distant places due to comparable
local influences, whether social, cultural, or economic? By the same token, how
do we interpret the marked sentiments of courtly love in the Georgian national
epic *The Knight in the Panther's Skin*, composed by poet Shota Rustaveli around
the end of the twelfth century? "This could not have been due to Western influence—it is scarcely conceivable that Provence should have traveled into the
Caucasus," concludes Peter Dronke. "Georgia makes her own Provence freshly
and unaided, her own *cour d'amour* around her beautiful, much-worshipped
queen." Or, heading farther east, what should we make of the *geji*, or "song courtesans," of the Song Dynasty of China, whose combination of beguiling music
and prostitution seems to match a cultural type found everywhere from medieval Europe to early twentieth-century New Orleans? Are these similarities signs
of some larger convergence in human institutions, or a matter of geographical
dissemination, or merely coincidences?

In Japan, shortly before the rise of the troubadours, we encounter another of
these striking parallels. Here we find a tradition of music-making among nobles
that exhibits both a stylized aesthetic beauty and a direct connection to matters
of love and courtship—so much so that we are inevitably reminded of the musical revolution soon to emerge in southern France. *The Tale of Genji*, written
by Japanese noblewoman Murasaki Shikibu in the early eleventh century, offers
insights into a feudal society where the ability to play music and compose lyrics
rank among the most honored skills, not just in providing entertainment but
also in matters of romance, both licit and illicit. In fact, this thousand-year-old
novel, with its rich tapestry of physical and psychological details, gives us greater
insight in the specifics of musical performance in a court society than any comparable Western document from the period.

Songs and lyrics took on particular importance in the romance and courtship of the Japanese ruling class of this period because more direct connections
between men and women were strictly controlled, and sometimes specifically
prohibited. Male suitors in *The Tale of Genji* often complain that they must
address their beloved through some intermediary, a gentlewoman or messenger.
In many instances, the man's contact is so limited that he has no idea what the
woman looks like, and if he hears her voice, she is often hidden behind a screen
or curtain. In such settings, relationships were frequently established through

music, which reaches beyond the curtain where the suitor cannot go, as well as via the exchange of poetic verses, referred to here as songs—*uta* (a song), *tanka* (a short song), or *waka* (a Japanese song). Sometimes a lover composed an original poem, but often the text was borrowed or adapted from a preexisting verse. The physical qualities of a work were as important as originality of content: a poem might be admired for the beauty of the handwriting, the nature of the paper, the fragrance of the scented stationery, the colors chosen for the message, and any accompanying flowers or gifts. The words themselves avoided the expression of intense feelings—which was frowned upon—and dealt more with what we would today call mood-setters or ambience. The evening mist, the moon in the sky, a blossom, the call of a bird—these and other images served as evocative building blocks in an indirect language of love:

> Now that ninefold mists must keep you and me apart, lovely plum blossom,
> Shall I never have from you the least breath of your perfume.

Or:

> How sadly I haunt the slopes of Mount Irusa, where the crescent sets,
> Yearning just to see again the faint moon that I saw then.

Unlike the troubadours of southern Europe, the singers of love songs in feudal Japan could rely on an older, established, and unsuppressed tradition of romantic and even erotic expression in lyrical form. Certainly similar songs must have existed in the West before the year 1000 but, as we have seen, they were castigated by the Church wherever they were found, extirpated if possible, and preserved only in the rarest circumstances. In contrast, love and sex are recurring themes in the *Man'yōshū*, the oldest surviving collection of Japanese poetry, compiled in the late eighth century but including sections that date back to the fourth century. The frankness here in matters of the heart has no equivalent in sanctioned European literature of the era:

> If I despised you, who are as beautiful
> as the murasaki grass,
> would I be longing for you like this,
> though you are another man's wife?

And from the woman's perspective:

> Whose words are these,
> spoken to the wife of another?

Whose words are these,
that bade me untie
the sash of my robe?

Around half of the poems in the *Man'yōshū* are anonymous, but in the northeast of India, we find creators of love songs of such renown during the late medieval period that we are not remiss in comparing them with the more prominent Occitan troubadours. Here with Vidyapati, from the present-day region of Bihar, and Chandidas from West Bengal, we find not only love lyrics of profound soulfulness, but also an uncanny focus on the same thorny sociological and theological issues that are familiar to us from our study of the secular songs of Europe. Such troubling questions: Must the singer and lover renounce the erotic in order to secure the higher delights of love? Can a dialogue take place across the apparent divide between spiritual and carnal love? Are these two spheres inevitably at odds, or can a pure heart partake of both? And, at an even more basic level, what are the proper words for such songs? Does the singer hold on to the traditional language of the past—Sanskrit in this instance—or embrace the vernacular of the people?

These are, of course, the identical questions that bedeviled Dante, but only a few decades after the Tuscan master's death, the courtier poet Vidyapati and the mystic priest Chandidas wrestled with the same dichotomies in their much different social milieu, far from the bastions of Christendom. And just as Western singers of love mixed in elements of the cult of the Virgin Mary into their concepts of romance, Vidyapati and Chandidas drew on a divine love story that would have been well known to their audiences. The love affair of the Hindu deity Krishna— himself a musician and often depicted playing a flute—with the *gopi* (cowherdess) Radha, had been the focus of the *Gita Govinda*, an epic by the twelfth-century poet Jayadeva. This work, akin to the Song of Songs from the Judeo-Christian tradition, presents the familiar trappings of love relationships in a manner suitable for symbolic reinterpretation along spiritual lines. Krishna's straying from Rudha and his later reconciliation with her can be seen as emblematic of the faithlessness of human souls and their subsequent return to union with the divine.

Building on this precedent, the Indian poets of the late medieval period created new vernacular love songs inspired by the well-known story. They celebrated a divine passion that would also have reminded listeners of the romances of everyday life. Even today, the love songs Vidyapati composed more than a half-millennium ago are performed at marriages in his native region. In the day before advice columns and how-to books, many young couples no doubt consulted these lyrics as a guide to satisfactory conjugal relations.

Oh friend, what should I say of his wantonness?
He desired unlawful pleasure.

Thinking my twin breasts hills,
he held them with his hands
lest they should fall upon his heart.
Leaving my modesty aside,
I was excited with love,
and my anklets kept on tinkling.

Vidyapati concludes: "Knowing his desire the girl was pleased."

Chandidas, born several decades after Vidyapati, creates problems for biographers because he was *too* popular. Other poets borrowed his name for their own works, or took credit for their famous predecessor's achievements—even in the modern day singers present his songs as their own. As a result, we struggle to determine which of the many lyrics attributed to Chandidas were written by the fifteenth-century poet, and which came from his epigones. We know little of Chandidas's life beyond what he reveals in his songs, and even these facts may present a composite figure incorporating elements of the different poets who adopted this name. He was, we are told, a mystic and a priest—two villages in West Bengal claim him as a native son and point to ruined temples where he supposedly served—whose mixture of spirituality and eroticism scandalized many members of Hindu society. His religious associations notwithstanding, his worldview is permeated with what we would today call humanism. His most often quoted phrase proclaims:

Man is the greatest Truth
Of all,
Nothing beyond.

Bengali ethnomusicologist Deben Bhattacharya, who translated the poet's lyrics into English in the 1960s, visited the Birbhum district of present-day West Bengal, where Chandidas lived so many centuries ago. There he found a surprisingly vibrant tradition that still echoed the native son: "By the roadside singers frequently render, in return for copper coins, Birbhum folk songs, more often than not distorted versions of songs by Chandidas. Chandidas is everywhere—in the villages, in the countryside, even on the roads."

The torn and incomplete manuscript of the Bengali poet's *Shreekrishna Kirtana*, discovered in a cowshed in 1909, ranks among the oldest surviving works in that language. As with Vidyapati, Chandidas's lyrics in this verse drama celebrate the love affair of the divine couple Radha and Krishna. But the legacy of the poet also includes a real-life romance, not dissimilar to the stories of Dante and Beatrice and Petrarch and Laura. In the case of Chandidas, the role of the beloved is filled by Rami, a young washerwoman, who defied convention and incurred condemnation through her affair with the Brahmin singer—although here we may be dealing with a biographical element from one of the later poets who claimed the name Chandidas. In any event, the desire of popular tradition to merge these sacred and profane elements into a single body of work by a composite figure is revealing. It reflects the same ambitious recalibration and attempted merging of the sacred and profane we see at work in the love songs of late medieval Europe. The spirit is willing, the flesh is weak, but both somehow manage to join hands in singing of a love that bridges the chasm between the two.

But for the most celebrated exponent of a spiritualized love and its attainment through music and dance in the late medieval era, we must turn our gaze to the the Persian city of Vakhsh, in present-day Tajikistan, where Jalâl al-Din Rumi was born in the year 1207. Rumi's influence spans poetry, theology, jurisprudence, mysticism, and the arts. During the same epoch when the troubadours of western Europe attempted to find a place for the music of love within a dominant religious culture, Rumi explored what he saw as love's mystical and spiritually charged essences. For Rumi, poetry, music, and dance served as pathways to the divine love, a spiritual journey that allowed the seeker to live with ardor and compassion amid the manifest world and its inhabitants. He writes, in words of ecstatic praise:

> Love makes the sea boil like a kettle;
> Love crumbles the mountain like sand;
> Love cleaves the sky with a hundred clefts;
> Love unconscionably makes the earth to tremble.

Despite the vividness of these comparisons and Rumi's skills as a poet, he believed that this supercharged sense of love resisted expression in mere words—an extraordinary claim from someone who left us around sixty thousand lines of poetry, more than Dante's *Divine Comedy*, Petrarch's *Canzoniere*, and Chaucer's *Canterbury Tales* combined. For Rumi, this divine love was approached most successfully in silence, or through dance and music.

Rumi's musical pathway to spiritual love was realized through the practice of *sama*, a ritualized approach to divine perfection via sound and movement. The word *sama* is sometimes translated as 'listening', a misleading descriptor of a ritual so filled with rapturous movement, or as 'audition' with its unfortunate associations of preliminary tryouts for a real performance at a later date. Those who have witnessed the Whirling Dervishes, those famous practitioners of *sama* of the Mevlevi order in present-day Turkey who trace their origins back to Rumi, would hardly latch on to such insufficient labels in describing this dizzying and dazzling hybrid of musical expression and spiritual practice.

Rumi is often cited as the originator of *sama*, and the story is told of the poet breaking into a spontaneous dance in response to the rhythmic pounding of the metalworkers in the marketplace. In truth, the roots of this Islamic spiritual practice predate Rumi's birth by at least two centuries. Teachers and scholars had long argued over the propriety of music and poetry in the mosque. Some had forbidden any poetry, others approved certain kinds, and in some instances even love poems were permitted. In other situations, lyric poetry could be recited but not sung. Sufi scholar Ali Hujwiri aimed to prove, back in the mid-eleventh century, that the Prophet had permitted song and music, enjoyed poetry, and encouraged the chanting of the Koran. Ali Hujwiri had reservations about "dancing," but claimed that this term did not apply to the ecstatic movements of the dervishes in *sama*.

Rumi nonetheless faced opposition to his practice of *sama*, and critics reminded him of works of Islamic law that warned against music and dance. But he persisted in this singing and whirling pathway to divine love, and in his poetry urged others to do the same:

> The wise men tell us that we take these tunes
> from the turning of celestial spheres
> these sounds are revolutions of the skies
> that man composes with his lyre and throat.

Or:

> When they free themselves from their own clutches
> when they can leap right out of their own flaws:
> they clap their hands and they do a dance.

As part of his modernization plans for the newly founded Republic of Turkey, Kemal Atatürk abolished the Mevlevi order in 1925 and prohibited the spinning ceremony—a ban that lasted more than a quarter of a century. When the Whirling Dervishes were finally allowed to resume their cherished ritual in the mid-1950s, the performances were now presented as a folk dance, primarily for the entertainment of tourists. During one of the first revivals, the police even issued a warning when one of the old dancers began praying as he moved. Yet the wording of the legal code and the presence of curious onlookers can hardly change the embedded significations—or, even more to the point, the physiological and psychic realities—of this potent and time-honored ritual. Politicians may have their agendas, but the legacy of Rumi has not been so easy to constrain.

In fact, his fame and influence today are greater than ever before, but they show up in musical settings where Rumi himself would be surprised—or even alarmed—to find them. You will encounter him at "spiritual aerobics" classes where a well-heeled paying clientele, sometimes including Hollywood celebrities or wealthy matrons, listens to Rumi's poems intermixed with rock music while working up a sweat. Deepak Chopra has recorded Rumi's love poems with the help of some famous friends, including Madonna, who turns from "Material Girl" to "Metaphysical Girl" when singing and reciting the mystic poet's impassioned lyrics. And what would Rumi have made of composer Steven Flynn's music for Robert Davidson's dance production *Rapture Rumi*? Here, according to the marketing copy, "hot rhythms and yearning melodies combine to make songs that speak of the desires of both body and soul," and the soundtrack serves as the perfect music for "listening or dancing, meditation or love-making."

Turning Rumi into a master of eroticism may draw an audience, but it represents a gross misinterpretation of his significant role in the long history of love. Since the days of Plato's Symposium, few had undertaken such an ambitious program of reclaiming love from the carnal realm, transforming it into a pathway to the transcendent, and purifying it into what John Coltrane would later call "a love supreme." Rumi is aligned, despite doctrinal differences, with Dante and St. Francis, Vidyapati and Chandidas, and other mystics and musicians, in pursuing one of the most grand, perhaps quixotic ventures of the late medieval period—nothing less than the reconciliation of the body and soul, eros and spirit.

What a surprising turn of events! After a millennium during which religious leaders had opposed and repressed love songs, the late medieval period found the most visionary spiritual minds, East and West, attempting to co-opt the romantic elements their predecessors had been unable to eradicate. In the poems and visions of Hadewijch, a thirteenth-century mystic living in the vicinity of Antwerp, union with Jesus is described in starkly sensual terms—and we are left to ponder which is stranger, this mixture of erotic fantasy and devotion, or the fact that devout churchgoers found it perfectly acceptable. Half a world away, ghazal singers often celebrated a love ambiguous in scope, perhaps centered on God, but possibly indicating a partner in romance. In other instances, the religious intent of the song is obvious, yet the language is charged with imagery and language drawn from the traditions of secular love songs. In the Zohar, the influential Kabbalistic work that first appeared in Spain during this same period, sexual and religious elements come together in an overarching mythology, with God's relationship to the world echoed in the union of human couples. The local circumstances differ markedly, but the overall trend is clear: theology champions the ideals of romance, but with the goal of infusing them with elements of the divine. The moral tone that dominated courtly love, the merging of the cult of the Virgin Mary into the earthy tales of the *Cantigas de Santa Maria*, the love songs drawing on the story of Radha and Krishna, the canticle of St. Francis, the luminous mixture of scholasticism and romance of Dante—each of these, in their different ways, aimed to disarm Cupid and enlist him in the ranks of angels.

The attempt was inspiring, and gave us magnificent works of poetry and song. But from a historical standpoint, it must ultimately be considered an abject failure. Love, and its music, proved too powerful in its erotic allure, too resistant to spiritualization. Theology could not master them—nor, for that matter, have civil authorities, parents, or anyone else who has tried. As we continue with our story of love songs, we will occasionally encounter dreamers and mystic who still believe in this 'love supreme', but they will increasingly be outliers or renegades from the mainstream culture. The love song had a different destiny as a secular force—built on its potency in shaping people's private lives and most intimate relations to a degree that few other cultural forces, and certainly no other style of music, could match. In short, we have now arrived at the dawn of the modern history of love, and of a different tone in the love song: beguiling, de-spiritualized, often overtly pandering in its eroticism. From now on, songs will occasionally deal with other subjects, but romantic, carnal love will be their dominant theme. Even God and the state, and other vested interests, will defer to its precedence. As they continue to do, even in the present day.

CHAPTER 10

Profane Love

The folk song was an object of mirth and of mockery, though also of a
secret yearning to descend into the lower sphere of supposed vulgarity and
of what was certainly a quite unambiguous obscenity.—Alfred Einstein,
The Italian Madrigal

At the dawn of the Renaissance, the spiritualized love celebrated in Italy by
St. Francis and Dante is displaced by an earthier, sometimes coarse attitude. The
secularizing impulse, seen in so many other spheres of society, inevitably finds
expression in poetic and musical matters, and the love song climbs down a few
rungs on Plato's ladder, happily expressing the carnal impulses that for so long
had to contend with the proprieties of courtly love or the theological concerns
of Christian authorities.

This shift can be seen most clearly in the music of the streets, and especially
during festive periods when the moral authority of Church and state were at
their weakest. In carnival season, groups of costumed young men—dressed as
pilgrims, tradesmen, or sometimes women—would sing ribald songs under ladies' windows. "They are seen and heard by everyone," writes Anton Francesco
Grazzini in the dedication of his 1559 collection of these works, "they can be sent
wherever one wants and they can be made a spectacle for everyone, including
even the young maidens in their houses, who, making for themselves a screen or a
curtain, can see and hear it all without being seen by anyone." Grazzini notes that,
after the celebration, the songs are "sent not only all about Florence and to all the
cities of Italy, but also to Germany, Spain and France to relatives and friends."

Texts to more than five hundred of these songs have survived, testifying to
their popularity, although in most instances we have only words and no music.
The subjects are informal and often abusive; more than two dozen, for example,
are the so-called *canti dei lanzi* (soldier songs), whose main focus is to ridicule
the German mercenary soldiers who served in Florence. The foreigners' clumsy
use of the Italian language is mocked, and they are depicted as more interested in
womanizing and drinking than military matters. "We come from Germany because

we have heard it said that Italians are good companions," relates one such song, "therefore we wish to come and drink with all of you, and we are all the best at teaching Italians how to play trombone." But this trombone lesson is rife with double meanings:

> Although our trombones are bent
> we can quickly straighten them
> and make them of great length or short;
> when we *lanzi* wish to play,
> we push it in and pull it out
> and play the whole range,
> and we are best at teaching
> Italians how to play trombone.

Lorenzo de' Medici not only condoned these performances, but wrote some of his own carnival songs. When the fire-and-brimstone preacher Girolamo Savonarola came to power after the exile of the Medici in 1494, he suppressed the songs and instead organized processions of youngsters singing lauds. In the purified carnival of 1496, thousands of these youths, between the ages of six and sixteen, sang praises to the Lord in place of the coarse refrains that had previously held sway. But this chastening of public life could hardly last—nor could Savonarola, who was excommunicated the following year, and executed in 1498. After the return of the Medici in 1512, the carnival celebrations resumed, but the *canti carnascialeschi*, as these songs were known, would lose much of their populist flavor in ensuing years. They persisted more as a literary tradition and less as a vibrant expression of the musical life of the city. Sometimes the songs survived in strange new guises—for example, many of the popular carnival melodies served as the basis for devotional music. The connection was frequently direct and deliberate: Lent immediately follows carnival in the calendar, and the chastened religious words could be sung while the melodies were still fresh in the ears of the recent revelers.

Carnival songs give us insights into a fluid and informal culture of love and marriage that bears little resemblance to stereotyped views of Renaissance relationships, where every aspect of a couple's coupling, from courtship to the wedding ceremony, was supposedly controlled and codified. Scholars Silvana Seidel Menchi and Diego Quaglioni have examined documents in Italian church archives on marriage and discovered a surprising range of customs—or, to some extent, lack of customs—in conjugal matters. "People got married in stables or in a tavern, in the kitchen or in the vegetable garden, in the pasture or on the attic, in a wood or in a blacksmith's shop, under the portico of one's house or near the public fountain." Music at wedding festivities was just as varied, and could encompass anything from the rustic bagpipe and hurdy-gurdy to stately vocal polyphony...or eventually (as we shall see in the following chapter) the production of an opera.

The Church's advocacy of mutual consent as the basis of marriage in the late medieval period had created a loose system in which such agreements were often accepted as the *sole* requirement for a binding union. A church setting, or even the participation of a priest, were optional, as were other practices most of us believe are essential ingredients to a proper wedding—such as the presence of witnesses or the exchange of rings. Secret marriages, usually undertaken to deceive interfering parents, were common. At the other extreme, the most elaborate procedures and protocol might accompany these unions. A guide to nuptials written in Rome by Marco Antonio Altieri in the early sixteenth century outlines a whole series of rituals, exchanges, and pledges. But whether the ceremony was grandiose or makeshift, the couples now felt more in control of the process, less beholden to Church or tradition, and freer to follow the dictates, or even mere whims, of love.

This loose and sometimes transgressive quality can also be seen in the biographical details of the composers of love songs from the period, and what we hear of their lives and times often has a strikingly modern flavor, akin to the scandals associated nowadays with rockers and rappers. Bartolomeo Tromboncino, the leading composer of Italian popular songs during the late fifteenth and early sixteenth century, was famous for his songs, but even better known for murdering his wife in 1499, after finding her in the embraces of a lover. He was never punished for the crime, and his bloody reputation did not prevent him from finding favor with prominent ladies, including Isabella d'Este, one of the most influential patrons of the arts during the Renaissance, as well as the infamous Lucrezia Borgia, the prototypical femme fatale and alleged poisoner with a nasty reputation of her own. Given his personal history, Tromboncino's contribution to the Venetian carnival of 1430 strikes an especially sour note: his entertainment presented three youths debating whether it was best to have a love affair with a young lady, a married woman, or a widow. They eventually decide that the widow is the superior lover.

A similar infamy surrounded composer and lutenist Carlo Gesualdo, who murdered both his wife and her lover—but the latter happened to be the Duke of Andria. In a gesture of defiance, the enraged musician left the mutilated bodies in front of the duke's palace. Like Tromboncino, Gesualdo was never punished or even arrested for the widely publicized murders. But not all musicians escaped unscathed from their crimes and indiscretions. Serafino dell'Aquila, acclaimed for his skills as a performer and improviser, no doubt took one chance too many in pursuing an affair with "a woman of questionable virtue named Laura." According to a biographical account from 1504, "she was the wife of the Milanese gentleman

Pietro da Birago and was a very sweet and graceful singer; in his love for her he composed the airs and words of several *strambotti*. But overindulging in such ways, he was seriously wounded in the face one night by an assailant whose identity and motive could not be discovered." Perhaps the motive might be guessed, no? Serafino wore the scar from this encounter for the rest of his life.

Tromboncino, for his part, may have benefited from the bad blood between d'Este and Borgia. These two leading ladies of Renaissance Italy were bitter rivals, and their competitiveness encompassed everything from clothes and jewelry to culture and the arts. Isabella's passion for music knew no bounds. She played clavichord and lute and sang with great skill; she even had musical symbols sculpted into the wall of her room and embroidered on her attire. Her correspondence with poets finds her constantly demanding verses for musical settings, so much so that "her insistence amounted almost to an obsession," remarks scholar Walter Rubsamen. Borgia may well have felt some satisfaction at engaging the services of a composer so recently in her rival's employ. Certainly Tromboncino was a prize catch and a versatile artist. He could compose and entertain, was acknowledged as a first-rate lutenist, and when poets finally delivered their lyrics to d'Este, she knew that he could do the best job in setting them to music. Surviving records indicate that Tromboncino earned three times as much as the next best paid musician in Borgia's service—and almost ten times as much as Borgia paid her chief cook and chaplain.

His great rival as a composer of love songs was Marchetto Cara, who unlike Tromboncino was a peaceful man, even "fearful and cowardly" according to a surviving account. Yet Cara was daring in the themes he tackled in his amorous songs—his works include a Latin ode on syphilis for four voices, composed to cheer up his patron Marchese Francesco Gonzaga, who had contracted the disease during his dalliances with prostitutes, and would eventually succumb to it in 1519. Castiglione praises Cara in his *Book of the Courtier*, mentioning him alongside Leonardo da Vinci and calling attention to the plaintive sweetness of his songs.

Tromboncino and Cara were, in the words of musicologist Alfred Einstein, "perhaps the first truly modern musicians," and he explains the impunity with which the former murdered his wife as a result of the public's deference to the artist's talent. A new freedom was granted to the creative spirits of the Italian Renaissance, and this liberty extended to both their lifestyle and artistic works. Michelangelo could rebuff the pope and, if some sources can be believed, even put coded insults to the papacy in his frescoes in the Sistine Chapel. In his autobiography, Benvenuto Cellini bragged of committing murder and admitted to a host of other crimes. Caravaggio, known for his ill temper and brawling, also killed a man, and needed to flee Rome—which didn't prevent him from getting arrested and imprisoned for a later altercation in Malta. These excesses, far from hurting the reputations of the artists, confirmed the public's view that the creative temperament played by its own rules, and the very emotional intensity that inspired their masterpieces could wreak havoc with their private lives. Even if the public and patrons criticized the sins and occasionally demanded punishment for the crimes, they admired the artistry all the more.

Tromboncino and Cara made their reputations as masters of the *frottola*, the most popular form of Italian secular song during the late fifteenth and early sixteenth century. Although they were typically composed for four voices (or melodic lines), counterpoint played a minimal role in this music, with the melody in the soprano part standing out, ensuring comprehensibility of the words that would be less marked with the later rise of the madrigal. The bass parts, with their roots and fifths, and the middle 'voices' served primarily as harmonic support. Documentary evidence suggests that these songs were typically performed by only one singer, with accompaniment likely supplied either by a lute, harp, or other chordal instrument, or by a consort of bowed string instruments (*viole da braccia* and *da gamba*). Lute accompaniment was favored when the writing was spare and chordal; but if it were dense and contrapuntal, the three lower melodic lines might be played by viol. A cappella performances no doubt also took place—the frontispiece to Andrea Antico's *Canzoni Nove* (1510) probably illustrates just such a rendition, with its depiction of four brutish gentlemen, looking more akin to a gang of robbers than a vocal ensemble, all singing from the same bound volume of music, and no instruments in sight.

The *frottola* reflected the musical tastes of the broader public. Its simple compositional elements, narrow melodic range, dance rhythms, and uncomplicated poetry—often derided by later commentators for its singsong banality—impart a populist authenticity to this musical tradition. Even the nomenclature conveys the humble trappings of this music: *frottola* probably derives from the Latin *frocta*, which signifies a motley collection, and was often used pejoratively. And still is today—in modern Italian, the word *frottola* refers to a fib or white lie. The name is fitting: the popular collections of *frottole* published by Petrucci actually contain a wide range of lyrical and compositional types, even some settings of Latin texts. But the chief aim of this music was to delight and entertain, and sophistication—whether in the words or the music—was often sacrificed in favor of clarity, vitality, repetition, and ease of execution.

Love was the predominant, indeed the obsessive, topic of secular song and poetry of the day. Olimpo da Sassoferrato, a contemporary of Tromboncino, compiled a booklet of poetry containing a series of *strambotti* praising each separate part of his beloved's body—beginning with her head and working down to her feet. Even religious authorities got caught up in the romantic spirit of the day. When Pope Pius II visited Florence in 1460, part of the entertainment devised for him by his host involved Piero di Cosimo de' Medici's daughter Bianca, only fourteen, performing love songs in the courtly tradition for the pontiff.

As such anecdotes make clear, the Church of Rome had by now grown complacent, even acquiescent, in the face of the public's insatiable appetite for love songs—and with the rise of the madrigal, Rome would emerge as one of the key centers of activity. There were occasional setbacks. Palestrina had to apologize for publishing his love songs, and this indiscretion may have caused his dismissal from the papal choir. On the other hand, Monteverdi continued to publish madrigals even after joining the priesthood in 1632, without any negative repercussions. But Protestant culture adopted a more severe stance than the Vatican. "This kind of music were not so much disallowable if the poets who compose the ditties would abstain from some obscenities which all honest ears abhor," writes English composer Thomas Morley in *A Plaine and Easie Introduction to Practicall Musicke* (1597). He laments the "blasphemies" of the love songs of his day, citing the Italian lyric "ch'altro di te iddio non voglio" ("other than thee, I'll have no God") as an especially alarming example. Even earlier, Calvin had warned that music had the power "to intoxicate mind and heart with present pleasures" that were "far removed from a lawful use of God's gifts." Huldrych Zwingli, leader of the Reformation in Switzerland, went further, forbidding even liturgical music. Choirs were disbanded, organs were removed from churches, and religious services took on a new, sober tone—in stark contrast to the festive rituals sanctioned across the border in Italy. Martin Luther, by comparison, showed far less hostility to music, and as a composer and musician himself was not ashamed of its emotional power. But even Luther acknowledged that it was best to protect young people from certain kinds of music, giving them "something to wean them away from love ballads and carnal songs and to teach them something of value in their place."

These ongoing skirmishes may have led to a more upright moral tone in the north, but they also ensured that innovation in love songs would now come from the south. Yet the rise of musical publishing would prove even more important than the tolerance of the Catholic hierarchy in legitimizing and disseminating the secular love song throughout Italy and elsewhere in Europe. By the time the *frottola* arrives on the scene, we can measure its popularity by the alacrity with which music publishers met the public's demand. The influential Italian printer Ottaviano Petrucci published eleven collections of these songs between 1504 and 1514, with four volumes issued in 1505 alone. During this same period Petrucci released nine books of masses, giving us some measure of the relative popularity of ecclesiastical and amorous music at the time, at least among those likely to purchase printed scores.

Perhaps the most surprising development in love songs during the High Renaissance is the extraordinary popularity of lyrics by Petrarch—who, by now, had been dead for almost a century. The style and imagery of his anguished love poetry exerted a pervasive influence, especially after the publication of Pietro

Bembo's 1501 edition of the *Canzoniere*. Even when the work of other poets was set to music, their ability to imitate the mood and phraseology of Petrarch was often crucial to the acceptability of their lyrics. Audiences seemingly never tired of hearing about beleaguered Petrarchan lovers, suffering from chills and fevers, aches and pains, and a melancholy so great that the poor fellows often longed for death.

Here is some typically over-the-top Petrarchan versifying from a work by Tromboncino:

> Within the fire I shiver and burn in the midst of ice
> Without moving, I run and continue running;
> To escape from my bonds I seek out the trap,
> In weeping I laugh and I cry laughing.

The irony is that Petrarch's beloved, Laura—probably inspired by the real-life Laura de Noves (1310–48)—was the actual victim of fever and pains. Her early death suggests that she fell victim to the Black Plague. Petrarch himself lived a long, comfortable life and died in his library at home while perusing a book, the day before his seventieth birthday. Dante, as we have seen, had already set the example for doomed love through his fatalistic attraction to Beatrice, who married a banker and, like Laura, died at young age—the closest Dante got to her was in his imaginary visit to Paradise in his *Divine Comedy*. Boccaccio, for his part, praised his Fiammetta, probably based on Maria d'Aquino, the illegitimate daughter of King Robert of Naples, and another victim of the Black Death. Tromboncino's case was somewhat different—his wife also died at a comparatively young age, but only because he murdered her. He survived, enjoying acclaim and patronage, for another three decades. In each of these instances, despite differences in details, the luckless lovers fared far better than the ladies to whom they were devoted with such apparent pain and suffering.

A music fan of the current day can hardly comprehend the zeal with which early sixteenth-century songwriters imitated the role model of a fourteenth-century poet. We are inclined to savor the newest fads and fashions in the popular arts, and even those who harbor a nostalgic admiration for a bygone era hardly expect the old styles to rise to the forefront. Yet the composers of love songs in the Renaissance had a different perspective, assuming that their predecessors possessed a more poetic appreciation of the finer sentiments, a deeper allegiance to romantic ideals. When *frottola* master Marchetto Cara received verses from Federico Gonzaga, the composer praised them for their *antique* style, which evoked "the time of the learned Dante and the delightful Francesco [Petrarch]." Surviving correspondence from Isabella d'Este shows her eagerness to secure copies of Petrarch's works and to have his poetry, or efforts imitating it, set to music.

Perhaps here we witness the first stirrings of the modern quest for "authenticity" in music, a familiar obsession with re-creating the aesthetic impulses of an earlier day, when singers were closer to some imaginary source of potency and emotional honesty.

These lyrics still pay lip service to aspects of the courtly love tradition, especially to the notion of vassalage and devotion to the beloved. But in other ways, the tone of the love song has changed since the days of the troubadours. The chivalric and soldierly pride of the warrior, so evident in the lyrics of those Provençal predecessors, has gradually softened. The composers of these lyrics were more likely to be scholars than soldiers, the declamatory firmness of their declarations now replaced by a moody sensitivity, one that would gradually take on more psychological depth, even as it lost its robust worldliness. The stories of knights in shining armor and their highborn ladies would continue to find a ready audience for some time, but the growing disconnection with early Renaissance social structures was already imparting a tinge of unreality to these tales— one that Cervantes would later lampoon in *Don Quixote*. The lovers (and poets) of the Renaissance still wanted to play the part of the courtly suitor, and they remained captivated by the elegance of this tradition, but the innocent vigor and ingenuous charm of the troubadour's art was growing harder and harder to evoke with a straight face in verse and song.

The love song was thus at a crossroads. Its practitioners could hardly be satisfied with mimicking a past—laden with the imagery and stylized attitudes of feudal times—that was increasingly outdated and even open to mockery. The imperative of the Renaissance, which had started as a rekindling of classical arts and knowledge but increasingly idealized the fresh and new, demanded innovation and the confident exploration of more true-to-life modes of artistic expression. Above all, a greater psychological depth and self-awareness, evident in all spheres of social and cultural life, inevitably required exploration in musical form. Just as the allegory of Everyman from the late fifteenth century gave way to the psychological riches of Shakespeare in the late sixteenth, so did the love song need to find a more perspicacious form of expression.

The end result of this tumult in the music of love was the madrigal. The fixation on the past is reflected in its name—as you will recall, the madrigal was the label given to an Italian vernacular song style of the early fourteenth century, the age of Petrarch. Two hundred years later, the term 'madrigal' returns, although now applied to a new movement in Western music. If the *frottola* was simple and direct, the madrigal was more complex and multifaceted. The intricacy of the counterpoint, with different syllables clashing on any given beat, sometimes made it difficult, and occasionally impossible, to comprehend the words sung. Even when the lyrics dealt with the most heated passion, they might just as well have been a laundry list or the Code of Hammurabi as far as many listeners were concerned. What exactly was the lover telling his lady? Who knew! Not that you would ever consider using a madrigal in an actual courtship: the need for multiple singers to deliver the polyphony undercut the intimacy of any rendition. The through-composed approach of the madrigalists, who showed little patience for the repetitions and catchy melodies that appeal to rank-and-file listeners in any era, further emphasized the growing distance between late Renaissance love songs and their humbler predecessors, those amorous tunes that flourished in medieval villages and hamlets, despite the hostility of the Church in an earlier day. As a result, the refinement of the madrigal, for all its artistry, came at the expense of love itself, with the foreplay of romance now forced into subservience to the free play of music and the creative imagination.

Alfred Einstein, in his massive three-volume study of the Italian madrigal, contends that the *frottola*, which often relied on instrumental accompaniment, evolved into the all-vocal madrigal—a view that has been opposed by Iain Fenlon, James Haar, Anthony M. Cummings, and other, later commentators. Certainly the *frottola* was one strand of influence, but other factors also played a role in the rise of madrigal: the influence of polyphony from the Franco-Flemish composers of the day; the publication of hundreds of French chansons in Italy during the early sixteenth century, and the presence of numerous French singers there as well; the taste for more sophisticated lyrical poetry spurred by the revival of Petrarch and other factors; and the flourishing of Renaissance patrons and institutions eager to sponsor the composition and performance of secular music of the highest quality. Yet the most decisive factor may have been a non-musical one, a pervasive sense among the creative minds of the time that all fields of human endeavor—artistic, economic, scientific, cultural—must progress, must embrace new, and typically more subtle and complex, techniques and perspectives. If the Renaissance began as an attempt to emulate models from the past, by now it had unleashed other, less controllable forces, challenging hierarchies both secular and ecclesiastical along the way. Read Giorgio Vasari's biographical sketches of the great painters—written during the same period that the madrigal was on the rise—and you can see this new notion taking shape. For the first time in Western history, the artist must do more than aspire to beauty or truth, must do more than master a craft, serve a patron; instead the artist must advance, must move forward, must constantly reinvent the rules of engagement.

The first appearance of the term *madrigal* to describe a printed collection of vocal music dates from 1530, with the publication of the *Madrigali de diversi musici libro primo de la Serena*, but the key elements of the new style already can be heard in earlier secular compositions from musicians active in the Rome of Pope Leo X, such as Bernardo Pisano, Sebastiano Festa, and Carpentras. Philippe Verdelot, considered the father of the Italian madrigal, visited the court of Clement VII in Rome and may have been influenced by the work of

Festa, but we know too little about the circumstances of this visit to propose a Roman school of madrigalists that preceded their better known Florentine successors. The early masters of the madrigal were well-traveled men, and, except for Francesco de Layolle, few of them were native Tuscans. Verdelot hailed from France, Jacques Arcadelt and Adrian Willaert probably came from Belgium, and Costanzo Festa, like his possible relative Sebastiano, from Piedmont. Costanzo spent most of his career in Rome, where he maintained a long association with the Sistine Chapel choir, but his fame no doubt traveled even farther—in the prologue to the fourth book of Rabelais's *Gargantua and Pantagruel*, he is the only Italian mentioned in a passage that refers to almost sixty illustrious musicians.

If we hear a greater depth, a more pronounced inwardness, emerge in the love songs of the sixteenth century, this should not surprise us. The two best known guides to conduct published in Italy during the early decades of the Cinquecento, *The Prince* and *The Book of the Courtier*, both based their advice on the assumption that our inner life often varies, sometimes considerably, from external behavior. Accepting such disjunctions would have been deeply unsettling to the medieval mind. During the Middle Ages and early Renaissance, psychological states were most successfully described in the form of allegory: here a character who embraced prudence might be named Prudence, just as one who exhibited bravery would be called Bravery. In the fifteenth-century morality play *Everyman*, we encounter characters named Discretion, Strength, Fellowship, and Knowledge. When love came to the forefront of artistic works, it might actually be in the form of Cupid shooting arrows at the unwary—indeed, Edmund Spenser still relied on this tired device in *The Faerie Queene*, long after the rise of the madrigal. For a culture that lacked the niceties (or naughtiness) of modern psychology, these forceful, straightforward representations of the inner life allowed for the clearest form of communication and contemplation of abstract states of being. This approach must seem clumsy or banal to us nowadays, but we perhaps also view with wistful longing a time when the life of the mind possessed such imposing, if specious, clarity and solidity.

When Castiglione described the banter of men and women at the Court of Urbino, he and his contemporaries still clung halfheartedly to this ideal. "Using various ways of concealment," he relates, "those present revealed their thoughts in allegories." But around the time of Castiglione's death, in 1529, the madrigal was already on the rise, delighting with its confessional attitudes and a laying bare of the heart's hidden impulses. And the freedom of the form allowed for a more daring use of musical devices to accentuate the meaning of the lyrics. The Italian madrigal, in the words of scholar Susan McClary, offered "elaborate mock-ups of inwardness for public delectation.... This genre revels in the simulation of complex inner feelings." By the same token, McClary finds it revealing that some of the first madrigals were composed for Machiavelli's love triangle play, *La Mandragola*, and suggests that the new love songs relied on the "same discrepancy between interiority (thought, feeling, desire, intention) and public behavior that also spawned modern political theory."

We lack the tools to measure the psyches of long-dead generations, but even the visual cues and second-order evidence available to us confirm this marked shift. *The Lute Player*, a painting by Caravaggio from 1596, presents the image of a dreamy-eyed musician staring directly at the viewer. Lorenzo Costa's painting of three singers from the late fifteenth century depicts a similarly arresting emotional appeal from the performers to the audience. In the words of art critic Jonathan Jones, such images capture the "frisson of excitement and desire at the moment of performance." They convey a sensuality invariably purged from modern-day concerts of Renaissance music which, Jones points out, "sound like church music, they are so harmonious and pristine." These paintings, in contrast, make clear that what we now call 'early music' "could be a dangerous, daring drama, with deep issues of love and longing."

Such images reflect a stark turnabout from earlier European paintings featuring musical performers—where the music almost always accompanies something grander happening elsewhere in the picture. Angels were typically assigned this supportive role: singing, playing trumpets or lutes, entertaining or heralding, serving as messengers or praise-givers, but rarely taking center stage. During the course of the Renaissance, these angelic performers begin to adopt more prominent roles. In Piero della Francesca's *Nativity*, in the National Gallery in London, the five singing angels (two playing lutes) are located in the center of the canvas, dominating the proceedings, and stand gazing directly at the audience as though they are performers on a stage. The kneeling Virgin and prostate infant Jesus are presented as attendant figures, even their postures suggesting an inferior, supplicant role. An equally surprising shift of musical performers into the forefront of a religious image can be seen in Paolo Veronese's *Marriage at Cana* (1563), now housed at the Louvre—where it is the largest painting in the museum's collection. Here the musicians are actually placed in front of Jesus and Mary. Were it not for the telltale halo on the seated Christ, we might even conclude that the wedding band is the central subject of the painting.

In works such as these, we can gauge the rising social status of musicians, the growing prestige of the public performer, and the emergence of a more modern relationship between artist and audience. Even if we had only these pictures for evidence, we could tell that a remarkable shift is taking place, that the musician, previously employed to give praise and honor to others, is now increasingly the recipient of such adulation. Yet even more striking in these paintings is their depiction of the musician as a person of especially potent emotional depth and power. The musician not only sings about love, but also seems to embody the audience's own longing and desires. Performance situations now shift in response to this new state of affairs. In the 1570s Alfonso II, Duke of Ferrara, decides that the madrigal might be improved if, instead of relying on the amateurs at his court as performers, he hires beautiful women to sing in the privacy of his apartment. "The madrigal's audience changed from participants in sexual play to a select group of noble voyeurs," writes musicologist Laura Macy, who notes that these female performers "were praised in contemporary accounts at least as often for their looks as for their voices." With the rise of the opera, the general public will share in this spectacle of the love song as an occasion to gaze on beautiful singers, who increasingly rise above the level of low-caste entertainers, gaining prestige and power by inflaming passions and serving as magnets for the erotic imagination.

Composers who proved their skill at tapping into these emotional currents, delivering madrigals that caught the proper balance between refinement and sensuality, were recognized and rewarded in the marketplace. Jacques Arcadelt's *Il primo libro di madrigali* was published in more than fifty editions, its compositions probably better known among the general public than any of the mass settings of Palestrina or Lassus. They formed, in the words of Susan McClary, "a core repertory of sixteenth-century 'standards,' the tunes all performers—vocal and instrumental, professional and amateur—had tucked away in their memories to draw upon at a moment's notice." Arcadelt's admirers included Michelangelo, who hired him to set some of the artist's own poetry to music; he rewarded the composer with a valuable piece of satin. But Arcadelt was just one of many rising stars of the new musical style. Philippe de Monte published at least thirty-four books of madrigals as well as another five collections of spiritual madrigals. And Claudio Monteverdi, one of the most famous composers of his day, owed much of his early renown to his madrigals, which he continued to compose for more than a half century. Certainly simpler love songs in the tradition of the *frottola* continued to find an audience—for example the *villanella*, which originated in Naples around this same period, and the *canzonette* that started to appear in print in the 1560s and 1570s—but, judging by the published anthologies, both performers and public favored the more intricate madrigal form. Between 1530 and the end of the century, a stunning two thousand volumes of madrigals were published, this enormous output not only playing a key role in the dissemination of these popular love songs but also serving as a major spur to the nascent music publishing industry.

As the century drew to a close, the madrigal traveled to distant lands, much as earlier troubadours had done—but now with the added assistance of these publishers and their distributors. Even Britain, which had never matched the enthusiasm of France and Italy for the stylized fare of the troubadours and *trouvères*, not only embraced this new style of love song but was revitalized by it. "Among the contemporaries of Shakespeare," writes Einstein, these imports from Italy produced "an artistic flowering such as, in the field of music, England has never seen before or since." Consider this a kind of British Invasion in reverse, a popular mania for a fresh and passionate new way of singing about love that, instead of spreading from port cities of England, arrived there from afar, and changed everything in its wake. In 1588, Nicholas Yonge published *Musica Transalpina* in London, a collection of Italian madrigals, with words translated into English. *Musica Transalpina* had such a lasting impact on British music that some forty years later, when William Heather, founder of the music professorship at Oxford, had his portrait painted, he was depicted with his hand resting on a copy of this seminal work.

But the same qualities that made the madrigal so popular also led to its eventual decline. Audiences raised on the confessional tone, musical flexibility, and emotional immediacy of the madrigal found that all of these qualities could be accentuated to an even higher pitch in the spectacle of opera. Indeed, the opening of the first public opera house in Venice in 1637 could almost serve as the symbolic end point of the Age of Madrigals. Love songs could now be embedded in love stories enacted on the stage, the power of the music intensified by the most titillating circumstances—affairs, scandals, illicit encounters, betrayals and infidelities, duels and deceptions, marriages and murders, courtships and seductions. Say goodbye to the courtly knight and his lady, to the Dantesque image of a love supreme, and the Petrarchan lover suffering for his beloved. We have now left the conventions of courtly love far, far behind—and even if its pageantry and idealism continue to arouse our nostalgic imagination, they can no longer hold center stage. Profane love now comes to the forefront, and finds in opera its most complete and satisfying form of artistic realization.

CHAPTER 11

Divas and Deviancy

The study of opera singers is as much the study of fantasies and ideologies attached to performances of femininity as it is the study of historical women.—Heather Hadlock

With the rise of opera, the most popular love songs increasingly came embedded in elaborate spectacles, presented on stage for patrons and paying customers. These songs originated as parts of stories, but would also thrive as stand-alone performance pieces sung in other settings, at concerts and recitals, in homes, and even out in the streets. Some of the least likely locales would eventually serve as impromptu venues for these impassioned melodies. My father often recalled, with nostalgia, his childhood in Italian-American communities where chefs sang arias while cooking and sometimes came to the table to serve up a musical accompaniment to their meals. In fact, he mentioned this so often that my siblings and I hired an opera singer as a surprise for our parents' fiftieth anniversary, and gave him the unexpected instructions that he must dress in a cook's outfit and make his entrance from the kitchen before launching into his love songs for our stunned mom and dad. My father was delighted, but not every opera fan applauds this crossover from the stage to everyday life. "Verdi and Bellini at their worst," griped a nineteenth-century British tourist in Venice after encountering one of the city's famous serenading gondoliers—a sentiment no doubt shared by other purists over the years. But it is testimony to the allure and impact of these songs that they have come to enjoy such a vibrant life outside the opera house.

From the start, opera was linked in the audience's imagination with love and courtship—and here too much of the romance took place offstage. Many of the earliest operas made their debut in conjunction with wedding festivities, the tender relationships depicted for entertainment echoing the happy nuptials celebrated by the onlookers. The characters in Giovanni de' Bardi's *Pellegrina*, an important precursor of opera staged for the 1589 wedding of Ferdinando de'

Medici and Christine de Lorraine, even offered their scripted blessings to the real-life wedding couple, enhancing the event's pleasant intermingling of truth and fiction. An even grander Medici marriage—between King Henri IV of France and Marie de' Medici in Florence in 1600—led to the debut of Giulio Caccini's *Il Rapimento di Cefalo* in the Uffizi, and *Euridice* composed by Jacopo Peri with additional music by Caccini, in the nearby Palazzo Pitti. The latter is the oldest opera to survive in its entirety. The music to an earlier (and by modern standards the first) opera by Peri, *Dafne* (1597), has not been preserved in full, but this musical love story no doubt made enough of an impression on the Medici family to spur their sponsorship of the later work.

Bardi was amazed that the Medici would present such objectionable material to their honored guests. *Il Rapimento di Cefalo* (literally "The Rape of Cephalus") revolves around Aurora's desire for the hunter Cephalus, a lust so all-consuming that she abducts the man. Our hero forgets his mortal sweetheart and is convinced instead to enjoy a fast-and-loose coupling with a goddess. More than a few onlookers must have seen a parallel between this story and that of the wedding they were celebrating: Henri IV was a reluctant groom (and didn't even attend the Florentine festivities) forced into marriage with the Medici by financial necessity. Unlike Cephalus, however, Henri kept his mistresses and reputation as a womanizer even after marrying his wealthy 'goddess'.

Almost from the start, opera divas grappled with romantic complexities in their private lives nearly as great as those they presented in their theatrical roles. The profession of opera singer did not exist in the earliest days of the art form, and instead of enjoying the prerogatives of divas, the performers were often reminded of their subservient status. The vocalist Angela Zanibelli, for example, worked as a weaver or embroiderer for the Marquis Enzo Bentivoglio when she was "borrowed" by the Duke of Mantua for the 1607 performance of Marco da Gagliano's *Dafne*. Unless a female singer could find some other means of employment—and it's worth noting that the typical career for a vocalist, serving in a church choir, was a path available only to males—this dependency could come at the cost of her reputation or worse. "If the Lord Duke wants to have me killed or raped he can do so, I know, believe it," Adriana Basile complained to the agent of the Duke of Mantua, and—in true operatic style!—fell in a faint at the conclusion of her outburst.

Very early in the history of opera, female singers gained a reputation as loose or kept women, not always unfairly. Seeking or requiring the support of wealthy patrons, the leading ladies often pursued affairs offstage that may have given them valuable experience in enacting similar affairs onstage. "Women who excelled in music-making were often assumed to be courtesans," writes scholar Bonnie Gordon. She adds: "Not surprisingly, Venice, the capital of courtesanship, would also become the first space to commercialize music in the form of opera." The literature of the time includes many references to the seductive power of the female singing voice, and not always in the context of musical performance. Just a few years after the birth of Italian opera, Venetian Ferrante Pallavicino published a satirical parody of a Jesuit manual, *La Retorica Delle Puttane* (The Whores' Rhetoric), in which an older prostitute advises her apprentice of the importance of singing in the sex trade. The implied connection between the two professions was so deeply ingrained in the public's mind that, in 1603, Duke Vincenzo I of Mantua stubbornly insisted that thirteen-year-old vocalist Caterina Martinelli undergo a medical examination to confirm her virginity before she could be hired as a singer at his court—a bizarre requirement, at first glance, but no doubt due to the duke's fear that he might be employing a courtesan. Martinelli's father initially objected to the implicit insult to his daughter's honor, but eventually all parties accepted the necessity of certifying the singer's chastity.

As opera moved from private settings to public theaters, the economic prospects of star performers improved markedly. By the 1640s, a successful opera singer in Venice could command a salary five times that of a leading soloist at St. Mark's Cathedral. But the emergence of opera as lavish public spectacle hardly lessened the aura of scandal and romantic intrigue that surrounded the art form. Jean de Tralage wrote in 1690 that the Paris opera house, whose official name was the Academy of Music, deserved rather to be called the Academy of Love. During their moments offstage, female singers would visit men in their private boxes, and male admirers would hang around after the performance in hopes of arranging an assignation.

How did the religious authorities of the day look upon these profane proceedings? At first, with some trepidation. Any significant artistic development in Europe eventually made itself felt in Rome, and opera found an especially enthusiastic patron in Pope Urban VIII, a member of the wealthy Barberini family of Florence and a prominent supporter of the arts. But the Church attempted to remove the more scandalous elements from the new art form even as it offered support. Only men and castrati were allowed to perform as opera singers, and the subjects of the productions had to be sufficiently uplifting. *Sant'Alessio*, a celebrated opera by Stefano Landi from 1632, not only focused on a fifth century saint for its subject, but even featured a libretto written by a future pontiff, Giulio Rospigliosi—who would become Pope Clement IX in 1667. Other operas from this period focused on Saint Didymus, Saint Theodora, Saint Boniface, and Saint Eustace. Yet even the Vatican needed to retreat in the face of the secularizing tendency of this new type of musical spectacle. "If God were omnipotent, the ecclesiastical authorities were not," observes historian Daniel Snowman. Six years after *Sant'Alessio*, the Palazzo Barberini in Rome witnessed the debut of the first comic opera, *Chi Soffre, Speri* (Let He Who Suffers Hope), and the subject this time came from a love story by Boccaccio.

Although opera was a new art form, its earliest practitioners prided themselves on resurrecting the glories of the ancients. Peri's collaborator Ottavio Rinuccini, the first opera librettist, noted in his dedication to *Euridice* that "the tragedies put on the stage by the ancient Greeks and Romans were sung throughout." But like many of the other early creators of opera, Rinuccini preferred stories of love, and even while he drew on classical subjects, he favored those with a bit of romance that he could develop, or indeed exaggerate. *Euridice* begins with a wedding in Act 1, and when Orpheus descends to the Underworld to bring back his departed wife, he is joined by Venus, goddess of love—an odd twist on the old legend. Instead of the familiar ending, in which Orpheus violates the demand that he not gaze at Eurydice until they have returned to the upper world (and thus loses her a second time), Rinuccini substitutes a happy ending, allowing the two lovers to rejoice at their unexpected reunion. So much for reviving ancient tragedy!

The composers of these works knew what their audiences expected, namely a story more akin to a Harlequin romance than *Oedipus at Colonus*. Who could be surprised when the leading composer of love songs of the day, Claudio Monteverdi, embraced the new art form of opera around the time of his fortieth birthday? He now had a much larger platform than the madrigal for presenting the conflicts and resolutions of amorous entanglements that audiences associated with his music. He too turned to the story of Orpheus for his debut effort, and his *Orfeo* from 1607 is the art form's first masterwork. Here again we find a festive wedding scene with the happy couple singing of their mutual love, and though Eurydice is held back at Hades in Act IV, she is given a chance for one last love song before disappearing. Monteverdi's librettist Striggio insisted on keeping true to the original Orphic myth, and even portrayed his hero murdered and dismembered by enraged followers of Dionysus. But once again, a happier ending must have been deemed more suitable: when the score to *L'Orfeo* was published in 1609, the opera now featured a charmingly romantic resolution. In the revised version, Apollo transports Orpheus to heaven, where he will forever see his beloved among the stars.

This obsession with rewriting the history of love was hardly restricted to the opera. The narrative of romance took on new guises in other art forms during this same period. *Don Quixote*, written by Cervantes at the same time Monteverdi was creating his first operas, turned the old stories of courtly love into the subject of ridicule and parody. Shakespeare did much the same, although in a different manner, and by the time he had made his contribution to the demystification of romance, his audience's image of the knight tended more to Falstaff than Lancelot. *The Merry Wives of Windsor*, Shakespeare's most incisive critique of knightly values, was written during the same period that witnessed the first opera performances, and the conjunction is hardly a coincidence. Just as the older accounts of courtly love were examined and found wanting, a new narrative of romance, cleansed of the etiquette and proprieties of medieval times, emerged to take its place. Opera would serve as it most spectacular platform.

A whole conjunction of events prodded and nudged the cultural life of Europe toward a more intensely individualistic and frank realism. Descartes's *Discourse on Method*—published the same year the first opera house opened its doors—promulgated the shocking idea that truth arose in the individual consciousness at the present moment, not the doctrines and dogmas of the past. The novel, whose emergence and rise in popularity follows a timeline similar to that of the opera, built its particular brand of realism on the same premise. And here, too, love emerged as the centerpiece of this new form of storytelling. Madame de Staël went so far as to insist that the ancient Greeks and Romans did not write novels for the simple reason that they *didn't understand romantic love* and the actual emotional relationships of men and women. The novelists who dominated European literary life in the aftermath of Cervantes and Shakespeare certainly would not make this same mistake. Instead of myth or idealized romance, they sought to present affairs of the heart in all the tawdry and messy realism they could muster—so much so that Denis de Rougemont quipped that, judging by the novel, adultery must be the chief occupation of modern man. "Few are the novels that fail to allude to it....Without adultery what would happen to imaginative writing?"

The same fascination with scandal and illicit love soon came to dominate the opera. True, adulterous relationships had been depicted on the stage since the days of Aeschylus and Sophocles, yet the ancient Greeks had focused on the psychological ramifications of these affairs more than their titillating dramatic possibilities. Now these relationships were exploited specifically for their erotic overtones, with the emphasis squarely on the passion of the lover, not the guilt of the transgressor. When opera composers turned to models from antiquity, they downplayed the sobriety of the Greek tragedians and preferred instead the more scurrilous tales drawn from Ovid, the most controversial of the great ancient poets as well as the classical author most fixated on matters of love. Just a few years before the first operas were staged, some Jesuit schools were still cutting out the objectionable parts of the *Metamorphoses*. But this equivocal work now emerged as the most popular source of opera and dramatic plots. Scholar Frederick W. Sternfeld notes that the influence of Ovid on opera is "four times as great as that of Virgil"—an assessment that has also been applied to Shakespeare's use of mythological themes—and adds that "one could easily arrive at a list of well over one hundred pieces" by musical composers of stature that borrow in some degree from the *Metamorphoses*.

Of course, Ovid was hardly the only source of plots for early opera. But even the most admired and decorous ancient text needed to yield a love story if it hoped to become a favorite with opera audiences. Virgil and Homer, the cherished masters of the ancient epic, may have gained renown for their tales of heroism and valor in battle, but when their stories were adapted by opera composers, the romantic subplots in their epics now took center stage. The affair between Aeneas and Dido plays a subsidiary role in Virgil's *Aeneid*, but serves as the main focus of Henry Purcell's *Dido and Aeneas*, one of the first English operas. The same love story shows up in Francesco Cavalli's opera *Didone*, Henri Desmarets's *Didon*, Giuseppe Sarti's *Didone Abbandonata*, Niccolò Piccinni's *Didon*, Hector Berlioz's *Les Troyens*, and other works. When Monteverdi drew on Homer's *Odyssey* for his 1639 opera *Il Ritorno d'Ulisse in Patria*, he similarly focused on the romantic reunion of Odysseus with his wife, Penelope, and later operatic composers who favored Homeric storylines turned to Circe or Helen of Troy for an appealing love angle. Even the Bible could, in a pinch, provide a seductive love story, as Verdi would show with *Nabucco*, Rossini with *Mosè in Egitto*, and Saint-Saëns with *Samson and Delilah*.

Eventually the mythological and historical trappings of opera began to feel burdensome to both opera composers and their audiences, and they demanded the same freedom to deal with modern love stories enjoyed by novelists, dramatists, and ballad singers. From an early point in its evolution, opera seemed destined to supersede these other forms of narrative in its bold depiction of human relations, not just in the emotional intensity of plot and character, but with evocations of sexual complexities that even the most daring novelist could hardly have broached. Why did even the most masculine roles, asks scholar Sam Abel-Palmer, "belong to tenors, men with voices closest to the female range; and, before that, to castrated men, sometimes with voices higher than the heroines? Why do women in operas play men's roles so often....And how can opera get away with staging sexual transgressions such as adultery and incest with so little protest from the audience," managing to be "thoroughly subversive in its eroticism behind a mask of sexual normalcy?" These very facets of the genre, its role in the cultural marketplace as the grandest and boldest spectacle of love—whether tragic, transcendent, or transgressive—spurred the art form's liberation from rehashing old stories, and its embrace of new ones specifically designed to showcase these varied relationships and their possible outcomes.

Can we still talk about a "hidden history" of the love song at this point in our survey? After all, these large-scale productions were putting it *all* out on stage. Even if the attendees at these operas worked hard to maintain a certain decorum and decency in their own love lives (or at least the appearance thereof), when they sought out musical entertainment, they wanted a full dose of erotic intrigue, forbidden entanglements, and scandal. I suspect that this very contrast played a decisive role in the popularity of opera throughout Christian Europe. Opera put the spotlight on the secret side of human relationships. It was almost as if the operagoer had been invited inside the confessional to hear, alongside the priest, the admission of those sinful details of their neighbors' lives that they never talked about, that they worked hard to keep out of sight. In other words, the love song still probed into hidden matters during the glory years of European opera, but for the price of a ticket you were empowered to experience them in all their raw, unfiltered honesty.

This voyeuristic quality in opera demanded stories that reflected the most immoral and debased side of everyday life. When John Gay tapped into this latent desire with *The Beggar's Opera* (1728), he not only was rewarded with the biggest hit of his day, but changed the course of popular entertainment. Almost two centuries after its debut, *The Beggar's Opera* would still draw record crowds: the 1920 production at the Lyric Theatre in Hammersmith enjoyed a run of 1,463 performances—a record at the time for London musical theater. Less than a decade later, Bertolt Brecht and Kurt Weill would draw on Gay's example for *The Threepenny Opera* (1928), frequently staged and widely translated in subsequent years. It would enjoy a remarkable run of 2,707 performances in Greenwich Village during the late 1950s, setting a record for New York musical theater. But in his own day, Gay had even more imitators. His success created an insatiable demand for ballad operas, freewheeling musical productions that mixed the familiar songs of the streets with satire and low-class characters. The protagonists in these productions violated each and every moral precept, but especially those dealing with lust and coveting thy neighbor's wife. Or, in the case of *The Beggar's Opera*, his unsuspecting daughter.

We will examine the folk ballad tradition in the next chapter, but suffice it to say that these songs of the streets reveal a surprising congruence with opera, at least in terms of plots and complications. Love and violence were the two dominant themes of the folk ballad, and offered the same voyeuristic enjoyment to commoners that opera provided to cultural elites. Class distinctions might have suggested that these two genres were incompatible. Opera, after all, served as diversion for the more affluent and sophisticated, who attended these productions not just for entertainment but also to assert their own status. Why would they buy an expensive ticket to hear the same music offered for free in the public square, or see the worst elements of society paraded on stage? But Gay's genius lay in understanding the inherent compatibility between the salacious ballads of taverns and street corners and the finely crafted love plots that drew audiences to the opera house. Nowadays we are familiar with creative works that deliberately blur the boundaries between highbrow and lowbrow art—give credit to Gay, who presciently understood the potential for these provocative mashups at the dawn of the Georgian era.

Ballad opera never found the following on the continent that it enjoyed in Britain, but the popularity of comparable genres—such as *singspiel* in Germany, *burletta* in Italy, and *comédie en vaudeville* in France—testified to the allure of musical entertainments with fewer highbrow pretensions than the grand mythological and historical operas of the past. In its land of origin, the ballad opera continued to delight audiences until the middle of the eighteenth century—as documented by the publication of more than a hundred operas and surviving accounts of numerous other productions. But the intense popularity of these entertainments accelerated their eventual decline, especially because the same melodies were used over and over again. What better way to imitate the success of *The Beggar's Opera* than to use the identical tunes that Gay featured? Similar plots, settings, and character types were also recycled. By 1750 theatergoers had grown tired of this predictable fare, the spark of originality that had given impetus to the movement now forgotten amid innumerable copycat efforts.

But opera was changed forever by this injection of lowlife vitality. In its early days, no one would have thought to build an opera around a barber, but just such a character fit perfectly with the new scope and tone of the art form. Thus Figaro, a barber of Seville reminiscent of the commedia dell'arte low-class rogue Brighella, now shows up in operas by Mozart, Rossini, and others. Just as earlier opera composers had repeatedly told the story of mythological characters, an Orpheus or Medea, they now returned again and again to a Figaro or Don Juan or other appealing commoners. In fact, these stories exerted such appeal that even today *The Barber of Seville*, *The Marriage of Figaro*, and *Don Giovanni* rank among the ten most frequently staged operas.

Did the romances and affairs depicted in the opera houses influence the love life of the members of the audience? Certainly many believed in a cause-and-effect connection. Operas were subject to strict censorship, and the actions of lovers presented onstage were carefully regulated well into the twentieth century. Prohibitions varied depending on time and place, but a general suspicion of opera's corrupting influence was pervasive. Cromwell allowed the performance of Italian operas because the unintelligibility of the foreign language prevented them from undermining the morals of the populace, but the spread of these scandalous musical productions in the native tongue in various countries raised grave concerns. In Vienna, for example, lovers could not kiss on stage or exit from a scene in tandem. A 1795 memo by censor Franz Carl Hagelin specified the many ways a theatrical or operatic production could offend public morals. The censor even suggested substitute words for prohibited ones: the term *prostitute* should be avoided, with *wench* offered as an alternative; a *pimp* must become a *broker, provider*, or *mediator*; a cuckold could never be described as "wearing horns," but a reference to "injuring faithfulness" was permitted; no "secret illness" could be mentioned, etc., etc.

Opera composers found audiences receptive to precisely those aspects of defiled love most upsetting to the upholders of public and private virtue. Many of the nineteenth-century and early twentieth-century operas that constitute the core repertoire reveal this fascination with the seamy side of romance, and sometimes posed a direct challenge to the moral precepts espoused from the pulpit or by the censors. The purity of heart and unrecognized nobility of the kept or ailing woman shows up repeatedly in classic operas from this period. In *La Traviata*, Verdi builds his opera around a prostitute with a debilitating illness—precisely the subjects that most alarmed the censor Hagelin in an earlier day—and instead of subtly hinting at her cohabitation with her lover, begins Act 2 with the couple living together in their home outside of Paris. In *Carmen*, Bizet, delivers a fully developed female antihero, not far removed from those depicted in Hollywood films today. Traditional morals were not only violated in these works; they were turned on their head. The rise of feminism has perhaps added new dimensions to our appreciation of the plight of victimized or manipulated heroines in these love stories, but a critique of conventional values, gender roles, and power structures can be found already waiting for us in a *Carmen* or *La Bohème*, a *Madame Butterfly* or *Salome*.

Love still is an important part of the show, but other themes now begin to challenge its supremacy in the opera houses of Europe. In Verdi, we encounter fewer love duets between a hero and heroine, and when he does turn to them, he undermines the sensuality with other priorities, such as accusations of cruelty or indifference. Verdi prefers to let his lovers make music together only after the glory of their passion has faded, and real-life couples who modeled their own relationships on these onstage partners would soon be making an appointment with a divorce lawyer. In Gilbert and Sullivan, the love plot often serves as a pretext for political satire or a comedy of manners. The verismo movement from this same period, which would reach its peak with the works of Giacomo Puccini, sought a more scrupulous realism, with special attention to the dark and gritty side of everyday life, including issues of poverty and violence—an approach that encompassed love affairs, but now embedded in a complex web of economic and social factors.

But no figure exemplifies these expanding ambitions for the art form more fully than Richard Wagner. He could hardly avoid love as a subject matter given the opera tradition he inherited, and in the case of *Tristan und Isolde*, he even returned to the time-honored practice of constructing an opera around a famous mythological couple. But, as music historians Carolyn Abbate and Roger Parker note, "with the exception of *Tristan und Isolde*, he became increasingly clumsy at depicting romantic passion in opera." By the time we get to the *Ring*, "hunger for power and the nature of greed are the predominant themes, so much so that the sexual couplings seem contrived largely for dynastic purposes." Such was the spirit of the times that critics sometimes went even further than the composers in their distaste for sentimentality. "I confess to a positive dislike for this brief love-song," writes H. T. Finck with regard to "Winterstürme" in *Die Walküre*, "which seems to me a cheap tune, as unworthy of Wagner's genius as the *Lohengrin* Wedding March." Thus are two famous paeans to romance in Wagner's work dismissed in a single sentence!

Even during opera's period of peak popularity, many of Europe's leading composers looked to other settings to present their love songs. Franz Schubert, Robert Schumann, and Hugo Wolf never enjoyed much success with their operas. Johannes Brahms and Gustav Mahler considered possible opera projects—and in the case of the latter, started and abandoned several operatic works—but never brought one to fruition. Frédéric Chopin was urged by his friends to compose operas but resisted their proddings. Yet each of these composers wrote love songs for voice with piano accompaniment, as did many of their contemporaries. The German term *Lieder*, signifying ballads or songs, is often used to describe these works, and they flourished with particular splendor in German-speaking parts of Europe—at the close of the nineteenth century Berlin hosted an average of twenty public song recitals, or *Liederabende*, per week. Many of the most popular texts for these songs came from German poets, notably Goethe and Heine. But we find similar developments among leading composers in other nations during this period.

In France, Charles Gounod and Hector Berlioz brought *mélodies*, the French equivalent of *Lieder*, into prominence, and in later years Jules Massenet, Gabriel Fauré, Claude Debussy, Maurice Ravel, Francis Poulenc, and others continued this tradition. Mikhail Glinka and Alexander Dargomyzhsky helped establish a robust school of Russian art songs in the early nineteenth century, and a host of other composers followed in their footsteps, including Alexander Borodin, Modest Mussorgsky, Nikolai Rimsky-Korsakov, and Pyotr Ilyich Tchaikovsky. In England, we find art songs by Frederick Delius, Ralph Vaughan Williams, Benjamin Britten, and many others. In Italy, Verdi, Rossini, and other leading opera composers also devoted energy to composing these more intimate songs for public recital. Edvard Grieg in Norway, Thomas Moore in Ireland, Enrique Granados in Spain, Antonín Dvořák in Bohemia (now part of the Czech Republic), and other leading composers in various locales, drew on both indigenous traditions and international currents in crafting works of lasting merit.

Schubert is often given credit for setting off this golden age of finely crafted, poetic songs for public recitals. "The 'birthday' of the *Lied*," writes singer and scholar Carol Kimball, "is said to be October 14, 1814—the day Schubert composed 'Gretchen am Spinnrade.'" In truth, secular songs for one voice accompanied by a single instrument had never disappeared from the purview of Europe's leading composers, even during the period of peak popularity of the madrigal and the rise of the opera. John Dowland was Monteverdi's contemporary, but focused his attention on melancholy songs for voice and lute, such as "Flow My

Tears" and "I Saw My Lady Weepe." We find secular songs for voice and key-board accompaniment among the works of Haydn, Mozart, Beethoven, and Bach—but in this instance, Carl Philipp Emanuel Bach, who was one of the most prolific composers of such pieces in eighteenth-century Germany, adopting a much simpler style in these works than we find in his father's famous contrapuntal efforts.

Several developments gave rise to a more intense interest in this type of music in the early decades of the nineteenth century. To some degree, music changed due to the economic and technological impact of the Industrial Revolution, which led to the spread of better and more affordable pianos, which in turn spurred demand for simpler compositions suitable for household performance. But new attitudes toward music perhaps exerted even more influence, for example the growing interest in traditional folk songs discussed in the next chapter. In many instances, composers of art songs self-consciously aimed at emulating the sound and style of the traditional music of the common people. But we cannot ignore the powerful new zeitgeist emerging outside the music world, especially in literary and philosophical spheres, which we have come to call Romanticism. Wherever its ethos was felt, the leading creative spirits of the day were celebrating emotional intensity, fostering the poetic and passionate, and searching after transcendence, especially via the arts.

Composers turned to the poetry of the day to find material for their love songs—and with good reason. Perhaps at no other point in Western history have poets and the poetic sensibility possessed such prestige and influence. "Poets are the unacknowledged legislators of the world," Percy Shelley wrote in 1821, almost at the same moment that Schubert was publishing his first songs. In the current day, when few if any living poets are household names, we might smile over such bold claims, but in that age of Goethe, Shelley, and Byron, heroic figures in their time, a different hierarchy of renown prevailed. And just as opera allowed composers to draw on the power of theater and drama, art song served as the meeting point of music and poetry and the springboard for a more intimate mode of expression. Poets often returned the favor, praising the power of melody to uplift their efforts. Goethe himself declared that all poetry was incomplete until set to music.

These songs often express romantic yearnings and the laments of the love-lorn. This, at first glance, was hardly a new development in Western music. But the scope of these yearnings and feelings tend to be far more expansive than those found in most troubadour lyrics, madrigals, and other traditional love songs. In the supercharged poetic sensibility of the period, a nature scene, running water, or a rainbow in the sky could inspire powerful emotions, described in terms very similar to those applied, in other songs, to the beloved. Intensity of feeling was sought out, nurtured, and dissected, irrespective of whether the song is addressed to the lovely miller's daughter, flowers, or a bubbling brook—as all are during the course of Schubert's song cycle *Die Schöne Müllerin*; or even when the most desperate emotions are evoked, as in the same composer's setting of Goethe's "Der Erlkönig," which describes a father bringing home his dying child. In "Der Hirt auf dem Felsen," composed by Schubert for soprano Pauline Anna Milder-Hauptmann in the final weeks of his life, the absent sweetheart is mentioned only once; the rest of the text is devoted to describing a valley scene, echoes from the ravines, the coming of spring, plans for a journey, and the singer's loneliness and melancholy. Given the spirit of the age, all-consuming feelings were essential to an art song, but a love story merely optional.

Yet even when the time-honored memes of the love song appear, they can take on strange new guises. In "Gretchen am Spinnrade," a woman sings while working at the spinning wheel—the same motif that initiated so many *chansons de toile* in the twelfth and thirteenth century, and various spinning and weaving songs about love from other times and places. In Schubert's updating, however, the piano accompaniment threatens to take over the song, spinning its own web with a nonstop flurry of sixteenth notes, while the singer responds to the romantic advances of Faust with a longing tempered by pathos and fear. This is a multivalent love song, supercharged with emotions, yet refusing to fit into the Petrarchan mold that dominated the melancholy romantic outpourings of an earlier day.

For all their virtues, these ambitious songs often encountered resistance from music publishers. As noted earlier, the spread of home pianos spurred demand for simple, sentimental songs, and even the greatest composers found themselves pressured to adapt to the needs of the marketplace. Schubert was repeatedly asked to transpose his works into more user-friendly keys. But even in the key of C, his songs could impose daunting challenges on amateur performers. Hear, for example, "Du bist die Ruh," in which the vocalist is required to deliver two formidable crescendos ending on a held high A—in the context of a meditative song about a tranquil love in which any sign of strain or tension in the melody disrupts the effect. Sometimes music critics joined in condemning the complexities of the more challenging songs of the period. Schubert's *Winterreise* stands out as one of the defining works of vocal music of the era, and a milestone in the history of love songs; but even here, critics griped about the composer's "sudden modulations," "labored" melodies, and "overly weighty accompaniments."

Music publisher George Thomson, whom we will encounter again in a later chapter, even dared to write a letter to Beethoven complaining that the music the maestro had provided was simply "much too difficult for *our* public. Indeed there is not one young lady in a hundred here who wants to look at the accompaniment of an air if it is even the least bit difficult. I flatter myself, therefore, that you will not be offended by the request that I make of you to send me another arrangement."

Although Beethoven had previously assured Thomson that he could compose in an "easy and pleasant style," he now rebuffed the publisher: "I am not in the habit of rewriting my compositions. I have never done it, being convinced that any partial alteration changes the character of the entire composition."

The gap between art song and popular song widened over the course of the century, but romantic love continued to inspire both idioms. Even composers who expressed reservations about this music found themselves drawn to its expressive power, especially when in the grip of a passionate love affair. In 1839, Schumann admitted to a friend that he "always considered music for the human voice inferior to instrumental music and never thought of it as great art." But around this same time, Schumann and pianist Clara Wieck, whom he would marry on September 12, 1840, began collecting poems they felt were suitable for setting to music. In May, when he embarked upon his *Liederkreis*, a series of songs based on the poetry of Joseph Eichendorff, Schumann wrote to his future spouse announcing that this "cycle is my most Romantic ever," adding: "It contains much of you in it." At the first Christmas following their marriage, she responded by sharing three songs she had composed for him.

The history of the art song is filled with many comparable examples. Brahms often found inspiration for songs in his relationships with specific women—including Clara Schumann, fourteen years his senior, who stirred his heart, performed his music, and may have been his lover after the death of her husband. Berlioz composed songs inspired by his love for actress Harriet Smithson. Wagner took time out from writing his most romantic opera *Tristan und Isolde* to compose songs inspired by his affair with poet Mathilde Wesendonck. Richard Strauss's marriage to soprano Pauline de Ahna lasted for more than a half-century, and most of his *Lieder* were composed for her voice. Grieg claimed that all his songs were written for his wife, Nina, a lyric soprano who was also the composer's first cousin. "I do not believe I have more talent for song-composition than for any other genre in music," he wrote. "From whence does it come then, that the song plays such a prominent role in my output?" The answer, he surmised, was love. "I fell in love with a young girl with a wonderful voice and similarly wonderful interpretation. This girl became my wife and life's partner right to this day. She has been for me—I may certainly say—the only true interpreter of my songs." Much of the allure of Romanticism, for both audiences and artists, came from this bold insistence on breaking down the boundaries between creative impulse and biographical circumstances. To some extent, our sense of the composer as a real, flesh-and-blood person, filled with passion and emotion, colors our perception of all the musical masterpieces of the era, but especially the art songs, where the cause-and-effect connection between the inner life and these external manifestations of it stands out in such sharp relief.

Although the songs of Schubert and Schumann were not without their challenges, in both the vocal and piano parts, many of them remained within the reach of amateur singers. Composers and publishers of the period worked to support the vibrant tradition of *Hausmusik*, music-making in homes and other informal settings by nonprofessionals of works that didn't make too many demands on the performers. But over the course of the century, the growing obsession with concert hall virtuosity tended to displace the populist leanings that had supported the *Hausmusik* movement. "The composer by then had in mind the professional singer and the large public he hoped to win for himself," explains singer Dietrich Fischer-Dieskau. "The amateur at home must have felt himself to be a mere shadowy imitator." By the time we get to Brahms's *Lieder*, we encounter more formidable challenges for both singer and accompanist, yet even here the composer hoped that nonprofessionals would embrace his music. But when we arrive at the art songs of Mahler and Wolf, we have left the priorities of *Hausmusik* far behind. With these composers and their successors we encounter even bolder use of chromaticism, chords with ambiguous functional roles or that never resolve, splintered rhythms and syncopations, and other progressive elements. Even if we set aside the considerable technical hurdles of this music, we are left with an aesthetic vision out of alignment with the demands of the mass audience and growing middle class, whether they were seeking songs to sing in the home, enjoy during an evening out, or listen to via the latest innovation in entertainment, sound recordings.

Other powerful currents were now shaping the love song. Publishers and the emerging record labels continued to respect, and sometimes support, the leading composers of classical music, but they seldom turned to artists with the pedigree of a Beethoven, Mahler, or Wolf in hopes of finding popular songs suitable for the mass market. Only a handful of composers—for example, George Gershwin or Kurt Weill—would prove capable of straddling these two different worlds in the post-Romantic period, bridging the gap between the music of highbrow culture and the hit songs of the general public. Opera and art songs would, of course, continue to flourish in subsequent decades, but now with less impact on the evolution of the love song. This is partly due to the growing emphasis on repertory works in these idioms—a survey of the most frequently produced operas is heavily tilted toward works by long-dead composers, and nineteenth-century art songs continue to figure prominently at vocal recitals. But in addition, many of the late-modern and contemporary composers best positioned to establish their own works in the repertory, such as John Adams and Philip Glass, have shown less interest in love stories and romantic scenes than their nineteenth-century predecessors. Post-1950 classical composers didn't entirely forget about love, as, for example, the works of Ned Rorem and Leonard Bernstein make clear—the latter even achieved a commercial hit with *West Side Story*, a reworking of the most famous love story of them all, *Romeo and Juliet*. But the days when the most popular romantic songs enter the public sphere via the opera house or classical recital are now behind us. If the chefs in my father's childhood sang arias while cooking and serving, they now are more likely to listen to popular music on the radio or their personal playlist.

This transition marks an important milestone in our history. The hierarchies that drive musical culture will soon topple—indeed, they will eventually get inverted. From this point on, we will rarely deal with nobles, wealthy patrons, and other elites, leaving them behind, perhaps, with a sigh of relief. Going forward, the love song will enjoy its greatest vitality when the leaders of the establishment aren't paying attention. They sometimes join along in the proceedings, usually late in the game, and invariably try to make a buck off the innovations in this music. *That* part of the story probably will never change. But the catalysts for innovation will now come from the least expected places, blindsiding those who look to the wealthy and privileged as arbiters of musical taste. In short, the love song will return to its roots as a music of the people, whose shifting attitudes and impulses now take center stage in our survey.

CHAPTER 12

Folk Songs and Love Songs

Humans vent great passions by giving themselves over to song.
—Giambattista Vico

Around the time Mozart was composing his first operas, German philosopher Johann Gottfried Herder discovered folk music, and liked what he heard. Perhaps it would be more accurate to say he liked the *idea* of what he heard. Herder was enamored with the concept of the *Volk*, the common people whose vitality and creative energy offered a much-needed alternative to the cold rationalism brought about by the Enlightenment. Where others saw only an unseemly rabble, crass and uneducated, Herder found 'authenticity' and drew on its example to define an aesthetic attitude that today we would call, "return to the roots."

It's easy to poke fun at Herr Herder, who made a big commotion about something the *Volk* had been doing in plain view for many centuries. After all, the Roman historian Tacitus wrote about German folk music before AD 100, and Emperor Julian also tried his hand at Teutonic ethnomusicology. "I have observed that even the barbarians across the Rhine sing savage songs composed in language not unlike the croaking of harsh-voiced birds," the emperor noted, although he conceded that the noisy vocalizing probably sounded better to the performers themselves than it did to him. Some 1,400 years later Herder, arriving late on the scene, not only noticed the singing, but gave it his fervent blessing, championing the robust *Kultur des Volkes* (folk culture) over the sterile *Kultur der Gelehrten* (learned culture). Perhaps in emulation of the Roman emperor, Herder admitted that non-Germans, even "savages," might have their own glorious folk music. "Europeans have everywhere been keenly touched by the crude sounds of lamentation of the savages," he wrote with enthusiasm, and even found words of praise for their primitive love songs (or, in Herder's words, their "heartfelt, inarticulate screams of affection").

At least as far back as the time of the *Shijing*, circa the sixth century BC, cultural elites showed an interest in songs of the common people, and took steps to preserve them. If we can believe traditional accounts, Confucius might even deserve

our praise as the first ethnomusicologist. Not every ruler or sage was similarly receptive to this music, but even during periods of repression and prohibition, the
songs of the folk continued to find an eager audience and attract new generations
of performers. Yet, in most times and places, only a tiny portion of this music was
preserved, and the scholar who wants to uncover the songs of everyday life in
earlier ages must probe deeply and cross conventional boundaries between disciplines to find even scraps of relevant information. This will now change.

The rise of the printing press gave more visibility to the songs of the streets and
countryside, and though the earliest publications after Gutenberg's revolution
were religious in nature, popular songs and poetry soon followed—eventually
in huge quantities. Published on single sheets as broadsides, or in inexpensive
booklets known as chapbooks, these works were sold in the streets or door-to-
door and found a ready audience, especially in Britain, well into the nineteenth
century. We will never know how many songs were disseminated in this form,
but clearly thousands were published and hundreds of thousands, if not millions, of copies were sold. Just one collection, that of Samuel Pepys, now held
at Magdalene College, Cambridge, contains more than 1,800 broadside ballads.
Book-length compilations of popular songs also appeared before Herder discovered the music of the *Volk*. By any measure, he was late to the party.

Yet Herder's importance should not be minimized. He was more than a song
collector or music historian, but an influential cross-disciplinary thinker who
played a decisive role in shaping the methodology of the social sciences at a key
juncture in their development. And he not only celebrated and legitimized folk
music—which, in itself, would have been a significant milestone in the history of
these songs—but went further in announcing its superiority to the artistic productions of those at the top of the cultural hierarchy. This flip-flop of traditional
aesthetic values continues to reverberate in our current discussions of music and
other arts, and Herder's impact can still be measured on a host of hot issues and
fierce debates: on the conflict between highbrow and lowbrow culture; on the
problematic role of primitivism in the arts; on authenticity and inauthenticity
in musical performance; indeed, on the significance of pop culture in general.

Nor should we mock other cultural elites who, since the time of Herder,
have suddenly "discovered" the music of the common people. These songs, ostensibly in plain view, can prove dauntingly difficult to find and document. In
that regard, folk songs of the past are not much different from the music in a
modern-day household, where parents can be oblivious to the most cherished
melodies of their children, and vice versa—even though the songs coexist under
the same roof. "The folk-song is like the duck-billed platypus," Charles Marson
has explained: "you can live for years within a few yards of it and never suspect
its existence." Marson, who helped Cecil Sharp collect ballads in Somerset in
southwest England, noted that during eight years residence he had stumbled

upon only one folk ballad, "The Seeds of Love," sung by the gardener at the parsonage; but once the hunt began in earnest, hundreds were offered by the local populace. The most celebrated song hunter of them all, Francis James Child—the core repertoire of English and Scottish ballads is still called "Child ballads" in reference to his late nineteenth-century collection of 305 songs—complained of the obstacles facing the seeker after the songs of the common folk. Scouring the "immense collections of Broadside ballads," he griped that they were "dunghills in which, only after a great deal of sickening grubbing, one finds a very moderate jewel." And even the most ardent researchers, who believe they have discovered the music of the people, can still miss the most obvious examples at their doorstep. The same Cecil Sharp who relentlessly sought folk music on song-hunting expeditions to the United States, tended to ignore the African American population, and showed even less interest in the music of Native Americans. He wanted folk music, but not from *those* folks.

As Sharp's preoccupation with the Anglo-American ballad makes clear, the history of folk songs and their gatherers is not easy to separate from issues of nationalism and political ideology. Even if those seeking the love songs of the folk have little interest in, say, German exceptionalism (another hot button for Herder) or the proletariat seizing the means of production, they will find that many who collected, documented, and disseminated the songs of the people put great stock in such concepts, and their concerns have inevitably shaped the surviving evidence we turn to in assessing the music of romance, courtship, and sexuality. I won't go so far as folklorist (anti-folklorist might be a better term) Dave Harker, who has ridiculed the supposedly authentic traditional folksong as "fakesong," or others who, in more recent years, have cast a skeptical eye on the quest for authenticity in traditional music—let's be honest, even the revisionists in this debate have their own cherished ideologies—but I must caution anyone joining me on this journey into the love songs of the 'common people', handed down to us only after many have filtered and 'purified' them, that almost every effort at preservation has been accompanied by a not-so-hidden agenda.

For example, between 1834 and 1880, police in conjunction with England's Society for the Suppression of Vice seized a staggering total of "28,000 obscene songs and circulars." These songs circulated among the same population that provided Child and other folk song collectors with their cherished English ballads. But one group of songs was deemed suitable for publication and scholarly study, while the other music was prohibited and burned. In our hidden history of love songs, the tunes that went up in smoke must rank as the most hidden of them all! And the Old World had no monopoly on these forbidden songs. An account published in March 1888 notes that "C. R. Bennett of San Francisco, the efficient agent of the Californian Society for the Suppression of Vice, reports...the seizure of 244 obscene pictures, 34 obscene figures, 108 obscene songs, 28 articles for immoral use," and a long list of customers for the above items. These raunchy songs were no doubt heard throughout the Western world, and hardly needed a printing press for their circulation. In his 1858 study *The History of Prostitution*, William Sanger quotes from a "researcher" whose anonymous pamphlet "Prostitution in Berlin" describes a spirited brothel scene that includes a guitarist performing obscene songs, and patrons, apparently familiar with the words, singing along with great enthusiasm. Sanger also provides the following list of prohibited items confiscated and destroyed by the Vice Society, as the English organization was commonly known, during a three-year period:

Blasphemous and impure books	279
Obscene songs (on sheets)	1,495
Obscene publications	1,162
Obscene prints	10,493

In other words, the "dirty songs" were even more popular than "dirty books" (although both lost out, by a wide margin, to the "dirty pictures").

Song collections published during this period often include specific reference to the naughty tunes omitted from their pages. For example, the compiler of *The Parlour Companion or Polite Song Book*, published in Philadelphia in 1836, boasts that "there is nothing in them (the songs) to tinge the cheek of modesty with the slightest blush" or cause "the tear to tremble in the eye, and the heart to tremble in the bosom of the sensitive and intelligent." The same disclaimer is repeated at the opening of the *Bijou Songster*, issued by a different publisher four years later, reflecting either plagiarism, collaboration, or perhaps just unanimity of opinion on this vital matter.

Yet many of the folk songs that found their way into books were shocking in their own way. Among the 305 traditional ballads collected by Child, we repeatedly encounter subjects that even the most transgressive contemporary singer would hesitate to mention. Rape takes place frequently, and sometimes leads to marriage. Other romantic relationships are initiated by abduction. Incest, adultery, illegitimacy, murder, extortion, suicide, dismemberment—they are all here, sometimes presented in lavish detail. Even the most jaded soap opera scriptwriter would refuse to fill his meretricious dramas with so much dysfunctional behavior. Take, for example, the ballad "Child Owlet," number 291 of the Child ballads. Here Lady Erskine tries to seduce her nephew Child Owlet, and her come-on line leaves nothing to the imagination: "Ye must cuckold Lord Ronald." When the young man refuses—"How would I cuckold Lord Ronald, / And me his sister's son?"—Lady Erskine responds by slashing herself with a knife. She tells her husband that Owlet cut her while attempting rape. Owlet is taken prisoner, and rewarded for his virtue by getting torn to pieces by wild horses. I challenge anyone to find another song that, in just forty-eight short lines, deals with incest, seduction, adultery, self-mutilation, rape, torture, and murder. One wonders what took place in the songs seized by the authorities, if the ballads approved by the scholars broached such taboos.

Child was an unlikely champion of this music. The most famous collector of English folk music, Child himself was an American citizen born in Boston, a city famous for primness and prudery during his lifetime. The son of a sail-maker, he earned a scholarship to Harvard, where he excelled at a wide range of subjects and gave the valedictory address to his graduating class. After earning his bachelor's degree in 1846, Child was hired by Harvard as a tutor in mathe-matics, but five years later he was appointed Boylston Professor of Rhetoric and Oratory. In 1876, he was named Harvard's first professor of English, and taught courses on Shakespeare and Chaucer. But Child's most famous work had little connection with any of these subjects. At a time when no university in the world employed a professor of folklore or ethnomusicology, he focused his attention on the traditional ballads of England and Scotland. The project began with mod-est ambitions when Child decided to include "traditional" ballads in a series of books he edited that collected the works of eminent British poets. He eventually formed the plan of gathering all the significant English and Scottish ballads, in their different versions, and making them available to the public.

Child published the results of this research in a series of volumes that included the ballads, their variants, and commentary—a hefty collection that weighs six pounds on the scale and even more heavily on the minds of balladeers and folk song collectors. More than a century after his death, Child is still revered as the preemi-nent source of traditional songs in the English language with scholars and perform-ers citing a song's "Child number" the way an aficionado of Mozart might refer to a Köchel number or a Confucian commentator might identify one of the songs in the *Shijing* (a collection that, curiously enough, also includes exactly 305 songs). Yet Child's work is far from exhaustive or above criticism. Most of his research took place in libraries and archives, and though he occasionally enlisted the help of those who collected songs from the actual lips of performers, he had little confi-dence in this method of research. He tended to assume that older versions were better than newer versions of songs, as if ballads were tainted by each additional person involved in its transmission—a not uncommon view among champions of "authenticity" in music, yet hard to reconcile with the celebration of the "wisdom of the common people" that Child shared with Herder and others. This attitude led him to view with suspicion many of the works of professional ballad writers and exclude lyrics that used fancy words or showed their creator's literary preten-sions. But songs of the folk were also excluded from his collection if they failed to match his notion of what constituted a 'true' ballad. A song might be too brief, too vulgar, or fail to provide the kind of narrative structure he cherished. Ballads in which animals figured as protagonists, such as "Froggy Would A-Wooing Go," were excluded—perhaps Child thought the music of the people must be, literally, about *people*. His criteria were often strange or unclear, or applied inconsistently.

Yet for all these limitations, the publication of Child's massive collection stands out as a milestone event in the history of music scholarship. The very fact that a prominent Harvard professor, whose erudition encompassed Shakespeare and Chaucer, had devoted so many decades to collecting and codifying this music went a long way toward legitimizing the study of vernacular song styles. Numerous other scholars and song collectors were inspired by Child's example, and worked to build on his work and fill in the gaps where he had missed or deliberately neglected valuable material. Nor should we overlook the significance of an American professor devoting so much energy to collecting British songs. This may seem like a small matter, but given the intensely nationalistic ideologies that would often dominate (and sometimes distort) research on traditional music both before and after Child, his willingness to devote himself to the preservation of a culture other than his own paved the way for the later emergence of ethnomusicology as a respected academic discipline.

But we are interested in Child for what his ballads say about love and its many manifestations. And he has much to tell us about how non-elites in Britain—and elsewhere, since many of these ballads were sung in other English-speaking countries, and have close counterparts in continental Europe—sang about courtship, romance and sexuality. Perhaps most surprising is the similarity between the concerns of these songs and the plots of 'sophisticated' operas. As with opera, the Child ballads reveal an obsession with two subjects: love and violence. In fact they end up in a virtual dead heat when we try to determine which of these two themes was most popular. I analyzed and tabulated the plot elements in all 305 Child ballads, and found a love angle in 67 percent of the songs, while violence, real or threatened, figured in 68 percent. And more than 40 percent found a way to include both love *and* violence.

But the ways love is presented here are even more important, for our purposes, than its mere prevalence. At first glance, these ballads seem to harken back to the days of courtly love, with their fanciful stories of romances between lords and ladies, knights and princesses. These may be the songs of the common people, but the majority of them deal with nobility. True, a few focus on love relationships between commoners, usually with a fellow named Willie making advances on a young woman named Annie, Margaret, Janet, or, in a surprising number of instances, with no name at all. But the more common scenario finds a man with an impressive title—at a minimum Sir, even better Lord, and in a few instances King—playing the part of romantic lead.

Stories about nobles falling in love with commoners must have been especially popular with the audiences of these ballads. In "Brown Robin" (Child 97), a king's daughter runs off with her lover of lowly birth, after first disguising him in woman's clothing. In "Lizie Lindsay" (Child 226), a young man comes from the Highlands to court a young woman in Edinburgh. When she returns with him to his home, she learns that he is a lord and she is now lady of a "bonnie braw castle." But not all romances between different social classes end happily in these ballads. In "The Jolly Beggar" (Child 279), for example, a poor man comes to a farmhouse asking for shelter. One of the daughters rises late at night to find the visitor standing naked before her. He seduces her, and she berates him afterward; she thought he was a gentleman, the young lady complains, but instead he rudely took her maidenhead. At this, the beggar lifts a horn to his lips, and when he blows it, two dozen knights come to do him service. Before departing, he scolds the daughter, telling her that if she had been a good woman, he would have made her a lady of eight or nine castles.

As these brief summaries make clear, the noble protagonists of the Child ballads often neglected the proprieties of courtly love. You may recall, from our examination of the troubadours, that their stylized conception of love was based on well-defined rules of behavior. Modern readers of troubadour lyrics are often surprised by the chaste sentiments and moralizing tone of many of these songs, but these were inseparable from the late medieval age's notions of romance. Of course, the prescribed code of conduct was not always followed to the letter—both the lyrics and real behavior were known to fall short of the ideal—but all the participants in this romantic undertaking understood the way the game was *supposed* to be played. A dose of eroticism was allowed to enliven the proceedings, but it was decked out in a pleasing garb of courtesy, humility, and other acceptable virtues. Above all, the singers of these songs were quite familiar with the concept of a love that did not seek sexual consummation—and, in many instances, could hardly envision such a union since the woman praised in the lyrics was frequently the boss's wife. The feudal lord may have enjoyed these songs, but only so long as they stayed within certain boundaries, and a troubadour who crossed the line was lucky if the only thing he lost was a patron. These rules of decorum lingered on, in song if not real life, for centuries. But now they are replaced in the folk ballads with a gritty, and often exaggerated, exploration of the dark side of human relations.

The Child ballads are filled with knights and fair ladies, princesses of the realm, and lords of the land. But they clearly follow a different set of rules from those espoused in the annals of courtly love. By my tabulation, more than a third of the Child ballads refer to sex. And as some of the song descriptions above make clear, much of the fornicating is illicit or reprehensible. Prince Heathen, in Child ballad 104, holds a young woman captive, rapes her, and forces her to bear his child. In one variant, he tells her how he murdered her family:

I killd your father in his bed,
And your gay mother by his side,
And your seven brothers, ane by ane,
And they were seven pretty men.

Yet the ballad ends with the prince declaring his love for his captive, violated lady. In "The King's Dochter Lady Jean" (Child 52), the heroine is raped by a stranger in the woods. They then discover that they are siblings. In one variant the brother solves this embarrassing situation by stabbing his sister to death with a penknife. "The Bonny Hind" (Child 50) presents a similar story of an incestuous relationship between the daughter and son of a lord, but in this instance the woman wields the blade, killing herself after leaving her brother to grieve the loss of his "bonny hind." We find this incest-and-death plot repeated in "Sheath and Knife" (Child 16) and "Lizie Wan" (Child 51). The "hero" in "Brown Robyn's Confession" (Child 57) takes this discordant theme to a new level, admitting to fathering two children with his mother and five with his sister.

Occasionally these crimes and scandals are accompanied by a bit of moralizing. But the lessons drawn from these stories aren't the ones you might expect. At the conclusion of "Crow and Pie" (Child 111), women are advised that they need to take more care in avoiding rape:

But, all medons, be ware be rewe,
And lett no man downe yow throwe;
For and yow doo, ye wyll ytt rewe,
For then pe pye wyll pecke yow.

The pecking of the magpie in the last line is a fairly crude sexual metaphor, but very much aligned with the tone of the rest of the narrative. In other ballads, stories of romantic betrayal and violence are concluded with flippant advice—for example, English men should not court Scottish women, or Scottish women should trust Highland men but avoid the false men from the Lowlands. If one tried to sum up the ethical tenor of such songs, the first phrase that comes to mind is "blame the victim."

Long after Child's death, the songs he compiled incurred the wrath of censors. When The Dubliners recorded Child ballad number 274 ("Our Goodman") in 1967 under the name "Seven Drunken Nights," the track was banned by the BBC—but became a top-five hit after it was picked up by pirate station Radio Caroline. As strange as it may seem, at that same moment in history, the Rolling Stones were enjoying a huge hit with their sexually charged song "Let's Spend the Night Together," but a Child ballad was considered too dicey to share with the general public. Did Child go out of his way to track down and canonize the

most salacious and sensationalistic songs he could find? Or were all folk ballads like this? Certainly Child was no prude by Victorian standards, but he was
hardly a dirty old man in professor's garb. Indeed, the sources he relied upon for
his collection probably presented many of the lyrics in cleansed and tidy versions that changed or removed more offensive passages, and Child himself had
his own concerns over questionable content. If we often find the published texts
outrageous or disturbing, the songs actually performed by the common folk
themselves may well have been even more scandalous.

When we turn to the broadside ballads, so scorned by Child (although he
wasn't above drawing on them for his work), we encounter the same fixation
on love and violence that we previously noted on the opera stage and in Child's
collection. Pepys organized his enormous collection of broadside ballads under
eleven different headings, but found it necessary to assign multiple categories to
texts about romance and courtship. The full list provides some insight into the
concerns of the people who made and bought these broadsides:

> Devotion and Morality
> History—True and Fabulous
> Tragedy—viz Murders, Executions, Judgments of God
> State and Times
> Love—Pleasant
> Love—Unfortunate
> Marriage, Cuckoldry, etc.
> Sea—Love, Gallantry & Actions
> Drinking & Good Fellowship
> Humour, Frollicks, etc.
> Small Promiscuous Supplement—Miscellaneous

Those who prefer happy endings will take some solace in knowing that
"Love—Pleasant" contains the most ballads. It represents around one-third of
the entire collection. But Pepys is quirky in his distinctions, and many of the
lovers presented here are lonely and bemoan the complications besetting their
supposedly 'pleasant' romances. The ballads included under "Love—Unfortunate" deal with a number of ways relationships can go bad, whether through broken promises, stubborn parents, or fickle fate, among other disruptive forces.
But these texts also show a recurring fixation on sexual matters, especially the
virginity of the female protagonists, which is linked to unhappiness in many
different ways. Sometimes the young lady sacrifices her innocence, only to find
herself abandoned by a false lover, or she insists on chaste relations and makes
her frustrated companion the 'unfortunate' party. But what does it say about
love in general, or Pepys in particular, that he separates love and marriage into

separate categories? Or that his marriage ballads are filled with so many misbehaving spouses, who spend their leisure hours in drunken revelry, spendthrift behavior, and adultery? As if this were not enough, unhappy romances also show up in the "Sea" and "Tragedy" categories. Indeed, as with operas and the Child ballads, the combination of crime and love figures prominently in the broadside ballads. For example, the murder of a husband by his wife was a fairly rare occurrence in everyday life, but was a popular subject in these ballads. In fact, a whole sub-genre of "sweetheart murder ballads" flourished during this period—and such fare would continue to find an enthusiastic audience long after the broadsides disappeared, whether in blues or popular songs such as "Frankie and Johnny" and "Tom Dooley."

Even Child, who includes so many naughty stories in his collection, must have found some of these broadside texts too vulgar for inclusion. In "The Helpless Maidens Call to the Batchellors," for example, a key word is left out but implied by the rhyme scheme:

> Few Maids have met with so good luck
> As to encounter the first pluck,
> Oh this would tempt young girls to ——
>   there again, there again,
> Oh! This would tempt young Girls to Marry.

The British, of course, had no monopoly on obscene broadside ballads. The following parody of Yankee Doodle dates from the late eighteenth century.

> Yankee Doodle, keep it up.
> Yankee Doodle dandy,
> Mind the action and the pep,
> And with the girls be handy!...
>
> And there was Cap'n Washington
> With gentle whores about him;
> They say his cock's so 'tarnal proud
> He cannot ride without 'em.

Many other well-known traditional songs circulated with similarly bawdy alternative lyrics—although few of them found publishers—with everything from "Turkey in the Straw" to "On Top of Old Smoky" serving as fodder for the public's erotic imagination.

How common were such crude sexual references in traditional folk songs? We will probably never be able to answer this question with any certainty. But

I suspect familiarity with this material varied significantly according to class and gender, vocation, and location. Surviving accounts indicate that sailors and soldiers knew many shocking songs, and because these professions involve frequent travel over great distances, they probably did a good job of disseminating them—at least to port cities and other stops on their itinerary. Even the most prim and proper must have gotten an earful in the barracks or tavern or forecastle of a merchant ship. But in other settings, such tunes were no doubt kept under wraps or completely unknown. If, as the anecdote about Charles Marson cited earlier makes clear, educated people could be unaware of even the most innocent folk songs in their midst, how less likely were, say, the local minister and his spouse to know the dirty songs?

But no one could avoid hearing love songs, which were literally sung for sale in the streets, even if the dicier lyrics were withheld from innocent ears. Wherever folk song collectors have found lyrical expression of personal feelings, the love song has played a role, and often predominated. "Nearly all of these minyō or folk-songs are short lyrics or simple poetic expressions of experiences of the individual and of common humanity," writes Iwao Matsubara in *Min-Yo: Folk Songs of Japan*. "The themes are, of course, varied; but love, in all its phases, and with all its attendant hopes and fears, joys and sorrows, is the most common and out-numbers all others." "The richest area of Russian lyric songs are songs about love and family life," states noted folklorist Vladimir Propp in his 1961 study of these traditional texts. He continues with a summary of the typical scenarios of these songs, which will by now be quite familiar to us. "The songs are about unhappy love more often than happy love. Unhappy love is caused by obstacles. These obstacles may be of an interior nature, consisting of the complexities of mutual relationships, or they may be of an exterior nature, that is, in the power that the elders have over the young." Antoinet Schimmelpenninck, in her study *Chinese Folk Songs and Folk Singers*, acknowledges that over half of the lyrics collected for the work were about "one or another aspect of love"—in other words, a proportion comparable to what we find in the Child and Pepys collections. Schimmelpenninck adds that these expressions of romance and courtship were more than twice as common as any other type, such as riddles (13.7 percent of lyrics collected), work songs (8.3 percent), or narratives about historical and legendary figures (6.7 percent). One villager, discussing the *shan'ge*—folk songs, often performed outdoors, sometimes during work—passed on an old saying: "Out of every ten *shan'ge*, nine are about love."

I could cite many other examples, but they would not add much to our store of knowledge on the love song. What strikes us about the songs included in these collections is how *little* they surprise, how much they remind us of what we have already encountered in other times and places. Though researchers in local musical customs have rarely focused on universals, preferring to champion (but seldom explicitly) the view that each culture's songs are incommensurable and inextricably embedded in local practices and traditions, the careful student of love songs is struck by the exact opposite phenomenon—namely, that the people who created these songs seem to be consulting the same playbook, even to the extent of drawing on similar comparisons and metaphors, and describing almost identical emotional states. Perhaps the strongest evidence that Darwin was correct about the evolutionary necessity of our love songs comes from these collections of folk music, works situated far outside the purview of most scientists, but presenting an enormous body of data that converges on an inescapable truth. We do not choose the love song; it chooses us.

Can we conclude that our conception of love itself varies little from society to society, or at a minimum shows marked similarities in the ways it is understood and expressed? William Jankowiak and Edward Fischer undertook a detailed cross-cultural comparison, seeking examples of romantic love in 166 different cultures. They eventually identified clear examples in 148, or 89 percent, of these situations, concluding that romantic love constitutes a universal or near-universal aspect of human behavior. This near uniformity is all the more surprising when we consider the constant and overwhelming pressure from authority figures throughout history to build our intimate human relationships on something more solid and enduring than romance. The ruling powers want the youngsters to construct their lives on the basis of duty, community needs, family wishes, economic realities, and other such weighty considerations. But the youngsters never listen. They want romance, and almost always find a way to get what they want.

What happens when this desire for romance is thwarted? If we trust the songs and stories, the frustrated lovers often kill themselves. We see this documented in the surviving British ballads, where the suicide of an unhappy lover is a familiar meme, but similar stories are told in other cultures as well. In Japan during the Edo period—the same time frame that saw the peak popularity of broadside ballads in the English-speaking world—popular songs and dramas of unhappy romance often ended with the lovers' suicide. Among the Lahu in Tibet, where a rigid moral code presides over the relationships of men and women, lovers sing "love-pact suicide songs to each other outside the village at night." In continental Europe in the aftermath of Goethe's *Sorrows of Young Werther*, young people were not only fascinated with a similarly fatalistic suicide story, but more than a few imitated Goethe's protagonist, who took his life after suffering rejection from the woman he loved. Even today sociologists use the term *Werther effect* to describe copycat suicides.

The Werther effect reverberates in both the lives and work of many composers influenced by Goethe and the spirit of Romanticism. Schubert, an ardent admirer of Goethe, repeatedly evokes a melancholy in his love songs that approaches in intensity the Freudian death wish, or *Thanatos*, as his successors have named it—an urge toward self-destruction that the Viennese theorist saw as the opposite of *Eros*, a quest for love, life, and sexuality. The journeyman protagonist in Schubert's song cycle *Die schöne Müllerin,* a setting of poems by Wilhelm Müller, drowns himself after his beloved gives her affections to another man. Schubert's friend and collaborator Johann Mayrhofer, whose writings served as the basis for dozens of the composer's songs and two operas, revealed a comparable obsession with death in his poetry, one eerily echoed in his early demise. Mayrhofer tried to drown himself in the Danube in 1831 but was rescued; five years later, he committed suicide by jumping out of the window of an office building. Schumann, who composed music for Heine's poetic evocation of a lover pushed to the brink of suicide, "Der arme Peter," attempted to kill himself by jumping into the Rhine in 1854. Suicide almost became part of the definition of love for composers pushing the limits of Romanticism. In Wagner's great love opera *Tristan und Isolde,* Tristan attempts suicide at the end of *each* of the three acts.

Do these songs and stories tell us anything about the nature of love? Do young people frequently kill themselves because social norms, family, or other obstacles interfere with their romantic aspirations? Or is this tendency exaggerated beyond recognition in songs and stories about love? Both anecdotal accounts and academic studies can be mustered to support a connection between love and suicide, at least in some social milieus. In her cross-cultural study of suicide among young people, Louise Jilek-Aall identified comparatively high rates among young females in Japan—it was the most common cause of death for women between the ages of twenty and twenty-nine—and noted that 20 percent are due to conflict with parents over marriage partners. In recent years, a large body of evidence has been gathered to suggest a connection between societal and parental constraints and suicides among gay and lesbian teens. Therapist Paul Gibson, in his survey of available research, concluded that these youths are two to three times more likely to attempt suicide than heterosexual teens, and may account for as much as 30 percent of youth suicides. Although cause-and-effect is impossible to measure with precision, the conflict between social pressures and romantic or sexual aspirations clearly plays a role in many real-life suicides, and not just in songs about love.

The student of this music inevitably notices the popularity of story songs about suicidal lovers in cultures where intense pressures for conformity on the micro level or economic or military advancement on the macro level are felt by the rising and striving masses, whether in England and Germany during the Industrial Revolution, in Japan during its period of rapid GDP growth, or in war-mongering nations greedy for expansion. More than a century and a half after Goethe wrote about Werther, German newspapers during the Nazi era gave extensive coverage to lovers' suicides, committed either by unhappy individuals or by couples facing parental opposition. When Rome was striving to conquer the world, its citizens were equally fascinated with stories about lovers who committed or threatened suicide, such as Ovid's account of Pyramus and Thisbe, or Virgil's tale of Dido's fatal attraction to Aeneas. Perhaps these tragic songs served as a release valve for emotional pressures that had few other outlets in these cultures, or maybe the militaristic values of these societies, where self-sacrifice was often praised on the battlefield, came to pervade civilian relationships. To some degree, even parents and other authority figures must have found functional value in such songs, seeing in them useful warnings to the young against succumbing to emotional ties that could lead to such destructive results.

Parents play a surprisingly prominent role in folk songs about love, although rarely a positive one. In his study of the Santals of eastern India, W. G. Archer devotes a lengthy chapter to "conflict with parents" and songs that express the frustrations of their unhappy children. In their collection of songs of the Great Lakes sailors, Ivan Walton and Joe Grimm note that "a common theme" of these lyric is "the lovestruck beauty and her meddling mother." Simon Harrison explores a similar phenomenon in his study of Avatip love songs from Papua New Guinea, aptly entitled *Laments for Foiled Marriages*. "Although my subject is the Avatip love-song, or *namai*, it is not my purpose here to discuss Avatip courtship and marriage," he writes at the start of his work; "in fact my starting-point is the rejection of offers of marriage, the breakdown of marriage negotiations—in short, what happens when things go wrong." He finds an unseemly collection of interfering relatives, haughty lovers, frustrated suitors, and secret intentions dragged painfully into the light—in short, all the trappings familiar to Western audiences, whether watching Shakespeare's *Romeo and Juliet* or Robert De Niro in *Meet the Parents*. Countless other examples could be cited, and many have been shared earlier in this book.

The time, place, and language may be different, but the same story is repeatedly told in these traditional songs. For example, the love songs of the Omaha tribe of Native Americans, as related by Alice C. Fletcher from her late nineteenth-century visits, seem to mimic the medieval troubadours in their combination of formalism and melancholy protestations. Fletcher writes of courting songs reminiscent of the *paraklausithyron*, the lament of the suitor left outside the door of the beloved—a theme we have already encountered in ancient Egypt, Greece, and Rome. "The lover, however, is apt to haunt the abode of his sweetheart to watch her movements from some hidden vantage point," writes Fletcher, "and at the dawn his love-song may be heard echoing over the hills. Sometimes he sings in the evening to let the maiden know of his presence.... All this little drama takes place covertly, no elder is made a confidant." Perhaps Fletcher is imposing her own Harvard-trained sensibilities on her sources. Certainly love songs are not as prominent in traditional Native American music as in European culture after the rise of the troubadours. Yet other researchers have also identified intriguing examples that present subjects and situations congruent with those found in Europe, Asia and elsewhere. Frances Densmore, for example, documented a number of love songs among the Chippewa, and her descriptions are not much different from what Propp tells us above about Russian love songs, or Pepys about British broadside ballads. The Chippewa songs tended to be mournful melodies chronicling unhappy affairs. Typical lyrics, translated into English by Densmore: "I sit here thinking of her. I am sad as I think of her." Or: "I go around weeping for my love." Petrarch could hardly have put it more succinctly!

However, the Chippewa were not all starry-eyed in their musical relationships. Densmore also found four "divorce songs" used by the tribe. I mentioned above how seldom traditional love songs surprise us, and more often follow predictable expressions of romantic longing. Yet divorce songs perhaps fall into the category of musical surprises. Although five-times-married Tammy Wynette enjoyed a number one country single with "D-I-V-O-R-C-E" in 1968, few songwriters have gotten much traction from tunes about the termination of marriage, custody battles, or the allocation of community property. For my own part, I don't take much delight in such songs or the broken marriages they commemorate. But in my research, I have gained a degree of hard-won satisfaction in finding these and other unexpected variations in the music of our most intimate relationships. I applaud, for example, the Jewish tradition of love songs presented in the form of riddles—a practice that can be traced back to ancient times. I was enchanted to discover that the Temiar of Malaysia believe that certain rhythms of their rain-forest home, such as the calls of birds and sounds of insects, move in time with the beating of the human heart, creating longing. They play their bamboo tube percussion in similar rhythms, hoping to evoke this same sense of desire. I learned, with curious apprehension, that Slovakian herders court young maidens by cracking their whips, and I am fascinated by Alan Merriam's assertion that the Flathead Indians of Western Montana do not sing love songs when they are lonely—they have a special group of "lonesome" songs for that situation, and these are performed only by women. Authentic love songs, in their view, are provided by guardian spirits, and are believed by some tribal members to exert magical power over the beloved.

I am also intrigued to learn that, among the Maori, love songs and laments are "functionally and textually often identical," according to ethnomusicologist Mervyn McLean—a puzzling discovery, at first glance, but congruent with the Western musical traditions of the dying-and-rising fertility god, in which eroticism and mourning for the dead are inextricably mixed. At recording sessions, Maori singers were frequently unsure how to determine which of the two categories, *waiata aroha* (love songs) or *waiata tangi* (laments), should be used to describe the song they were performing. Yet the one type is sung because of an illness or after the death of a relative, while the other may be merely about an unrequited love. The Maori word for love (*aroha*) also signifies "pity" or "sympathy"—further evidence of the unhappy nature of romance, at least in the music and language of this culture. Yet another type of song, the *waiata whaiaaipo*, or "sweetheart song," is more lighthearted and is addressed by a woman to a man she claims to love. But even here, the depth of the commitment can be questioned, since in many of the *waiata whaiaaipo* lyrics, the woman asserts that she is in love with *several men*, singing to each in turn.

But my favorite variant on the love song is the magical melody that *compels* the reluctant object of romantic advances to reciprocate the singer's affections. We are familiar with love charms in our own culture, if not from real life at least from our literary heritage—they show up in highbrow culture, from Shakespeare to Wagner, as well as in myths and folklore. In fact, 20 percent of the Child ballads include some element of the magical or supernatural in their plots, often in the context of a love story. But the historical and anthropological accounts of musical love magic are filled with many variations. Among the *yilpintji* (love-magic) ceremonies of the Pintupi in Australia, for example, the sound of the bullroarer plays an important part in rituals that enhance the sexual attractiveness of the men and inspire desire among the women. One singer told ethnomusicologist Richard Moyle that the sound of the bullroarer had such force it could affect a woman at the distance of some eighty kilometers. The women practice a comparable ceremony, the *yawulyu*, but unlike the men's rite, this tradition consists mostly of body painting—which might take up as much as three and a half hours in a four-hour ceremony. Yet women in the tribe also recognize the power of musical charms, and some claim that their singing alone can bring a man to them, or put him in a state of sexual arousal. Moyle, who witnessed many of these ceremonies, writes: "On one occasion at Balgo, a man, apparently unaware of the performance, blundered out of the scrub on to the ceremonial area. The women immediately jumped to their feet, calling out for him to come right over to them; this was the living proof of the *yawulyu's* power! With a look of utter terror, though, he fled."

We may laugh at such stories, but are we really so different from the Pintupi and other cultures who place their trust in the functional power of music to secure the affections of the beloved? Sociologist Tia DeNora interviewed fifty-two British and American women in the late 1990s and asked them about the use of music in their intimate moments with a loved one. These women described in great detail the care and consideration that went into the selection of music in these settings, and the concerns they had over the efficacy of different kinds of songs. The convergence of their opinions was striking. "Of the fifty-two women interviewed for the music and daily life study," DeNora reports, "not one indicated fast-paced or high-volume music as something they associated with intimacy." (I note, in passing, that Densmore in her study of Chippewa music described above, found that songs used as love charms were noticeably slower in tempo than other tribal music.) DeNora's respondents preferred, to quote their own terms, "romantic," "relaxing," or "smoochy music." But even as they tried to articulate their decision-making process, these women struggled to describe the ineffable and even explicitly supernatural quality at play when this music accompanied their romantic encounters. "It's a kind of magical, mystical type thing," explained one of the women, who added that her belief in "non-traditional religion" had a bearing on her choice of music in these settings. As such statements suggest, we haven't entirely resigned ourselves to the notion that love songs are just background music to our courtships and couplings. We still believe (or at least hope) that music can charm and seduce. We even tend to gravitate to the same kinds of songs, acknowledging their efficacious powers, and scorning other melodies that have no comparable potency.

In this regard, the love song follows a pattern of evolution similar to what we see in other types of folk or indigenous music. In many traditional cultures, songs are prized for their inherent power, for their ability to transform and enchant. The songs actually *do* things. I'm reminded of the statement of the Motu tribal member in New Guinea, who insisted to a researcher: "No drums are beaten uselessly. There are no dances that are merely useless." Such songs have been cherished and preserved by traditional societies for many reasons, but perhaps most often for their inherent powers. They played a decisive role in healing or worship; they inspired warriors in battle or prepared hunters for the chase; they coordinated physical labors or made work less burdensome; they could preserve history or teach lessons; they brought communities together in solidarity. And, of course, they assisted in matters of courtship, love, and romance, perhaps even casting a spell of enchantment. If our modern culture has tended to marginalize and ignore these multifaceted roles, and focus on music as mere entertainment, we still haven't forgotten the powers inherent in song. As researchers such as Tia DeNora and John Sloboda have shown, people still employ music to *make things happen* in their day-to-day lives, especially in matters of love.

But from this point on in our story, a new force will come into play, indeed will dominate the music, namely the profit motive. We have already encountered it, especially in our exploration of the madrigal, opera, and other musical forms that required the intervention of business interests in order to spread through Europe. Yet even after the rise of large-scale capitalism, the folk song still persisted as a style of popular music that could find an audience without relying on a financial transaction to seal the deal. Businesses did get involved, of course, as we have seen with the broadside ballads and ballad operas, but these songs didn't need an entrepreneur or angel investor to help them go viral, let alone YouTube and Facebook. They were shared in family settings, in informal social gatherings, at celebrations and community events, and were woven into the day-to-day life of millions of people.

But now the 'folk' will increasingly become the audience for mass-produced music designed for the purposes of commerce. They still play an essential role—after all, someone must buy the music in order for this profit-driven model to work. And, for a time, the folk will still have creative input into the process. Many households will own pianos or other instruments, and the songs they buy from retailers will be integrated into personal or family rituals and recreations. But gradually this creative input will lessen, and the 'folk' will find themselves transformed, almost completely, into consumers.

The love song will still thrive in this new model. Even more, it will emerge as the leading profit generator for the music business. But it must also change, become less quirky, more homogenized, and in other ways made suitable for that new arbiter of tastes, the now ascendant 'listening public'.

CHAPTER 13

Love Songs for the Mass Market

When you play music you have to remember that just about everything composed has to do with love and courtship.—Oscar Hijuelos, *The Mambo Kings Play Songs of Love*

The folk only gradually realized that they also represented the core commercial *audience* for music. For most of history, the folk created their own musical entertainment, or turned to family members and neighbors to do it for them. The very notion of an audience separated from performers is unknown in many traditional societies—as ethnomusicologists have noted, communities with vibrant musical cultures often don't have (or need) a word for *audience*. Even in the industrializing nations of the modern world, this distinction sometimes seemed arbitrary until very recently. Are the dancers at a traditional wedding part of the performance or members of the audience—or does this starkly posed alternative miss the holistic nature of what actually transpires in such a setting? When parishioners in early America sang hymns at church, were they creating the music or receiving it? How can you tell the difference? When Victorian-era British football fans broke into a chant or melody to urge on their team, did they lose their status as audience members and become performers? How do we classify children singing while playing a game, or the shepherd playing the flute with only the sheep at hand? Are laborers singing at work really performers? Does the overseer monitoring their progress represent the audience?

A well-known music writer once insisted to me that "all music is performed with an audience in mind." Yet my impression is the exact opposite. Throughout history and prehistory, most music has been embedded in social, community, and ritual occasions in which the notion of an audience has no place. Today we take for granted that people either 'consume' or 'create' popular entertainment—certainly this model accurately describes the economic reality of music-making in the twenty-first century. But this state of affairs emerged only gradually, and after many fits and starts.

Love songs played a key role in this process. Perhaps in a now distant day, these songs belonged to the lovers themselves, but at a very early stage the music of romance and courtship turned into a kind of spectacle—delighting those who, much like audiences today, took vicarious enjoyment in passions and intimate affairs experienced at second hand. Indeed, the love song may have played a decisive role in creating our modern notion that music serves primarily for entertainment and diversion. At every juncture in the evolution of the singer-songwriter in the West, the love song has typically served as the main attraction. It has adapted to changing tastes and passing fads, as well as new methods of musical dissemination and emerging technologies of performance and preservation. In many instances love songs have led the way, other styles of music following in their wake.

But this process of dissemination was much slower before the rise of modern mass media. Songs may have gone 'viral' but not with the speed of the current day. In chapter ten, we explored the synergistic relationship between the madrigal and the emerging industry of music publishing. As we saw, the love song helped finance this business model, and thus made it possible for other types of music to reach a larger audience. But consumers for these music books represented only a tiny subset of the population. A typical print run for a music publisher during the age of the madrigal was five hundred copies; for an especially popular work this might rise to a thousand copies or slightly more. When compared to platinum records or videos with a billion views, this attempt to monetize music via the printing press was minuscule.

Sales figures from earlier centuries are almost impossible to trace with any precision, but many experts believe that the first published song to sell more than a million copies was "After the Ball," written by Charles K. Harris in 1891. Like so many subsequent hits, this popular waltz was a love song, sentimental and saccharine in the style of that era. But consider the date. Yes, the music publishing industry waited more than four hundred years before enjoying its first million seller!

Why did it take so long? Supply and demand, those two pesky forces dominating our day-to-day life, actually had little to do with it. Melodies have never been in short supply, and demand for love songs (and other music) is as old as human society itself. The bottleneck came at the meeting point between supply and demand: the performer. You can't sell sheet music in large quantities unless you have a large number of people who can play it. Music-making couldn't evolve into a sizable commercial music business until households started owning pianos and other instruments, and the people living in these homes learned how to use them. In short, music had always been a powerful social force, but needed lots of help before emerging as a potent *economic* force.

Perhaps this helps explain why the music publishing industry stagnated during the seventeenth century. But the rise of the bourgeoisie and the emergence of a large urban middle class in Europe gradually expanded the ranks of skilled amateur musicians. Even in the sixteenth century we hear of bakers, tanners, and other artisans paying for music lessons for their children. But this process unfolded slowly, over the course of decades. Although we see music teachers advertising their services, the leading composers still turned to religious institutions, nobility, and the wealthy to advance their careers. Even so, the spread of middle-class musicianship can be measured by the increasing mention of lutes, guitars, and other instruments in inventories of dowries and wills.

Of course, love songs still were perceived by many as dangerous—a popular 1605 narrative poem by Juan de Salinas is filled with double meanings linking music-making with seduction, a connection that would have been familiar to his audience. Salinas clearly had firsthand experience of the dark side of love, if not from his poetry certainly from his job as superintendent of a hospital that specialized in treating syphilitics. Many parents must have felt uneasy about bringing this passion-filled music into their homes. Yet ambitious families were increasingly willing to run that risk, viewing music as an accomplishment that could help a child, especially a daughter, make a better match. Indeed, the seductive quality of the music was part of its allure—provided it could be channeled in parentally approved directions.

And the key to unlocking the potential of mass-market music was the keyboard. More than any other development, the widespread acceptance of the piano as the home entertainment center for the aspiring classes created an economic platform for the emergence of music as a large-scale business. The composers themselves are evidence for the new pecking order in music. Until the late seventeenth century, the leading musicians and composers of Europe tended to be singers or performers on string instruments. There were exceptions, of course: William Byrd, Girolamo Frescobaldi, Gottlieb Muffat, and others wrote for the keyboard, but the more typical career path for a rising music star began in a church choir, or perhaps with a lute in hand. Yet around the time of Johann Sebastian Bach and Domenico Scarlatti—both born in 1685—a shift is evident. From this point on, most of the leading composers of Europe will compose for keyboard instruments, and often play them with virtuosity. At the same time, technological improvements will lead to the evolution of the modern piano, an instrument perfectly suited both for public performance and private music-making in the home. Improvements in manufacturing and economies of scale gradually make these pianos more affordable, and the rising bourgeoisie will emerge as the target market for this new industry.

Even with all these trends in place, the music business expanded very slowly. As late as 1770, if we can believe music historian and traveler Charles Burney, no music shops existed in Vienna, nor did he find any during his sojourn in Italy. Music publishing was in such a feeble state that customers often found it necessary to purchase handmade scores from copyists. *The Well-Tempered Clavier*, today considered the definitive keyboard work of the century, circulated widely in manuscript, but no professionally printed version arrived on the market until 1801—almost eighty years after it was composed. Of course, Bach didn't possess the fame and name recognition he would later acquire, but even Handel, perhaps the most renowned composer of the mid-eighteenth century, relied on copyists to fill orders for his many unpublished works. Music historians often refer to Haydn's success in the free market economy of London at the close of the century, but we need to remember that the composer did not make this daring move until he had secured a pension from the Esterházy family, his noble Hungarian patrons. Mozart survived, barely, as what we nowadays would call an 'freelancer', but even he would have preferred a court appointment over the opportunities (or lack thereof) provided by the marketplace.

This changes in the closing years of the eighteenth century, with the arrival of the piano in countless households. Families had many reasons for making this expensive purchase—the piano served as an attractive piece of furniture, a signal of prosperity, a token of culture, and even occasionally a source of music. But if we could give these long-departed bourgeoisie a truth serum, I suspect that many would admit that they bought the piano to marry off their eligible daughters to promising bachelors. Numerous authorities of the period stressed the importance of music in a young lady's education, but many instruments were dismissed as "unbecoming the Fair Sex," as John Essex explained in 1722. Wind instruments could "look indecent in a Woman's Mouth," and even the dainty flute was "very improper, as taking away too many of the Juices, which are otherwise necessarily employ'd to promote the Appetite, and assist Digestion." The piano had none of these defects. No juices were expended. No oral contact required.

By almost any measure, the piano seemed custom-made for a respectable courtship—all the more so due to its lack of portability. If a musical seduction took place, it would occur in the household's music room, where inquiring parents could keep tabs on its progress. The guitar, well known as the instrument of seducers, was a much dicier proposition. The unaccompanied human voice, like the Sirens of ancient myth, might lure young men into rash actions in places where no cooler-headed adults could intervene. But entrenched on a piano bench in the parlor, a budding young woman could perform the most romantic songs, enflaming desire even while offering no means of satisfying it short of a formal proposal.

Under such circumstances, music could afford to become more overtly romantic—in fact, the marketplace demanded it. Given the evolution of musical styles, this change would have happened anyway. It was, after all, the age of Romanticism with a capital R, and intense emotions and extravagant passions, so feared by the sober-minded of earlier generations, were increasingly cultivated as heroic attributes by cultural elites. But the less-than-heroic middle-class consumers of piano music also found this stylistic shift congenial to their purposes. Instead of fugues and sonatas, which rarely set hearts aflutter with notions of love, they preferred to purchase nocturnes, romances, and other evocative works of mood music. Yet if a pianist sought the most impassioned and amorous music of the era, this meant opera, and savvy intermediaries found ways to translate the heady emotions of La Scala and Covent Garden to the humble home keyboard. "One can see the changing tastes reflected in the catalogues of a publisher such as Pleyel," music historian Hans Lenneberg notes, "the titles of which are aimed at a new public with its rage for arrangements, fantasies, variations, and what-have-you on operatic themes, most often for piano or for solo instrument with piano accompaniment."

But opera soon had a rival. The waltz, nowadays considered a symbol of primness and restraint, was the dirty dancing of its era, abhorred by upholders of moral virtue even as it took over the parlors and ballrooms of Europe. In time, waltz rhythm would serve as the underpinning for countless romantic songs, but even when performed without lyrics, as was typical in these early days, its connection with love and courtship was the key to both its appeal...and its scandal. A character in Sophie von La Roche's 1771 novel *Geschichte des Fräuleins von Sternheim* expresses the reaction of many high-minded onlookers to this new spectacle on the dance floor: "When he put his arm around her, pressed her to his breast, cavorted with her in the shameless, indecent whirling-dance of the Germans and engaged in a familiarity that broke all the bounds of good breeding—then my silent misery turned into burning rage."

Germany, the source of this indecent innovation, had long been more tolerant of close-contact dancing than its neighbors to the south. Montaigne describes a dance he witnessed in Augsburg in 1580, where the "gentleman took the lady's hand, kissed it, and placed his hand on her shoulder; he then clasped her securely, holding her so close that they were cheek to cheek." Another visitor to this town, Hans von Schweinichen, noted that "young men may embrace the damsels with whom they are dancing. The young men often bribe them to do so frequently, and many a hug may be had for half a thaler."

In the closing years of the eighteenth century, the rest of Europe learned to love, or at least tolerate, the waltz and the intimate physical contact it offered. Here too capitalists assisted in the evolution of romance-driven art. By 1797, nearly seven hundred public dance halls were active in Paris alone, allowing patrons to enjoy the pleasures of clasping, turning, and engaging in close face-to-face contact with a member of the opposite sex. But no city would show more fervor for the waltz than Vienna. The Apollo Palace, opened in 1808, could accommodate up to six thousand dancers, and the Odeon, inaugurated in January 1845, gained renown as the biggest dance hall in the world—with capacity for at least eight thousand patrons and an eighty-piece orchestra. But working-class dancers found opportunities to waltz in less opulent settings. They could be seen dancing at small local ballrooms, restaurants, coffee houses, and public parks.

Composers attuned to this new style of musical courtship no longer needed to rely on religious institutions or wealthy patrons to support their careers, and many now rose from the ranks of dance bands to win the public's acclaim. The self-taught Joseph Lanner, son of an Austrian glove maker, started working in Michael Palmer's popular ensemble when he was only twelve, and by seventeen enjoyed enough of a following to launch his own group. His "Die Schönbrunner" waltz ranked among the most popular compositions of its day—at his last performance the audience demanded twenty-one encores of this prototype for the modern hit song. In 1823, Lanner hired Johann Strauss, destined to emerge as his leading rival. The two later separated after a bandstand brawl, covered in all the newspapers, which anticipated the band breakups of the current day. Strauss achieved international acclaim for his waltzes, and as a touring star brought the Viennese sound to Germany, Belgium, the Netherlands, and England. But his band would also serve as a launching pad for a more successful competitor, in this instance his son Johann Strauss Jr. Far from feeling paternal pride, the father was so upset when Dommayer's Casino booked his offspring as a headliner that he refused to play the venue again.

The sounds of the ballroom inevitably entered the home, where countless amateur musicians performed waltzes and other styles of dance-oriented music at the family piano. Yet another innovation of the era may have had even more influence in laying the groundwork for the modern music business, namely the so-called *parlor song*. In many instances, the early anthologies of these songs resemble the collections of the ballad hunters discussed in the previous chapter. But the demands of commerce increasingly forced music publishers to 'improve' the songs handed down to them by the past, making them more suitable for public consumption, or in many instances supplementing them with original works. George Thomson, who published the popular *Select Collection of Original Scottish Airs for the Voice* in six volumes between 1799 and 1841, prodded poet Robert Burns to replace unsatisfactory old lyrics in the songs he contributed, and hired Peter Pindar to create new works for the anthologies. One angry critic denounced the inclusion of "new words by contract" in these volumes—thus anticipating the champions of authenticity in our own day—but was forced to add that the "practice, however ingenious, is by no means unprecedented." Yet even the musical notes needed to change to meet the requirements of the marketplace. As we saw in chapter eleven, Beethoven was chided by this same publisher, who complained that young ladies could not play the piano parts he had been hired to write.

The parlor song arose to meet this demand for simpler musical fare for household use. The same families who purchased pianos for their homes and paid for music instruction for their children served as the target market for these sentimental tunes, works designed to pull on the heartstrings without requiring inordinate support from the fingers at the keys. True, these same songs could be heard in public performance—they were, after all, the popular music of the day—but the business model for the parlor song required purchase by amateur musicians, the more the better, and the works were designed with this consumer in mind. Some might laud such a shift as a democratization of the arts, while for others it represents the moment when 'dumbing down' started in our musical culture. But for the music publishers of the day such exemplary simplifications, the pruning and training that gets us from Schubert's *Winterreise* to "I'll Take You Home Again, Kathleen," were hardly philosophical or aesthetic matters, merely the ground rules for market expansion.

Many of these songs were advertised as *ballads*—we find that word again and again on the covers of the sheet music—and the people who wrote such works were often referred to as "ballad composers." But in this context, the term conveyed a meaning different from that encountered in our survey of the Child ballads. For Child, the ballad told a story, preferably an old story preserved by tradition, and presented in the form of a third-person account of events occurring in the distant past. The ballad collector Cecil Sharp emphasized that such songs were "above all, impersonal, that is to say, the singer is merely the narrator of events with which he personally has no connection and for which he has no responsibility." But even Sharp recognized the existence of another type of song cherished by the 'folk', which he described as "a far more emotional and passionate utterance" and "usually the record of a personal experience—very frequently of an amatory nature." Long before Sharp wrote these words, this type of lyrical expression of intense emotion, presented as though from the intimate experience of the singer, had emerged as the primary focus for the parlor song. This shift represents the birth of our modern ballad, with all its romantic associations and audience expectations.

The parlor song would enjoy its greatest success in the United States, where it fueled the growth of the American music industry during the nineteenth century. But this homegrown business started on a very modest scale. During the first several decades following the nation's independence, most of the parlor songs purchased by American consumers were composed overseas, and often imported directly from London. When a few leading music retailers began publishing their own scores, they typically preferred to reprint works that had already been issued in Britain. By the same token, an American composer or performer with a London pedigree found it easier to secure work in the New World than did homegrown talent. Even in patriotic songs, where American origins added to the authenticity of the tune, music was lifted from British antecedents, as demonstrated in "The Star Spangled Banner," "My Country, 'Tis of Thee,"

"The Liberty Song," and other early expressions of national pride. The War of Independence may have secured political autonomy for the United States, but in cultural matters its citizens were still in thrall to their past masters.

In the sphere of musical romance, however, American lovers took a more active stance than their European counterparts. Many visitors from overseas were astonished by the prevalent Yankee custom of bachelors serenading outside the homes of eligible young ladies. Although this practice was known in Europe, young men in the New World seemed to embrace it with particular fervor. "This is a common practice in many parts of the States," wrote one visiting Englishman, "every sort of music being employed from the voice and guitar up to the German band... to perform before the houses of young ladies of their acquaintance." Swedish tourist Carl David Arfwedson experienced this practice firsthand during his stay in the in the early 1830s. He explained that "a custom very prevalent in Boston is to perform serenades at night time for the edification of the fair sex." Invited to participate on one of these evening outings, Arfwedson later jotted down his observations:

> Provided with a guitar and a flute, we started about midnight, and proceeded, in the first instance, to a house in the lower part of town, the residence of one of the belles of the city. In full imitation of the Italian fashion, we were wrapped up in cloaks, and formed a group exactly under the window stated to belong to the bedchamber of the lady.... Within a few moments our attention was arrested by the noise of a window softly opening.

Although Arfwedson tried to peer into the window, he found it impossible to discern the reactions of the "fair sex" to these serenades, or even who was listening to the music. But a few days later, a number of ladies told him that they had noticed his contribution to the music-making.

These same Americans who impressed visitors with their ardent desire to perform love songs would, just a few decades later, make their mark as the leading consumers of the same. In 1800, only around eighteen publishers of sheet music operated in the entire United States, but by 1860 this number had grown to almost one hundred. So many songs came on the market that amateur musicians needed help figuring out which ones to play. Many subscribed to magazines that promised to pick the best of the best, and deliver these superior tunes to the home mailbox. Annual collections, published around Christmas each year, were especially popular and often given as presents. Some consumers made their own compilations, purchasing individual songs and binding them together in elegant volumes, a kind of scrapbooking for the musically inclined. Even *Godey's Lady's Book*, the most popular woman's magazine of its day and the forerunner of the modern fashion magazine, included sheet music along with its color illustrations of dresses and coverage of the latest happenings in American society. Professional performers adopted these same songs, and even touring opera singers from Europe soon learned that audiences wanted to hear some sentimental local melodies mixed in with classics from afar.

Musical tastes in the New World differed from those across the ocean, and this inevitably impacted the kinds of songs favored in the American marketplace. These consumers preferred simple expressions of heartfelt affection over extravagant declarations of passion. The virtuosity of European performers may have been admired, but was often viewed with suspicion. In 1827, when Francis Courtney Wemyss was preparing to leave London for theatrical bookings in the United States, he received a letter from a Philadelphia promoter with advice on how to hire a singer that would appeal to the American public. "High musical attainments are not so essential as expression, feeling and vivacity." As a result a "good singer" was often preferred over a "superior singer." But vulgarity of any sort must be avoided—"this deficiency has been the cause of the failure of many" previous visiting performers. Audiences in Philadelphia would expect "polished manners, good exterior, and a guarded sense of decorum."

These same words could be used to describe the formula for writing a love song for an American music publisher during this period. "By far the most popular theme in the parlor ballads is affection," writes Nicholas E. Tawa, a specialist in this period of American song. But this affection need have no connection to romance. It could attach to a sibling or an aging parent, to a familiar household object, or a favorite pet. Stephen Foster might celebrate his fondness for "Oh! Susanna," but he was just as likely to sing about "My Old Kentucky Home" or "Old Dog Tray." Those seeking deep passions and extravagant displays of emotion were advised to stick with Italian opera or British broadside ballads. Lovers in the published American popular songs of the period did not commit murders out of jealousy. They did not abduct, seduce, or emulate any of the other transgressive activities of the protagonists in traditional folk songs. These decorous suitors were more likely to make bland statements about Cupid and his arrows, or refer wistfully to the one "who has learned to love another" whose "voice I must forget." In most songs of the pre–Civil War era, "the lovers neither kiss nor clasp each other," Tawa explains. "Those few songs which treated love as a physical passion were quite unpopular. Contemporary writers on music seldom mention them as being in public performance; musical amateurs scarcely ever purchased them." As noted in the previous chapter, the publishers of song collections often included specific statements about the works excluded from consideration—for example, The Singer's Own Book, issued in Philadelphia in 1832, which assured purchasers that nothing in its pages would "offend the nicest modesty, or mantle the cheek of beauty with the faintest blush."

Judging on the basis of these paeans to primness, one would hardly predict that the United States would soon emerge as the most influential force in popular music. Europe offered a much more tolerant and vibrant platform for love songs, whether in the British music halls, which started to draw large audiences during the middle decades of the nineteenth century, or the Parisian cabarets that flourished in the 1880s and are still major tourist attractions today. In this louche environment, songwriters and performers didn't worry about matching their fare to the needs of young ladies playing the parlor piano or the expectations of their watchful parents. Entertainment and revelry took precedence, accompanied by food, drink, tobacco, and sometimes illicit sex. During the 1880s, the number of prostitutes registering with the French police declined, but this hardly indicated a rise in male chastity and fidelity, rather the inroads of a new breed of professional, women who worked as dancers or in some other capacity at these popular nightspots, but also took on paying customers for more private services. The cabarets proved so successful as a place where prostitutes could meet clients, that owners of traditional brothels saw a marked decline in their business, and some madams responded by turning their establishments into centers of musical entertainment.

Both the songs and the style of singing changed in these erotically charged environments. The cabaret chanteuse aimed for a greater sense of intimacy in her delivery, sometimes moving from singing to speaking in midperformance and drawing on every possible tool—gestures, poses, facial expressions, costumes, or, if the audience's attention drifted, lifting up her skirt—to intensify the impact of a song. The sensuality of this music had few counterparts in the New World, but even the cynicism and irony of the words would have been out of place on American soil. Not everyone approved of such songs, but even the harshest critics realized that something new was happening in the music world. A French journalist, writing about the famous chanteuse Yvette Guilbert in 1894, described her as "the quintessence of feminine neurosis, the fatal corollary of the general degeneration where our admirable society is putrefying." Guilbert was "a simple pretext for morbid germs, where brains go berserk in strange lustfulness." But the writer also saw in this same performer "the feverish gropings of the modern spirit."

The British music halls operated under closer police scrutiny. Even the arrival of one unescorted female customer could provoke authorities into closing the premises—on the assumption that she might be a prostitute looking for clients. The owners of these establishments also practiced self-censorship. A contract from an Islington music hall specifies that entertainers must submit new songs for approval by the manager a week in advance of their debut, and that "giving expression to any vulgarity" was cause for immediate dismissal. Yet British music hall owners also understood that a dose of vulgarity was not displeasing to the clientele. A government report from 1892 notes that "a famished manager" might "prefer to seek in scandal and indecency the means of replenishing an exhausted treasury"—and adds, in an interesting aside, that this kind of fare was especially popular with "richer, idler and more fashionable audiences." Love songs, in such an environment, often aimed for hints of salaciousness that stopped just short of indecency, as for example in Arthur Lloyd's 1873 song "It's Naughty but It's Nice":

> I kiss'd her two times on the cheek,
> I would have kissed her thrice,
> But I whispered, ain't it naughty?
> She said, Yes, but it's so nice.

The mixture of music, alcohol, and sensuality would prove a winning formula throughout Europe during the late nineteenth and early twentieth century. Germany embraced the cabaret lifestyle with a vengeance, and in time Berlin would almost rival Paris as a center for this type of entertainment. But cabarets also opened in Amsterdam (1895), Barcelona (1897), Vienna (1901), Cracow (1905), Budapest (1907), Moscow (1908), Prague (1911), Zurich (1916), and many other continental cities. Love songs were only part of the attraction of these establishments, where everything from political satire to bohemian culture found a fertile breeding ground, but the overt eroticism of these settings served as an especially powerful magnet for well-heeled customers, fun-seeking revelers who might never read a manifesto or attend a gallery opening. And soon, with the rise of commercial recordings, other European national and regional traditions, each with its own distinctive take on love—the melancholy moods of *fado* in Portugal, the underground and criminal associations of *rebetiko* in Greece, *cante flamenco* in Spain with its assertions of love and love betrayed, and other popular song styles—spread across borders and cross-fertilized other idioms with greater ease than ever before.

How could the United States even begin to compete with these innovations in love songs? Almost everything in American cultural life seemed to conspire to keep popular music trapped in a circle of shallow sentimentality, whether we consider the often puritanical attitudes of civic life or the determination of publishers to match their songs to the needs of parents and their innocent daughters. Well, almost everything. The United States did possess one advantage over Europe in musical innovation, and it would eventually prove decisive. In a strange twist of fate, this future determinant of American dominance of popular music earned little respect during the nineteenth century—in fact, it was widely disparaged and despised. But for readers of this 'hidden history' it will be a familiar source of innovation in music in general and love songs in particular. Once again, the spark that sends everything into a flurry of motion comes from Africa, and not willingly, but in bondage.

CHAPTER 14

The African Connection (Again)

Q. Is the blues a song of sorrow?
A. No, it is a song of romantic failure.
—Duke Ellington, *Music Is My Mistress*

The impact of black musicians on American song is a familiar story. We encounter it every day, on television and radio, in live performance or streaming over the web. But readers who have traveled this far in our history of the love song may now see this influence in a new light. Again and again, we have uncovered the often hidden role of slaves and other outcasts in shaping innovations in music, whether in the theatrical productions of ancient Rome or among the *qiyan*, the female singers of the Islamic world during the early Abbasid era. Now, in the closing decades of the nineteenth century, the same pattern is about to play out again, as the lowest class of American society lays the groundwork for a revolution in song that is still reverberating in the current day.

The role of slaves as innovators in the history of music is often minimized and sometimes completely ignored—I have a whole shelf of books on European troubadours in front of me, and not a single volume mentions the *qiyan*, whose songs anticipate so many of the themes of the famous poets of Provence. Even within European culture, almost every example of the vernacular love songs of the lower classes from the pre-troubadour period—thousands of songs, by any reasonable estimate—is lost to us. We know they existed, indeed must have flourished, because of the fierce and repeated denunciations from the pulpit over a period of centuries, but few histories of Western music mention them. Only when the European vernacular love song garnered the support and advocacy of the nobility did it emerge from the shadows.

But focusing on the contribution of slave culture to music history is more than just a matter of fairness. The very *essence* of Western song has been shaped by the mentality of the indentured and outcast. We are likely to misunderstand the meaning of these songs if we fail to comprehend the dynamic process at work. The idea that the ruling elite might want to sing *as if they were slaves* is, at first glance, puzzling. Yet now we find it again, in the New World, played out in ways that are sometimes plaintive, but often grotesque.

As we have seen, this slave mentality permeated Western song and poetry long before minstrel shows and blues songs showed up in American cities. In fact, we encounter it in every song or poem that presents the lover in service to the beloved, that treats romance as a kind of bondage to the object of affection. In the West, this attitude took on the label of courtly love, but almost every rule and sentiment included in this noble code was anticipated by earlier songs of slaves. To some degree, the love song evolved in the manner of early Christianity, a system of conduct initially propagated by the outcasts of the classical world, who found that it imparted a much-craved dose of dignity and grandeur to what, from another perspective, was merely the debasement of the victim. Turning the other cheek and giving away one's possessions were peculiar notions, but even the ruling class eventually felt compelled to join in affirming (although not always practicing) these extraordinary injunctions. Perhaps, as some have suggested, the rulers merely realized the usefulness of a worldview that gave the poor a reason to feel good about poverty. But I believe this perspective underestimates the allure of the outsider or the piquancy of a rulebook that flip-flops hierarchies of value. Certainly in the case of song, the noble singers of the troubadour era took particular delight in a carefully cultivated stance that turned them into servants and slaves of their cherished ladies. Even if real relationships bore little resemblance to these imagined ones, the play-acting imparted an erotic charge not dissimilar to the kind dispensed by a dominatrix to her paying customers in our modern metropolises.

Is this just a quirk of history? Absolutely not! The slave and outsider are innovators for the simple reason that they enjoy a freedom of behavior that others in their society do not possess. In a paradoxical way, the slave is sometimes freer than the master. I don't think it is mere coincidence that the Latin term for a freed slave, *libertinus*, serves as the source for our modern word *libertine*, a person who is free from moral restraints, especially in sexual matters. As we saw in chapter six, the *qiyan* of the Islamic world were often granted liberties forbidden to free women—to wear stylish clothing, for example, or leave their faces uncovered. In China during the Han dynasty, we hear of slaves purchased as entertainers for wealthy households, and who could be found for sale in the marketplace wearing lavish embroidered clothing and fancy silken shoes. In ancient Rome, slaves could enjoy the frisson of performing on stage, but members of the ruling class were discouraged from doing so because of the shame associated with such pursuits.

And what about the slaves of antebellum America? Did they enjoy freedoms unknown to their masters? This is harder to determine, because the liberties involved here are psychological and attitudinal, and to trace their history requires us to speculate on the mental states of people long dead. At first glance, African Americans in bondage had no advantages over their owners. Everything they possessed, their closest family relationships, even their life, could be destroyed on the whim of a callous master. Yet their very exclusion from the dominant culture freed them from the stiffness and decorum that made so many of the songs of white America seem vapid and sentimental by comparison. Above all, the slave wasn't hemmed in by the deep-seated Western shame—our inheritance from ancient Rome, as amply documented in chapter four—at expressing heartfelt emotions in public or in the form of song. Few aspects of their African heritage remained in their day-to-day lives, but music stood paramount among these intangible possessions, and here they held this outsider's advantage. Their psychological distance from Western manners opened up paths of expression and delight that were largely closed to the ruling class. No, antebellum slaves received no special freedoms from the hand of the master, but this one they already owned, and no one could wrest it from their grasp.

Perhaps we now also understand why this history of love songs is a *hidden* history. If I have dwelt frequently on outsiders and the excluded in this book, this simply reflects the strange nature of the love song in the Western world. This strangeness can be summed up very simply: we feel compelled to sing about love but are deeply embarrassed by this compulsion. We need the outsider to extricate us from our shame. That's just as true today as it was two thousand years ago. Most hit songs are about love, but you would hardly guess it from the prevailing discourse on popular music, which avoids the subject as though romance were some unspeakable taboo. The especially 'mushy' songs receive endless ridicule—although they are always there, rising up the charts, finding an audience, infuriating earworms we can't get out of our head. Yet the love song is just as resilient as it is shameful, although sometimes it takes an outsider, immune to these attitudes of propriety and decorum, to innovate and disseminate. We focus on these outsiders in this history not to redress past wrongs or impose ideology on the subject, but because the course of history has forced the rest of us to turn to them to learn how to sing about love.

Black Americans played this role of the innovating outsider in the New World. The slave traders and owners never intended this. Their goal was to enrich themselves, not the musical culture of the Americas. Unlike masters in the Islamic world, who sometimes sent promising slaves to a school or teacher in order to develop latent skills as a performer, plantation owners in antebellum America would have derided or feared such concessions to the human chattel that supported their economy. In some instances, legislators forbade musical performances by the slaves. The lawmakers of Georgia instituted fines for any master or overseer who allowed slaves "to beat drums, blow horns, or other loud instruments." In St. John the Baptist Parish in Louisiana, slaves were prohibited "from beating the drum or dancing after sundown." In North Carolina, the state assembly outlawed slave gatherings "for the purpose of drinking and dancing." But some kinds of music-making found encouragement. Work songs tended to improve plantation productivity, and thus supported the slave economy. Music for recreation, provided it did not get out of hand, might also contribute to the efficiency of a well-ordered plantation. Although some owners tried to prevent their slaves from receiving religious instruction, many inculcated Christian values among their captive workforce; as a result, hymns and spirituals flourished, and church music in the United States gained immeasurably from the contributions of African Americans.

Yet black creativity proved so great that it began to displace the musical culture of the masters. Even before the War of Independence, slaves performed for their owners' dances and parties. A slave with a particular gift as a fiddler was a prized possession and could command a premium price on the market. By the mid-nineteenth century, slaves dominated the musical life of the American South. By some accounts, almost every farm had a black fiddler, and one visitor to Charleston, South Carolina claimed that in his trip from Washington, D.C., he had not encountered a single white orchestra south of the Potomac.

Yet even after the Civil War and emancipation, white America was hardly ready to hear love songs from the mouths of former slaves. Songs about work or God might meet with the public's approval. White attendees at a dance might applaud a black band's accompaniment to their revels. But any black man invited to entertain a white audience knew, without being told, to avoid frank expressions of romantic longing, let alone erotic desire. Even as American parlor songs broached these subjects more frequently in the late nineteenth and early twentieth century, the leading African American performers tended to offer the same kind of repertoire that had served them during the days of slavery. I have a collection of songbooks of "authentic" (or so their editors claim) black music from this period, but as I page through these compilations, I find few songs that deal with courtship and romance. Of the 129 songs in English presented by William Francis Allen in his collection *Slave Songs of the United States* (1867), only two deserve to be called love songs—and even these make only the most fleeting reference to romance. I can't find a single love song in *Cabin and Plantation Songs*, first published in 1874 and released in an expanded edition in 1891. Nor are there any love songs in *Calhoun Plantation Songs*, first published in 1901, with an expanded edition appearing in 1907. In Natalie Curtis-Burlin's collection *Negro Folk Songs*, published in four books in New York in 1918 and 1919, I find one love song, the last song in the last volume, "Liza-Jane":

Come ma love, an' go wid' me, Li'l Liza Jane,
Come ma love, an' go wid' me, Li'l Liza Jane,

O, Eliza! Li'l Liza Jane!
O, Eliza! Li'l Liza Jane!
I got a house in Baltimo', Li'l Liza Jane,
Street car runs right by my do', Li'l Liza Jane....
Come, mah love, an' live with me, Li'l Liza Jane,
An' I'll take good care of thee, Li'l Liza Jane.

Is it possible that black Americans didn't sing of love before the days of street cars in Baltimore? That can hardly be true. A commentator writing about slave music in Charleston in 1819 describes them as "plaintive love songs." We also find love themes in nineteenth-century black work songs and other informal kinds of music-making not intended for white audiences. At the conclusion of Allen's 1867 collection of slave songs, we find several love songs in a French dialect contributed by a "lady who heard them sung before the war, on the 'Good Hope' plantation, St. Charles Parish, Louisiana." In other words, black Americans sang about love even during the days of slavery, but not on stage or in public performance.

Our closest approach to African American attitudes to love in nineteenth-century popular music comes to us via the minstrel song. But this version of black culture is distorted by so many agendas that we must exercise great caution before drawing any conclusion from it. These simple tunes embody so many paradoxes and contradictions. Minstrel performers ridiculed African Americans even as they sought to draw on their creative power and vitality; they parodied black culture but often wanted credit for the authenticity with which they represented it; whites "stole" from blacks, yet the blacks also took back from the whites, performing in their own blackface minstrel troupes. As a result, we seek in vain for the proper vantage point that might allow us to find the core of "real" black music in this mish-mash. The people who made these songs weren't purists or preservationists, and a host of other motives—among them, opportunism, elitism, crass commercialism, and out-and-out bigotry—bedevil our efforts to see behind the blackface performers on stage to the music-making of daily life that gave rise to these often grotesque spectacles. But one fact is indisputable: namely, the pervasiveness and popularity of the minstrel song.

Musicologist Dale Cockrell has documented more than five thousand blackface performances on American stages before the year 1844—and about half involve minstrel-type songs. He notes that his sources are sketchy, and suggests that he may have captured only one-quarter of the actual blackface performances from this period. Thomas Rice's enormous success with his caricature of black speech, dance, and music, most notably in his 1828 song "Jump Jim Crow," showed how white performers in blackface could achieve fame and fortune through these crude evocations of plantation life. The 1843 New York appearance of Dan Emmett and his Virginia Minstrels served as a major turning point. Here the entire troupe of performers, including the band, wore blackface, and presented not just a few skits or musical numbers, but an entire show of plantation-type material. Every aspect of the entertainment, from costumes and facial expressions to 'plantation' instruments such as bones, tambourine, and banjo (which advertisements claim were manufactured by the players themselves) served to accentuate the ludicrous and primitive aspect of the spectacle.

The people who attended these performances weren't looking for love songs. But the exaggerated emotional demonstrations of the minstrel idiom were not, strange to say, incompatible with expressions of romantic longing. Even before the Civil War, songwriters had attempted to blend elements of the minstrel idiom with the love song, a tendency most notable in the works of Stephen Foster. The most successful songwriter of his day, Foster had little firsthand exposure to southern or plantation life, but he specialized in crafting tunes that drew on the sentimental attitudes and stereotypes of the region, many of them still widely known today—such as "Camptown Races," "Old Folks at Home" (also known as "Swanee River"), and "My Old Kentucky Home." But his most famous song, "Oh! Susanna" (1848), made clear that elements of black culture, even when reflected through the distorting lens of minstrelsy, could add to the emotional impact of a love song. Here Foster introduces both elements—romance and stereotype—at the very start: "I come from Alabama, wid my banjo on my knee, / I'm gwyne to Louisiana, my true love for to see." By any measure, this is a strange song, although it is such a familiar bit of Americana most of us don't notice it peculiarities. Many of the words are clumsy if not contradictory ("it rain'd all night the day I left, the weather it was dry") and some of the lyrics are so weighted down with racial caricature that they are simply omitted, and rightly so, when the song is performed nowadays. But the public's receptivity, indeed extraordinary enthusiasm, for a minstrel *love* song about a separated black couple is both surprising and revealing in the context of mid-nineteenth-century America. Anticipating the later rise of blues, gospel, and other popular styles of commercial music, the success of "Oh! Susanna" indicates that even in the days of slavery, white audiences intuitively felt that the emotional authenticity of a song, its ability to move beyond sentimentality into a deeper expression of feeling, was enhanced by a black perspective, even a *faux* one adopted second-hand by a white composer. At a time when sales of five thousand copies constituted a huge hit, "Oh! Susanna" allegedly sold 100,000 copies, and in the two years following its release at least thirty different versions by sixteen publishers flooded the market—although Foster may have made little or no money from these copycat editions (anticipating the future of black American music in this manner as well).

Many odd hybrids have surfaced in American music over the years, from Hawaiian guitar in tango bands to German polkas played by Mexican Americans in Texas, but the marriage of love song and minstrelsy must rank among the most awkward and unlikely. Yet in *Minstrel Songs Old and New*, published in 1882, almost 20 percent of the compositions are love songs, and by the time we get to the series of *Famous American Coon, Lullaby and Plantation Songs*, a compilation of minstrel tunes released in several volumes in England around the turn of the century, close to half of the works selected are about romantic relationships. The minstrel song would never serve as a trustworthy or suitable vehicle for expressing the black perspective on love, or other matters, but its evolution makes clear that even an idiom that aimed to ridicule and denigrate the culture of the nation's former slaves needed to adapt as commercial interests grasped the broader possibilities of African American music.

A series of events from the turn of the century hint at the ways black Americans would revolutionize the love song. The fad for ragtime music, for example, allowed black composers a different kind of fame, as instigators of a new performance style marked by its intricacy and technical demands. Although ragtime is best known as instrumental music, its leading exponents often composed love songs, with rag rhythms or in other styles. Even Scott Joplin, the most famous exponent of this music, published two love songs in waltz time—"Please Say You Will" and "A Picture of Her Face"—four years before he released his first rag, and would continue to write romantic songs long after he achieved considerable fame for his syncopated piano pieces. We know less about the first stirrings of jazz music, heard in New Orleans around this time, but love songs clearly figured in the repertoires of the early bands. Meanwhile, other black songwriters composed mainstream popular songs in the style of sentimental parlor ballads, or wrote minstrel-style works with less denigrating stereotypes and more plausible emotional content.

But the big breakthrough took place outside of the major cities and centers of commerce, in the most impoverished rural communities of the American South. Here a completely new style of love song emerged virtually unnoticed by the music industry, a harsh and poignant style of lyrical expression that we now call the blues. This bold, unapologetic style would serve as the antidote to the excessive sentimentality and clichés of parlor ballads, and impart a new vitality to American popular music. In time, the blues sensibility would impact more mainstream styles, imparting an edgier and sassier tone to American commercial music, and with decisive results. Instead of falling behind the Europeans, whose frank and satirical cabaret songs seemed destined to set the tone for twentieth-century popular culture, the U.S. music business now had something different to offer, even more daring and unconventional, and with the potential to blend with other idioms and thus set the stage for a series of future musical innovations—spawning R&B, rock 'n' roll, and other vibrant performance styles.

But all this is still far in the future. In its earliest days, blues had no name, and hardly registered in the public consciousness. Record companies didn't market blues recordings until the 1920s—when the enormous success of Mamie Smith's "Crazy Blues" turned this previously little-known musical style into an important commercial category. But blues music had been around for at least two decades by that time. Howard W. Odum, a scholar who started collecting African American folk music in the rural South around 1909, believed that an important change had taken place shortly after the turn of the century, when secular songs gained in popularity in black communities where religious music had previously predominated. What subjects came to the forefront in these "social songs," as Odum described them? "Woman holds first place among the themes sung by the Negro," he wrote, adding that one could learn a great deal about the prevalent conceptions of love and sex from this body of music. These were different from the hackneyed love songs played in the parlors and social gatherings of white America. Odum noted that these secular songs of rural blacks could include both the "filthiest thoughts" and "loftiest sentiments."

Other listeners encountered this new type of song, frequently in unexpected locales, and were often surprised by what they heard. In 1901 and 1902, Harvard archaeologist Charles Peabody spent time in Mississippi supervising a dig, and was so struck by the singing of his hired workers that he wrote an article about it for the *Journal of American Folk-Lore*. He noted the prevalence of "hard luck tales" and "love themes" in these songs, and provided examples that show how far these lyrics departed from the sentimental tone of commercial popular music. A typical example: "The reason I loves my baby so, / 'Case when she gets five dollars she give me fo'." Around this same time, circa 1903, W. C. Handy discovered the blues at a train station in Tutwiler, Mississippi, where he heard a black musician singing an eerie lament while accompanying himself on slide guitar played with a knife to bend the notes. In New Orleans, probably during this same period, jazz pianist Jelly Roll Morton heard his first blues song, performed by a woman named Mamie Desdunes:

> If you can't give a dollar, give me a lousy dime,
> Can't give a dollar, give me a lousy dime.
> I wanna feed that hungry man of mine.

Jazz musicians in New Orleans paid close attention to blues music of this sort, even as most of urban America remained ignorant of it. We lack many details of the specific circumstances that gave birth to jazz, but clearly the incorporation of blues music into the repertoires of local bands played a key role in this process. Histories of early jazz tend to focus on instrumentalists, the horn players and pianists who led the most famous bands, but vocal blues and other brazen love songs were part of the allure of this music from the very start. Buddy Bolden, often acknowledged as the first jazz musician, performed numerous songs of this sort, for example his version of "Make Me a Pallet on the Floor":

> Make me a pallet on the floor,
> Make it soft, make it low,
> So your sweet man will never know.

Or "Careless Love," another staple of Bolden's repertoire:

> Ain't it hard to love another woman's man.
> You can't get him when you want him,
> You have to catch him when you can.

Several sources testify to the importance of blues in Bolden's repertoire. The details are sketchy and no recordings have survived, but the evidence suggests that this artist played a key role in concocting the recipe that would propel American music of the ensuing decades—a mixture of the syncopated rhythms of ragtime with the bent notes and the frank lyrics of blues music.

Audiences in mainstream America, circa 1900, would have been shocked and outraged by love songs of this sort. In any event, music publishers and the early recording companies didn't care to find out whether a commercial market existed for such fare—at least not yet. The most innovative African American love songs ignored the proprieties of the day. They would eventually shake up everything with their bawdiness and cynicism, their shameless admission (and sometimes celebration) of adultery and infidelity, but not until two decades had elapsed. In the meantime, mainstream American listeners satisfied themselves with maudlin love songs, such "A Bird in a Gilded Cage" (1900), "I Love You Truly" (1901), "Sweet Adeline" (1903), and "In the Shade of the Old Apple Tree" (1905)—each one a million-seller. Here's what a love song in white America sounded like at the turn of the century:

> I love you truly, truly dear,
> Life with its sorrow, life with its tear
> Fades into dreams when I feel you are near
> For I love you truly, truly dear.

With the benefit of hindsight, we can see how tepid fare of this sort would eventually get displaced by the more robust music of black America. The only questions were how and when.

When a love lyric of this period broached dicey topics, as did Hughie Cannon's "Won't You Come Home Bill Bailey" (1902), with its hints of adultery, the song required a dose of blackness before it gained acceptance from the general public. "Bill Bailey" was frequently performed in blackface, and the cover of its sheet music prominently featured an image of a feuding black couple. Two years later, the same composer published "Frankie and Johnny," drawing on preexisting material, and once again consumers needed assurance that this ballad about murderous lovers, perhaps a pimp and his prostitute, referred to African American domestic troubles. Cannon published the song under the name "He Done Me Wrong," adapting the lyrics and adding the subtitle "Death of Bill Bailey" to indicate that the black man immortalized in his previous hit song had finally got his comeuppance. To seal the deal, the sheet music featured a photo of blackface performers Lambert & Pierce.

Nothing in the usual lyrics to "Frankie and Johnny" indicates the skin color of this unhappy duo, but even without seeing the sheet music, many would have simply assumed they were black. According to most accounts, the song drew on a real incident involving an African American couple in St. Louis, although some parts of it seem to predate that event. (In a curious historical twist, the location where the shooting occurred is on roughly the same spot where the St. Louis Blues, a professional hockey team named after the musical idiom, plays its home games.) Some years later, when Thomas Hart Benton painted a scene from the story of "Frankie and Johnny" as part of his mural project at the Missouri State Capitol, he made this assumption explicit, depicting a black woman shooting a black man in the buttocks. Some public outcry resulted, but not due to the racial stereotypes involved—citizens were outraged because the artist had dared portray a black lowlife couple on the wall of a respectable government building.

Real black love songs would soon trump all this, standing out as even more transgressive and unconventional than these white imitations. Around a decade after "Bill Bailey," blues music first arrived in the households of mainstream America, initially in the form of sheet music and later via recordings. These works may have struck early listeners as a novelty or passing fad in the music business, but the blues market demonstrated remarkable versatility and staying power. In time, the many success stories—of W. C. Handy, Mamie Smith, Bessie Smith, Blind Lemon Jefferson, and others—proved that black songs composed and performed by black Americans had more commercial potential than even the most artful minstrel works. But the importance of blues goes far beyond matters of music industry finances or even racial equality. The very nature of the love song in the modern world would now change as a result of the emergence of this new musical style.

I would go so far as to claim that black music of this period signals the most important shift in songs about romance—perhaps even in *attitudes* about romance—since the dawn of the troubadours. The delicate sensibilities and chaste sentiments of American parlor songs now seemed stale and clichéd in the face of this new music, which willingly broached each and every type of love entanglement, whether innocent or lustful, sanctioned or forbidden, caressing or violent, uplifting or degrading. The tone of these songs proved as variable as the subject matter. A wistful sentimentality sometimes predominated, but also cynicism, irony, or out-and-out anger. A blues song might include empty promises, bald-faced lies, dirty double meanings, taunts, boasts, ridicule, even violent threats, all in the name of love.

The music business sometimes imposed limits on what could be described in these songs—for example, Lucille Bogan's dirty version of "Shave 'Em Dry" went unreleased for a half century—but I'm just as surprised at what was allowed. Even explicit sexual references showed up on these records, provided they were cloaked in the thinnest of metaphors. Listeners quickly figured out that Ma Rainey wasn't really singing about fishing when she declared:

> If you don't like my ocean don't fish in my sea.
> Don't like my ocean don't fish in my sea.
> Stay out of my valley and let my mountain be.

And the same is true of Bessie Smith's testament to her lover's swimming skills:

> He's a deep-sea diver with a stroke that can't go wrong.
> He's a deep-sea diver with a stroke that can't go wrong.
> He can touch the bottom and his wind holds out so long.

Maggie Jones offered to let anybody try her cabbage. Bessie Smith wanted a little sugar in her bowl. Lonnie Johnson bragged about the quality of his jelly roll. Victoria Spivey declared that her handy man could thread her needle and chop her meat.

But these songs did more than just breach sexual taboos. The blues soon proved as transgressive in presenting images of violence as in conjuring up scenes of eroticism. "My man beat me last night with five feet of copper coil," Ma Rainey sings in "Sweet Rough Man," and proceeds to describe the various injuries inflicted by her lover, presented with a vivid masochism unprecedented in early styles of commercial music: "He keeps my lips split, my eyes as black as jet, / But the way he love me, make me soon forget." But in other Ma Rainey songs, the woman is the aggressor. In "Leaving This Morning," she brags about packing a Gatling gun, the predecessor of modern automatic weapons, to handle her no-good man. And in "Broken Hearted Blues," she murders the man, and apparently innocent bystanders as well: "Good morning, Judge, Mama Rainey's done raised sand, / She's killed everybody, Judge, she's even killed her man."

Guns appear with surprising frequency in this new style of love song. In his "22–20 Blues," Skip James boasts about his willingness to cut his woman "half in two" with his firearm. "If I send for my baby and she don't come," he sings, "all the doctors in Wisconsin, they won't help her none." There is no 22–20 gun, but this doesn't stop James from asserting the superiority of his firearm. But other blues musicians preferred different guns—for example Roosevelt Sykes who, in his "44 Blues," complains about getting a sore shoulder from packing heat in the name of love. Robert Johnson, probably inspired by James, recorded "32–20 Blues," another infidelity song in which the gun gets as much attention as the unfaithful lover. By the time we get to Louisiana Red's "Sweetblood Call," frequently requested by fans at his performances, love is but a dim memory, obliterated by a deranged jealousy: "I'll have a hard time missing you baby with my pistol in your mouth / You maybe thinking of going North but your brains are staying South."

Guns may have been favored, but knives also had their advocates among black singers during the early days of the blues. In "A to Z Blues" (1924) Billy Higgins threatens to cut Josie Miles's head "four different ways, long, short, deep and wide"—an image that proved so popular Blind Willie McTell adopted the song and recorded it on several occasions. Geeshie Wiley wants to slit her lover's throat and stare at him while he dies; Peg Leg Howell has similar plans, but adds that he wants to drink his woman's blood. In "If You Want Me to Love You," Georgia Tom declares:

> You got to take all your money, throw it against the wall
> You take what sticks, and I'll take what falls....
> If you want me to love you, the last thing you got to do...
> Take a butcher knife, cut off your head,
> Send me a telegram that your heart is dead.

I note, for what it's worth, that Georgia Tom is better known under the name Thomas Dorsey—he is frequently acknowledged as the "father of gospel music" and is best remembered for songs such as "Peace in the Valley" and "Take My Hand, Precious Lord."

Not every love song by a blues artist delved into taboo or unsavory subjects. Many blues drew on the same themes and imagery addressed in traditional lyrics of romance, not much different from what we find in Petrarch or the *Carmina Burana*. The themes of loneliness, the pain of separation, and the anguish of rejection were even more prominent in blues music than eroticism and boastful violence. If anything, these time-honored symptoms of lovesickness were heightened or magnified in the context of this new performance style—so much so that the very term *blues* came to signify an emotional state, an agony akin to what St. John of the Cross called "the dark night of the soul," only transferred here to purely secular settings. The "dirty parts" may have spurred record sales during the 1920s and 1930s, with the condemnation of family members and church leaders only adding to the allure of these sultry songs, but over the long term blues thrived as a musical idiom and gained respect as an artistic force because it delved further and deeper into complex "feelings" than other genres of love music. Ostensibly the most carnal kind of tune, the blues also demanded respect as the most acutely *psychological*, with all the contradictions that term came to symbolize in the modern age.

The blues entered the American mainstream in several distinct waves. In its first manifestation, the blues showed up in retail outlets in the form of sheet music, and though some of these compositions, most notably W.C. Handy's "St. Louis Blues" (1914) would enjoy enormous success—ASCAP would later claim that Handy's work was the second most frequently recorded song during the first half of the twentieth century, trailing only "Silent Night"—this popularity was slow in building. Three years after writing his most famous song, Handy was still working with a band at a country club, and hoping to get another hour in his time slot so that each musician could make an extra dollar. The breakthrough for Handy, as for so many other musicians and composers, came via recordings, which tapped into a much larger potential audience, many of whom would never purchase sheet music or own a musical instrument. Year later Handy recounted his astonishment at the royalty check he received for Earl Fuller's 1917 recording of his "Beale Street Blues," and even remembered the exact amount: $1,857 (equivalent to around $35,000 in current dollars). He adds that he spent the next day celebrating, and paying off all his debts.

Recordings of blues music soon turned other black artists into national stars. Mamie Smith's "Crazy Blues," recorded in August 1920, sold seventy-five thousand copies within the first month and inspired a host of imitators. "One of the phonograph companies made over four million dollars on the Blues," a writer announced in *The Metronome* a few months later. "Now every phonograph company has a colored girl recording. Blues are here to stay." Paramount hired Ma Rainey and featured her on close to a hundred tracks during the 1920s. Columbia backed Rainey's protégée Bessie Smith, whose first release, "Downhearted Blues," sold more than 750,000 copies in just six months, and helped turn this blues diva into the highest-earning black entertainer of the era. Black Swan, founded by Handy's partner Harry Pace, recorded Ethel Waters. Victor promoted Sippie Wallace and Victoria Spivey, and the latter also recorded for Okeh. Alberta Hunter made records for *all* of these labels. Even Thomas Edison jumped on the bandwagon, and though he had little impact on the blues market, the entry of the inventor of the phonograph into the market for "race recordings" (as the new category of black music targeted at black consumers was called at the time) showed how much the business had changed in the face of this new type of song.

The fame generated by these recordings was supplemented by expanding opportunities for blues stars to perform on the road. At its peak in the 1920s, Theater Owners Booking Association (TOBA) flourished as the leading promoter of African American live entertainment, and its more than one hundred members in both the North and South constituted a vaudeville circuit for blues singers and other black performers. Working conditions and financial dealings stirred up complaints—entertainers on the circuit, run mostly by white owners, often quipped that TOBA stood for "tough on black asses." But the rise of TOBA and the emergence of race records signaled a turning point in American music. The black audience now represented a large enough commercial market for its tastes and demands to support businesses, attract entrepreneurs, and turn a few performers into well-known stars.

But a different kind of blues, even more raw and untamed, showed up in American households during the late 1920s. This style of music, sometimes called "country blues" or "folk blues," came out of some of the poorest, least urbanized parts of the South. Unlike the "classic blues" (as the music of Ma Rainey and Bessie Smith is now known), this less polished idiom was performed mostly by men who accompanied themselves on guitar. They didn't rely on professional songwriters or sheet music for their repertoire but created it themselves, or borrowed it from other local musicians, or shared it as part of an oral/aural tradition. The songs themselves represented a rejection of many of the most cherished and time-honored practices of Western music. The formal structures were fluid: a song might follow a twelve-bar blues form, then switch to an eleven- or thirteen- or twelve-and-a-half-bar chorus. The individual notes, both sung and played on guitar, often got bent or distorted in ways that conventional music notation could not convey. To create these characteristic sliding sounds, a guitarist might play his instrument with a knife, comb, bone, or bottle-top—something stronger than weak human flesh—torturing the strings to make them speak the truth. The frailties of the flesh also figured in the lyrics, which often combined the sensibility of a love song with the fervor of a religious exhortation, appealing to listeners with their willingness to probe pathos and despair, and occasionally exhilaration and epiphany, with an immediacy few commercial songwriters could match.

This rural music had lingered at the margins of American society for a long time, perhaps a quarter of a century or longer, before the record industry paid attention to it. But in 1926 Paramount took a chance on Blind Lemon Jefferson, an itinerant blues singer who often played on the streets of his native Texas. His recordings sold so well that Jefferson rose to the top of Paramount's roster—he would be their biggest star for the rest of the decade, and inspire the label and its competitors to find other country blues singers who might generate hit recordings.

Between 1926 and 1930, record companies made frequent field trips to southern cities seeking to discover black talent with commercial potential. They traveled to New Orleans to record local musicians on seven occasions, made eight trips to Dallas, visited Memphis eleven times and, their favorite destination, Atlanta seventeen times. These companies also brought black musicians north to record at professional studios. Some of the artists they promoted, such as Charley Patton and Blind Blake, sold well, while others, such as Son House and Skip James, left behind powerful recordings now considered classics but mostly ignored at the time of their release. Robert Johnson (1911–38) stands out as the most famous of the singing blues guitarists, his reputation enhanced by an oft-told tale about his selling his soul to the devil in exchange for his musical talent. But by the time he made his recordings in 1936 and 1937, the boom in blues music had already subsided, a victim of changing tastes and the economic impact on the music business of the Great Depression.

But blues left a lasting impact on how commercial musicians sang about love—and would continue to do so for many years to come. We will explore in the next chapter how rock stars of the 1950s and 1960s turned to blues musicians for inspiration as they rewrote the rule book of love songs during the Cold War era. But this same process of assimilation also took place, albeit in a different direction, back in the 1920s and 1930s. Jazz musicians were the first to learn from the blues; indeed, they had done so long before record labels recognized the importance of either style. The two idioms were close enough that jazz players could mix effortlessly with blues stars—hear, for example, Louis Armstrong accompany Bessie Smith or Coleman Hawkins alongside Mamie Smith. But as it evolved, jazz offered a slightly different perspective on courtship and romance, echoing some of the concerns of the blues, but adding new angles as well.

I doubt that jazz players of the 1920s and 1930s thought much about their impact on American attitudes toward love. Many of the early jazz stars focused on playing the horn or the piano, and left the crooning of romantic lyrics to others. But when they did sing, these musicians—and the tunesmiths who wrote for them—made clear that the Jazz Age had unleashed new attitudes about relationships between the sexes. Did jazz create these freer, looser ways of courting? No, not entirely. But the musicians and songwriters of the era announced these changes more stridently than anyone else, and by giving them such ardent expression, they imparted momentum and, perhaps more important, a degree of *glamour* to the changes afoot. I will stop short of claiming that blacks taught the rest of America a new way of loving, but clearly black creative talent (and whites who imitated or drew inspiration from them) set the tone at every step in this process.

Many individuals played a part in this transformation. A precise measurement or even a provisional ranking is impossible, but the roster of innovators must include George and Ira Gershwin, Irving Berlin, Fats Waller, Bessie Smith, Louis

Armstrong, Bing Crosby, Cole Porter, Al Jolson, Ethel Waters, and many, many others. I can't prove the chain of cause and effect, but I suspect that many Americans started talking and thinking about romance in different ways because they heard a song performed or composed by one of these artists. In many instances, the words may have been written by a Jewish songwriter, such as Berlin or Ira Gershwin, or another outsider to black culture. But the lyricist had clearly observed African American music and attitudes at close hand. This process took place repeatedly, day after day, at the heart of the American music industry...and the result is something we now call the Jazz Age. No, I can't prove any of this, and others might reverse the whole process, postulating a social ferment that started among the general public and only gradually found expression in popular song. Yet the end result, in either scenario, is the same: Americans thought differently about courtship and love, and their songs celebrated this new state of affairs.

How do we describe this new attitude? It's sassy and irreverent. Bold and confident. Frequently curt and in-your-face, but not without a touch of irony or self-reflection. The values of parents and community leaders are rarely attacked directly in these songs; rather they have simply disappeared from view. The moral tone is harder to pin down These tunes tended to avoid vulgarity but often delighted in hints of indecency. Mainstream audiences enjoyed this suggestive ambiguity, exemplified in songs such as "Oh, Lady Be Good!," "Ain't Misbehavin'," "Sweet Georgia Brown," "How Come You Do Me Like You Do?," or "I Wish I Could Shimmy Like My Sister Kate." True, jazz players occasionally touched on a pathos approaching that of the deep blues, as in "St. James Infirmary," a love song delivered to a corpse, or "(What Did I Do to Be So) Black and Blue." But these explorations of despair proved the exception. If the blues recordings of the era showed a kinship with old-school tragedy, the jazz sensibility fit more comfortably with the Bacchanalian excesses of the day. Jazz music encouraged you to party, even if sometimes it was just a party of two.

I'll explore these issues in more detail in the next chapter. But before moving on, we need to take a look elsewhere in the Americas, where we find musical developments similar to those playing out in the United States. Wherever large numbers of African slaves had been brought—in Central and South America, and throughout the Caribbean—new song styles emerged that would eventually enter and influence the broader currents of Western music. Not all of this music dealt with love. Many of the musical innovations of Africans in the New World came to the forefront in instrumental performances for dancers (although here, too, the songs influenced romantic relationships). Some of the most vibrant vocal traditions, such as calypso in Trinidad and samba in Brazil, frequently served up political commentary or dealt with issues of communal pride and solidarity. In the Dominican Republic, the dictator Rafael Trujillo could even rely on *merengue* music as a form of propaganda and social control, with songs praising his achievements, the futility of his enemies, the grandeur of the nation under his rule. At the other extreme, some of the *mento* songs from Jamaica—predecessors of ska and reggae—describe food and recipes, or address other humble aspects of everyday life. But in every setting, the transplanted Africans and their progeny eventually found ways of merging their new musical perspectives with the timeless dialogue about love and sex. And even when they didn't sing about it, the music itself struck many listeners—and religious leaders—as inherently erotic, perhaps morally dangerous. The lyrics themselves might seem innocent or innocuous, or perhaps the song didn't even have words. But the rhythms themselves gained a reputation as instigators of licentiousness.

The association of sin and black dance in the Americas probably dates back to the arrival of the very first slaves. The Jesuit Peter Claver (1581–1684), later canonized and acknowledged as the "patron saint of the slave," allegedly felt such compassion for the Africans in bondage in Cartagena that he pressed his lips to their ulcerous sores—yet he also prohibited their dances and seized their drums. In 1763, the Bishop of Popayán banned several types of "dishonest and provocative" dances under "pain of excommunication." Commenting on the exciting dances he saw while visiting Peru in 1865, Louis Moreau Gottschalk noted that "although very picturesque," these were "not such as prudent mothers permit their daughters to indulge in." Indeed, community and religious leaders had many reasons to fear black dancing. Even when it didn't lead directly to fornication, it made them uneasy with its pagan associations and ecstatic qualities. But, again and again, we find them reacting specifically to the erotic aspects of these dances, and the threat they posed to public morals.

These were mostly local skirmishes, but the furor over the tango developed into an international incident. This dance and its accompanying music even today stand out in popular culture as the prototype of musical eroticism, and if the tango is no longer quite so scandalous, it has hardly lost its reputation as sensual and seductive. As with jazz and blues, the tango's origins are difficult to unravel. Yet the new dance clearly drew, in varying degrees, on a hodgepodge of European, African, and Latin American elements. We can trace the influence of the Cuban *habanera*, the Uruguayan *candombe*, and the homegrown Argentine *milonga*, the immediate predecessor of the tango, each of these African-European hybrids boasting its own complex genealogy. Yet a German instrument would eventually supply the trademark sound of the tango, the bandoneon, a relative of the accordion and concertina. Exponents of the tango clearly borrowed, as well, from the pervasive European social dances of Argentine nightlife—the waltz, the polka, the mazurka, the schottische, and other styles that Buenos Aires immigrants had brought with them from the Old World. The words of tango songs, typically expressive of passionate and sometimes tragic love, were very much in keeping with the Western tradition of romantic lyrics, but often also revealed that particular intensity and fatalism, tinged with allusions to violence and the libido, already familiar to us from our look at the blues. Indeed Ramón Gómez de la Serna's striking description of this distinctive Argentine style inevitably reminds us of the American blues tradition. "One plays and sings other music to heal emotional wounds," he explained. "One plays and sings the tango to open and stir a wound."

The tango first conquered Buenos Aires, starting in the working-class neighborhoods but later finding its way into the most elegant dance halls and formal balls. Long before U.S. labels paid attention to jazz or blues, their Argentine counterparts jumped on the tango bandwagon, recording hundreds of tracks, while publishers captured the faddish new sound in sheet music. Both the music and its dance, with its close and often intimate body contact—almost more an embrace or swoon than a pattern of footwork—soon attracted fanatical fans, and equally fervent critics, outside Argentina. Perhaps, as some suspect, Argentine sailors brought the tango with them to the port city of Marseille. Or the many Buenos Aires natives in Paris shortly after the turn of the century, such as pianist Alberto López Buchardo and dancer Casimiro Aín, may have laid the groundwork for France's later tangomania. Certainly a milestone event took place around 1907, when the Buenos Aires–based music company Gath & Chaves decided to record tango music in Paris featuring Ángel Villoldo, Alfredo Gobbi and his wife, Chilean Flora Rodríguez. Yet even at this stage, few Europeans knew about this music. Perhaps the decisive turning point came a few years later, when Argentine playboy and author Ricardo Güiraldes shocked and delighted onlookers by demonstrating the tango at a fashionable Parisian salon.

In any event, by 1913 Parisians not only knew about tango but were deeply divided by it. "It has spread all over Paris," announced caricaturist Sem (Georges Goursat), who decided the city ought to be renamed "Tangoville." "There are tango tea parties, tango exhibitions, tango lectures. Half of Paris rubs against the other half. The whole city jerks: it's got the tango under the skin." And soon London, Berlin, Rome, and the other cultural centers of Europe followed the example of Paris. Letters filled with outspoken opinions about the new fad poured into the offices of *The Times* in London, and numerous magazines covered the controversy. Even royalty got involved in the debate. When Grand Duke Michael of Russia hosted a ball at Kenwood in Hampstead during the summer of 1913, the tango was omitted from a demonstration of new dances planned for the event—out of deference to Queen Mary. But the queen expressed such disappointment at this decision that an impromptu tango was organized, much to the delight of the royal onlooker, who declared herself charmed by the proceedings.

But even a queen's blessing could not stifle opposition in other quarters. Kaiser Wilhelm II prohibited German officers in uniform from dancing the tango, or even attending social gatherings where others engaged in such scandalous behavior. Bishops and cardinals attacked the sinful dance, and eventually the pope was called upon to offer a verdict. Pope Pius X asked for a private demonstration of the new fad sweeping Christendom, but even the restrained rendition of the tango staged for his consideration proved too much for the pontiff. He wondered why Christians would adopt the "barbarian contortions of Negroes and Indians," and suggested that young people ought to dance the *furlana*, a comparatively tame folk dance that hailed (like the pope himself) from northern Italy, a pleasing alternative in which physical contact went no further than clasped hands. This proclamation from the Vatican was widely covered in the press, but efforts by the devout to replace the seductive tango with the "pope's dance" failed to halt the rising popularity of the Argentine import.

Even the United States, which tango lyricist Cátulo Castillo had declared a "country unreachable for the tango," was now embracing the dance. Maurice Mouvet, who had learned the tango in Paris, opened a New York dance studio in 1911, where he taught his tango techniques for $25 per hour. But Vernon and Irene Castle had even more impact when they danced a tango in a 1913 Broadway production. A reviewer at the time announced that this show-stopping interlude had "eliminated the waltz from the musical comedy stage and substituted a vogue for dances of Western origin." But even this success paled in comparison to the sensation caused by Rudolph Valentino when he danced a highly eroticized tango, with lots of crotch-to-crotch contact, in the 1921 film *The Four Horsemen of the Apocalypse*. One of the most popular movies of its era, this film brought the tango into Middle America. In 1924 a survey of American high school students asked them to name their favorite film, and both teenage boys and girls agreed on their top pick: *The Four Horsemen of the Apocalypse*. For better or worse, the tango and its celebration of sexualized dancing had not only gone mainstream, but now turned up in the romantic fantasies of millions of young Americans.

Was this the moment when the genie got out of the bottle? Is this when American youth decided that popular culture offered a better blueprint for personal fulfillment than the advice dispensed by parents and pulpit? We can never answer that question with any finality. But clearly a change was taking place. The counterculture of the 1960s may get more attention nowadays as the perpetrator of the generation gap, but almost every element of this later disjunction was prefigured in the 1920s. Certainly from this point forward, popular music will increasingly set the tone for generational conflict and debates on the 'sins' of the youngsters. And almost every later controversy on music and morals will follow the same pattern we have traced here in our exploration of the blues and tango.

In fact, this conforms to the pattern we've witnessed over and over again in previous chapters of this book. A disruptive force enters into the DNA of the love song, almost always inserted by outsiders to the power structure, whether a woman from Lesbos, a Muslim invader of Europe, or a slave from Africa. Almost as often, the path of dissemination moves from south to north, from Provence or the Mississippi Delta or Buenos Aires or North Africa. At some undefined moment, a tipping point arrives, and the elites take over (and often take credit for) this new way of singing about love. A radical idea has moved from the margins into the center of musical culture and enjoys its moment of triumph. But not for long. For the same process is destined to happen again and again and again.

Let's call this the dialectic of the love song. A cultural force turns into its opposite, the evil songs of sinners get transformed into the approved soundtrack for the power brokers and the morally upright. In ancient times or the Middle Ages, the process by which this turnabout took place was almost always hidden from view. The songs don't show up on our historical radar screen until they have already gained admittance to the palace precincts. Much of the evidence for their earlier disreputable evolution was either left undocumented or destroyed after the fact. In earlier chapters, I've tried to cut through this smokescreen, piece together the facts and show the ways in which the scandalous love songs of outsiders got incorporated into the respected cultural inheritance of insiders; but, as you have seen, considerable sleuthing and questioning of conventional historical accounts is required. But from this moment on, the process of change and assimilation is well documented and the evidence easy to gather. The ensuing revolutions in the love song mounted by outsiders—whether a poor kid named Elvis from Tupelo, Mississippi; long-haired lads from Liverpool; punkers at CBGB; or hip-hoppers in the South Bronx—are not only well known and often discussed. They are, in fact, cherished as milestones of modern liberation and generational coming-of-age. In short, the recurring turmoil in the evolution of the love song, once hidden from view, will now take center stage in pop culture.

CHAPTER 15

Crooners, Torch Songs, and Bobby-Soxers

Swing music is nothing but orchestrated sex...a phallic symbol set to sound.—Blue Barron

Technology changes everything, even the love song. At the most obvious level, technology-driven entrepreneurs built large businesses on the preservation and dissemination of these songs—first through the publication of musical scores and later via the magic of recordings. But innovation even altered the tone and mood of these songs, impacting both the ways they were sung and how audiences heard them.

The scientists who developed improved microphones and systems for electronic sound amplification during the 1920s had no notion that they would intensify the emotional impact and eroticism of popular music. But they did just that. These new devices managed to capture more nuances in vocal delivery, both in the recording studio and live performance. Before this technical assistance came to their rescue, singers entertaining large audiences had to bellow, shout, and project their voice to the back row. You can hear this, for example, in Bessie Smith's recordings, or the early vocal work by Louis Armstrong—in his 1926 performance of "Georgia Grind," he and his wife Lil Hardin Armstrong are singing their duet with such forcefulness that any flirtatiousness in their give-and-take is overwhelmed by the sheer power of their delivery. But just a few years later, Armstrong, and a whole generation of popular singers, had learned to take full advantage of the emerging technologies. Compare Armstrong's 1926 effort with his "Body and Soul" and "Confessin'" from 1930, or "Star Dust" and "I Surrender, Dear" from 1931, and see how far the American love song had changed in just five years. A new intimacy has entered the music.

And the same thing happened at the receiving end. Many music historians have described the growth of radio during the 1920s, but I would call attention to the first automobile radio, offered as an option by Chevrolet in 1922, as an equally important milestone in the history of the love song. A quarter of a century elapsed before most American cars came equipped with sound, but from the start this innovation seemed destined to accelerate the romantic learning curve of the general public. The automobile itself opened up possibilities of intimacy to a degree unknown to previous generations of couples, who often conducted every step in their courtship under watchful eyes. This now changed. When I proposed marriage to my wife, I spent a considerable amount of time planning how and where to pop the question for the maximum effect—I eventually made my move on the middle of the Golden Gate Bridge during a rainstorm (the storm was not part of my plan). But I first did some research, and learned that the most common location for a marriage proposal is inside an automobile. How dreary, I thought—but then realized that the car was perhaps the most appropriate place to make that final commitment, since so many of the preliminaries had probably taken place in that same confined, quasi-private spot. And if the car on its own changed American romance, imagine what happened when Detroit added romantic music on the radio.

Many of the early efforts to create a sexier soundtrack to modern life now seem laughable in retrospect. Rudy Vallée sang through a megaphone so that he could impart a warm, confidential tone to his phrases, and avoid the shouting of his peers. As technology advanced, Vallée was reluctant to give up the device—a prop that fans associated with this celebrity—but he eventually had his megaphone wired and amplified. This might seem a mere gimmick or stunt, but Vallée's makeshift was a genuine innovation, nothing less than the introduction of intimacy into live performances of pop music. And fans—especially female fans—responded with unprecedented enthusiasm, indeed almost hysteria. Here we see the first stirrings of the crowd manias that would recur in popular music in decades to come. Women sometimes screamed so loudly during Vallée's performances that his voice couldn't be heard over the din. When reporter Jane Dixon tried to get backstage to interview Vallée after a Brooklyn performance, she had to fight her way through "a hundred or more women suffering from the Vallée complex" just to get to the stage door. When she finally reached the star, he entertained her with numerous anecdotes about over-the-top lady fans, including the woman who "insists she is already Mrs. Vallée, and her husband and five children cannot persuade her she is wrong." Another female admirer from the western United States sent the singer letters every day, sharing marriage plans, and when she traveled to New York tried to move into Vallée's apartment. "The fact that she is already married and has a daughter older than myself doesn't mean a thing to her," the singer added.

I don't think it's a coincidence that the first commercial vocalist to popularize singing in an understated, conversational manner set off such an intense reaction. Music writers who dismiss Vallée and his megaphone as a corny figure from the past are missing the point. He gave the public the first taste of what they craved: the fantasy of a one-on-one relationship with a music star. And for those who laugh at the megaphone, I'll note that Justin Bieber relied on it to sing from the balcony of Universal Music's Paris office in 2012, and a large group of female fans screamed their approval from below.

Around this same time, Al Jolson benefited from the greatest technology boost of them all—the introduction of talking (and singing) motion pictures. This brought direct connection with the star to a new level. Given the lead role in the first 'talkie', Jolson took full advantage of this new sensual medium, emoting for close-up shots and sometimes staring directly into the camera. Yet every other aspect of his performance still reeked of the nineteenth century: the declamatory singing style, the exaggerated gestures and, above all, the blackface evocation of minstrelsy. Jolson could make only a few faltering steps toward defining the new technology-driven love song for the modern age. Someone else, more visionary and less wedded to the past, with a hipper sensibility than either Vallée or Jolson, would need to take the next leap forward.

This prototype hipster would be Bing Crosby, an up-and-coming vocalist from Spokane, Washington, who pulled all these disparate threads together and set the tone for American popular singing in the 1930s. Crosby understood exactly what the new paradigm demanded, and delivered it to perfection. His conversational style of singing managed to intensify the emotional impact of the lyrics, even while he delivered the phrases with unprecedented relaxation and apparent nonchalance. He brought a similarly understated demeanor to Hollywood, and found the approach worked just as well on the movie screen. Crosby is often acknowledged as a major force in shaping the cool aesthetic, but the rise of this style was directly connected to the introduction of technologies that amplified and magnified even the tiniest vocal nuance or on-camera movement. Crosby mastered these small gestures and singing subtleties, but also drew on the high-octane energy of jazz. Then he took this whole package, all of it cutting edge, and presented it in a charismatic, unthreatening manner perfectly suited for mainstream America. No black entertainer, whether Bessie Smith or Louis Armstrong, or a white man in blackface such as Jolson, could have pulled off this feat.

At this juncture in history, the mass market craved understatement. The generation of radio fans and record buyers who came of age in the 1930s had grown up hearing vehement and vociferous vocalists with loud, declamatory styles. When the new technologies allowed for more low-key delivery of love songs, audiences responded with unrestrained enthusiasm, cheering for moderation and reserve to a degree that probably will never be replicated in popular music. In 1931 Crosby sang on ten of the top fifty songs of the year. He would eventually rack up more than forty number-one hits and release close to four hundred chart-bound singles. In 1932, Crosby took top billing in the film *The Big Broadcast* and would go on to appear in seventy-nine films—he reportedly sold

more than a billion movie tickets during his career, making him the most popular singing actor in history. His controlled, low-key sexuality allowed him to
play a remarkable range of roles, not just the romantic lead but also a comic foil
(most famously in a series of films with Bob Hope), a doctor, a professor, and,
on several occasions, a priest. By the same token, Crosby's recordings helped
to popularize many of the most famous love songs of the century—"Ghost of a
Chance," "I Surrender, Dear," "I'll Be Seeing You," "Out of Nowhere," "Too Marvelous for Words," and many, many others. Yet his biggest successes came via
two immaculately chaste holiday carols: "Silent Night," which eventually sold
some fifteen million copies, and "White Christmas," which earned a place in the
Guinness Book of World Records as the biggest-selling single of all time.

Not everyone loved this new way of singing love songs. In 1932 Boston's
Cardinal William O'Connell warned that "crooners make the basest appeal to
sex emotions in the young. Their songs are not true love songs; they profane
the name." An association of New York singing teachers concurred, declaring
that "crooning corrupts the minds and ideals of the younger generation." But
fans warmly embraced the new singers, perhaps for the very reasons these
critics specified.

Many vocalists contributed to the new naturalism in the performance of
love songs. Gene Austin, Russ Columbo, and Al Bowlly are little remembered
nowadays but enjoyed a large following during the heyday of crooning. When
Columbo died of a (probably accidental) gunshot at twenty-six, thousands of
fans went to the funeral services on Sunset Boulevard—my father, sixteen at
the time, was one of them. Even after the crooning fad stopped causing scandal,
the key breakthrough of this generation of singers, namely the beguiling illusion
that the vocalist was communicating directly and intimately with the listener,
remained an essential ingredient of popular music. Long before the close of the
1930s, the term *crooner* had fallen out of favor; the label probably even seemed
embarrassing to many music fans, much like *boy band* or *bubblegum music* in
a later day. But by this point even singers with big, flamboyant voices, such as
Louis Armstrong or Ella Fitzgerald, had mastered sweet cooing sounds and laid-
back phrasing.

No one would ever pigeonhole Billie Holiday as a crooner, yet she deserves
our recognition and applause as the key innovator who took this method of intimate, conversational delivery to the next level. More than any other singer of
her generation, Holiday showed how the tiniest rhythmic and melodic gestures
could amplify the emotional impact and eroticism of a love lyric. Perhaps this came,
as some suggested, from a troubled life—marked by abandonment, abuse, prostitution, and addiction—that gave Ms. Holiday a storehouse of inner pathos
she could channel into her melancholy songs, a kind of method acting for the
nightclub bandstand. Or maybe her mastery of microtonal sounds and behind-

the-beat phrasing were merely her ways of compensating for what she *didn't* have. Holiday's limitations were all too obvious. Her range, even in her prime, spanned a mere octave and a half. Her voice was small and could never have captured the attention of audiences in the days before amplification. She lacked the free-flowing improvisation skills of Fitzgerald and Armstrong and probably worked out many of her effects in advance. Yet I almost hesitate before listing any of these 'defects', for the simple reason that, when you hear Holiday sing, you aren't aware of any of them. She inhabits the feeling state of the song with such authority that the vocal virtuosos seem the ones who have fallen short, missing the deeper nuances that Holiday has held up for our inspection.

Even today, more than a half-century after her death, Holiday's oeuvre can serve as a starting point and touchstone for those who want to sing about love. During the late 1930s and early 1940s, she worked her magic, whether saddled with flimsy Tin Pan Alley novelty numbers and maudlin sentimental tunes—"Me, Myself and I" or "What a Little Moonlight Can Do" (where the rhyme with the title phrase is merely a sigh: "ooh, ooh, ooh")—or classic jazz standards, such as "All of Me," "Our Love Is Here to Stay," "I Can't Get Started," "Easy to Love," "A Fine Romance," and "I Cried for You." And then there are the songs that became jazz standards almost entirely due to Holiday's force of personality, both works she composed herself, such as "God Bless the Child" and "Don't Explain," as well as tunes so closely associated with her that they might as well have been her personal property, such as "Mean to Me," "Strange Fruit," "Good Morning Heartache," and "Lover Man." When still in her early thirties, however, Holiday already seemed on the decline, not just in her private life, where heroin addiction and its legal consequences added to her fame for all the wrong reasons, but also behind the microphone, where her voice often sounded strained and troubled. Yet even her late recordings, no matter how world-weary, are filled with a raw poetry and emotional honesty that enhanced her legend and enriched her legacy.

Even as interpretive styles evolved, the love songs themselves changed little between the close of the 1920s and the early 1950s. In fact, many of the songs recorded by Frank Sinatra, Nat King Cole, Sarah Vaughan, Peggy Lee, Dean Martin, Rosemary Clooney, and other star vocalists during the Eisenhower administration are the *exact same tunes* performed by Holiday, Armstrong, and Crosby two decades before. During this period, almost every romantic song came in a thirty-two-bar form, and the rhythmic flexibility and harmonic maximalism that jazz had introduced into popular music in the 1920s still held sway until the rise of rock 'n' roll. Lyrics broached a kind of sophisticated populist poetry, and the masters of the form—Cole Porter, Ira Gershwin, Johnny Mercer, Irving Berlin, Dorothy Fields, and Lorenz Hart, among others—practiced a seemingly carefree craftsmanship in which the passions of the heart were artfully balanced against wit and sassy repartee. Many consider this period the golden age of American popular song—indeed if love songs were judged like fine wines and praised for their complexity, subtlety, and a potency that intoxicated you in sweet, gradual steps, then this era deserves credit for producing our finest vintages. Certainly they have aged well.

Even so, the United States had no monopoly on the music of romance during these years. Some singing stars of the era, such as Chinese popular vocalist Zhou Xuan, never found a global audience; a few had a taste of transnational success— for example, Carlos Gardel, Maurice Chevalier, Marlene Dietrich, and Carmen Miranda. In most instances, the highest rung of global fame was reserved for stars willing to sing in English and play 'exotic' roles in Hollywood movies. Yet this exoticism occasionally bordered on the ridiculous and patronizing—Miranda, a beloved samba singer in Brazil, became more famous in Hollywood films for her campy fruit-laden headgear. Even as she achieved a new level of stardom, her movies were sharply criticized in Latin America for their demeaning portrayal of Miranda in particular and South American culture in general. Her film *Down Argentine Way* (1940) even got banned in Argentina, and when Miranda performed songs from her New York club act for a high-society audience in Rio de Janeiro that same year, she was booed after each number.

Edith Piaf, in contrast, managed to achieve international fame as a singer of love songs with very few concessions to the increasingly powerful U.S. movie and music interests. She occasionally sang in English, and put some effort into building an audience in America, but her onstage performances were distinctly Old World in flavor and came charged with an intensity and forthrightness that resisted campiness and faux exoticism. If we seek an American comparison, it is not with any Hollywood star, but rather Billie Holiday, Piaf's almost exact contemporary—they were born just a few weeks apart, and both died in their midforties. Piaf was a Parisian street urchin; like Holiday, she was raised by relatives and spent some of her youth in a brothel. In Piaf's case, her grandmother was the madam of an establishment in Normandy, but both her parents were entertainers, and in her early teens she too began performing as a street singer. She was discovered by a cabaret owner in the Pigalle area of Paris, who put her on stage, and before her twentieth birthday Piaf was already a rising star. Her delivery captured the anguish of love and heartbreak, those oldest subjects of lyric expression, with an immediacy that half-convinced listeners she had been the first to explore these dark corners of the soul. But if the great American singers of the era built their appeal on the intimacy made possible by microphones and amplification, Piaf gave full scope to her powerful voice, a sharp contrast to her less-than-five-foot stature. Her most famous songs, such as "La Vie en Rose" and "Non, Je ne Regrette Rien," somehow managed to retain the flavor of a whispered confession even as they were delivered with melodrama and authority, like national anthems for the new independent state of romance.

The term *torch song* is often applied to the work of singers such as Holiday and Piaf. The term entered the popular vocabulary in the 1920s, referring to an especially intense love song—and probably derived from the use of the phrase "carrying a torch" to describe a passionate and unrequited love. In November 1927, *Vanity Fair* magazine explained to its readers that "when a fellow 'carries the torch' it doesn't imply that he is 'lit up' or drunk, but girl-less. His steady has quit him for another." The same article, which cites columnist Walter Winchell as its source, notes that singer Tommy Lyman introduced his performance of "Come to Me, My Melancholy Baby" as "my famous torch song," and that the phrase was now used in "Broadway late places" when a patron made "a request for a ballad in commemoration of a lonesome state." Others, perhaps more erudite or merely imaginative, have tried to link the phrase back to the torches carried by ancient Greek revelers at the wedding processions discussed earlier in this book.

In any event, this style of song, marked by a confessional first-person perspective and a degree of emotional force that went beyond the sentimentality of most commercial tunes, predated the *torch* label. Composer and music writer Alec Wilder praises Spencer Williams's 1915 song "I Ain't Got Nobody" as the first significant torch song. This work, in Wilder's words, marked the "emergence of a new, more personal point of view." Marion Harris, a white singer from Kentucky, had great success with her early recordings of this composition, which became her signature song; but I note that the cover of the 1916 sheet music for "I Ain't Got Nobody" features a blackface performer—another example of the tendency, detailed in the preceding chapter, for especially demonstrative and emotionally charged songs of that era to be associated with blackness. But Spencer Williams was hardly the first to tap into this sensibility. A decade before "I Ain't Got Nobody," Bert Williams achieved enormous success with "Nobody," a semi-spoken lament with a tragicomic attitude that anticipates the emotional tone of the later song. His recording of "Nobody" sold in huge quantities—probably more than 100,000 copies—and Williams, the most celebrated African American entertainer of his day, was obliged to sing this prototype of a torch song at every performance for the rest of his life.

Yet when music fans talked about torch singers in the 1920s and 1930s, they almost always referred to female vocalists. Since the early days of blues recordings, black women had made their mark as specialists in love gone bad, but they now had to share the acclaim with other ladies who aimed to probe the melancholy side of romance with microphone in hand. A Jewish white woman such as Fanny Brice (singing "My Man") or Annette Hanshaw, an ingénue with movie star looks and a Betty Boop voice, found favor as torch singers—as would, in later years, European stars such as Dietrich and Piaf. Many of the leading torch singers of the era are forgotten nowadays, but their classic performances have not lost their poignancy. Listen, for example, to Ruth Etting sing "Love Me or Leave Me," Helen Morgan deliver "Can't Help Lovin' Dat Man," Libby Holman interpret "Body and Soul," or Lee Wiley perform "Time on My Hands," and you can hear how the ethos of these well-aged recordings anticipates the frankness and confidential tone of many later and current-day performances. When I chart the use of the term *torch singer* in Google's database, I find that it reached its peak in 1938 and then declined steadily until around 1970, when its usage starts to rise again. This resurgence doesn't surprise me: in many ways, the singer-songwriters who flourished in the 1970s built on the foundations laid by these forerunners from the Jazz Age and Great Depression. And this torch still burns, at least in some corners of the contemporary music world—many of the mannerisms and attitudes refined by these pre-World War II stylists still show up in song interpretations today, especially when the tempo is slow and the mood intense.

Why did torch singers fall on hard times in the late 1930s? The rise of the Swing Era, with its celebration of hot jazz, probably played the key role in this shift. Benny Goodman's audience-rousing performance at Hollywood's Palomar Ballroom in August 1935 often gets mentioned in the history books as the breakthrough moment when mainstream America discovered swing music. The idea that fans switched overnight to hot jazz is a bit of an exaggeration, but Goodman's amazing popularity—the press soon dubbed him "King of Swing"—clearly signaled a change in musical tastes among teens and young adults as profound as that unleashed by Elvis and the Beatles in later years. A host of other bandleaders flourished by serving up high-octane dance music during this same period, many of them newcomers to hot jazz, a few such as Ellington and Armstrong pioneers of this style back in the 1920s. Some alarmists made dire predictions and issued strident warnings—medical authorities were cited to prove that dance tempos faster than a typical human pulse rate could weaken moral restraints, and the New York legislature even considered a law prohibiting swing music. But to no avail. Before the close of the decade, jazzy dance music was everywhere, an incessant soundtrack to the leisure hours of the younger generation.

Heart-on-sleeve love songs could coexist with the emerging style, but would never serve as the main attraction during the Swing Era. Many of the bestselling records from this period were instrumentals, and even when a popular tune had words, the poetry of the lyrics had less impact than the dance beat or riff-like insistence of the melody line in separating the hits from the misses. The singers who flourished in this environment often enjoyed huge sales with tunes that had nothing to do with love—for example, Ella Fitzgerald's "A-Tisket, A-Tasket," which is closer to a nursery rhyme than a torch song, or Doris Day, who sang about a "Sentimental Journey," or the Andrew Sisters, who harmonized over the virtues of the "Boogie-Woogie Bugle Boy," or Nat King Cole who enjoyed a big hit with "Straighten Up and Fly Right." Even a psychologically charged singer such as Judy Garland, who could deliver a torch song with as much smoldering fire as any of her contemporaries, achieved some of her biggest successes during this period with love-free songs—for example, "Over the Rainbow," "It's a Great Day for the Irish," and "On the Atchison, Topeka & Santa Fe." As I look back at this era, and the shift from torch songs to swing and novelty numbers, I am reminded of the similar transition in the 1970s from the introspective singer-songwriters who dominated the first half of the decade to the campy disco acts that flourished in its closing years. In both instances, a style of performance that prided itself on the revelation of romantic longings and the inner life got displaced by a more carefree music driven by a danceable groove.

Yet the romantic ballad survived this shift in the public's taste, and even reached a new level of sophistication in its aftermath. But credit here is due largely to the achievement and influence of a single performer, namely Frank Sinatra. Sinatra assimilated the innovations of the crooners and torch singers, while incorporating new elements that, previously, had played little part in the popular love song. He added new layers of irony, sometimes outright cynicism, to the emotional immediacy of the torch singers, and the end result was something new: a performance that delivered the inner meaning of the lyric while also offering an arch commentary on it. Watching a Sinatra concert, audiences saw two contrary levels of interpretation somehow coexisting, both an acceptance of vulnerability to the feeling state of the song, and a macho assertion of independence from its jurisdiction. Today we have come to accept this kind of multivalent approach to singing about love—some even scorn interpretative styles that avoid its complexities—but before Sinatra, those who delivered these lyrics rarely journeyed so far from their surface meanings. Occasionally a bold performer—Louis Armstrong, Fats Waller, perhaps even Bing Crosby—could add a dose of humor or nonchalance to a love song, but these were rare exceptions to the general rule that the ego of the performer must be made subservient to the psychological implications of the words. With Sinatra, in contrast, these two forces battled as equals for control of the music, and the conflict revealed unexplored depths in even the simplest songs, almost akin to the way Freud showed how our supposedly unified psyches contain within them opposed forces, conflicts never resolved but potentially a source of creativity and surprising degrees of self-expression.

I must admit to some ambivalence in the face of this change in popular singing. My own aesthetic preference is for intense emotional immersion in the mood and ambience of the lyric—in the manner of Billie Holiday or the great blues singers such Son House and Robert Johnson. Irony, I fear, is a corrosive element in a love song, and must be handled with great care. Yet even my skepticism is overcome by the sheer brilliance and bravado of Sinatra's breakthrough. Hearing him deliver one of the classic standards—such as "I've Got You Under

My Skin" or "I Get a Kick Out of You," or "A Foggy Day"—I find the experience exhilarating, even as I remain unsure whether the main course here is the Porter or Gershwin song, or Sinatra himself. I suspect that other music lovers are equally torn, and for every listener who dreamily muses over the love story presented in the song, an equal number fantasize about what it would be like to *be* (or be with) Frank Sinatra.

Did Sinatra's frenzied fandom signal the moment when the popular music audience became more obsessed with the celebrity performer than with the songs themselves? Certainly we have already seen stirrings of this new attitude to the love song in the public's response to Rudy Vallée and the crooners; and historians of music can point to previous examples of a "cult of personality" among concert audiences—Liszt, for example, stirred such a frenzy among his admirers that contemporaries branded it as a kind of mania. But these outbursts were rare exceptions, or at least they were until the middle of the twentieth century. Benny Goodman may have caused a sensation with his swing jazz, but the movement got named the *Swing Era* after the music, not after the man. No one needed a word such as *Goodman-o-mania* to describe the popularity of big band dance music. But even before we arrive at the Beatlemania of the 1960s, a new attitude to the love song is evident. Of course, the music doesn't lose its importance—even if one sometimes struggles to hear it over the screaming fans—but the most obvious expression of love and sexuality is no longer centered in the lyrics, but rather in the relationship between the adoring audience and the erotically charged performer.

In the case of Sinatra, the mass movement took its name from his fans. Newspapers wrote about *bobby-soxers*—the term came from the rolled-down-to-the-ankle hosiery, often worn with poodle skirts and saddle shoes, favored by the young female admirers of the popular vocalist. Perhaps their screaming and swooning for Sinatra originated, as some have insisted, in the wily machinations of a publicist who paid young women to make as much noise as possible for the singer's 1942 appearance at the Paramount Theater. But hundreds of other hysterical fans, not on the payroll, contributed to the pandemonium. The bobby-soxer phenomenon soon eclipsed the most ambitious publicist's wildest dream and turned into a demonstration of the power of crowd psychology. When Sinatra returned to the Paramount in 1944, tens of thousands of fans showed up, and those who couldn't get inside blocked traffic in the street. Hundreds of police officers and reserves were called in, and when the singer appeared on stage, the uproar was so deafening that the music got lost in the outbursts from the audience. *The New Republic*, appraising this extraordinary scene, described it as a "phenomenon of mass hysteria that is seen only two or three times in a century."

But if the journalist correctly diagnosed the hysterical quality of the response, he was wrong about its rarity—at least in the new world of fandom. Similar scenes took place when Sinatra showed up in Chicago, Boston, and other cities. And later superstars of popular music stirred up equally strong emotions. Young women screamed for Elvis Presley, and they screamed for the Beatles. They still scream for the latest pop sensation today, although music critics no longer reach for medical or sociological explanations—nowadays, this is just how fans are expected to act. Yet the mystery remains: Why do the ladies scream? The research on crowd psychology offers various possible explanations. The desire to imitate others runs strong in crowds, so the excessive response of a few emotionally over-wrought individuals may spread through the audience with the rapidity of 'the wave' moving around a football stadium. Or perhaps the musician of the present day is akin to the religious figures or political leaders of yesteryear, exerting an irresistible charisma that overwhelms onlookers. Or perhaps concerts have come to fill the role of the bacchanalian rituals of ancient times, also marked by their musical intensity, which allowed participants a rare opportunity to *let go*, throw off the restraints of everyday life, and enjoy the ecstasy that can be found only in a crowd of similarly uninhibited supplicants. But I tend to believe the opinion of a different expert, the source I turn to when mystified (as I often am) by female psychology: namely, my wife. She tells me that these screaming young ladies just want to get noticed by the musician. They are screaming for attention. Darwin would have liked that explanation too. It supports his controversial hypothesis that music is, at bottom, just part of the game of sexual selection for the propagation of the species.

In any event, fans will play a more active role in the final chapters of our history. Even as the entertainment industry exerts unprecedented influence over the musical tastes of the general population, audiences seek much more from music than just entertainment. During the second half of the twentieth century, songs increasingly will serve as lifestyle accessories, as tools of self-expression, even self-actualization. The very word *lifestyle*—which didn't exist in English until around the time Frank Sinatra attracted his legion of bobby-soxers—— starts showing up everywhere during the second half of the twentieth century, and with it comes the related notion that our everyday existence can morph into a kind of work of art. Music plays a key role in this process, not just as a soundtrack in the background, but as a constitutive ingredient in generational identity and the individual's sense of self.

The love song doesn't disappear in this highly charged context—if anything, it takes on new power. But its role changes. It must change. Even the music industry powerbrokers soon see that the *listening public*, a term that gained widespread use with the rise of radio, now wants to do more than just listen. The listeners insist on participating, and with the rise of rock 'n' roll, they will get a chance to do just that.

CHAPTER 16

Rock 'n' Roll and the Summer of Love

There are more love songs than anything else. If songs could make you do
something we'd all love one another.—Frank Zappa

By the midpoint of the twentieth century, the swing-driven big band sound had
already lost much of its mojo. Pop singers serving up dreamy ballads and novelty tunes now dominated the charts. Number-one hits from 1950 include Nat
King Cole's "Mona Lisa," Patti Page's "The Tennessee Waltz," and Sammy Kaye's
"Harbor Lights." Bing Crosby and Frank Sinatra still sold lots of records, but
their biggest successes that year were, respectively, "Rudolph the Red-Nosed
Reindeer" and "Goodnight, Irene." Pop music now served as comfort fare, and
even Mom and Dad could join in on the G-rated fun. Record labels, for their
part, envisioned the future of the love song in the simplest demographic terms:
appeal to the mass market with sentimental, inoffensive tunes that touched the
heartstrings of all generations, and offended no one.

Of course, they proved wrong. Everyone would realize this before the decade
came to a close. But even in 1950, less inhibited love songs were on the rise—
but mostly in black communities. The previous year, *Billboard* started using the
term *rhythm and blues* as a category name, and the biggest R&B hit of the year
was "The Hucklebuck," as famous for its erotically charged dance steps as for the
song itself. In 1950 songs about infidelity or adultery—Johnny Otis and Little
Esther's "Double Crossing Blues" and "Mistrustin' Blues" and Ivory Joe Hunter's
"I Almost Lost My Mind"—held the top spot in the R&B chart for most of the
early part of the year. But the Dominoes pushed even further with "Sixty Minute
Man," a hit single recorded at the end of December:

> There'll be fifteen minutes of kissin'
> Then you'll holler "Please don't stop" (Don't stop!)
> There'll be fifteen minutes of teasin'
> Fifteen minutes of squeezin'
> And fifteen minutes of blowin' my top.

When the Federal label released this track the following May, many radio stations banned it from the airwaves. But this hardly hurt the popularity of the "Sixty Minute Man." The single skyrocketed to the top of the R&B chart and stayed there for fourteen weeks. (Some time later, the band followed up with "Can't Do Sixty No More," but this soulful song about sexual exhaustion didn't get enough lift to even reach the charts.)

Some things never change in the history of love songs. In twentieth-century industrialized societies, as in medieval communities, censors and others concerned with public morals continued to take an active interest in the songs of the day, and aimed to save impressionable youth, or even mature parents and grandparents, from exposure to sexualized content. Their decisions showed amazing inconsistency at times. For example, NBC Radio refused to mention the title of the 1930 song "Body and Soul" on air, fearing that the very word *body* hinted at too much. Yet a few years later, the Columbia label allowed Count Basie to release a track entitled "Upright Organ Blues"—you hardly need to know that only pianos, not organs, come in upright consoles to find something suggestive in *that* title. Yet a general tendency could be detected amid this confusion—namely, that black musicians and black audiences got a little more wiggle room. When Cole Porter faced a public backlash over the sinful implications of his song "Love for Sale," featured in the 1930 Broadway musical *The New Yorkers*, he found the controversy abated somewhat after the song was assigned to Elizabeth Welch, a black singer, instead of white actress Kathryn Crawford. To finish the makeover, the backdrop for the song changed from the façade of a Madison Avenue restaurant to the front of Harlem's Cotton Club. With these alterations, a song about a prostitute no longer seemed quite so objectionable. When white vocalist Dottie O'Brien released "Four or Five Times" in 1951, many radio stations banned it, although black singers had been performing this song for many years without any outcry. At the dawn of the 1950s, Dean Martin enjoyed top-twenty hits with "If" and "I'll Always Love You," but when he released "Wham! Bam! Thank You Ma'am," many broadcasters refused to play it, and the tune (unlike "Sixty Minute Man," issued at almost the same time) never even appeared on the *Billboard* chart.

The whole attempt to segregate the commercial music market into white and black segments proved impossible to enforce. Audience crossover had always taken place, even in the days of slavery and increasingly after the rise of ragtime, blues, and jazz. But in the mid-1950s, the obsession of white youngsters with black music took on a new degree of intensity. Around the same time the Supreme Court handed down its *Brown v. Board of Education* decision, ending state-sponsored school segregation, American teens started to shake up the segregation of the music marketplace. They surprised radio deejays, jukebox operators, and record store owners with their interest in rhythm-and-blues. Jukebox owners may have been the first to see the change coming. Tracking demand a dime at a time, these close observers of youth behavior quickly learned that even white neighborhoods needed access to the black R&B hits. Many retailers catering to white consumers had previously not carried these records in their inventory, but most now put them in stock in response to this rising demand. Influential radio deejays—Alan Freed in New York, Dewey Phillips in Memphis, Bill Randle in Cleveland, and many others—also recognized the changing landscape of American popular music, and helped accelerate the rise of the next new thing: white singers who took their inspiration from the most uninhibited exemplars of black R&B music. Phillips is credited as the first radio host to play an Elvis Presley record on the air, and Freed even claimed to have originated the term *rock 'n' roll*. In the face of these ardent advocates with airwave access, no Supreme Court decision was necessary to integrate the popular music favored by American teens.

In hindsight, the decision of a whole generation of youngsters to embrace raucous, dance-oriented music, whether black rhythm-and-blues or white rock 'n' roll, seems an inevitable response to the tepid pop music of the early 1950s. Yet this changing of the guard did not take place without a struggle and backlash—especially from those who feared the moral contagion of the new music. Thousands of citizens complained to elected officials, and Congress briefly considered a bill that would ban the shipment of obscene rock 'n' roll records via the postal service. Police in some communities confiscated jukeboxes and imposed fines on their owners. Church groups put pressure on disk jockeys to keep objectionable records off the air, and some members of the music business suggested the creation of censorship committees or review boards. Records were burned. Concerts got canceled. But singer Pat Boone may have had the most ingenious solution to the problem at hand: he recorded cover versions of hot black R&B and rock 'n' roll tunes, inserting squeaky-clean words in place of suggestive lyrics.

Some thought the problem might just go away on its own. An old hipster friend, who hung out with Kerouac and played jazz in the 1950s, once confided to me: "When this rock 'n' roll sound took off, we all thought it was a passing fad. We figured it would disappear in a few months." In 1955 and early 1956, rock 'n' roll *did* seem like a novelty sound. Fans who tuned in to the radio inevitably heard Bill Haley's "Rock Around the Clock," but they also encountered comparatively tame chart-topping singles such as Bill Hayes's "The Ballad of Davey Crockett," Mitch Miller's "The Yellow Rose of Texas," or Tennessee Ernie Ford's "Sixteen Tons." Then came Elvis Presley, who proved bigger than all of these artists combined, releasing hit after hit—"Heartbreak Hotel," "Hound Dog," "Love Me Tender," "All Shook Up," and many others. Between 1955 and 1958, Presley had ten singles that topped the sales chart. And when he didn't hold the number-one position, some other rock 'n' roll song inevitably did.

The critics feared the erotic energy of these songs, yet the lyrics often had nothing to do with sex, or even romance. Often the words simply referred to dancing—"The Twist," "Rock Around the Clock," and "At the Hop" were among the most popular recordings of the era. Other chart-topping hits served up nonsensical lyrics, for example "The Purple People Eater" or "Tequila." But who knew what meanings lurked behind cryptic phrases? The FBI scrutinized the Kingsmen's 1963 recording of "Louie Louie" in search of obscenity, and eventually compiled a hundred-page file on the tune—but their experts found the song unintelligible. The most interesting section of this FBI report, to my mind, is the sheet of paper confiscated by a junior high principal, which contains the words young males *thought* Kingsmen vocalist Jack Ely sang on the hit single. As in so many instances with early rock 'n' roll, the musicians didn't need to supply the dirty stuff; the receptive attitude of the audience ensured the sexualization of this music.

Who can be surprised that widespread rumors persisted, hinting at secret sexual messages hidden in the grooves of rock 'n' roll records? Even when the words to a rock 'n' roll song seemed innocent, the primal beats and pelvic thrusts of dancers spelled out S-E-X in big bold letters, at least for those inclined to fear for the morals of the younger generation. Over the course of a tumultuous decade, parents watched in dismay as a series of dance fads swept through the popular culture—the Twist, Watusi, Mashed Potato, Frug, Boogaloo, and others—dances that usually drew onlookers' attention down below the waist. And if these movements could inspire lust in the observers, what desires did they spur in the teenage dancers themselves?

The turning point in this public debate arrived with Elvis Presley's famous September 1956 appearance on *The Ed Sullivan Show*. This singer had the misfortune to possess an unusual first name that rhymed with "pelvis"; but no doubt his below-the-belt movements would have spurred jokes and scandal under any circumstances. Sullivan, for his part, had previously declared Presley's prurient performances incompatible with the family values of his viewers, but changed his mind after his rival TV host Steve Allen enjoyed enormous ratings success with an Elvis appearance. Presley's first visit to the Sullivan show proved far more popular than anyone had anticipated. More than 80 percent of the U.S. television audience tuned in that evening to see the hot young singer. CBS gave viewers only a few glimpses of the famous pelvis, focusing on Presley's upper body for most of the shots. But audiences at home could imagine, from the screams of the young ladies in attendance, what they were missing. The moralists may have won this small battle over camera angles, but they lost the war. When Presley sang "Hound Dog" on a return visit to Sullivan's show four months later, the network allowed mainstream America a longer look at the singer's gyrating hips. They liked what they saw.

This musical revolution transformed youth culture in America (and soon elsewhere), but anyone listening to the most popular love ballads of the era would hardly appreciate the changes underway. When Presley sang "Love Me Tender," a number-one single from 1956 and one of his featured songs on *The Ed Sullivan Show*, he didn't deviate far from the pattern of old-fashioned love songs—in fact the music of this megahit came from the Civil War song "Aura Lee," and the maudlin lyrics remind us of the sentimental parlor ballads of the nineteenth century. The same is true of the Beatles, the next scream-inspiring musical act to dominate the pop charts. The tame sentiments expressed in the band's first chart-topping U.S. hit, "I Want to Hold Your Hand," don't come close to the raunchy fare served up by blues and R&B acts in previous decades. At this stage in their ascendancy, the band's boldest romantic demands were "Please Please Me" and "Hold Me Tight." Even in later years, the Beatles most experimental works—songs such as "A Day in the Life," "Revolution #9," "I Am the Walrus," "Strawberry Fields Forever," and other mind-expanding tunes—were seldom love songs. The band's most popular love ballads, bittersweet songs such as "Yesterday" and "Michelle," signaled no revolution. They often showed up in cover versions by veterans of the Swing Era or purveyors of "easy listening music," and parents and sometimes even grandparents could enjoy the results.

But if early rock love songs featured mostly tame lyrics, the performances came charged with unprecedented erotic energy—again supplied primarily by the audience. Screaming female fans no longer seemed quite so strange any more, after the long history of hysteria associated with Rudy Vallée, Frank Sinatra, and Elvis Presley. But with the Beatles, the shrieking and swooning took on an unprecedented level of intensity. By the fall of 1963, newspapers started using the term *Beatlemania* to describe the phenomenon. Women tried to climb on stage at the band's concerts, others tossed programs at the musicians with phone numbers written in lipstick. Some hurled themselves into the cordons of police, knocking off helmets and sending constables staggering in their attempts to reach the band. Even in in semi-rural cities, unfamiliar with manias of this sort, near-riots ensued. When the Beatles came to Cumbria to appear at the ABC Cinema in Carlisle, hundreds of schoolgirls confronted the bobbies in their zeal to get tickets, and some fans required medical treatment in the aftermath. That same day, the Beatles got mentioned for the first time in Parliament, when a member asked about the cost of police protection for the band.

When the Beatles traveled to the United States in February 1964, the same frenzy broke out before the band played a single note. Three thousand clamorous admirers greeted the lads from Liverpool on their arrival at New York's Kennedy Airport, and when the Beatles appeared on *The Ed Sullivan Show* two days later some fifty thousand people tried to get seats in an auditorium that could accommodate fewer than eight hundred. Seventy-three million Americans watched at home—a new record for TV viewership. In contrast to Presley's controversial debut, CBS offered plenty of full-body views of the band, but the real show took place in the studio audience. After Sullivan introduced the group, the camera turned immediately to the screaming fans, almost entirely young women. The focus then shifts to the band, but a few seconds later, the camera reverts to the wild fans once more, centering on a schoolgirl who appears to be hyperventilating. At the end of the song, the camera pans through the audience again; the few young men in attendance show a modicum of restraint, while the ladies exhibit all the signs of collective hysteria. Every song the Beatles played on *The Ed Sullivan Show* that evening was a love song, but their romantic fervor hardly matched the devotion shown by the onlookers.

Those seeking transgressive love songs found edgier fare in the music of the Rolling Stones, soon to emerge as the leading rival of the Beatles for the affection of rock fans. The Stones had stronger ties to the blues tradition—when Keith Richards reconnected with his old schoolmate Mick Jagger at a train station in 1961, a chance encounter that led to the formation of the band, he was most impressed with Jagger's knowledge of American blues and R&B artists. In a letter Richards wrote to his aunt a few months later, he enthused: "He's got every record Chuck Berry ever made and all his mates have too, they are rhythm and blues fans, real R&B I mean (not this Dinah Shore, Brook Benton crap), Jimmy Reed, Muddy Waters, Chuck, Howlin' Wolf, John Lee Hooker all the Chicago bluesmen real lowdown stuff, marvelous.... Besides that Mick is the greatest R&B singer this side of the Atlantic, and I don't mean maybe." Soon teenagers on both sides of the Atlantic would get a taste of this same "real lowdown stuff" in the music of the Rolling Stones. If the Beatles, despite their modishly long hair and extraordinary fame, still seemed like young men you could bring home to meet mom and dad, the Stones represented the bad boys best kept out of sight of parents. Both bands spurred adolescent and teenage fantasies, but in the case of the Rolling Stones, these romantic daydreams were more likely to get an R rating.

"(I Can't Get No) Satisfaction" proclaimed the Stones' first chart-topping U.S. single, but back in Britain many fans heard the record only on pirate radio stations, due to the song's sexually charged lyrics. Yet when the band released "Let's Spend the Night Together" in 1967, even many American deejays refused to play it on air, and the song on the flip side of the single, "Ruby Tuesday," rose to the top of the chart instead. The Rolling Stones insisted on playing the prohibited song on *The Ed Sullivan Show*, and the ensuing conflict between host and band was resolved only when Jagger agreed to substitute the words "let's spend some time together." Moralists (again) won the battle, but lost the war: the Stones benefited from their reputation as purveyors of forbidden love songs. Fans rewarded them by pushing their later lust-ridden singles "Honky-Tonk Women" and "Brown Sugar" to the number-one position in the *Billboard* chart.

But don't count out the Beatles, who responded with the most ambitious move of all—nothing less than an attempt to recraft the love song in the spirit of the age. During the second half of the 1960s, the words *love* and *peace* had turned into turbocharged mantras of the youth movement. John Lennon and Paul McCartney realized sooner than most of their peers that their songs needed to change in response to this broadening of the concept of love—a term that now signified much more than romance or sex, but also expressed a social movement, a generational identity, and a groovy cosmic force. When the Beatles debuted their new song "All You Need Is Love" on a global TV link on June 25, 1967, some 400 million people watched the satellite broadcast. In a brilliant move, Lennon came up with a song title that also served as a catchy slogan—as he would do again in later years with "Give Peace a Chance" and "Power to the People"—and to emphasize the communal, participative ethos of the mandate, the band performed surrounded by young fans, almost as though they were leading a sing-along rather than showcasing a new work. When "All You Need Is Love" was released as a single a few days later, it jumped to the top of the charts in both Britain and the United States.

Perhaps those next three months would have turned into the Summer of Love even without the Beatles setting the tone. When school got out that June, the Western world reverberated with the changes. The most striking upheavals of the love movement took place in San Francisco, where visitors were advised by a hit song of that summer to wear "flowers in their hair." The new spirit of love was in the ascendancy, and not just in the Haight-Ashbury district, where hippies and their lifestyle got covered as national news almost every day during that period, but also in Golden Gate Park, in Berkeley, and at the Monterey Pop Festival. Similar events took place on the other coast, in Greenwich Village and Central Park, even on the New York Stock Exchange, which Abbie Hoffman and the 'yippies' invaded in late August. London had its own share of Summer of Love events, for example the International Love-In that transpired at London's Alexandra Palace in July. But everyone with access to a transistor radio, the most pervasive handheld device that summer, could pick up some of these vibes no matter where they lived, could hear the new ethos broadcast round-the-clock via hit singles such as "Groovin'," "Feelin' Groovy," "Happy Together," "(Your Love Keeps Lifting Me) Higher and Higher," "A Whiter Shade of Pale," or "Up, Up and Away," with their promises of a transcendent coming together much higher on the Platonic ladder of love than anything dreamed of by Bing Crosby or Frank Sinatra or any other pop singer above the age of thirty. Even the gatekeepers of family entertainment jumped on the bandwagon, with Broadway hosting the hippie-inspired musical *Hair*, which ran for 1,750 performances and spawned a cast album that sold three million copies, and Hollywood releasing dozens of youth rebellion and counterculture films, from the ridiculous (Disney's 1968 comedy *The Love Bug*) to the sublime (Peter Fonda and Dennis Hopper's classic *Easy Rider* from 1969).

The older generation tended to view with suspicion these entreaties, musical and otherwise, for youngster to join the *love-in*—a term that first appeared in the national discourse in 1967, referring to any gathering where the emerging ethos predominated. Wasn't this just the age-old call to sexual promiscuity, dressed up in psychedelic garb? But the most representative love songs of this short-lived season were more than just musical eroticism. They somehow managed to combine elements of spirituality and mind-expanding social awareness along with the sexual charge. Those who have followed along with this history will recognize the similarity to the late medieval attempts of Rumi, Dante, Francis of Assisi, and others to create a new kind of love song, which also tried to take listeners "higher and higher." At the close of 1964, John Coltrane captured the same spirit with his recording of *A Love Supreme*, an album that anticipated the Summer of Love mind-set by more than two years. At this point in his career, a typical John Coltrane release would sell around thirty thousand units, but before the end of the decade music fans had purchased a half million copies of *A Love Supreme*. In retrospect, the whole notion of rewriting not just the rules of the love song, but also its social and political context, must seem wildly idealistic and doomed to inevitable failure. Yet during the late 1960s, just such a transformation entranced and inspired not only visionaries and hippies, but a huge portion of the younger generation.

By the time they got to Woodstock, they were half a million strong, but this celebrated August 1969 rock festival on Max Yasgur's dairy farm in upstate New York signaled the end of the era rather than the arrival of a new age of music-driven love and peace. Woodstock may have defined a generation, but who could agree on the meaning of the definition? Yes, some observers celebrated Woodstock as the vanguard of a higher kind of love, but just as many viewed it as an outgrowth of the drug culture, or the culmination of 1960s protests, or a utopian interlude of youth-driven euphoria, or merely the self-worship of a narcissistic generation. A few may even have considered it as a milestone musical event. But whatever the verdict, the times were now a-changin', albeit in a surprising new direction, as different from Woodstock as it was from the old-time rock 'n' roll of Elvis & Co. In the early 1970s, popular music took an inward turn, led by a new generation of singer-songwriters who favored personal expression and self-actualization over dreams of love-inflected social engineering.

The groundwork for this shift had been laid in the 1960s through the efforts of a handful of visionaries who had risen to the top of the pop-rock hierarchy as individual artists, even as most of the music world focused on brash bands with colorful names. Bob Dylan had drawn on a wide range of sources of inspiration—folk ballads, blues, protest music—outside of the sphere of rock 'n' roll and the

American popular songbook, and the result was a more expansive style of song-writing in which poetry blended with pop, and broader social concerns played as prominent a role as the personal musings that had traditionally dominated commercial music. Paul Simon would soon follow a similar path, first in conjunction with his partner in pop Art Garfunkel, and later as a successful solo act. Yet the huge radio hits for both these artists in the 1960s rarely dealt with love. The cover of *The Freewheelin' Bob Dylan* was cherished by fans for its romantic image of Dylan snuggling up to his girlfriend Suze Rotolo, but the most famous songs on the LP, "Blowin' in the Wind" and "A Hard Rain's a-Gonna Fall," for all their lyricism, are anthems of social protest, and "Don't Think Twice, It's Alright" is a breakup song without the heartache, merely a curt dismissal of so long and fare-thee-well. Nor did Dylan get much closer to romance in most of his other hit singles of the period, standout tracks such as "Mr. Tambourine Man," "The Times They Are A-Changin'," and "Like a Rolling Stone." True, Dylan was capable of dealing with more intimate matters, and doing so brilliantly—just hear "Lay Lady Lay" from 1969 for evidence thereof—but one always had the sense that, like Bartleby the scrivener, he would rather not.

The same is true with Paul Simon, the other forerunner of the 1970s singer-songwriter renaissance, who enjoyed hit after hit in the 1960s with mostly romance-free songs about surprising topics such as a boxer, a visit to the zoo, and the sound of silence. Can we classify "Homeward Bound" or "I Am a Rock" as love songs? How about "Feelin' Groovy" or "The Dangling Conversation"? Well, perhaps, but the romance here plays a subsidiary role, at best. When Simon & Garfunkel's song "Mrs. Robinson" got featured in the hit film *The Graduate*, the movie added elements of cross-generational seduction and eroticism to the tune that are nowhere to be found in the song itself. Even so, an unmistakable tone of emotional transcendence can be detected in these songs, perhaps most notably in the Simon & Garfunkel megahit "Bridge over Troubled Water," released in the very first days of the 1970s, which hints at a kind of higher love akin to that celebrated in the more metaphysical Beatles songs.

But personal love, in all its ecstasy and messiness, would emerge as the dominant theme of the singer-songwriters of the early 1970s. The period from 1970 to 1975 still stands out as the great moment of lyrical and poetic pop music in the modern era, and I am hardly surprised that the term *troubadour* started showing up again in music criticism and the daily conversations of fans. Indeed, the Los Angeles nightclub at the vanguard of this movement was even named The Troubadour—and though it had been called that since the 1950s, the title now captured with uncanny exactitude the artists who performed on its stage. These included Joni Mitchell, Elton John, Carole King, James Taylor, Van Morrison, Neil Young, Cat Stevens, Neil Diamond, Billy Joel, Randy Newman, Laura Nyro, John Denver, Jackson Browne, Linda Ronstandt, Gordon

Lightfoot, Don McLean, Kris Kristofferson, Carly Simon, and many others who helped shape the more intimate, confessional style of musical expression of the period. Only a few years before, plugged-in rock groups with outlandish names, from Animals to Zombies, had dominated the airwaves, but now individuals, each with their own personal and sometimes quirky take on matters, but primarily romantic love, took center stage in the world of popular music.

Some of the hit songs from this period were woeful ("Feelings . . . wo, wo, wo feelings!") or cringe-inducing ("You're having my baby!") or maudlin ("Alone again naturally") or just plain strange ("Bye, bye Miss American Pie"). But the freedom accorded to artists, who could take chances and explore their own inner psyches, on stage and over airwaves, to a degree unprecedented in popular music, tended to compensate for the epic fails and embarrassing moments. The extreme demands of the format, which required a composer who could also perform (usually on acoustic guitar or piano), sing, and exude a modicum of on-stage charisma, forced record labels to reward talent to a degree they have not always matched in more recent decades, and the best of the artists who rose to prominence during this period—say, a Joni Mitchell or Elton John—are worthy of comparison with the finer songwriters of the so-called Golden Age of American popular song. A knowledgeable fan could hear affinities between, for example, Cole Porter and Randy Newman or Harold Arlen and Carole King, and surmise that even in an age of musical revolution, a certain continuity with the longer history of the love song was maintained.

But this inward, psychological turn also could be detected in other styles of romantic pop music during this period. Among the record labels that focused on African American entertainment, for example, the formulas of rhythm-and-blues had gradually been replaced by a newer style known as "soul music." And just as the rock bands of the 1960s gave way to the individual performers of the early 1970s, soul music also experienced a similar shift to megastar solo artists. Diana Ross left the Supremes to pursue a successful solo career in 1970 and never looked back. Around this same time, Smokey Robinson departed from the Miracles, Eddie Kendricks quit the Temptations, and Michael Jackson began pursuing a solo career in addition to his ongoing work with the Jackson Five. Stevie Wonder, the most successful African American popular musician of the period, had flourished as a solo artist from the start of his career, but even his music took on a more individualistic tone. He had previously worked with professional songwriters and within a tightly controlled format imposed on him by the Motown label, but now he showed he could achieve greater acclaim not only by writing his own material, but often playing multiple (or sometimes all of the) instruments on his tracks via overdubbing. Other leading black music luminaries of the era—such as Marvin Gaye, Bill Withers, and Roberta Flack—further blurred the line between soul artist and the emerging crop of singer-songwriters.

At this juncture, anyone considering the future of popular music in general, or the love song in particular, would have predicted a happily-ever-after of poetic solo artists tapping their deep inner selves. and weaving their lyrical effusions in harmonically rich ballads or appealing groove tunes. But these prognosticators would, once again, have been dead wrong. As the 1970s passed by, the spotlight in popular music turned instead to glam rockers, disco acts, funk, and punk. The singer-songwriters never died, merely faded away…or changed allegiances. Joni Mitchell embraced jazz; Randy Newman evolved into a composer of film scores; Van Morrison recorded albums of meditation music; Cat Stevens perhaps made the most radical career shift of them all, changing his name to Yusuf Islam and abandoning his pop music career to devote himself to various causes in the Muslim community. Each story was different, but the overall trend was clear: the age of moody, introspective troubadours had passed, maybe never to return. Perhaps the move most symbolic of the changes afoot came from Elton John, who just a few years earlier had triumphed as a singer-songwriter on the stage of The Troubadour, where he made his U.S. debut in August 1970. John now reinvented himself as a glam rock icon, performing in outlandish costumes, peculiar hats, and oversized eyeglasses. He sometimes showed up on stage adorned in ostrich feathers, or dressed up to resemble the Status of Liberty or Mozart, or in some similar attention-attracting attire.

A campy gay sensibility as well as the deliberate evocation of sexual ambiguity tapped into the audience's demand for something edgier and more transgressive than James Taylor or John Denver, or others of their cohort of low-key singer-songwriters, could offer. *Star Wars* may have been the biggest movie box office hit of the period, but the film that really peered into the future wasn't any high-budget, special effects–driven sci-fi flick, but rather *The Rocky Horror Picture Show* from 1975. This cult classic starts where most romance movies end—with a happily engaged heterosexual couple; but a flat tire forces these unsuspecting lovebirds to seek refuge at a strange castle, where their horizons are broadened by a cast of gender-bending, cross-dressing, and otherwise nonconformist characters. This film did poorly in most cities on its initial release, but went on to enjoy an extraordinarily successful afterlife, primarily in midnight showings on weekends in college towns and major cities. In some instances, cinemas continued to screen the film for years, and showings turned into happenings, with an unprecedented degree of participation from the audience—who sometimes became more of an attraction than the movie itself.

Just as jazz musicians had played a key role in ending segregation in earlier years, rock performers now took the lead in introducing mainstream society to outside-the-mainstream conceptions of gender and sexual self-definition. In 1972, English pop-rock star David Bowie developed the on-stage persona Ziggy Stardust—a mixture of science fiction concepts, androgyny, and bold coiffure and costume choices. Around this same time, Marc Bolan, leader of the band

T. Rex, started putting glitter on his cheekbones and wearing feather boas, and subsequently strutted his way to chart-topping success. In 1970, Bryan Ferry scraped by in London as a pottery teacher and furniture restorer, but a short while later, with the help of fake leopard skin and a generous application of makeup, he was fronting the hot new band Roxy Music, an ensemble that seamlessly merged appealing pop-rock melodies and futuristic fashion statements. Lou Reed, after leaving the Velvet Underground, brought on Bowie as a producer for his *Transformer* album, and its resulting hit single "Walk on the Wild Side" could serve as anthem for the emerging ethos. A host of other bands and artists were walking on this same wild side, and the music industry was abuzz with talk about "glam rock" and "glitter rock." These labels implied a superficial showiness to the proceedings on-stage, yet this could hardly disguise the profound social changes now in play that brought elements of entertainment previously limited to drag shows and other under-the-radar venues into the homes and on to the turntables of teens and twenty-somethings.

This shift in values and attitudes could be seen even more clearly in the disco movement that took center stage in the music world during the late 1970s. Here again the real action occurred among the audience rather than with the musicians on the bandstand—in fact, there usually were *no* musicians on the bandstand, as nightclubs replaced live performers with deejays spinning dance records. From the perspective of love and romance, the songs themselves held few surprises. The lyrics offered only the tiniest amount of guidance to couples, shorthand advice such as "Get Down Tonight" or "Shake Your Booty." "Love's Theme" by Barry White's Love Unlimited Orchestra, one of the first disco love songs to top the chart, had *no* lyrics, merely offering a danceable accompaniment to the love fantasy of your own choosing. After the outpouring of cosmic, expansive love of the late 1960s and the poetically passionate expressions of the early 1970s singer-songwriters, this was thin gruel indeed. Fortunately, the audience compensated for the limitations of the repetitive recordings by building their own expansive ambitions for romantic conquests and sexual fulfillment on the flimsy musical foundations of the disco craze. The Bee Gees may have enjoyed the biggest selling disco album of all time with their soundtrack to *Saturday Night Fever*, which stayed atop the *Billboard* album chart for almost six months, but—unlike the Beatles and Elvis, who took the starring roles when they made movies—the band didn't figure in the film itself. The story instead featured a hardware store worker living with his parents who reinvents himself as the king of the disco when he arrives on the dance floor. John Travolta, who played the starring role, looked a bit like a young Elvis, and the implication was clear: the real stars of this new dance fad were the paying patrons at the discotheque. *Saturday Night Fever*, for all its shallow theatricality, captured the essence of disco's appeal: a promise of personal transcendence and wish fulfillment set to a throbbing, hypnotic beat.

This sense of liberation at the disco took on particular resonance within the gay communities of major cities, where only a few years before same-sex dancing had been strictly prohibited. In the Stonewall Riots of 1969, patrons at a gay dance club in New York's Greenwich Village fought back against the police, and gained the support of many bystanders and community members. Their resistance contributed to the rise of a vibrant gay rights movement and eventually led to a greater level of tolerance from legal authorities. Before that milestone event, patrons at gay bars had learned to expect regular police raids, and the close scrutiny of management, who intervened whenever men danced with other men, or even faced each other provocatively while on the dance floor. When the disco phenomenon emerged a few years later, gay men played a key role in virtually all aspects of the movement, serving as deejays, band members, patrons, and marketeers. "At one point gay men held the top three positions in the field of disco record promotion," pop music historian Alice Echols tells us. "Each worked at a different label, but the three shared an apartment where they convened after work and smoked grass, snorted coke, and strategized about their upcoming releases." In the emerging disco culture, new gender rules were applied to love songs. Sometimes the same record—such as Abba's "Dancing Queen" or the Bee Gees' "More Than a Woman"—could hold different meanings for straight and gay audiences, and an unambiguously homosexual band such as the Village People, whose single "Y.M.C.A." sold twelve million copies worldwide, could now cross over to mainstream pop success.

Yet even before the close of the 1970s, a backlash against disco could be detected, both among the general public and within the music industry. The linkage of discos to the gay lifestyle and hedonistic excesses of all sorts, including the liberal use of various illegal drugs, no doubt contributed to the criticisms and jokes directed at the music. But the genre itself showed signs of creative exhaustion. Disco hits were often self-referential, celebrating dancing and the disco lifestyle ("You Should Be Dancing," "Last Dance," "Get Up and Boogie"), sometimes with ludicrous associations ("Disco Duck," "Disco Inferno"). When the leading artists in the genre wanted to address other subjects, whether love or social issues, they typically needed to condense their message into the simplest phrases—the biggest dance hits embraced repeated mantras, an emphatic sloganeering set to a predictable rhythm, almost always falling between 110 and 140 beats per minute. In its early days, rock 'n' roll had also shown signs of falling into inane, self-referential formulas, but that music had outgrown "Rock Around the Clock" and "The Twist," evolving into *The White Album* and *Exile on Main Street*. In contrast, disco failed to rise above the recipes that created its early hits, and even ardent patrons at the dance clubs soon started seeking something new and different.

During the course of the 1980s, other styles took over the loudspeakers at these venues—house music, techno, trance, acid jazz—but these failed to replicate the mainstream success of the disco fad. The rave party represented perhaps the most daring attempt to reinvigorate the connection between dance music and couples coupling, but the attendees at these uninhibited free-for-alls didn't need familiar hit songs to fuel their festivities, or even nightclubs, for that matter. Raves might take place in almost any setting, from meadows to abandoned industrial buildings. Music played a role at these parties, but a more subsidiary role than in the dance halls of earlier days. Rave deejays aimed for minimalist effects, replacing lyrics and traditional song structures with beats and programmed sounds. These stripped-down faux tunes contributed to the hypnotic ambience, and though love and (perhaps more often) sex were part of the ecstatic temperament of these events, along with powders and pills to cast a quasi-aphrodisiacal glow over the proceedings, participants didn't look for cues from romantic songs and dreamy ballads. All ravers needed was the momentum of a mesmerizing beat; they could supply the rest.

Many fans craved something stronger, less formulaic, and just plain *nastier* than electronic dance music, and even before disco had run its course, punk rock and new wave had emerged as bolder alternatives, serving as magnet and lifestyle inspiration for the rebellious, the radicalized, and other disaffected members of the younger generation. The rise of bands such as the Sex Pistols, Ramones, The Clash, and Talking Heads showed that the original vision driving the rock revolution, namely its promise to shock, surprise, and subvert, had lost none of its allure. Although some individual singer-songwriters, such as Patti Smith, Joe Jackson, and Elvis Costello, adapted to the new ethos, this was primarily a time for new bands high on energy and low on Freudian superego. These ensembles prided themselves on their frankness, their willingness to confront all subjects, and a sound with even fewer frills and less instrumental virtuosity than the most primal early rock bands. In the punk idiom, fancy guitar solos were frowned upon, and lyrics often shouted rather than sung. The spirit of rebellion sometimes gave way to unvarnished nihilism—the Sex Pistols even turned the slogan "No Future" into a mantra, much as John Lennon had once brandished the phrases "All you need is love" or "Give peace a chance."

At this late stage in the rock revolution, was it still possible to cross new boundaries, to sing about things never sung about before? These bands built their reputations on just such a covenant with their fans. The Sex Pistols celebrated Queen Elizabeth's silver jubilee with "God Save the Queen," a caustic in-your-face track that was banned by the BBC and almost certainly would have led to criminal prosecution in an earlier day. For their debut single, the group chose "Anarchy in the UK"—band member Johnny Rotten explained that the idea for singing about an anarchist came from the need to find a rhyme for "anti-Christ." No, the words don't really rhyme, but in the spirit of the time, combining *anarchist* with *anti-Christ* possessed an inner punk logic than no fan could deny. If any band could find a taboo that hadn't been crossed yet in popular music, they turned it into a song, as the Ramones demonstrated with "Now I Wanna Sniff Some Glue," the Talking Heads with "Psycho Killer," Devo with "Mongoloid."

These same artists who seemed capable of handling any subject, tended to avoid the key topic of popular music for the previous thousand years: love. From the time of the first troubadours to the rise of Beatlemania, the love song had held the central place in the music enjoyed by vast majority of listeners. But now it all but disappeared from the repertoires of the hot up-and-coming bands. Even more surprising, genuine eroticism was almost as elusive in the punk and new wave pantheon, despite ensembles that called themselves the Sex Pistols, Buzzcocks, and The Slits, among other naughty names. True, sexual references in the lyrics played an occasional role, but typically as a way of establishing the transgressive credentials of the band. The whole notion of intimacy is foreign to this music. The assertive and often angry punk stance precluded it. "Punk rock's attitude to the sex act itself was not libertarian but puritan," argues punk rock historian Jon Savage. "The body was not something to be celebrated but...objectified through fear." To some degree, this new tone in rock reminds me of the attitudes of the ancient Romans, who found something unmanly and disgraceful in the love song. But the punk ethos took this stance to a new level, infusing it with politically charged rebellion and devising a new type of popular music in which disillusionment and sometimes outright rage trumped romance.

The marvel of the punk movement was how it could say so much about sex without conjuring up any hints of sensuousness or human connection. Thus we find a song about abortion on the Sex Pistols' *Never Mind the Bollocks* LP; the first single released by the Buzzcocks after signing with United Artists, "Orgasm Addict," deals with masturbation; the opening track on The Clash's debut album, "Janie Jones," is about a brothel madam. Elvis Costello released the single "Alison" to promote his first album *My Aim Is True*, but some have suggested that this apparent love song (which includes the album title, with its ostensible gun reference, in its lyrics) is actually about murder. Costello denied it, but the spirit of the age was such that a hit song about killing your lover wasn't so unlikely. Around this same time, Nancy Spungen, girlfriend of Sid Vicious of the Sex Pistols, died of a knife wound. Vicious was arrested and charged with murder but died of an overdose before the case came to trial. The story of Sid and Nancy got mythologized and scrutinized in the aftermath, much as happened in an earlier century with Abelard and Heloise (a romance that also, oddly enough, ended with a knife wound). For better or worse, this unseemly tale persisted as the most famous punk love story.

The more polished ensembles that came to the forefront around the dawn of the 1980s, such as The Police, Culture Club, Joy Division, and The Smiths, tended toward a crafted pop sensibility, but even here the anti-romantic tone stood out as a defining element. The love songs most appealing to their fans were often strange or cynical or flippant—marked, for example, by the awkward flirting of The Smiths' "This Charming Man," the resignation of "Love Will Tear Us Apart" by Joy Division, or the general weirdness of Culture Club's "Karma Chameleon." Morrissey, lead singer with The Smiths, claimed in interviews that he was celibate, and though his later revelations called that assertion into question, an affirmation of asexuality seemed very much aligned with the mood of late 1970s and 1980s progressive pop-rock. In his 1978 song "Lipstick Vogue," Elvis Costello announced that love was a tumor and needed to be cut out. A year later, the band Gang of Four compared love to a case of anthrax. Not every rock star went quite so far, but a general rejection of the utopian 1960s vision of love and sex could be seen in a wide range of works, from the neutered tone of Brian Eno's minimalism to My Bloody Valentine's shoe-gazing sounds. And when sex wasn't forgotten, it usually tended toward kinkiness. The Police, who racked up the most sales of any of these 1980s artists, encompassed a whole range of fetishes and hang-ups in their hit singles, which included the masochism of "King of Pain" and "Wrapped Around Your Finger," the taunting stalker's boasts of "Every Breath You Take," and the creepy Humbert Humbert evocations of "Don't Stand So Close to Me."

Not since the medieval era had romantic music fallen into such disfavor. Yet even as punk rockers and new wave bands renounced softer sentiments, an unexpected factor entered into the equation. A few months after Sid Vicious's death, an ex-deejay named Robert Pittman and former CBS news radio manager John Lack made a pitch to their corporate overseers at Warner Amex Satellite Entertainment Company, seeking $20 million in funding to support a bold plan to marry cable television, hit songs, and video footage. At the end of the presentation, the suits conferred and agreed to commit the cash, ensuring the launch of MTV. I doubt whether these instigators even mentioned love or sex in their strategic plan, but the folks making the videos soon figured out the value of placing these ingredients prominently in their fare. And just as punk rock and its aftermath had worked to remove eroticism and romance from commercial music, MTV and the video format brought them back into the forefront with a vengeance, constructing a new formula for popular entertainment that would redefine the love song in the modern age. To some degree, we are still dealing with the fallout.

CHAPTER 17

As Nasty as They Wanna Be

There's no religion but sex and music.—Sting

It's hard to claim that sexiness ever falls out of style, but anyone who judged matters on the basis of cutting-edge popular music in the late 1970s and early 1980s might have speculated that a new puritanism had infected the leading rock bands. Not since the age of the castrati had asexuality risen so high in the charts, and arousal levels sunk so low. Punkers and New Wave stars eschewed romance—David Byrne of Talking Heads summed up the sentiment, announcing in his song "Life During Wartime": there's "no time for dancing, or lovey dovey; I ain't got time for that now." The romantic flame didn't burn much brighter in the sythnpop or glam metal bands of the day. When Mötley Crüe released its debut album in 1981, the band members wisely chose the title *Too Fast for Love*, and many fans applauded their priorities. The disco scene, in particular, now found itself subject to frequent parody, by everyone from Frank Zappa to Sesame Street, and the erotic clichés of the idiom spurred an angry backlash even among music industry insiders. A San Jose radio host inspired many imitators by playing a few bars of a 'sexy' disco hit ("Macho Man," for example), speeding up the song to squeaky gibberish, then adding the sound of a flushing toilet or a person vomiting—followed by a quick switch to a loud heavy metal track. Other deejays in other cities invented their own anti-disco stunts; the most ambitious may have been Disco Demolition Night at a 1979 Chicago White Sox doubleheader at Comiskey Park, during which a reported fifty thousand dance records were destroyed in a midfield explosion.

Of course, the music industry continued to release songs about love and sex, and many had airplay success. But increasingly these were attacked or ridiculed by critics and fans. When Rod Stewart released his single "Da Ya Think I'm Sexy?" in 1978, he was hammered by rock purists for selling out. Olivia Newton-John sold two million copies of "Physical," but many millions more laughed at the cutesy sensuality of her performance. Meanwhile a surprising number of hit pop

246

singles put aside romance in favor of chaste or simply strange subjects, such as Christopher Cross's paean to "Sailing," Dolly Parton's song about the workaday "9 to 5" job, Queen's "Another One Bites the Dust," Frankie Valli's "Grease," or Randy Newman's "Short People." In a few years, the AIDS epidemic would cause many to think twice about casual couplings, but even before medical authorities and media identified this situation, a noticeable retreat from intimacy could be heard over the airwaves.

Despite these precedents, sexy music came back with a vengeance over the course of the 1980s, but record labels and performers get little credit for this turnaround. The instigators were technology and consumer decisions on home entertainment. The emergence of the music video and the spread of cable television transformed the love song into a visual genre, and the most successful artists of the decade—Michael Jackson, Madonna, Prince, Whitney Houston, and others—took full advantage of the new format. Few were paying attention when MTV started broadcasting music videos in August 1981. Only a quarter of U.S. households had access to cable television at the time, and the concept of filming performances of hit songs was anything but new—Hollywood had done this as far back as the 1920s. But the rapid spread of cable during the 1980s and the increasing focus by the music industry on elaborate video presentation of potential hits combined to transform the relationship between performer and audience. No one back then could have predicted the later rise of YouTube and web-driven viral videos, but the groundwork was laid during the MTV era, when song turned into spectacle, and recording artists put aside their instruments to strut, dance, and shake their way to superstardom.

The love song inevitably changed in response to this upheaval in the music business. Record labels had always favored talent with good looks and sex appeal, but these now turned into paramount attributes. The ability to play an instrument or compose songs no longer mattered quite so much. After the ascendancy of MTV, Paula Abdul could emerge from the ranks of cheerleaders for the Los Angeles Lakers as a hit music star, and the move made perfect sense given the new emphasis on sexiness and cool dance steps. The pop act Milli Vanilli, invited to join Abdul on the Club MTV tour which took video stars on the road, couldn't even sing their own songs, but they looked good on camera and danced with lots of energy—if they had done a better job of hiding their lip-syncing, which eventually turned them into a music industry joke, they might have continued to enjoy their video-driven stardom.

In truth, even the legit stars needed to rely on outside help as music turned into a multimedia pageant. Michael Jackson, Madonna, and other celebrity performers not only required the support of a filmmaking entourage to mount their dazzling videos, but also delegated composing, arranging, and playing instrumental parts to a degree never seen before in the music business; yet the finished product showed the wisdom of this team-oriented approach. When they appeared in the MTV rotation, these artists exuded the charisma of Hollywood stars, and their every step was choreographed, rehearsed, and polished to perfection. The songs played a part in creating an ambience of romance and eroticism, but now only a modest part in expensive productions that drew on every possible tool to maximize the sex appeal of the star. Some griped that music was turning into a bump-and-grind show—and, in truth, many of the dance moves in the hit videos had originated not with George Balanchine or Martha Graham, but in strip clubs and burlesque shows. Yet the very nature of the medium inescapably required the transformation of the love song into a physical demonstration, and the compact nature of the form, typically of three or four minutes in duration, made a nuanced love story almost impossible to convey. Occasionally an artist would stretch out the form and add a narrative setup to the song-and-dance routine—as did, for example, Michael Jackson in 1982 with his thirteen-minute *Thriller* video, produced with an outlay of a half million dollars—but few musicians had the budget or inclination to tell structured stories. The video format usually required performers to cut to the chase, and in matters of love, this meant less courtship and foreplay, and more thrusting hips and crotch-centered camera shots.

Not all of the songs featured in MTV videos dealt with love and sex, but after casting, choreography, and costuming were completed, even the least romantic tunes, invocations to "Walk Like an Egyptian" or "Express Yourself," had been markedly eroticized. An increasingly common device paired fully dressed men, often in formal evening attire or official uniforms, with women in lingerie or bikinis. The music video had no monopoly on this formula, nor did it originate it—I give choreographer Bob Fosse the most credit for its popularity. (You can see an early example in Fosse's mid-1950s staging of "Whatever Lola Wants" for *Damn Yankees*, and he was still working out variations of the suit-meets-undies routine two decades later in his stylized work for *Cabaret*, *Chicago*, and *All That Jazz*.) But this dance meme soon turned into a MTV staple and, for all its incongruity, proved irresistible to audiences. In Cher's video for "If I Could Turn Back Time," she prances around the battleship USS *Missouri*, backed by a cadre of uniformed sailors, while wearing an outfit better suited to lap-dancing than nautical pursuits. David Lee Roth sings "California Girls" to more than a dozen attractive young women in skimpy swimwear, but he is fully dressed, complete with stylish vest and bowtie. Madonna adopted a similar concept, portraying a peepshow entertainer in her video "Open Your Heart."

These exercises in musical titillation each resulted in impressive record sales. Even so, artists found it harder and harder to achieve a sufficient level of shock and awe given the endless repetition of these sexually charged formulas. How could a megastar push the envelope without running afoul of MTV censors? Madonna found the combination of eroticism and Christian iconography stirred up some protests—and a healthy dose of publicity and sales. Some artists tested the waters by including homoerotic content, for example British band Frankie Goes to Hollywood, whose initial video for their hit song "Relax" was set in a gay S&M club. But edginess failed in its purpose if a video went beyond the established boundaries of cable TV fare. In the case of "Relax," the band needed to shoot a second, much tamer video for their song.

Most of the controversies of the era arose from the visual images, not the songs themselves. I speak of songs here, but the artists of this period increasingly focused on creating recordings, not compositions, and often the recording itself was conceived from the start in conjunction with the potential for video realization. Anyone who simply studied the sheet music would almost always come away disappointed by the flimsy foundations on which hits were constructed, but by the time the team of experts and handlers had created the final product, the meager song had undergone a magical transmutation into an extravagant vehicle for the star performer. The themes presented in the lyrics of the leading songs were often highly conventional, recycling the same sentiments and imagery favored in decades past. The words of Robert Palmer's "Simply Irresistible" and "Addicted to Love" could hardly be more banal, but viewers were captivated by flickering images of the artist, dressed like a successful banker, backed by a cadre of deadpan miniskirted and braless lovelies who looked as if each had been cloned from the same DNA. The tune "Rhythm Nation" is little better than an awkward chant for an imaginary country that couldn't afford a real national anthem, but Janet Jackson's leadership of a sexy paramilitary troupe of dancers turned it into one of the most riveting videos of the era, a kind of sensual steampunk for MTV viewers. Madonna's song "Cherish" not only reuses the title of a chart-topping single by The Association from more than twenty years earlier, but even mimics its opening words; and the reference to Romeo and Juliet in the lyrics—allegedly the song was partly inspired by Shakespeare—draws on an even older, if by now banal and predictable, romantic symbolism. Even so, the finished recording is catchy and danceable, and its strikingly Hollywood-ish video, with rolling-in-the-sand romance overtones of *From Here to Eternity*, brought this appealing taste of pop-music candy to places the Bard of Avon never envisioned. Such was the fate of most of the popular love songs of the MTV age: the words embraced tired clichés, but the spectacle proved simply irresistible.

Technology also spurred the rise of rap music during this period, but instead of high-budget video tech the early exponents of this genre relied on mix-and-match equipment and do-it-yourself audio innovations, much of it driven by the humble record turntable. The disco craze had legitimized the shift from live bands to recorded entertainment at clubs and events, and rappers took advantage of these new rules of engagement. In disco culture, the recording artists still got the accolades, not the person operating the sound system or spinning the disks at the club; but now at block parties and sundry gatherings in the Bronx and other urban areas the creative use of multiple turntables and rapping over prerecorded beats turned the deejay or emcee (or more often DJ and MC, as they now came to be known) into the main star of the event.

The basic elements of this revolution had long been in place. Many radio hosts had made a specialty of inserting their smooth or hip talk over the beat on the intros of hit songs, and soul artists such as Barry White and Isaac Hayes had turned this kind of stylized monologue into a key component of their records. New York's Caribbean community had long hosted "back-a-yard" social events where powerful bass and drum–driven sounds, low on melody and high on volume, dominated the proceedings. Club deejays had already mastered the use of multiple turntables, techniques that allowed for a nonstop transition from song to song. Now the rappers drew on all these precedents, meanwhile adding a few new tricks of their own, and with such skill and success that they turned the hierarchy of the music business on its head. The physical record, the 'star' who made it, and the equipment to play it, all became subservient to the needs and purposes of the rapper, who used these ingredients as a springboard to a new creative product. "Lots of times we'd give shows with rappers and get bigger crowds than if we had a guy with just records," producer Russell Simmons later recalled. "The more flyers and stickers and posters that you could get your name on, the more popular you'd become as a rapper."

The crossover success of early rap hits such as Sugar Hill Gang's "Rapper's Delight" and Kurtis Blow's "The Breaks" proved that this music could appeal to audiences outside of the black community or, for that matter, outside of the United States—"Rapper's Delight" even reached the top chart spot in the Netherlands, and got to the number-two slot in Sweden and Norway. Some in the music industry no doubt dismissed these as novelty hits, flukes fueled by a different sound that would come and go, as had other music fads in the past. But rather than fading, rap spawned a series of megastar acts over the next several years, including Run-DMC, LL Cool J, Public Enemy, and the Beastie Boys.

Love was rarely the focal point of these early rap hits, and when it came to the forefront, as on Spoonie Gee's "Love Rap" from 1979, the attitude downplayed romance in favor of the more typical rap boasts about being a *player*. This is the same artist who, when describing himself in another track from period, rhymed "baby-maker" with "heartbreaker" and "woman-taker"—a far cry from Shakespeare's sonnets or even your usual Valentine's Day card formulas. LL Cool J, the stage name of James Todd Smith, who adopted that moniker as an abbreviation of "Ladies Love Cool James," had more success in crafting genuinely romantic rap ballads, notably his hit "I Need Love" from 1987, which adopted an intimate and insinuating delivery unusual for the genre. But perhaps the most surprising rap love saga of the era originated with the band U.T.F.O. which released the single "Roxanne, Roxanne" in 1984, a familiar "complaining lover" song that spurred dozens of responses from other artists. Rap fans even started talking about the "Roxanne wars" as different rappers offered up the perspective of Roxanne herself, or her parents or brothers or some other commentator on this failed relationship.

These tracks, however, ran counter to the dominant tendencies of the idiom. The in-your-face attitudes of most rap performers, with sweeping gesticulations and declamatory shout-it-out delivery, had little in common with the time-honored techniques of musical seduction. Even the guy with the biggest collection of rap records must have felt a sense of genuine panic trying to find an album to play as background music when he brought his date back to his cool hip-hop pad. With the rise of gangsta rap around this same time, romantic themes were pushed even further into the background. The defiant stances of N.W.A., Public Enemy, and the other politically charged rap acts of the day left little room for flirtatious banter or postcoital pillow talk. This music required a tougher tone. Its fans wanted street talk, not sweet talk. You can even quantify it at the Rap Genius website, which offers a statistical measure of the frequency with which various terms show up in rap lyrics. The site's database, which goes back to 1988, shows that in every year the term *bitch* appeared more often than *woman* or *girl* or *lover*. The word *romance* is all but absent from the database, although *guns*, *cars*, and *money* figure as recurring references. Occasionally a female perspective came to the forefront of hip-hop culture, with Salt-n-Pepa, Queen Latifah, and other rapping ladies emerging in the late 1980s to counter the male-dominated tone, but never with enough influence to change the macho culture of the genre.

We have already seen something similar in our look at punk rock. Exponents of a defiant, testosterone-charged musical style take pride in their uncompromising attitudes and truculent tropes, but struggle to find a way to address the more intimate side of human relationships. And hostility to romance, for all its appealing badass vibe, tends to limit sales potential. Yet, unlike the punks, the rappers found a solution to this problem. The men of rap filled their videos with lots of scantily clad ladies, who twisted and writhed and shook their rumps as if they were horse riders without the horse. Lyrics spilled over with sexual references, often described in the coarsest terms. Few rap acts did more to advance this explicit strain in the music—or to spur demands for censorship and album warning labels—than 2 Live Crew, whose aptly named 1989 LP *As Nasty as They Wanna Be* made history not only as a double-platinum seller, but as the first album in U.S. history to become certified as obscene by a district court (a decision later overturned by the Eleventh Circuit Court).

This band was hardly the first to shock with dirty rap—Blowfly, a specialist in sexualized parodies of popular songs, had even released a song called "Rapp Dirty" almost a decade before *As Nasty as They Wanna Be*. But the notoriety of

2 Live Crew contributed to the growing pressure on the music industry to police the profanity in its releases. In the years leading up to this turning point, a host of albums with explicit lyrics, edgy content, or dicey cover art—including many outside the hip-hop genre, by artists such as Frank Zappa, Prince, Megadeth, and Guns N' Roses—had stirred up controversy and spurred demands for political or industry action. But the new craze for sexy rap tilted the balance irremediably in favor of those calling for intervention. Finally in March 1990, the Recording Industry Association of America introduced its "Parental Advisory" warning label. The follow-up 2 Live Crew album *Banned in the U.S.A.*, marketed as a solo album by group member Luke with the rest of the band receiving supporting credit, was the first album to wear it.

Album cover stickers kept these releases off the shelves of some retailers and outside of a few households, but they did little to halt the production of songs with pointed sexual references or videos featuring exposed flesh. The meme of the fully clothed man singing to (or dancing with) a mostly exposed woman went mainstream during the 1980s and 1990s. You could find it everywhere, from fashion magazines to TV award shows. Even the older generation of rock and soul stars learned how to play this game. During his televised duet with Tina Turner at the 1985 Live Aid benefit concert, Mick Jagger tore off his partner's skirt midsong, and few believed his later explanation that the disrobing was unintended. Nowadays we have a term for these crowd-pleasing mishaps, the *wardrobe malfunction*, but long before the 2004 Super Bowl halftime show that brought this phrase into the popular vocabulary, the basic formula was established. A male star dresses to kill, and his female collaborator undresses to thrill.

Mainstream culture had shifted, and attire that once would have resulted in arrest for subverting public morals now helped boost ladies to stardom as dancing divas. Yet listeners seeking prim, simple, and sex-free love songs still had many options, especially in more wholesome music genres. Demand for country music surged in the 1990s, perhaps as a reaction to these trends, and here audiences could enjoy sentimental tunes conveying heartfelt love with little to offend even delicate sensibilities. You could hardly imagine a more cloying love song than "Achy Breaky Heart," released by Billy Ray Cyrus in 1992, but audiences rewarded its declarations of sanitized, maudlin longing by purchasing twenty million copies of the *Some Gave All* album that contained this often derided and parodied track. When Garth Brooks sang "Unanswered Prayers" on his *Double Live* recording from 1998, it sounded as if tens of thousands of women in the audience knew the lyrics and were joining in the performance of this mawkish tune about a guy who prefers his wife to the old high school sweetheart he meets at a hometown football game. Judging by the 100 million records Brooks sold during the decade, fans probably did know the words to "Unanswered Prayers," and most of the other songs he played on stage. Even as the world grew more urbanized and cowboys disappeared from other spheres of popular culture—the movie and TV industries had all but abandoned the once flourishing western genre—country music flourished. Sales of country recordings doubled during the decade, and on radio it surpassed all other formats in many major markets, with around 2,500 U.S. stations devoted to its soothing strains. Even outside the United States, the music found a ready audience, notably in English-speaking countries, but also in locales that might seem resistant to this kind of music. "Achy Breaky Heart," for example, was a hit single in Austria, France, Germany, and Switzerland.

But music fans had plenty of other choices of genre and subgenre within a fragmenting music industry. Back when Frank Sinatra or Elvis Presley rose to fame, audiences tended to share the same popular culture—disseminated via a small number of radio and TV stations and other vehicles of mass media. I remember my amazement, as a tiny child, that my ancient grandfather, born during the Teddy Roosevelt administration, could do a killing vocal parody of Elvis—how did he even know the words to "Hound Dog"?—but such was the cross-generational visibility (although not necessarily appeal) of stardom in a day when households possessed only a few entertainment options. Yet during the second half of the twentieth century, a series of technological advances broadened these choices almost to infinity: first the spread of FM radio, then the channel proliferation of cable and satellite TV, and finally the rise of the labyrinthine World Wide Web. Along the way, manufacturers of consumer electronics provided new ways to personalize your listening experience, whether via the Walkman, Discman, iPod, or some other device. The terms *mixtape* and *playlist* were coming out of the mouths of even average music consumers, as the ideas of personalization and customization gained more and more adherents. By the final years of the century, mass media had turned into a proliferation of countless micromedia options.

How did this impact the love song? At first glance, the onlooker struggles to find some common thread in this unraveling. Consumers in the 1990s could pick almost any kind of love song, fine-tuned to aesthetic rules of their own choosing. They could opt for bracing grunge rock, romantic jazz standards, the increasingly popular merging of rap and R&B, boy bands or girl bands showcasing more sex appeal than talent, different variants of electronic dance music, nu metal or old metal, and a host of other styles, many of them now incorporating the term *alternative* or *alt* in their name. In truth, almost every kind of sound was an 'alt' sound in this era, except for the few megastar artists who could rise above the fray and achieve genuine across-the-board stardom that even grandpa and grandma acknowledged, however grudgingly. You could choose music that celebrated chaste love, dirty love, agape love, and any other variant or fetish that floated your boat.

Yet amid this proliferation of single-person soundscapes a few important general considerations jump out. The concept of a shared music celebrating a transformative communal love—those blissful and no doubt unrealistic dreams that spawned the Summer of Love and Woodstock—had by this point mostly disappeared from view. Music was now an assertion of individuality, a lifestyle choice, or at best an admission ticket to some fringe subgroup of society. At some point songs began losing their mystique as rallying cries to a grand utopian collective, whether potential or actual; instead, like most consumer products, they were increasingly fine-tuned and targeted at specific segments of the marketplace. With the proliferation of choice and genre, it's doubtful whether any kind of love song can now "speak for a whole generation," as had been the case during the Swing Era or the Age of Rock. The shift has been gradual, but the end result is unmistakable. When comedians in the 1960s and 1970s made fun of the social pretensions of music, they often laughed at people sitting in a circle singing along to "Kumbaya," but the joke at the dawn of the twenty-first century was more likely at the expense of the clueless jogger or pedestrian with earbuds, blissed out on a self-contained soundtrack for an audience of one.

The arrival of the Internet, with its endless opportunities for customization and isolation, merely accelerated the adoption of trends already in place, and furthered the separation of music consumption from the traditional locations where courtship and romance had taken place—the ballrooms, nightclubs, and social gatherings where couples of an earlier day had met and flirted, dated and danced. YouTube and streaming services take the primitive concept of personalized music, born with mixtapes and the Walkman, and pump it up on steroids. High tech headsets and other immersion technologies enhance the experience, but also its detachment. If fans showed their appreciation of Sinatra or the Beatles by clapping and screaming, they now do the same for the hot new millennium acts by clicking and streaming. In the twenty-first century, a young lover can still take a date out to hear live music or dance, sharing in the seductive sounds while advancing a personal romantic agenda. But with the rise of virtual entertainment, this kind of coupled music consumption is rarer and rarer. Technologies of music dissemination instead aim at reaching the audience one member at a time, and as an inevitable result the chasm between courtship and listenership grows wider and wider. In such an environment, the music of love gradually frees itself from the rituals of lovers, and gets more entrenched in our fantasy lives, our moments alone with our preferred digital interface.

On the one hand, these new platforms for music are liberating and empowering. New love songs flow around the world with surprising speed and unpredictability, so that J-Pop or K-Pop can compete with the most heavily promoted releases from the major U.S. and European labels. Artists from Australia and New Zealand go global with an ease impossible to imagine only a few years earlier.

With the smallest effort, I can hear the songs that are currently captivating listeners in Brazil or Mali or Russia or any other spot on the map. And aspirants to stardom from any locale can make their own love songs, filmed at home with their phone or some other inexpensive device, and shared with the whole world a few seconds later. We don't need to settle for passivity and mindless consumption; we can be creative agents and add our music to the mix. But in practice, the most salient result of the new technologies is to isolate and aggregate, to turn what we once called the "audience" into "metrics."

The proliferation of TV talent contests represents just another twist on this same formula. The invisible millions show their support for a favored singer or performance by pressing the right buttons, and sending their vote off for tabulation. The vocalist still sings for love, but now it's for *our* love, for the fickle viewer at home, deciding which candidate to back. The tunes themselves are a hodgepodge of old and new, with a heavy emphasis on familiar fare, and above all catchy love songs with mass appeal. Any aspirant to Idol-dom with a taste for the edgy, ironic, sarcastic, or transgressive rarely lasts long in such competitions. Nor does the emotional depth of a vocal interpretation, that Billie Holiday-ish ability to inhabit the feeling state of a lyric, play much of a role in these singer showdowns. Instead, stage presence, vocal pyrotechnics, and an aw-shucks willingness to please invariably determine the outcome. Yet the scale of these competitions, which make all previous talent shows look minuscule in comparison, demands our begrudging respect. Fans submitted close to 100 million votes in the season-seven finale of *American Idol*—many perhaps voting multiple times to ensure the victory of their favorite vocal gladiator. This obsession with TV singing competitions is a global phenomenon, the same formula adapted and repeated in market after market. The proliferation in China—where twenty TV talent shows were scheduled to launch in 2013—got so out of hand that the government issued restrictions on the competitions. Authorities justified the regulation by citing the need to "avoid extravagance, luxury, sensationalism and flashy programming, as well as formats that cause too much excitement."

But even these impressive metrics pale beside the mounting clicks that propel viral videos onto various homepages, social networking sites, and handheld devices. "Gangnam Style" would have struggled to reach a global audience in an earlier day, but effortlessly generated a stunning two billion plays on YouTube. A host of other music videos can count their views in the hundreds of millions. Here every consumer action is quantified and analyzed, each click and share, every listen and replay. Algorithms identify the trending tunes, and accelerate the dissemination of the trendy, consigning the rest to virtual obscurity. And what do the metrics tell us? The combination of a sexy singer-dancer with a brash rapper has proven especially popular—indeed, never before in the history of commercial music has the two-stars-for-the-price-of-one format found more success. A perusal of the list of the most viewed YouTube music videos of all time shows that roughly half of these megahits are built on paired celebrity perform- ers, usually a boy-and-girl combo, although boy-and-boy and girl-and-girl also work in a pinch. Jennifer Lopez and Pitbull quickly racked up more than a half- billion views for "On the Floor," as did Rihanna and Eminem for "Love the Way You Lie," while Justin Bieber and Ludacris got close to a billion hits for "Baby," which briefly ranked as the most viewed music video ever, until nudged aside by "Gangnam Style." Here, and in many other hit videos, we can identify the most successful formula for the love song in the present day, namely the combination of macho and sexy compressed into a few minutes of colorful footage, juiced up with plenty of camera cuts and gyrating hips. Even when a song has little or nothing to do with love, as in "Party Rock Anthem" (another video that climbed above the coveted half-billion-views mark), these same ingredients usually show up in the finished product. A student of the form could watch hit music videos for hours, and fail to find a single one that didn't include some erotic content that would have been banned from network television only a few decades ago.

"Sex sells," as I've heard over and over again. Whoever came up with that cynical two-word marketing plan must have worked in the music business. But even sex—or at least sexualized music—demands variety, and rising stars must find ways to work new variations on the oldest of themes. Girl bands in Asia now incorporate elements of cosplay, anime, action films, and gymnastics into their provocative performances. In the United States, Rihanna releases sexually charged videos dealing with everything from S&M to Russian roulette. Raising the ante still higher, Lady Gaga draws on the most extravagant elements of performance art, in both her music and public appearances, and discovers ever new ways of marrying the aural, the erotic, and the outrageous. As the situation warrants, she appears in a meat suit, inside a large egg, wearing a G-string and a bra made of seashells, or (Lady Gaga emulating Lady Godiva) nothing at all.

Perhaps the most powerful and recurring image in the twenty-first-century conception of the love song is that time-tested combination of the sharply dressed man with the mostly unclothed woman, the Fosse meme that refuses to die. This stylized conjunction of eye candy and fashion statement must somehow fulfill both latent male and latent female fantasies, or it wouldn't keep coming back to haunt us. And it somehow retains the power, at least in its most extreme forms, to shock. When music critic Dorian Lynskey, writing in *The Guardian*, announced that Robin Thicke's "Blurred Lines" was "the most contro- versial song of the decade," everyone knew that he wasn't really talking about the song. This piece of beat-driven dance music offered little new or different—in fact many commentators complained that it sounded like a rehash of a Marvin Gaye track from 1977. The real controversy came in the visual images accom- panying the Thicke recording. Two versions of the video were released, one in which the female models were barely clothed and the other in which they were mostly bare. In both instances, Thicke kept himself in natty attire suitable for a *GQ* shoot.

But these exercises in musical eroticism hardly made a stir when compared with Thicke's televised appearance with Miley Cyrus at the MTV Video Music Awards in August 2013. Cyrus, who came to fame as a sweet-as-pie teen actress on the Disney Channel series *Hannah Montana*, accompanied Thicke with dance moves that no doubt aimed at sexiness but achieved instead a strange rote and ritualistic quality, more like the courting ceremonies of marionettes. Turning her back on her dance partner, Cyrus bent over like a female cat in heat and rotated her buttocks in a move known as "twerking"—a word all but unknown before the broadcast, but heard everywhere in ensuing days. Wearing only skin-colored underwear, Cyrus sometimes accompanied her 'dance' moves by waving a large foam finger, akin to the exaggerated phallus representations in some ancient art, and sticking out her tongue.

Somehow we've come full circle in our history of love songs. As you may recall, when we looked at the songs of the ancient Mesopotamian fertility rites a few hundred pages ago, we found many scholars asking the pointed question: Do these really deserve to be called love songs? The sexual elements were so heightened and the romantic trappings so noticeably absent, that we hesitated before applying the word *love* to the proceedings. Today we wrestle with the same question with regard to the most successful 'love songs' and are forced to ponder how, several thousand years later, we got back to the starting line.

Is this the inevitable result of the leveling impact of the web and metrics-driven algorithms that now dominate the music business? Face it, for a video to generate hundreds of millions of views in a few days and rise to the top of the heap, it needs to offer something that transcends national boundaries, cultural differences, language barriers, and varying tastes—and nothing manages that better than the brute force of biology. Should we be surprised that, turbocharged by these global technology platforms, aesthetics blurs into the basic instincts? The message of these videos is universal, no subtitles required, our receptivity literally coded into our DNA.

So is this the endgame of the love song? Are we seeing the final validation of Darwin's claim that the drive to procreate plays the tune, and the rest of us just dance to the primal beat? Is survival of the sexiest the inescapable rule of the day, and every day to come—the formula for popular music that will always deliver superior metrics?

Perhaps. But I'm still not ready to write off romance. The rituals of court-ship and the heady euphoria of emotional surrender are, in their own way, as alluring as the provocative sex come-ons of our viral videos—and with perhaps even more potential for aesthetic transformation. The narrative of love, with its endless complications and resolutions, offers more variety than even the most skilled courtesan can invent or digital *Kama Sutra* contain. When compared with the tangible qualities and overwhelming physicality of sex, the ineffable metaphysics of love must strike us as insubstantial, perhaps even a burdensome preliminary to the main event. But the heartfelt love song, yes even the *wimpy* love song, has overcome far tougher odds in the past, and if it has managed to surmount religious, political, and cultural obstacles during the course of millennia, it can certainly find a way around YouTube algorithms and the conventional wisdom of our hormone-driven music business. As this history makes clear, love has spurred many musical revolutions in the past and thus can probably set off a few more in the future. But another lesson, documented here again and again, is that when the upheaval arrives, when *love* finally calls the tune, it almost always comes from the least expected direction—from the bohemian, the outcast, the excluded, the marginalized and least powerful folks, and the most hidden places.

NOTES

Introduction and Acknowledgments

ix The time for next things is past: Arthur C. Danto, *The State of the Art* (New York: Prentice Hall, 1987), 217.

xii risk accusations of sentimentality: David Foster Wallace, *A Supposedly Fun Thing I'll Never Do Again: Essays and Arguments* (Boston: Little, Brown, 1987), 81.

Chapter 1: Birds Do It!

1 primeval man, or rather some early progenitor: Darwin, *The Descent of Man*, 90.

2 drumming to the snipe's tail: Darwin, *The Descent of Man*, 391.
beautifully constructed stridulating organs: Darwin, *The Descent of Man*, 587.
Love is still the commonest theme: Darwin, *The Descent of Man*, 592–93.
have nearly the same taste: Darwin, *The Descent of Man*, 371.

3 a brown thrasher: Kroodsma and Parker, "Vocal Virtuosity in the Brown Thrasher." Kroodsma adds that this bird "was probably improvising on the wing, so to speak, so that he could sing an infinite variety of songs" (email to author, July 27, 2013).
In my opinion the simple beating: Wallaschek, *Primitive Music*, 245.
The howling of dogs: Herbert Spencer, "The Origin and Function of Music," in *Literary Style and Music*, 78–79.
obscene processes and prurient apparitions: Jonathan Smith, *Charles Darwin and Victorian Visual Culture* (Cambridge: Cambridge University Press, 2006), 168. Ruskin's refusal to have sex with his wife has been much discussed by commentators, who have offered various interpretations. Ruskin's own explanation, given in a legal deposition, was that "though her face were beautiful, her person was not formed to excite passion." Timothy Hilton, *John Ruskin: The Early Years* (New Haven, CT: Yale University Press, 2000), 118.
Edward Hagen and Gregory Bryant: Hagen and Bryant, "Music and Dance as a Coalition Signaling System."

4 ornithologist Douglas Smith: Smith, "Male Singing Ability."
J. R. Krebs demonstrated: J. R. Krebs, "Song and Territory in the Great Tit Parus Major," in Stonehouse and Perrins, *Evolutionary Ecology*, 47–62.
Even the apparently romantic: Wickler, "Duetting Songs in Birds." More recently Hall and Magrath, "Temporal Coordination Signals Coalition Quality," have shown that precisely coordinated duets between two magpie-larks are more effective at defending territories than uncoordinated duets.
In contrast to birds, singing behavior: Thomas Geissmann, "Gibbon Songs and Human Music from an Evolutionary Perspective" in Wallin et al., *The Origins of Music*, 112, 119.

5 **Musician Leonard Williams:** Williams, *The Dancing Chimpanzee*, 13.
   But just when Darwin's proposed: For the research mentioned here see Ukkola et al., "Musical Aptitude Is Associated with AVPR1A-Haplotypes"; Ukkola et al., "Association of the Arginine Vasopressin Receptor 1A (AVPR1A) Haplotypes with Listening to Music"; de Kloet, "From Vasotocin to Stress and Cognition"; Panksepp and Bernatzky, "Emotional Sounds and the Brain"; Lim and Young, "Vasopressin-Dependent Neural Circuits"; Murphy et al., "Changes in Oxytocin and Vasopressin Secretion During Sexual Activity in Men."
   Research conducted by Sarah Earp and Donna L. Maney: Earp and Maney, "Birdsong."
   increased singing by male sparrows: Goodson, "Territorial Aggression and Dawn Song."
6 **a survey of thousands of commercial recordings:** Geoffrey Miller, "Evolution of Human Music through Sexual Selection," in Wallin et al., *The Origins of Music*, 329–60.
   Music is what happens: Miller, "Evolution of Human Music," 349.
   men find higher-pitched female voices more attractive: Some researchers have tried to push this research further, demonstrating that women's voices become higher pitched immediately before ovulation, when they are most fertile. Could this serve as a signal to potential mates? Alas, female voices also move up in pitch right after ovulation, when they are less fertile, so the vocal cue is unreliable. See Fischer et al., "Do Women's Voices Provide Cues of the Likelihood of Ovulation?" For more on vocal pitch and perceived attractiveness, see Feinberg et al., "The Role of Femininity and Averageness of Voice Pitch"; Collins and Missing, "Vocal and Visual Attractiveness."
7 **hunter-gatherers in Tanzania:** Coren L. Apicella, David R. Feinberg, and Frank W. Marlowe, "Voice Pitch Predicts Reproductive Success in Male Hunter-Gatherers," *Biology Letters* 3, no. 6 (2007): 682–84.
   male and female subjects, presented with two photographs: Krauss et al., "Inferring Speakers' Physical Attributes from Their Voices."
   A recent study in France: Nicolas Guéguen, Sébastien Meineri, and Jacques Fischer-Lokou, "Men's Music Ability and Attractiveness to Women in a Real-Life Courtship Context," *Psychology of Music*, May 1, 2013, http://pom.sagepub.com/content/early/2013/05/01/0305735613482025.
   A similar study conducted in Israel: Sigal Tifferet, Ofir Gaziel, and Yoav Baram, "Guitar Increases Male Facebook Attractiveness: Preliminary Support for the Sexual Selection Theory of Music," *Letters on Evolutionary Behavioral Science* 3, no. 1 (2012): 4–6.
   The average male has seven: "New Survey Tells How Much Sex We're Having," NBC News, June 22, 2007, http://www.msnbc.msn.com/id/19374216/ns/health-sexual_health/t/new-survey-tells-how-much-sex-were-having/#.UOS527ZM70g. For Mick Jagger and Gene Simmons see Kiki Von Glinow, "Mick Jagger Sex Life: Rocker Has Slept with 4,000 Women, Biographer Says," *Huffington Post*, July 11, 2012, http://www.huffingtonpost.com/2012/07/11/mick-jagger-sex-life-4000-women_n_1666176.html; Gene Simmons interview with Terry Gross, *Fresh Air*, NPR, broadcast February 4, 2002, http://archive.org/details/TerryGrossInterviewWithGeneSimmons.
   Researchers have found a correlation: Primack et al., "Degrading and Non-Degrading Sex in Popular Music."
8 **Allan Bloom, who announced that:** Allan Bloom, *The Closing of the American Mind* (New York: Simon & Schuster, 1987), 73.

Chapter 2: Procreative Music

9 **There are in fact very few songs:** Williams, *The Dancing Chimpanzee*, 36.
   far from being basic human qualities: Colin Turnbull, *The Mountain People* (New York: Simon & Schuster, 1987), 32.
   There is no cuddling: Waipuldanya, as told to Douglas Lockwood, *I, the Aboriginal* (Sydney: Lansdowne, 1996), 107.

9 **Tell me of your marriage:** Quoted in Frederick E. Hoxie, *Parading through History: The Making of the Crow Nation in America 1805–1935* (Cambridge: Cambridge University Press, 1995), 190.

10 **Sir Laurens van der Post:** Laurens van der Post, *The Lost World of the Kalahari* (New York: William Morrow, 1958), 239.

11 **The rituals of music-making in these societies:** For these and other examples, see the chapter "The Hunter" in Gioia, *Work Songs*, 13–34.
    Folklorist Frank Hamel: Hamel, *Human Animals*, 30–31.

12 **a young bear was suckled:** Frazer, *The Golden Bough*, 2: 101–2.
    dance of the amorous mallard: Döpp, *Music and Eros*, 25.
    T. G. H. Strehlow witnessed: Strehlow, *Songs of Central Australia*, 305–27.

13 **the ugliest of the customs:** Herodotus, *The History*, translated by David Grene (Chicago: University of Chicago Press, 1987), 124. Much scholarly effort has gone into attempts to explain away this passage, for example by accusing Herodotus, in Jerrold Cooper's words, of "denigrating and exoticising the Oriental other." Yet Herodotus is ready to praise other Babylonian customs, and indeed many other foreign practices, in his work. And, as outlined in this chapter and elsewhere, a growing body of evidence supports his account. See Jerrold S. Cooper, "Sex and the Temple," in Kaniuth et al., *Tempel im Alten Orient*, 49–58. The student of love songs encounters many examples of scholars attempting to explain away references to sex in primary sources—the Song of Songs, the *Shijing*, Herodotus, Procopius, the vidas of the troubadours—and often on the basis of the scantiest evidence. This scholarly prudishness warrants scrutiny and critique.

16 **Surviving texts describe the king:** Kramer, *The Sacred Marriage Rite*, 62–66.
    Sumerian love songs are no exception to this tendency: For a recent summary of perspectives on whether intercourse accompanied the sacred marriage ritual, and other disputed aspects of the Sumerian tradition, see Pirjo Lapinkivi, "The Sumerian Sacred Marriage and Its Aftermath in Later Sources," in Nissinen and Uro, *Sacred Marriages*, 7–42.
    then and there she composes a song: Kramer, *The Sacred Marriage Rite*, 59. For more recent commentary on Kramer's work, and the sacred marriage ritual in general, see Lapinkivi, *The Sumerian Sacred Marriage*; Nissinen and Uro, *Sacred Marriages*.

17 **is a modified and conventionalized form:** Kramer, *The Sacred Marriage Rite*, 89.

18 **Yitzhak Sefati uses precisely that term:** Sefati, *Love Songs in Sumerian Literature*.
    Scholar Steve Tinney: Tinney, "Notes on Sumerian Sexual Lyric."
    The very existence of an ancient: Meador, *Inanna Lady of Largest Heart*, 5.
    in spite of all possible pitfalls: Rubio, "Inanna and Dumuzi."
    Your love is more delightful: Quotes from the Song of Songs are from the New International Version, 1:2, 15, 16.

19 **I love you through the daytimes:** Foster, *Love Songs of the New Kingdom*, 17.
    If only I were her Nubian maid: Fox, *The Song of Songs*, 37–38.

20 **This is a *fetish*:** For more on love magic and the connection between the spells and songs, see the chapter on magical incantations in Gioia, *Healing Songs*, 18–33.

21 **wrote a letter to Alfred Chester Beatty:** "It is unfortunate that the original story becomes very licentious at this point and I have felt it to be my scientific duty to translate the passages literally as it stands," Gardiner wrote to Beatty. Then added in further self-justification: "I need not say that the obscene passages were not of my seeking, but imposed by the material." See Charles Horton, " 'It was all a great adventure': Alfred Chester Beatty & the Formation of His Library," *Modern Ireland* 8, no. 2 (Summer 2000): 37–42.
    Scholar Erik Iversen: Iversen, "The Chester Beatty Papyrus," 84. The alternate translation is from Landgráfová and Navrátilová, *Sex and the Golden Goddess*, 168.

Chapter 3: Sappho and Confucius

24 **Barbara Johnson, a longtime:** Barbara Johnson, *The Feminist Difference: Literature, Psychoanalysis, Race and Gender* (Cambridge, MA: Harvard University Press, 1998), 114; Melissa Fran

Zeiger, *Beyond Consolation: Death, Sexuality, and the Changing Shape of the Elegy* (Ithaca, NY: Cornell University Press, 1997), 27.

25 **A scholiast commenting:** Willis Barnstone, ed. and trans., *The Complete Poems of Sappho* (Boston: Shambhala, 2009), 123–24.

One of our better sources: Campbell, *Greek Lyric*, 5.

all external and internal evidence: McEvilley, *Sappho*, 17.

26 **wrinkled and white-haired:** McEvilley, *Sappho*, 17. A previously unknown Sappho poem discovered in 2004, on the burdens of old age, tends to support this view.

An epigram attributed to Plato: This comment and the accompanying remarks about Sappho can be found in Campbell, *Greek Lyric*, 9, 13, 29, 49.

27 **What did Sappho of Lesbos teach:** Campbell, *Greek Lyric*, 43.

Last Tango in Paros: Peter Green made his "Last Tango in Paros" quip in the *Times Literary Supplement*, March 14, 1975, 272, cited in Davenport, *Seven Greeks*, 3. The passage from Davenport's translation of this poem quoted here is from the same volume, 28.

28 **The possibility I am suggesting:** West, *Studies in Greek Elegy and Iambus*, 27.

29 **I must think maidenly thoughts:** C. M. Bowra, *Pindar* (Oxford: Clarendon Press, 1964), 363.

On a papyrus of Alcman's work: Peter Bing and Rip Cohen, *Games of Venus: An Anthology of Greek and Roman Erotic Verse from Sappho to Ovid* (New York: Routledge, 1993), 64–65.

the inventor of the love song: David Mulroy, ed., *Early Greek Lyric Poetry* (Ann Arbor: University of Michigan Press, 1999), 55–56.

30 **young men of an age to marry:** Stehle, *Performance and Gender in Ancient Greece*, 32.

The songs came alive in performance: Ferrari, *Alcman and the Cosmos of Sparta*, 1.

The chorus does not act for itself: Calame, *Choruses of Young Women in Ancient Greece*, 89.

We find female choruses: For these and other examples of female choruses in ancient Greek rituals, see Calame, *Choruses of Young Women in Ancient Greece*, 89–206.

31 **She lived a tranquil life:** McEvilley, *Sappho*, 396–97.

to explain away Sappho's passion: Parker, "Sappho Schoolmistress," 313.

33 **Delicate Adonis is dying:** Campbell, *Greek Lyric*, 155.

To me it seems that man Rayor, *Sappho*, 44.

Love shook my senses: Rayor, *Sappho*, 50.

34 **On the throne of many hues:** Rayor, *Sappho*, 25.

I love again and do not love: Bing and Cohen, *Games of Venus*, 91.

love is at rest in no season: Andrew M. Miller, *Greek Lyric: An Anthology in Translation* (Cambridge, MA: Hackett, 1996), 97.

Tragedy's only significant depiction: Sue Blundell, *Women in Ancient Greece* (Cambridge, MA: Harvard University Press, 1995), 143.

35 **When Pindar speaks pridefully:** Bundy, *Studia Pindarica*, 3.

coarse and scurrilous enough: Prentice, "Sappho," 351.

36 **Oh, they will not lead you astray:** Confucius, *Analects*, 8.

37 **A very handsome gentleman:** Allen, *The Book of Songs*, 72.

There was a man so lovely: Allen, *The Book of Songs*, 75.

38 **ditties of the villages and backways:** Van Zoeren, *Poetry and Personality*, 228–29.

C. H. Wang, following in the footsteps: Wang, *The Bell and the Drum*. For Lord and Parry's work, see Lord, *The Singer of Tales*.

Marcel Granet has suggested: Granet, *Festivals and Songs of Ancient China*, 129.

39 **My sad heart is consumed:** Allen, *The Book of Songs*, 24.

The goddess comes not: Hawkes, *The Songs of the South*, 106–7.

40 **put all three hundred and five compositions:** From *Records of the Grand Historian (Shi Ji)*, circa 100 BC, quoted in Allen, *The Book of Songs*, 342.

If along the highroad: For this and the commentary below on "Along the Highroad," in the context of a survey of the exegetical tradition of *Shijing* scholarship, see Allen, *The Book of Songs*, 349–55.

An alternative tradition: Kern, "Beyond the Mao Odes."
When Confucius edited: Wong and Lee, "Poems of Depravity," 212.
41　strong resistance among scholars: Schimmelpenninck, *Chinese Folk Songs and Folk Singers*, 142–43.
　　Although women are often the main protagonists: Yasushi and Santangelo, *Shan'ge*, x.

Chapter 4: Love in Ancient Rome

44　The joke consists in taking it seriously: Lewis, *The Allegory of Love*, 6–7.
45　You can take it from me: Plautus, *Casina*, translated by Richard Beacham, in *Plautus: The Comedies*, edited by David R. Slavitt and Palmer Bovie (Baltimore: Johns Hopkins University Press, 1995), 1: 268, ll. 219–26.
　　ninety percent of the pop songs: Dave Hickey, *Air Guitar: Essays on Art and Democracy* (Los Angeles: Arts Issues Press, 1997), 15.
46　Romance is frivolous and stupid: Noah Berlatsky, "I'm a Guy Who Loves Romance Novels—and Jennifer Weiner Is Right about Reviews," *Salon*, April 21, 2014.
47　Cicero said that even if his lifetime: Translated by W. R. Johnson in the context of a valuable discussion of Cicero's "hostile indifference" to lyric poetry, in Johnson, *The Idea of Lyric*, 76.
　　The revolting pursuits of singing: Williams, *Roman Homosexuality*, 164.
　　Still I think I ought to be more emphatic: Quintilian, *The Institutio Oratoria of Quintilian*, translated by H. E. Butler (New York: G. P. Putnam's Sons, 1920), 1: 175.
48　around 15 percent of the populace could read: William V. Harris, *Ancient Literacy* (Cambridge, MA: Harvard University Press, 1991), 266–267.
　　If I didn't know that love: Plautus, *Miles Gloriosus*, in *Plautus: Three Comedies*, translated by Peter L. Smith (Ithaca, NY: Cornell University Press, 1991), 103, ll. 1284–88.
49　It seems to me highly probable: Landels, *Music in Ancient Greece and Rome*, 186–87.
　　Hellensitic music hall songs: For more on the sources of Plautus's songs, see Duckworth, *The Nature of Roman Comedy*, 375–83. For an outstanding recent overview of the music of Roman comedy, see Moore, *Music in Roman Comedy*.
　　separate their literary and musical cultures: Habinek, *The World of Roman Song*, 58–109.
　　Of all the figures used: Copley, "Servitium Amoris in the Roman Elegists."
50　The Theodosian Code went so far: Ruth Webb, "Female Performers in Late Antiquity," in *Greek and Roman Actors: Aspects of an Ancient Profession*, edited by Pat Easterling and Edith Hall (New York: Cambridge University Press, 2002), 295.
　　Often in the theater: Procopius, *The Secret History*, translated by G. A. Williamson (London: Folio Society, 1990), 41.
51　not a flautist or a harpist: Procopius, *The Secret History*, 40.
　　singing girls—man eaters: Eyben, *Restless Youth in Ancient Rome*, 118.
　　When Cicero wanted to attack: Anthony Corbeill, "Dining Deviants in Roman Political Invective," in *Roman Sexualities*, edited by Judith P. Hallett and Marilyn B. Skinner (Princeton, NJ: Princeton University Press, 1997), 122.
52　Plutarch describes the singing: Campbell, *Greek Lyric*, 45.
53　Propertius summed it up best: Vincent Katz, translator, *The Complete Elegies of Sextus Propertius* (Princeton, NJ: Princeton University Press, 2004), 107.
　　Cynthia's eyes ensnared me: David R. Slavitt, translator, *Propertius in Love: The Elegies* (Berkeley: University of California Press, 2002), 3.
54　I think this is what scholar Peter Dronke: Dronke, *Medieval Latin and the Rise of European Love-Lyric*, 1: 164.
　　Wallace called Updike: David Foster Wallace, *Consider the Lobster and Other Essays* (New York: Little, Brown, 2005), 51.
　　the prospect of dying without: Wallace, *Consider the Lobster*, 54.
　　Italians already had: Copley, *Exclusus Amator*, 28.

56 **"sacred sounds" and "sacred sights":** Burkert, *Ancient Mystery Cults*, 91–92.
57 **This is the purpose of the Bacchic initiation:** Burkert, *Ancient Mystery Cults*, 113.

Chapter 5: Debauched Maidens and Lustful Harlots

58 **thousands if not millions:** Haines, *Medieval Song in Romance Languages*, 67.
59 **Scholars of love lyrics have grown accustomed:** See Dronke, *The Medieval Lyric*, ix–xv; Dronke, *Medieval Latin and the Rise of European Love-Lyric*, 1: 264–65.
  the Devil should not have all the best tunes: Coulton, *Medieval Panorama*, 529.
  The Council of Chalon-sur-Saône: Klinck, *Anthology of Ancient and Medieval Woman's Song*, 4.
  An eighth-century ecclesiastic condemnation: Haines, *Medieval Song in Romance Languages*, 60.
  beguiling performances of titillating stories: Filotas, *Pagan Survivals*, 183.
  warnings against impure songs: For these and other condemnations of indecent songs at Christian celebrations, see Haines, *Medieval Song in Romance Languages*, 56–60.
60 **Three surviving continental penitentials:** Filotas, *Pagan Survivals*, 181.
  woman who dances in taverns: Quasten, *Music and Worship*, 127.
  How many peasants and how many women: Klingshirn, *Caesarius of Arles*, 185.
  choruses of women: Klinck, introduction to *Anthology of Ancient and Medieval Woman's Song*, 4.
  A woman might mix: Filotas, *Pagan Survivals*, 297.
  who take a live fish: Filotas, *Pagan Survivals*, 298.
61 **A strange thing hangs:** William Souter Mackie, ed., *The Exeter Book*, part 2: *Poems IX–XXXII* (London: Oxford University Press, 1934), 141.
  Benjamin Thorpe: Benjamin Thorpe, *Codex Exoniensis* (London: Society of Antiquaries, 1842), 527.
  Do not perform lewd and sensuous songs: This and below from Haines, *Medieval Song in Romance Languages*, 61.
  In the late sixth century, Caesarius: Haines, *Medieval Song in Romance Languages*, 62.
62 **beautiful porches:** Carl Holliday, "Concerning Marriage," *The Smart Set* 37, no. 2 (June 1912): 87.
63 **A woman's love, Jerome warns:** Jerome, *Against Jovianianus*, book 1, in *Nicene and Post-Nicene Fathers*, second series, vol. 6: *Jerome: Letters and Select Works*, edited by Philip Schaff and Henry Wallace (New York: Cosimo, 2007), 367.
  See, therefore, how the prostitutes: Haines, *Medieval Song in Romance Languages*, 65.
  A medieval municipal statute from Bagnols: Otis, *Prostitution in Medieval Society*, 81.
64 **I am not one of the *juglaresas*:** Judith R. Cohen, "Ca No Soe Joglaresa: Women and Music in Medieval Spain's Three Cultures," in Klinck and Rasmussen, *Medieval Woman's Song*, 68.
  the familiar song "Greensleeves": Leonard Ashley, *Elizabethan Popular Culture* (Bowling Green, OH: Bowling Green State University Popular Press, 1988), 119.
  Augustine, famous for his own wayward youth: Brundage, *Law, Sex and Christian Society*, 106.
65 **the custom of dancing is a leftover:** Dowden, *European Paganism*, 161–62.
  I avow the bond of your love: Dronke, *Medieval Latin and the Rise of European Love-Lyric*, 1: 197.
66 **The young scholars soon fell into a way:** Whicher, *The Goliard Poets*, 3.
67 **Dull and dour sobriety:** From Whicher's translation of "Estuans intrinsecus" in *The Goliard Poets*, 107–8.
68 **I am hot with flaming desire:** Translation of "Amor habet superos" from Walsh, *Love Lyrics from the Carmina Burana*, 95.
  Why does my mistress hold me: Translation of "Cur suspectum me tenet domina" from Walsh, *Love Lyrics from the Carmina Burana*, 129–30.
  The maiden has allowed me: Translation of "Grates ago veneri" from Walsh, *Love Lyrics from the Carmina Burana*, 44.

69 **Why not be brave and say:** From Whicher's translation of "Iam, dulchis amica" in *The Goliard Poets*, 25.

Scholar Peter Dronke, considering: Dronke, *Medieval Latin and the Rise of European Love-Lyric*, 1: 30.

70 **Alas, how seldom in these days:** Waddell, *The Wandering Scholars of the Middle Ages*, 137.

71 **Abelard refers to her as *nominatissima*:** Radice, *The Letters of Abelard and Heloise*, 277–78.

No distance over land: Clanchy, *Abelard*, 3.

What king or philosopher could match: Radice, *The Letters of Abelard and Heloise*, 115.

took cruel vengeance on me: Radice, *The Letters of Abelard and Heloise*, 75.

72 **Men call me chaste:** Radice, *The Letters of Abelard and Heloise*, 133.

Now the more I was taken up: Radice, *The Letters of Abelard and Heloise*, 68.

You left many love-songs and verses: Radice, *The Letters of Abelard and Heloise*, 115.

How many kisses from her lips did I steal: Translation of "Hebet sidus" from Walsh, *Love Lyrics from the Carmina Burana*, 192.

73 **jesters and other singers of filth:** Clanchy, *Abelard*, 134.

Before attempting to define the Middle Ages: Gilson, *Heloise and Abelard*, 143.

Chapter 6: The North African and Middle Eastern Connection

76 **Belgian musicologist François-Joseph Fétis:** Fétis, *Histoire Générale de la Musique Depuis les Temps Plus Ancient*, vol. 5, 9. The translation here is mine.

Our music has absorbed no influence from the Arabs: Quoted in Ribera, *Music in Ancient Arabia and Spain*, 19.

Again in the 1920s, scholar Julian Ribera: Ribera, *Music in Ancient Arabia and Spain*, 4.

a splendid collection of Arabic music: Ribera, *Music in Ancient Arabia and Spain*, 6.

The artistic Spain of olden times: Ribera, *Music in Ancient Arabia and Spain*, 9.

to read some poems from eleventh-century Spain: Menocal, *Shards of Love*, 27.

77 **My Lord Ibrahim:** Dronke, *The Medieval Lyric*, 88.

Don't bite me my love: Philip F. Kennedy, "Thematic Relationships between the Kharjas, the Corpus of Muwashshahat and Eastern Lyrical Poetry," in Jones and Hitchcock, *Studies on the Muwaššah and the Kharja*, 79.

No genuine lyrical poetry: Federico Corriente, "The Behaviour of Romance and Andalusian Utterances in the Kharjas under the Constraints of 'Arūd," included in Jones and Hitchcock, *Studies on the Muwaššah and the Kharja*, 67.

78 **A thirteenth-century Maghribi chronicler:** Zwartjes, *Love Songs from Al-Andalus*, 41.

Moses ibn Ezra, a Jewish philosopher: Zwartjes, *Love Songs from Al-Andalus*, 41.

79 **The (wine) cups went round and round:** Quoted in Zwartjes, *Love Songs from Al-Andalus*, 48.

How can I change my ways: Margaret Larkin, "Popular Poetry in the Post-Classical Period," in Allen and Richards, *The Cambridge History of Arabic Literature*, 206.

80 **Al-Jahiz, a ninth-century scholar from Basra:** Zwartjes, *Love Songs from Al-Andalus*, 154.

Ibn Sana' al-Mulk makes a similar comment: Zwartjes, *Love Songs from Al-Andalus*, 154.

I shout in the streets: Zwartjes, *Love Songs from Al-Andalus*, 198.

81 **Everybody, the elite and the common people:** Ibn Khaldun, *The Muqaddimah: An Introduction to History*, translated by Franz Rosenthal (Princeton, NJ: Princeton University Press, 1967), 458.

My lady, let us do what the spy suspects: Zwartjes, *Love Songs from Al-Andalus*, 191.

Come, my love, come this night: Zwartjes, *Love Songs from Al-Andalus*, 192.

There is usually the mood of the unhappy lover: Cantarino, "Lyrical Traditions in the Andalusian Muwashshahas," 217.

Scholar Linda Fish Compton enumerates: Compton, *Andalusian Lyrical Poetry*, 60.

Break my bracelet and loosen my belt: Zwartjes, *Love Songs from Al-Andalus*, 204.

Mess up my hair, rub my breast: Zwartjes, *Love Songs from Al-Andalus*, 203.

82 **He assaulted me and kissed my mouth:** For these passages and a description of sexual violence and reproaches in these songs, see Kennedy, "Thematic Relationships Between the Kharjas, the Corpus of Muwaššahat and Eastern Lyrical Poetry," 77–78.

    Raise my anklets up to my earrings: Zwartjes, *Love Songs from Al-Andalus*, 214.

    I shall not kill you but on condition: Zwartjes, *Love Songs from Al-Andalus*, 240.

    Lady, come, come, kiss and embrace me: Zwartjes, *Love Songs from Al-Andalus*, 230.

    secluded himself for several years with skilled singing girls: Amnon Shiloah, "Muslim and Jewish Musical Traditions of the Middle Ages," in *The New Oxford History of Music*, vol. 3.1: *Music as Concept and Practice in the Late Middle Ages*, edited by Reinhard Strohm and Bonnie J. Blackburn (New York: Oxford University Press, 2001), 7.

    Alas! Christians do not know their own law: Roger Wright, *Late Latin and and Early Romance in Spain and Carolingian France* (Liverpool, UK: Frances Cairns, 1982), 157.

83 **into the twenty-first century:** For an example, see Amelia Maciszewski, "Tawa'if, Tourism and Tales: The Problematics of Twenty-First-Century Musical Patronage for North India's Courtesans," in Feldman and Gordon, *The Courtesan's Arts*, 332–51.

84 **But the division was never clear cut:** Lesley Downer, "The City Geisha and Their Role in Modern Japan: Anomaly or Artistes?" in Feldman and Gordon, *The Courtesan's Arts*, 223.

    A surviving auction catalogue: Caswell, *The Slave Girls of Baghdad*, 15–16.

85 **Ethiopian priest:** Dronke, *Medieval Latin and the Rise of European Love-Lyric*, 1:27.

    O host of lovers how execrable: Caswell, *The Slave Girls of Baghdad*, 63.

    Sire, you have burdened me: Caswell, *The Slave Girls of Baghdad*, 117.

86 **Love, seduction and enslavement are forever linked:** Quoted in Caswell, *The Slave Girls of Baghdad*, 46.

    Neither happiness nor sadness: Caswell, *The Slave Girls of Baghdad*, 201–2.

87 **Muti has become ardent in love:** Caswell, *The Slave Girls of Baghdad*, 222.

    three ladies hold my reins: Caswell, *The Slave Girls of Baghdad*, 223.

88 **One commentator ranked Ibn Surayj:** See Hilary Kilpatrick, "Mawali and Music," in *Patronate and Patronage in Early and Classical Islam*, edited by Monique Bernards and John Nawas (Leiden: Brill, 2005), 336.

    delicate, attractive, tender and full of ideas: Kilpatrick, *Making the Great Book of Songs*, 81.

    Be quiet, ignorant boy: Rowson, "The Effeminates of Early Medina," 692.

89 **There are expert old women:** Liu and Monroe, *Ten Hispano-Arabic Songs*, 37.

90 **invented in bitter exile:** Menocal, *Shards of Love*, 91.

Chapter 7: The Troubadours

93 **Should we believe C. S. Lewis:** Lewis, *The Allegory of Love*, 4.

    or is at least as old as Egypt: Dronke, *Medieval Latin and the Rise of European Love-Lyric*, 1: xvii.

    should be interpreted as a collective fantasy: Boase, *The Origin and Meaning of Courtly Love*, 121.

    Denis de Rougemont: de Rougemont, *Love in the Western World*, 75–102.

95 **For her body is beautiful:** Translation from Topsfield, *Troubadours and Love*, 36.

96 **The art of arts is the art of love:** This and the passage below from William of St. Thierry, *The Nature and Dignity of Love*, translated by Thomas X. Davis (Kalamazoo, MI: Cistercian, 1981), 47–50.

    It seems that Thomas Aquinas: Dronke, *The Medieval Lyric*, 16.

97 **Queen Eleanor was asked to decide:** Ackerman, *A Natural History of Love*, 53.

98 **One has to assume:** Simon Gaunt, email to the author, dated August 11, 2013.

    If an author wished to know whether his work: Chaytor, *Script to Print*, 3.

100 **one of the greatest deceivers of women:** Margarita Egan, *The Vidas of the Troubadours* (New York: Garland, 1984), 45. Many believe this *vida* is the work of Uc de Saint Circ (1217–53).

Marcabru, the son of Lady Bruna: Simon Gaunt, Ruth Harvey, and Linda Paterson, *Marcabru: A Critical Edition* (Cambridge, UK: D. S. Brewer, 2000), 245.

101 **extended alba:** Gale Sigal, *Erotic Dawn-Songs of the Middle Ages* (Gainesville: University of Florida Press, 1996), 2.

If you want to compose a *descort*: Marianne Shapiro, *De Vulgari Eloquentia: Dante's Book of Exile* (Lincoln: University of Nebraska Press, 1990), 129.

If you want to compose a *retroncha*: Shapiro, *De Vulgari Eloquentia*, 128.

If you want to compose a *danca*: Shapiro, *De Vulgari Eloquentia*, 128–29.

A canso must speak agreeably of love: Shapiro, *De Vulgari Eloquentia*, 127.

102 **Arnold Hauser:** Hauser, *The Social History of Art*, 100.

103 **One night I'd like to take my swain:** Kehew, *Lark in the Morning*, 171.

Lady Carenza, taking a husband: Translated by Sarah White, in Bruckner et al., *Songs of the Women Troubadours*, 87.

104 **one of the strangest in the entire Middle Ages:** Dronke, *Medieval Latin and the Rise of European Love-Lyric*, 1: 221.

A lady's grace will grant whatever is reasonable: Dronke, *Medieval Latin and the Rise of European Love-Lyric*, 1: 226.

105 **It seems a troubling, difficult thing:** Dronke, *Medieval Latin and the Rise of European Love-Lyric*, 1: 475.

Andreas Capellanus describes Eleanor: Capellanus, *The Art of Courtly Love*, 20–23.

106 **tradition of shamanic music:** Gioia, *Healing Songs*, 49–88.

107 **such a fire was spread throughout the land:** H. J. Chaytor, *The Troubadours* (Cambridge: Cambridge University Press, 1912), 81–82.

Chapter 8: The Triumph of Romance

111 **Augustine, who documented his own struggles:** Augustine, "On Marriage and Concupiscence," in *Nicene and Post-Nicene Fathers*, first series, edited by Philip Schaff (New York: Cosimo Books, 2007), 5: 269.

In the trial of the prostitute Salvaza: Kenneth R. Bartlett, ed., *The Civilization of the Italian Renaissance: A Sourcebook*, 2nd edition (Toronto: University of Toronto Press, 2011), 148.

By the close of the Middle Ages, doctrine and dogma: Brundage, *Law, Sex, and Christian Society*, 447–49.

112 **The worldly woman is the organ of Satan:** Haines, *Medieval Song in Romance Languages*, 48.

arouses and praises the instinct of lust: Liu and Monroe, *Ten Hispano-Arabic Songs*, 8.

prose romances, chronicles, collections of anecdotes: Mullally, *The Carole*, 41.

113 **Their favorite stories were not, like ours:** Lewis, *The Allegory of Love*, 9.

114 **Were the world all mine:** Waddell, *The Wandering Scholars of the Middle Ages*, 237.

115 **I have elsewhere documented comparable examples:** Gioia, *Work Songs*, 79–98.

Women who are weaving, or disentangling: Dronke, *The Medieval Lyric*, 15.

116 **Daughter, I'd like, if you please:** Fowler, *Songs of a Friend*, 40.

119 **I have traveled far and wide:** Seagrave and Thomas, *The Songs of the Minnesingers*, 87–88.

Chapter 9: A Love Supreme

121 **beauties of the body are as nothing:** Symposium, translated by Michael Joyce, in Hamilton and Cairns, *The Collected Dialogues of Plato*, 562–63.

She must have been a kind of seer or priestess: Symposium, 553.

123 **Praised be You, my Lord:** Regis J. Armstrong, Ignatius C. Brady, and John Vaughn, *Francis and Clare: The Complete Works* (New York: Paulist Press, 1982), 38.

loved to sing his Provençal songs: Walter Nigg, *Francis of Assisi*, translated by William Neil (London: Mowbray, 1975), 27.

God's Troubadour: Sophie Jewett, *God's Troubadour: The Story of Saint Francis of Assisi* (New York: Thomas Y. Crowell, 1957).

124   *Cantigas* **are attributed:** Martínez, *Alfonso X, the Learned: A Biography*, 217–30.

125   **In all of the miniatures the principal musician:** Ribera, *Music in Ancient Arabia and Spain*, 225.

127   **Scholar F. Alberto Gallo:** F. Alberto Gallo, *Music of the Middle Ages II*, translated by Karen Eales (Cambridge: Cambridge University Press, 1985), 68.
         clever things can scarcely be: Quoted in Gallo, *Music of the Middle Ages II*, 68.
         You are at one and the same time: Bloch, *Medieval Misogyny*, 90.

130   **disorganized singing of unpolished people:** Elena Abramov-van Rijkp, *Parlar Cantando: The Practice of Reciting Verses in Italy from 1300 to 1600* (Bern: Peter Lang, A.G., 2009), 99.

131   **Love makes my heart languish:** Translation of "Loyauté vueil tous jours maintenir" from William Mahrt, "Male and Female Voice in Two Virelais of Guillaume de Machaut," in *Machaut's Music: New Interpretations*, edited by Elizabeth Eva Leach (Woodbridge, UK: Boydell Press, 2003), 227.

132   **Francesco, deprived of sight:** Weiss and Taruskin, *Music in the Western World*, 62.
         surpassed any organist in living memory: Filippo Villani, "The Life of Francesco Landini," in Weiss and Taruskin, *Music in the Western World*, 64.

133   **Rise up, gentle souls, eager for love:** Wilkins, *Music in the Age of Chaucer*, 52.

134   **Give me a kiss, sweet kiss, light of my eyes:** Dronke, *Medieval Latin and the Rise of European Love-Lyric*, 1: 12.
         This could not have been due to Western influence: Dronke, *Medieval Latin and the Rise of European Love-Lyric*, 1: 17.

135   **Now that ninefold mists:** Murasaki Shikibu, *The Tale of Genji*, translated by Royall Tyler (New York: Penguin, 2003), 539, 160.
         If I despised you: Ian Hideo Levy, trans., *Love Songs from the Man'yōshū* (Tokyo: Kodansha, 2000), 29, 57.

136   **Oh friend, what should I say of his wantonness:** Bhattacharya, *Love Songs of Vidyapati*, 91.

137   **Man is the greatest Truth:** Bhattacharya, *Love Songs of Chandidas*, 44.
         By the roadside singers frequently render: Bhattacharya, *Love Songs of Chandidas*, 17.

138   **Love makes the sea boil like a kettle:** Reynold A. Nicholson, trans., *The Mathnawí of Jalálu'ddin Rúmí: The Translation of the Fifth and Sixth Books* (London: Luzac, 1934), 164.

139   **The wise men tell us that we take these tunes:** Lewis, *Rumi, Past and Present*, 312.

Chapter 10: Profane Love

142   **They are seen and heard by everyone:** William F. Prizer, "Reading Carnival: The Creation of a Florentine Carnival Song," in *Early Music History: Studies in Medieval and Early Modern Music*, edited by Iain Fenelon (Cambridge: Cambridge University Press, 2004), 23: 188–89.
         We come from Germany: McGee and Mittler, "Information on Instruments in Florentine Carnival Songs."

143   **People got married in stables:** Bayer, *Art and Love in Renaissance Italy*, 3.

144   **a woman of questionable virtue named Laura:** Vincenzo Calmeta, "Life of the Fertile Vernacular Poet Serafino Aquilano," in Tomlinson et al., *The Renaissance*, 44.

145   **her insistence amounted almost to an obsession:** Rubsamen, *Literary Sources of Secular Music in Italy*, 9.
         fearful and cowardly: Einstein, *The Italian Madrigal*, 1: 51.
         perhaps the first truly modern musicians: Einstein, *The Italian Madrigal*, 1: 54.

147   **This kind of music were not so much disallowable:** Thomas Morley, "A Plaine and Easie Introduction to Practicall Musicke," in Tomlinson et al., *The Renaissance*, 201.
         Calvin had warned that music: John Calvin, *Institutes of the Christian Religion: 1536 Edition*, translated by Ford Lewis Battles (Grand Rapids, MI: Wm. B. Eerdmans, 1986), 180.

something to wean them away: From Martin Luther's preface to Johann Walter's *Chorgesangbuch* (1524) cited, in the context of a useful discussion, in Robin A. Leaver, *Luther's Liturgical Music: Principles and Implications* (Grand Rapids, MI: Wm. B. Eerdmans, 2007), 18.

148   **Within the fire I shiver and burn:** Prizer, "Games of Venus."
    the time of the learned Dante: Prizer, *Courtly Pastimes*, 222.
    correspondence from Isabella d'Este: Julia Cartwright, *Isabella D'Este, Marchioness of Mantua, 1474–1539*, vol. 2 (London: John Murray, 1907), 21–25.

150   **a view that has been opposed:** For Einstein's view on the evolution of the madrigal from the frottola, and responses from more recent scholars, see Einstein, *The Italian Madrigal*, 1: 107–27; Fenlon and Haar, *The Italian Madrigal in the Early Sixteenth Century*, 3–7; Cummings, *The Maecenas and the Madrigalist*, 3–13.

151   **Using various ways of concealment:** Baldesar Castiglione, *The Book of the Courtier*, translated by George Bull (New York: Penguin, 1976), 44.
    elaborate mock-ups of inwardness for public delectation: McClary, *Modal Subjectivities*, 39, 41.

152   **frisson of excitement and desire at the moment of performance:** Jonathan Jones, "Caravaggio Gives Us a Glimpse of Renaissance Rock 'n' Roll," *Guardian*, February 28, 2012.

153   **The madrigal's audience changed from participants:** Macy, "Speaking of Sex," 17.
    a core repertory of sixteenth-century "standards": McClary, *Modal Subjectivities*, 59.

154   **Among the contemporaries of Shakespeare:** Einstein, *The Italian Madrigal*, 1: 4.

Chapter 11: Divas and Deviancy

155   **Verdi and Bellini at their worst:** Robert C. Davis and Garry R. Martin, *Venice: The Tourist Maze. A Cultural Critique of the World's Most Touristed City* (Berkeley: University of California Press, 2004), 158.

156   **If the Lord Duke wants to have me killed:** Rosselli, "From Princely Service to the Open Market," 7.
    Women who excelled in music-making: Bonnie Gordon, "The Courtesan's Singing Body as Cultural Capital in Seventeenth-Century Italy," in Feldman and Gordon, *The Courtesan's Arts*, 189, 194.

157   **deserved rather to be called the Academy of Love:** Blanning, *The Triumph of Music*, 89.
    If God were omnipotent: Snowman, *The Gilded Stage*, 26.

158   **the tragedies put on the stage:** Weiss, *Opera*, 12.

159   **ancient Greeks and Romans did not write novels:** Watt, *The Rise of the Novel*, 135.
    adultery would seem to be the chief occupation: de Rougemont, *Love in the Western World*, 16.
    four times as great as that of Virgil: Sternfeld, "Orpheus, Ovid and Opera," 176.

160   **belong to tenors, men with voices:** Sam Abel, *Opera in the Flesh* (Boulder, CO: Westview Press, 1996), 11–12.

162   **The censor even suggested substitute words:** Lisa De Alwis, "Censorship and Magical Opera in Early Nineteenth Century Vienna," Ph.D. dissertation, University of Southern California, 2012, especially 21–32.

163   **with the exception of *Tristan und Isolde*:** Abbate and Parker, *A History of Opera*, 349, 358.
    I confess to a positive dislike for this brief love-song: Quoted in Ernest Newman, *A Study of Wagner* (New York: G. P. Putnam's Son, 1899), 10.

164   **The "birthday" of the *Lied*:** Kimball, *Song*, 39.

165   **Poets are the unacknowledged legislators:** Percy Bysshe Shelley, *The Works of Percy Bysshe Shelley in Verse and Prose*, edited by Harry Buxton Forman (London: Reeves and Turner, 1880), 7: 144.
    Goethe himself declared: Goethe's letter to Zelter, December 21, 1809, in *Goethe: Musical Poet, Musical Catalyst*, edited by Lorraine Byrne (Dublin: Carysfort Press, 2004), xx.

166   **sudden modulations:** For the reception to Schubert's *Winterreise*, see Susan Youens, *Retracing a Winter's Journey: Schubert's Winterreise* (Ithaca, NY: Cornell University Press, 1991), 45–49.

much too difficult for *our* public: Letter from George Thomson to Monsieur Louis van Beethoven, dated October 30, 1812, in *Letters to Beethoven and Other Correspondence*, vol. 1: *1772–1812*, edited and translated by Theodore Albrecht (Lincoln: University of Nebraska Press, 1996), 263.

167   **easy and pleasant style:** From the composer's letter to George Thomson, dated October 1, 1806, in A. C. Kalischer, ed., *Beethoven's Letters*, translated by J. S. Shedlock (New York: Dover, 1972), 62.

I am not in the habit of rewriting my compositions: Alexander Thayer, *The Life of Ludwig van Beethoven*, edited by Henry Edward Krehbiel (New York: Beethoven Association, 1921), 2: 246.

always considered music for the human voice: Jürgen Thym, "Schumann: Reconfiguring the Lied," in Parsons, *The Cambridge Companion to the Lied*, 122. Schumann wisely added the request "Please don't pass this on to anybody" to this curt dismissal of vocal music.

cycle is my most Romantic ever: Thym, "Schumann: Reconfiguring the Lied," 122.

I do not believe I have: Beryl Foster, *The Songs of Edvard Grieg* (Woodbridge, UK: Boydell Press, 2007), 10.

168   **The composer by then:** Dietrich Fischer-Dieskau, *The Fischer-Dieskau Book of Lieder*, translated by George Bird and Richard Stokes (New York: Knopf, 1976), 26.

Chapter 12: Folk Songs and Love Songs

170   **I have observed that even the barbarians:** Julian, *The Works of the Emperor Julian*, translated by Wilmer Cave Wright (New York: Macmillan, 1913), 2: 421–23.

Europeans have everywhere been keenly touched: Rousseau and Herder, *On the Origin of Language*, 97.

171   **We will never know how many songs:** Tessa Watt suggests that at least 600,000 copies of ballads circulated in England during the second half of the sixteenth century, and perhaps as many as several million. *Cheap Print and Popular Piety*, 11.

The folk-song is like the duck-billed platypus: Cecil J. Sharp and Charles L. Marson, *Folk Songs from Somerset* (London: Simpkin, Marshall, Hamilton, Kent, 1905), xiii.

172   **immense collections of Broadside ballads:** Sigurd Hustvedt, *Ballad Books and Ballad Men* (Cambridge, MA: Harvard University Press, 1930), 254.

Dave Harker, who has ridiculed the supposedly: Harker, *Fakesong*.

England's Society for the Suppression of Vice: Allison Pease, *Modernism, Mass Culture, and the Aesthetics of Obscenity* (Cambridge: Cambridge University Press, 2000), 51.

C. R. Bennett of San Francisco: Anthony Comstock, "Helps and Hindrances in the Suppression of Vice," in *Our Day: A Record and Review of Current Reform*, edited by Joseph Cook (Boston: Our Day, 1888), 223.

173   **William Sanger quotes from:** Sanger, *The History of Prostitution*, 247, 334.

there is nothing in them (the songs): *The Parlour Companion or Polite Song Book* (Philadelphia: A. J. Dickinson, 1836), iii–iv; *The Bijou Minstrel* (Philadelphia: Turner and Fisher, 1840), viii–ix. Both examples are cited with commentary and additional examples in Jackson, *Early Songs of Uncle Sam*, 124.

Ye must cuckold Lord Ronald: Child, *The English and Scottish Popular Ballads*, 5: 157.

177   **I killd your father in his bed:** Child, *The English and Scottish Popular Ballads*, 3: 113.

But, all medons, be ware be rewe: Child, *The English and Scottish Popular Ballads*, 3: 210.

178   **Devotion and Morality:** For more information about Pepys's distinctions between types of broadside ballads see the English Broadside Ballad Archive operated by the University of California at Santa Barbara, especially the page entitled "Pepys Categories," http://ebba.english.ucsb.edu/page/pepys-categories.

179   **Few Maids have met with so good luck:** "The Helpless Maidens Call to the Batchellors," English Broadside Ballad Archive, http://ebba.english.ucsb.edu/ballad/22458/xml.
      Yankee Doodle, keep it up: Vance Randolph, *Blow the Candle Out: "Unprintable" Ozark Folksongs and Folklore*, vol. 2: *Folk Rhymes and Other Lore* (Fayetteville: University of Arkansas Press, 1992), 616.

180   **Nearly all of these minyō or folk-songs:** Matsubara, *Min-Yo*, i–ii.
      The richest area of Russian lyric songs: Propp, *Down along the Mother Volka*, 11, 13.
      Antoinet Schimmelpenninck, in her study: Schimmelpenninck, *Chinese Folk Songs and Folk Singers*, 142.
      Out of every ten *shan'ge*, nine are about love: Schimmelpenninck, *Chinese Folk Songs and Folk Singers*, 71.

181   **William Jankowiak and Edward Fischer undertook:** Jankowiak, *Romantic Passion*, 4–5.
      Among the Lahu in Tibet: Shanshan Du, *"Chopsticks Only Work in Pairs": Gender Unity and Gender Equality among the Lahu of Southwest China* (New York: Columbia University Press, 1992), 182.

182   **Louise Jilek-Aall identified:** Louise Jilek-Aall, "Suicidal Behaviour among Youth: A Cross-Cultural Comparison," *Transcultural Psychiatry*, no. 25 (June 1988): 87–105.
      these youths are two to three times more likely: Paul Gibson, "Gay Male and Lesbian Youth Suicide," in *Report of the Secretary's Task Force on Youth Suicide*, vol. 3: *Prevention and Interventions in Youth Suicide*, edited by Marcia R. Feinleib (Washington, DC: Department of Health and Human Services, 1989), 110–42.

183   **W. G. Archer devotes a lengthy chapter:** Archer, *The Hill of Flutes*, 139–57.
      In their collection of songs of the Great Lakes sailors: Ivan H. Walton and Joe Grimm, *Windjammers: Songs of the Great Lakes Sailors* (Detroit: Wayne State University Press, 2002), 109.
      Although my subject is the Avatip love-song: Harrison, *Laments for Foiled Marriages*, 7.
      The lover, however, is apt to haunt the abode: Alice C. Fletcher, *A Study of Omaha Indian Music* (Lincoln: University of Nebraska Press, 1994), 15.

184   **I sit here thinking of her:** Frances Densmore, *Chippewa Music II*, Smithsonian Institution, Bureau of American Ethnology, Bulletin 53 (Washington, DC: Government Printing Office, 1913), 220–21. In the course of her fieldwork, Densmore also encountered complaints about love songs. "The words of modern Indian love songs usually express a lack of respect for women," she heard from her Pawnee informants, "and often boast of fascinations and conquests. They are connected with intoxication and are sung by young men of no standing among their own people." Frances Densmore, *Pawnee Music*, Smithsonian Institution, Bureau of American Ethnology, Bulletin 93 (Washington, DC: Government Printing Office, 1929), 93. Does this reflect that pernicious impact of outside influences on tribal music or perhaps just the familiar complaint of elders at the liberties taken by the next generation?
      love songs presented in the form of riddles: Rubin, *Voices of a People*, 91–93; Weinstein, *Marriage Rituals Italian Style*, 413–15.
      Temiar of Malaysia: Marina Roseman, *Healing Sounds from the Malaysian Rainforest* (Berkeley: University of California Press, 1991), 15.
      Slovakian herders court: Jan Ling, *A History of European Folk Music*, translated by Linda Schenck and Robert Schenck (Rochester, NY: University of Rochester Press, 1997), 23.
      Flathead Indians of Western Montana: Merriam, *Ethnomusicology of the Flathead Indians*, 59–60.
      among the Maori, love songs: Mervyn McLean, *Maori Music* (Auckland: Auckland University Press, 1996), 114.

185   ***yilpintji* or love-magic ceremonies:** Moyle, *Songs of the Pintupi*, 20, 23.
      Tia DeNora interviewed: DeNora, *Music in Everyday Life*, 116.

186   **No drums are beaten uselessly:** James Chalmers, *Adventures in New Guinea* (London: Religious Tract Society, 1886), 181.
      John Sloboda: John A. Sloboda and Susan A. O'Neill, "Emotions in Everyday Listening to Music," in *Music and Emotion: Theory and Research*, edited by Patrik N. Juslin and John

A. Sloboda (New York: Oxford University Press, 2001), 415–29; John Sloboda, "Empirical Studies of Emotional Response to Music," in *Cognitive Bases of Musical Communication*, edited by Mari Riess Jones and Susan Holleran (Washington, DC: American Psychological Association, 1992), 33–46.

Chapter 13: Love Songs for the Mass Market

189   **"After the Ball":** Furia, *The Poets of Tin Pan Alley*, 19–25, 47.

190   **no music shops existed in Vienna:** Lenneberg, *On the Publishing and Dissemination of Music*, 75–76.

191   **unbecoming the Fair Sex:** Richard Leppert, *The Sight of Sound: Music, Representation, and the History of the Body* (Berkeley: University of California Press, 1993), 67.

192   **One can see the changing tastes:** Lenneberg, *On the Publishing and Dissemination of Music*, 115–16.

   When he put his arm around her: Sophie von La Roche, *The History of Lady Sophia Sternheim*, translated by Christa Baguss Britt (Albany: State University of New York Press, 1991), 160.

   gentleman took the lady's hand: This and the quote below from Kirstein, *Dancè*, 139–40.

193   **new words by contract:** Joseph Ritson, *Scottish Songs* (Glasgow: Hugh Hopkins, 1869), 1: 105.

194   **above all, impersonal:** Olive Dame Campbell and Cecil J. Sharp, *English Folk Songs from the Southern Appalachians* (New York: G. P. Putnam's Songs, 1917), xii.

195   **This is a common practice in many parts of the States:** D. W. Mitchell, *Ten Years in the United States: Being an Englishman's Views of Men and Things in the North and South* (London: Smith, Elder, 1862), 88.

   a custom very prevalent in Boston: C. D. Arfwedson, *The United States and Canada in 1832, 1833, and 1834* (London: Richard Bentley, 1834), 1: 150–51.

196   **High musical attainments are not so essential:** Francis Courtney Wemyss, *Twenty-Six Years of the Life of an Actor and Manager* (New York: Burgess, Stringer, 1847), 125.

   By far the most popular theme: Tawa, *Sweet Songs for Gentle Americans*, 123.

   who has learned to love another: From the song "Thou Hast Learned to Love Another, or Farewell, Farewell, Forever" by Charles Slade, quoted in Tawa, *Sweet Songs for Gentle Americans*, 124–25.

   lovers neither kiss nor clasp each other: Tawa, *Sweet Songs for Gentle Americans*, 128.

   offend the nicest modesty: Emerson, *Doo-Dah*, 57.

197   **the quintessence of feminine neurosis:** M. Z., "Yves Guilbert à la Scala," *Le Courrier Français*, March 4, 1894, translated in Rae Beth Gordon, *Dances with Darwin 1875–1910: Vernacular Modernity in France* (Burlington, VT: Ashgate, 2009), 46–47.

   giving expression to any vulgarity: Scott, *Sounds of the Metropolis*, 76.

   a famished manager: Scott, *Sounds of the Metropolis*, 80.

198   **I kiss'd her two times:** Scott, *Sounds of the Metropolis*, 77.

Chapter 14: The African Connection (Again)

200   **In China:** Anne Behnke Kinney, *Representations of Childhood and Youth in Early China* (Stanford, CA: Stanford University Press, 2004), 126.

201   **to beat drums, blow horns:** For these and other examples and a discussion of prohibitions of slave music, see Epstein, *Sinful Tunes and Spirituals*, 60–62.

202   **one visitor to Charleston:** Robert Darden, *People Get Ready! A New History of Black Gospel Music* (New York: Continuum, 2004), 48.

   Come ma love, an' go wid' me: Natalie Curtis-Burlin, *Negro Folk Songs*, 160–67.

203   **plaintive love songs:** Blassingame, *The Slave Community*, 51.

   lady who heard them sung before the war: Allen, Ware, and Garrison, *Slave Songs of the United States*, 113.

Dale Cockrell has documented: Dale Cockrell, *Demons of Disorder: Early Blackface Minstrels and Their World* (Cambridge: Cambridge University Press, 1997), 15.

204   **"I come from Alabama":** Emerson, *Doo-Dah!*, 127–28.

206   **Woman holds first place among:** Odum and Johnson, *The Negro and His Songs*, 160, 148.

   The reason I loves my baby so: Charles Peabody, "Notes on Negro Music," *Journal of American Folk-Lore* 16 (July–September 1903): 148–52.

   If you can't give a dollar: Alan Lomax, *Mister Jelly Roll* (Berkeley: University of California Press, 1973), 270–71.

207   **Make me a pallet on the floor:** This and below from Donald Marquis, *In Search of Buddy Bolden, First Man of Jazz* (Baton Rouge: Louisiana State University Press, 1978), 107–8.

   blues in Bolden's repertoire: For a summary of the key sources, see Ted Gioia, *The History of Jazz*, Second Edition (New York: Oxford University Press, 2011), 33–35.

   I love you truly, truly dear: Carrie Jacobs-Bond, "I Love You Truly," in *Seven Songs as Unpretentious as the Wild Rose* (Chicago: Carrie Jacobs-Bond & Son, undated), first published circa 1901.

209   **If you don't like my ocean:** From "Don't Fish in My Sea," in Eric Sackheim, ed., *The Blues Line: A Collection of Blues Lyrics* (New York: Grossman, 1969), 47.

   He's a deep-sea diver: From "Empty Bed Blues," in Taft, *Talkin' to Myself*, 528.

   My man beat me last night: For these and other images of violence in Ma Rainey's music, see Sandra Lieb, *Mother of the Blues: A Study of Ma Rainey* (Amherst: University of Massachusetts Press, 1981), 116–19.

210   **If I send for my baby:** See my discussion of these lyrics in the context of other blues songs about guns in Ted Gioia, *Delta Blues* (New York: Norton, 2008), 144–45. The specification of Wisconsin in the lyric relates to the site of the recording session, Grafton, Wisconsin.

   I'll have a hard time missing you baby: Sterling Plumb, "Sweetblood Call: The Blues Purity of Louisiana Red," *Black World*, September 1975, 53.

   four different ways: Adam Gussow, *Seems Like Murder Here: Southern Violence and the Blues Tradition* (Chicago: University of Chicago Press, 2002), 41.

   You got to take all your money: From "If You Want Me to Love You," in Taft, *Talkin' to Myself*, 170. I've made some corrections to Taft's transcription, based on the 1932 recording by Georgia Tom and Tampa Red (Vocalion 1682).

211   **Handy recounted his astonishment:** Handy, *Father of the Blues*, 132–33.

   One of the phonograph companies: Quoted in Harrison, *Black Pearls*, 43.

215   **dishonest and provocative:** Peter Wade, "Black Music and Cultural Syncretism in Colombia," in *Slavery and Beyond: The African Impact on Latin America and the Caribbean*, edited by Darién J. Davis (Lanham, MD: Rowman & Littlefield, 1995), 132.

   although very picturesque: Louis Moreau Gottschalk, *Notes of a Pianist*, edited by Jeanne Behrend (New York: Knopf, 1964), 358.

216   **One plays and sings other music:** Döpp, *Music and Eros*, 205.

   It has spread all over Paris: Artemis Cooper, "Tangomania in Europe and North America 1913–1914," in Collier et al., *Tango!*, 74.

217   **barbarian contortions of Negroes and Indians:** Cooper, "Tangomania in Europe and North America," 91.

   country unreachable for the tango: Carlos G. Groppa, *The Tango in the United States* (Jefferson, NC: McFarland, 2004), 1.

   eliminated the waltz: Groppa, *The Tango in the United States*, 11.

Chapter 15: Crooners, Torch Songs, and Bobby-Soxers

220   **a hundred or more women:** Jane Dixon, "Rudy Vallée Tells of Pests Who Make Him Miserable," *Milwaukee Journal*, September 11, 1930, 1.

222   **crooners make the basest appeal:** Allison McCracken, "Real Men Don't Sing Ballads: The Radio Crooner in Hollywood, 1929–1933," in *Soundtrack Available: Essays on Film*

and Popular Music, edited by Pamela Robertson Wojcik and Arthur Knight (Durham, NC: Duke University Press, 2001), 116.

crooning corrupts the minds: Pitts and Hoffmann, *The Rise of the Crooners,* 21.

225 **when a fellow 'carries the torch':** Rosemarie Ostler, *Let's Talk Turkey: The Stories behind America's Favorite Expressions* (Amherst, NY: Prometheus, 2008), 237.

emergence of a new, more personal point of view: Alec Wilder, *American Popular Song: The Great Innovators 1900–1950,* edited by James T. Maher (New York: Oxford University Press, 1972), 21.

228 **phenomenon of mass hysteria that is seen:** Bruce Bliven, "The Voice and the Kids," *The New Republic,* November 6, 1944, reprinted in *The Frank Sinatra Reader,* edited by Steven Petkov and Leonard Mustazza (New York: Oxford University Press, 1995), 30.

Chapter 16: Rock 'n' Roll and the Summer of Love

230 **There'll be fifteen minutes of kissin':** The Dominoes, "Sixty Minute Man" (Federal 12022), composed by Billy Ward and Rose Marks, released 1951.

235 **He's got every record Chuck Berry ever made:** Keith Richards, *Life* (Boston: Little, Brown, 2010), 78.

242 **At one point gay men held the top three positions:** Echols, *Hot Stuff,* 40.

244 **Punk rock's attitude to the sex act:** Jon Savage, "Tainted Love: The Influence of Homosexuality and Sexual Divergence on Pop Music and Culture Since the War," in *Consumption, Identity and Style: Marketing, Meanings, and the Packaging of Pleasure,* edited by Alan Tomlinson (New York: Routledge, 1990), 111.

Chapter 17: As Nasty as They Wanna Be

250 **Lots of times we'd give shows with rappers:** Nelson George, "Rappin' with Russell: Eddie Murphying the Flak-Catchers," in Cepeda, *"And It Don't Stop,"* 44.

251 **The site's database:** The frequency with which various terms are used in rap lyrics can be measured at http://rapgenius.com/rapstats.

255 **The proliferation in China:** Lotus Yuen, "Too Popular for Their Own Good: China Restricts TV Singing Competitions," *Atlantic,* July 26, 2013.

256 **When music critic Dorian Lynskey:** Dorian Lynskey, "Blurred Lines: The Most Controversial Song of the Decade," *Guardian,* November 13, 2013.

BIBLIOGRAPHY

Abbate, Carolyn, and Roger Parker. *A History of Opera*. New York: Norton, 2012.

Abramov-van Rijk, Elena. *Parlar Cantando: The Practice of Reciting Verses in Italy from 1300 to 1600*. Bern, Switzerland: Peter Lang, A. G., 2009.

Ackerman, Diane. *A Natural History of Love*. New York: Random House, 1994.

Akehurst, F. R. P., and Judith M. Davis, eds. *A Handbook of the Troubadours*. Berkeley: University of California Press, 1995.

Alighieri, Dante. *La Vita Nuova*. Translated by Barbara Reynolds. New York: Penguin, 1969.

Allen, Joseph R., ed. *The Book of Songs: The Ancient Chinese Classic of Poetry*. Translated by Arthur Waley and Joseph R. Allen. New York: Grove Press, 1996.

Allen, Roger, and D. S. Richards, eds. *The Cambridge History of Arabic Literature: Arabic Literature in the Post-Classical Period*. Cambridge: Cambridge University Press, 2006.

Allen, William Francis, Charles Pickard Ware, and Lucy McKim Garrison. *Slave Songs of the United States*. Bedford, MA: Applewood Books, 1996.

Archer, W. G. *The Hill of Flutes: Life, Love and Poetry in Tribal India*. Pittsburgh: University of Pittsburgh Press, 1974.

Armistead, Samuel G. "A Brief History of Kharja Studies." *Hispania* 79, no. 1 (1987): 8–15.

Armstrong, Edward A. *Bird Display and Behaviour*. New York: Dover, 1965.

Armstrong, Edward A. *The Folklore of Birds: An Enquiry into the Origin and Distribution of Some Magico-Religious Traditions*. New York: Dover, 1970.

Bayer, Andrea, ed. *Art and Love in Renaissance Italy*. New York: Metropolitan Museum of Art, 2008.

Betz, Hans Dieter, ed. *The Greek Magical Papyri in Translation Including the Demotic Spells*. Vol. 1: *Texts*. 2nd edition. Chicago: University of Chicago Press, 1992.

Bhattacharya, Deben, trans. *Love Songs of Chandidas: The Rebel Poet-Priest of Bengal*. New York: Grove, 1970.

Bhattacharya, Pralay, trans. *Love Songs of Vidyapati*. New Delhi: Sterling, 1998.

Blanning, Tim. *The Triumph of Music: The Rise of Composers, Musicians and Their Art*. Cambridge, MA: Belknap, 2008.

Blassingame, John W. *The Slave Community: Plantation Life in the Ante-Bellum South*. New York: Oxford University Press, 1972.

Bloch, R. Howard. *Medieval Misogyny and the Invention of Western Romantic Love*. Chicago: University of Chicago Press, 1991.

Boase, Roger. *The Origin and Meaning of Courtly Love: A Critical Study of European Scholarship*. Manchester, UK: Manchester University Press, 1977.

Bonner, Anthony, ed. *Songs of the Troubadours*. New York: Schocken, 1972.

Bragg, Lois. " 'Wulf and Eadwacer,' 'The Wife's Lament,' and Women's Lyrics of the Middle Ages." *Germanisch-Romanische Monatsschrift* 39 (1989): 257–68.

Brown, Eleanor D., Susan M. Farabaugh, and Clare J. Veltman. "Song Sharing in a Group-Living Songbird, the Australian Magpie, Gymnorhina Tibicen. Part 1. Vocal Sharing within and among Small Groups." *Behaviour* 104, no. 1–2 (1988): 1–28.

Bruckner, Matilda Tomaryn, Laurie Shepard, and Sarah White. *Songs of the Women Troubadours*. New York: Garland, 2000.

Brundage, James A. *Law, Sex, and Christian Society in Medieval Europe*. Chicago: University of Chicago Press, 1987.

Bundy, Elroy L. *Studia Pindarica*. Berkeley: University of California Press, 1986.

Burkert, Walter. *Ancient Mystery Cults*. Cambridge, MA: Harvard University Press, 1987.

Calame, Claude. *Choruses of Young Women in Ancient Greece: Their Morphology, Religious Role, and Social Functions*. Translated by Derek Collins and Jane Orion. London: Rowman & Littlefield, 1997.

Campbell, David A., ed. and trans. *Greek Lyric: Sappho and Alcaeus*. Cambridge, MA: Harvard University Press, 1990.

Cantarino, Vincent. "Lyrical Traditions in Andalusian Muwashshahas." *Comparative Literature* 21, no. 3 (1969): 213–31.

Capellanus, Andreas. *The Art of Courtly Love*. Translated by John Jay Parry. New York: Columbia University Press, 1960.

Caswell, Fuad Matthew. *The Slave Girls of Baghdad: The Qiyān in the Early Abbasid Era*. London: I. B. Tauris, 2011.

Catchpole, C. K., and P. J. B. Slater. *Bird Song: Biological Themes and Variations*. Cambridge: Cambridge University Press, 1995.

Cepeda, Raquel, ed. *"And It Don't Stop": The Best American Hip-Hop Journalism of the Last 25 Years*. New York: Faber and Faber, 2004.

Chang, Jeff. *Can't Stop Won't Stop: A History of the Hip-Hop Generation*. New York: St. Martin's Press, 2005.

Chaytor, H. J. *Script to Print: An Introduction to Vernacular Medieval Literature*. London: Sidgwick & Jackson, 1966.

Child, Francis James. *The English and Scottish Popular Ballads*. 5 vols. Mineola, NY: Dover, 2003.

Clanchy, M. T. *Abelard: A Medieval Life*. Oxford: Blackwell, 1999.

Collier, Simon, Artemis Cooper, María Susana Azzi, and Richard Martin. *Tango! The Dance, the Song, the Story*. London: Thames and Hudson, 1995.

Collins, Sarah A., and Caroline Missing. "Vocal and Visual Attractiveness Are Related in Women." *Animal Behaviour* 64, no. 5 (2003): 997–1004.

Compton, Linda Fish. *Andalusian Lyrical Poetry and Old Spanish Love Songs: The Muwashshaḥ and Its Kharja*. New York: New York University Press, 1976.

Confucius. *Analects with Selections from Traditional Commentaries*. Translated by Edward Slingerland. Indianapolis, IN: Hackett, 2003.

Cooke, Brett, and Frederick Turner, eds. *Biopoetics: Evolutionary Explorations in the Arts*. Lexington, KY: International Conference on the Unity of the Sciences, 1999.

Cooney, Helen, ed. *Writings of Love in the English Middle Ages*. New York: Palgrave, 2006.

Cooper, Jerrold S. "Gendered Sexuality in Sumerian Love Poetry." In *Sumerian Gods and Their Representations*, edited by Irving L. Finkel and Markham J. Geller. Groningen, Netherlands: Styx, 1997.

Copley, Frank Olin. *Exclusus Amator: A Study in Latin Love Poetry*. Baltimore: American Philological Association, 1956.

Copley, Frank Olin. "On the Origin of Certain Features of the Paraclausithyron." *Transactions and Proceedings of the American Philological Association* 73 (1942): 96–107.

Copley, Frank Olin. "Servitium Amoris in the Roman Elegists." *Transactions and Proceedings of the American Philological Association* 78 (1947): 285–300.

Coulton, G. G. *Medieval Panorama: The English Scene from Conquest to Reformation*. New York: Cambridge University Press, 2010.

Cummings, Anthony M. *The Maecenas and the Madrigalist: Patrons, Patronage, and the Origins of the Italian Madrigal*. Philadelphia: Philadelphia American Philosophical Society, 2004.

Cummings, Anthony M. *The Politicized Muse: Music for Medici Festivals 1512–1537*. Princeton, NJ: Princeton University Press, 1992.

Curtis-Burlin, Natalie. *Negro Folk-Songs: The Hampton Series Books I–IV, Complete*. Mineola, NY: Dover, 2001.

Cyrino, Monica Silveira. *In Pandora's Jar: Lovesickness in Early Greek Poetry*. Lanham, MD: University Press of America, 1995.

Dalby, Liza. *Geisha*. Berkeley: University of California Press, 1998.

Darwin, Charles. *The Descent of Man*. Amherst, NY: Prometheus Books, 1998.

Davenport, Guy. *Seven Greeks*. New York: New Directions, 1995.

Davidson, Clifford. "Erotic 'Women's Songs' in Anglo-Saxon England." *Neophilologus* 59, no. 3 (1975): 451–62.

de Kloet, E. Ronald. "From Vasotocin to Stress and Cognition." *European Journal of Pharmacology* 626, no. 1 (2010): 18–26.

Delon, Michel, ed. *The Libertine: The Art of Love in Eighteenth Century France*. New York: Abbeville, 2013.

DeNora, Tia. *Music in Everyday Life*. Cambridge: Cambridge University Press, 2000.

de Rougemont, Denis. *Love in the Western World*. Translated by Montgomery Belgion. Princeton, NJ: Princeton University Press, 1983.

Döpp, Hans-Jürgen. *Music and Eros*. New York: Parkstone, 2008.

Doupe, Allison J. "Birdsong and Human Speech." *Annual Review of Neuroscience* 22 (March 1999): 567–631.

Dowden, Ken. *European Paganism: The Realities of Cult from Antiquity to the Middle Ages*. New York: Routledge, 2000.

Drinker, Sophie. *Music and Women: The Story of Women in Their Relation to Music*. New York: Coward-McCann, 1948.

Dronke, Peter. *Forms and Imaginings from Antiquity to the Fifteenth Century*. Rome: Edizioni di Storia e Letteratura, 2007.

Dronke, Peter. *Medieval Latin and the Rise of European Love-Lyric*. Vol. 1: *Problems and Interpretations*. 2nd edition. New York: Oxford University Press, 1968.

Dronke, Peter. *Medieval Latin and the Rise of European Love-Lyric*. Vol. 2: *Medieval Latin Love-Poetry*. 2nd edition. New York: Oxford University Press, 1968.

Dronke, Peter. *The Medieval Lyric*. Woodbridge, Suffolk, UK: D. S. Brewer, 1996.

Duckworth, George E. *The Nature of Roman Comedy: A Study in Popular Entertainment*. 2nd edition. Norman: University of Oklahoma Press, 1994.

Earp, Sarah, and Donna L. Maney. "Birdsong: Is It Music to Their Ears?" *Frontiers of Evolutionary Neuroscience* 4, no. 14 (November 28, 2012).

Easterling, Pat, and Edith Hall, eds. *Greek and Roman Actors: Aspects of an Ancient Profession*. New York: Cambridge University Press, 2002.

Echols, Alice. *Hot Stuff: Disco and the Remaking of American Culture*. New York: Norton, 2010.

Einstein, Alfred. *The Italian Madrigal*. Translated by Alexander H. Krappe, Roger H. Sessions, and Oliver Strunk. Princeton, NJ: Princeton University Press, 1971.

Elbert, Samuel H. "Chants and Love Songs of the Marquesas Islands, French Oceania." *Journal of the Polynesian Society* 50 (1941): 53–91.

Ellinwood, Leonard. "Francesco Landini and His Music." *Musical Quarterly* 22, no. 2 (1936): 190–216.

Emerson, Ken. *Doo-Dah!: Stephen Foster and the Rise of American Popular Culture*. New York: Simon & Schuster, 1997.

Epstein, Dena J. *Sinful Tunes and Spirituals: Black Folk Music to the Civil War*. Urbana: University of Illinois Press, 1981.

Eyben, Emiel. *Restless Youth in Ancient Rome*. New York: Routledge, 1993.

Feinberg, David R., Lisa M. DeBruine, Benedict C. Jones, and David I. Perrett. "The Role of Femininity and Averageness of Voice Pitch in Aesthetic Judgments of Women's Voices." *Perception* 37, no. 4 (2008): 615–23.

Feldman, Martha, and Bonnie Gordon, eds. *The Courtesan's Arts: Cross-Cultural Perspectives.* New York: Oxford University Press, 2006.

Fenlon, Iain, and James Haar. *The Italian Madrigal in the Early Sixteenth Century: Sources and Interpretation.* Cambridge: Cambridge University Press, 1988.

Ferrari, Gloria. *Alcman and the Cosmos of Sparta.* Chicago: University of Chicago Press, 2008.

Fétis, François-Joseph. *Histoire Générale de la Musique Depuis les Temps Plus Ancient,* Vol. 5. Paris: Firmin Didot Frères, 1876.

Filotas, Bernadette. *Pagan Survivals, Superstitions and Popular Cultures in Early Medieval Pastoral Literature.* Toronto: Pontifical Institute of Medieval Studies, 2005.

Fischer, Julia, Stuart Semple, Gisela Fickenscher, Rebecca Jürgens, Eberhard Kruse, Michael Heistermann, and Ofer Amir. "Do Women's Voices Provide Cues of the Likelihood of Ovulation? The Importance of Sampling Regime." *PLoS ONE* 6, no. 9 (21, 2011): e24490. www.plosone.org.

Fisher, Helen. *Why We Love: The Nature and Chemistry of Romantic Love.* New York: Henry Holt, 2004.

Foster, John L. *Love Songs of the New Kingdom.* New York: Charles Scribner's Sons, 1974.

Foucault, Michel. *The History of Sexuality.* Vol. 1: *An Introduction.* Translated by Robert Hurley. New York: Vintage, 1978.

Fowler, Barbara Hughes, trans. *Songs of a Friend: Love Lyrics of Medieval Portugal.* Chapel Hill: University of North Carolina Press, 1996.

Fox, Michael V. "Love, Passion, and Perception in Israelite and Egyptian Love Poetry." *Journal of Biblical Literature* 102, no. 2 (1983): 219–28.

Fox, Michael V. *The Song of Songs and the Ancient Egyptian Love Songs.* Madison: University of Wisconsin Press, 1985.

Frazer, James George. *The Golden Bough: A Study in Comparative Religion.* New York: Gramercy, 1981.

Fromm, Erich. *The Art of Loving.* New York: HarperCollins, 2000.

Frymer-Kensky, Tikva. *In the Wake of the Goddesses: Women, Culture and the Biblical Transformation of Pagan Myth.* New York: Fawcett Columbine, 1992.

Furia, Philip. *The Poets of Tin Pan Alley: A History of America's Great Lyricists.* New York: Oxford University Press, 1990.

Gagey, Edmond M. *Ballad Opera.* New York: Columbia University Press, 1937.

Gaunt, Simon. *Love and Death in Medieval French and Occitan Courtly Literature: Martyrs to Love.* New York: Oxford University Press, 2006.

Gaunt, Simon, and Sarah Kay, eds. *The Troubadours: An Introduction.* Cambridge: Cambridge University Press, 1999.

George, Nelson. *Hip-Hop America.* New York: Penguin, 2005.

Gilson, Etienne. *Heloise and Abelard.* Ann Arbor: University of Michigan Press, 1960.

Gioia, Ted. *Healing Songs.* Durham, NC: Duke University Press, 2006.

Gioia, Ted. *Work Songs.* Durham, NC: Duke University Press, 2006.

Gold, Barbara, ed. *A Companion to Roman Love Elegy.* Oxford: Blackwell, 2012.

Goldberg, Sander M. *Constructing Literature in the Roman Republic: Poetry and Its Reception.* New York: Cambridge University Press, 2005.

Goodson, James L. "Territorial Aggression and Dawn Song Are Modulated by Septal Vasotocin and Vasoactive Intestinal Polypeptide in Male Field Sparrows (Spizella pusilla)." *Hormones and Behavior* 34, no. 1 (1998): 67–77.

Gorrell, Lorraine. *The Nineteenth-Century German Lied.* Pompton Plains, NJ: Amadeus Press, 2005.

Granet, Marcel. *Festivals and Songs of Ancient China.* Translated by E. D. Edwards. London: George Routledge & Sons, 1932.

Greene, Ellen, ed. *Reading Sappho: Contemporary Approaches.* Berkeley: University of California Press, 1996.

Habinek, Thomas. *The World of Roman Song: From Ritualized Speech to Social Order.* Baltimore: Johns Hopkins University Press, 2005.

Hackett, Jo Ann. "Can a Sexist Model Liberate Us? Ancient Near Eastern 'Fertility' Goddesses." *Journal of Feminist Studies in Religion* 5, no. 1 (1989): 65–76.

Hagen, Edward H., and Gregory A. Bryant. "Music and Dance as a Coalition Signaling System." *Human Nature* 14, no.1 (2003): 21–51.

Haines, John. *Medieval Song in Romance Languages.* Cambridge: Cambridge University Press, 2010.

Hall, Michelle L., and Robert D. Magrath. "Duetting and Mate-Guarding in Australian Magpie-Larks (Grallina Cyanoleuca)." *Behavioral Ecology and Sociobiology* 47, no. 3 (2000): 180–87.

Hall, Michelle L., and Robert D. Magrath. "Temporal Coordination Signals Coalition Quality." *Current Biology* 17, no. 11 (2007): R406–7.

Hallett, Judith P., and Marilyn B. Skinner, eds. *Roman Sexualities.* Princeton, NJ: Princeton University Press, 1997.

Hamel, Frank. *Human Animals.* New York: Frederick A. Stokes, 1915.

Hamilton, Edith, and Huntington Cairns, eds. *The Collected Dialogues of Plato, Including the Letters.* New York: Pantheon, 1961.

Handy, W.C. *Father of the Blues: An Autobiography.* New York: Da Capo, 1991.

Harker, Dave. *Fakesong: The Manufacture of British "Folksong" 1700 to the Present Day.* Milton Keynes, UK: Open University Press, 1985.

Harrison, Daphne Duval. *Black Pearls: Blues Queens of the 1920s.* New Brunswick, NJ: Rutgers University Press, 1993.

Harrison, Simon. *Laments for Foiled Marriages: Love Songs from a Sepik River Village.* Boroko, Papua New Guinea: Institute of Papua New Guinea Studies, 1982.

Hauser, Arnold. *The Social History of Art.* Vol. 1: *From Prehistoric Times to the Middle Ages.* London: Taylor and Francis, 1999.

Hawkes, David, ed. and trans. *The Songs of the South: An Ancient Chinese Anthology of Poems by Qu Yuan and Other Poets.* London: Penguin, 2011.

Hitchcock, Richard. "The Kharjas as Early Romance Lyrics." *Modern Language Review* 75, no. 3 (1980): 481–91.

Hobbs, Dawn, and Gordon Gallup. "Songs as a Medium for Embedded Reproductive Messages." *Evolutionary Psychology* 9, no. 3 (2011): 390–416.

Hollis, Susan Tower, ed. *Hymns, Prayers, and Songs: An Anthology of Ancient Egyptian Lyric Poetry.* Translated by John L. Foster. Atlanta, GA: Scholars Press, 1995.

Holman Jones, Stacy. *Torch Singing: Performing Resistance and Desire from Billie Holiday to Edith Piaf.* Plymouth, UK: Altamira, 2007.

Iversen, Erik. "The Chester Beatty Papyrus, No. I, Recto XVI, 9–XVII, 13." *Journal of Egyptian Archaeology* 65 (1979): 78–88.

Jackson, George Stuyvesant. *Early Songs of Uncle Sam.* Boston: B. Humphries, 1933.

Jankowiak, William, ed. *Romantic Passion.* New York: Columbia University Press, 1995.

Johnson, W. R. *The Idea of Lyric: Lyric Modes in Ancient and Modern Poetry.* Berkeley: University of California Press, 1982.

Jones, Alan, and Richard Hitchcock, eds. *Studies on the Muwaššaḥ and the Kharja: Proceedings of the Exeter International Colloquium.* Reading, UK: Ithaca Press, 1991.

Kaniuth, Kai, Anne Löhnert, Jared L. Miller, Adelheid Otto, Michael Roaf, and Walther Sallaberger, eds. *Tempel im Alten Orient: Colloquien der Deutschen Orient Gesellschaft 7.* Wiesbaden: Harrassowitz Verlag, 2013.

Kehew, Robert, ed. *Lark in the Morning: The Verses of the Troubadours.* Chicago: University of Chicago Press, 2005.

Kay, Sarah. *Courtly Contradictions: The Emergence of the Literary Object in the Twelfth Century.* Stanford, CA: Stanford University Press, 2001.

Kelly, Douglas. *Medieval Imagination*. Madison: University of Wisconsin Press, 1978.

Kern, Martin. "Beyond the Mao Odes: Shijing Reception in Early Medieval China." *Journal of the American Oriental Society* 127, no. 2 (2007): 131–42.

Kern, Martin. "Lost in Tradition: The Classics of Poetry We Did Not Know." In *Hsiang Lectures in Chinese Poetry*, Vol. 5, edited by Grace S. Fong. Montreal: Centre for East Asian Research, McGill University, 2010.

Kilpatrick, Hilary. *Making the Great Book of Songs: Compilation and the Author's Craft in Abū l-Faraj al-Iṣbahānī's Kitāb al-aghānī*. London: Routledge, 2003.

Kimball, Carol. *Song: A Guide to Art Song Style and Literature*. Milwaukee, WI: Hal Leonard, 2005.

Kirkwood, G. M. *Early Greek Monody: The History of a Poetic Type*. Ithaca, NY: Cornell University Press, 1974.

Kirstein, Lincoln. *Dance: A Short History of Classic Theatrical Dancing*. Brooklyn, NY: Dance Horizons, 1969.

Klinck, Anne L. *Anthology of Ancient and Medieval Woman's Song*. New York: Palgrave, 2004.

Klinck, Anne L. "Lyric Voice and the Feminine in Some Ancient and Mediaeval Frauenlieder." *Florilegium* 13 (1994): 13–36.

Klinck, Anne L., and Ann Marie Rasmussen, eds. *Medieval Woman's Song: Cross-Cultural Approaches*. Philadelphia: University of Pennsylvania Press, 2002.

Klingshirn, William E. *Caesarius of Arles: The Making of a Christian Community in Late Antique Gaul*. Cambridge: Cambridge University Press, 2004.

Knighton, Tess, and David Fallows, eds. *Companion to Medieval and Renaissance Music*. Berkeley: University of California Press, 1997.

Kowalzig, Barbara, and Peter Wilson, eds. *Dithyramb in Context*. Oxford: Oxford University Press, 2013.

Kramer, Samuel Noah. *The Sacred Marriage Rite: Aspects of Faith, Myth and Ritual in Ancient Sumer*. Bloomington: Indiana University Press, 1969.

Krauss, Robert M., Robin Freyberg, and Ezequiel Morsella. "Inferring Speakers' Physical Attributes from Their Voices." *Journal of Experimental Social Psychology* 38, no. 6 (2002): 618–25.

Kroodsma, Donald E., and Bruce E. Byers. "The Function(s) of Bird Song." *American Zoologist* 31 (1991): 318–28.

Kroodsma, Donald E., and Linda D. Parker. "Vocal Virtuosity in the Brown Thrasher." *Auk* 94, no. 4 (1977): 783–85.

Landels, John G. *Music in Ancient Greece and Rome*. New York: Routledge, 1999.

Landgráfová, Renata, and Hana Navrátilová. *Sex and the Golden Goddess I: Ancient Egyptian Love Songs in Context*. Prague: Czech Institute of Egyptology 2009.

Lapinkivi, Pirjo. *The Sumerian Sacred Marriage in the Light of Comparative Evidence*. Helsinki: Institute for Asian and African Studies, 2004.

Legman, Gershon. "Erotic Folksongs and Ballads: An International Bibliography." *Journal of American Folklore* 103, no. 410 (1990): 417–501.

Lenneberg, Hans. *On the Publishing and Dissemination of Music 1550–1850*. Hillsdale, NY: Pendragon, 2003.

Lewis, C. S. *The Allegory of Love*. New York: Oxford University Press, 1970.

Lewis, Franklin D. *Rumi, Past and Present, East and West: The Life, Teaching and Poetry of Jalâl Al-Din Rumi*. Oxford: Oneword, 2008.

Lim, M. M., and L. J. Young. "Vasopressin-Dependent Neural Circuits Underlying Pair Bond Formation in the Monogamous Prairie Vole." *Neuroscience* 125, no. 1 (2004): 35–45.

Liu, Benjamin, and James Monroe. *Ten Hispano-Arabic Songs in the Modern Oral Tradition*. Berkeley: University of California Press, 1989.

Lord, Albert B. *The Singer of Tales*. Edited by Stephen Mitchell and Gregory Nagy. Cambridge, MA: Harvard University Press, 2000.

Macy, Laura. "Speaking of Sex: Metaphor and Performance in the Italian Madrigal." *Journal of Musicology* 14, no. 1 (1996): 1–34.

Manniche, Lise. *Music and Musicians in Ancient Egypt*. London: British Museum Press, 1991.

Marcus, Greil. *Lipstick Traces: A Secret History of the Twentieth Century*. Cambridge, MA: Harvard University Press, 1989.

Mariaselvam, Abraham. *The Song of Songs and Ancient Tamil Love Poems: Poetry and Symbolism*. Rome: Editrice Pontificio Istituto Biblico, 1988.

Marrocco, W. Thomas. "The Fourteenth Century Madrigal: Its Form and Content." *Speculum: A Journal of Medieval Studies* 26, no. 3 (1951): 449–57.

Martínez, H. Salvador. *Alfonso X, the Learned: a Biography*. Translated by Odile Cisneros. Leiden: Brill, 2010.

Matsubara, Iwao. *Min-Yo: Folk Songs of Japan*. Tokyo: Cosmo, 1946.

McClary, Susan. *Desire and Pleasure in Seventeenth-Century Music*. Berkeley: University of California Press, 2012.

McClary, Susan. *Modal Subjectivities: Self-Fashioning in the Italian Madrigal*. Berkeley: University of California Press, 2004.

McDonald, Nicola, ed. *Medieval Obscenities*. Rochester, NY: York Medieval Press, 2006.

McDowell, A. G. *Village Life in Ancient Egypt: Laundry Lists and Love Songs*. Oxford: Oxford University Press, 1999.

McEvilley, Thomas. *Sappho*. Putnam, CT: Spring, 2008.

McGee, Timothy J., and Sylvia E. Mittler. "Information on Instruments in Florentine Carnival Songs." *Early Music* 10, no. 4 (1982): 452–61.

McNeil, Legs, and Gillian McCain. *Please Kill Me: An Uncensored Oral History of Punk*. New York: Grove Press, 1996.

Meador, Betty De Shong. *Inanna Lady of Largest Heart: Poems of the Sumerian High Priestess Enheduanna*. Austin: University of Texas Press, 2000.

Menocal, María Rosa. *The Ornament of the World: How Muslims, Jews and Christians Created a Culture of Tolerance in Medieval Spain*. Boston: Little Brown, 2002.

Menocal, María Rosa. *Shards of Love: Exile and the Origins of the Lyric*. Durham, NC: Duke University Press, 1994.

Merriam, Alan P. *Ethnomusicology of the Flathead Indians*. New York: Wenner-Gren Foundation for Anthropological Research, 1967.

Moore, Timothy J. *Music in Roman Comedy*. New York: Cambridge University Press, 2012.

Moyle, Richard M. *Songs of the Pintupi: Musical Life in a Central Australian Society*. Canberra: Australian Institute of Aboriginal Studies, 1979.

Mullally, Robert. *The Carole: A Study of a Medieval Dance*. Burlington, VT: Ashgate, 2011.

Murphy, Michael R., Jonathan R. Seckl, Steven Burton, Stuart A. Checkley, and Stafford L. Lightman. "Changes in Oxytocin and Vasopressin Secretion During Sexual Activity in Men." *Journal of Clinical Endocrinology and Metabolism* 65, no. 4 (1987): 738–41.

Nissinen, Martti, and Risto Uro, eds. *Sacred Marriages: The Divine-Human Sexual Metaphor from Sumer to Early Christianity*. Winona Lake, IN: Eisenbrauns, 2008.

Odum, Howard W., and Guy B. Johnson. *The Negro and His Songs: A Study of Typical Negro Songs in the South*. Chapel Hill: University of North Carolina Press, 1925.

Olds, W. B. "Bird-Music." *Musical Quarterly* 8, no. 2 (1922): 242–55.

Ortega y Gasset, José. *On Love: Aspects of a Single Theme*. Translated by Toby Talbot. New York: Meridian Books, 1957.

Otis, Leah Lydia. *Prostitution in Medieval Society: The History of an Urban Institution in Languedoc*. Chicago: University of Chicago Press, 1985.

Panksepp, Jaak, and Gunther Bernatzky. "Emotional Sounds and the Brain: The Neuro-Affective Foundations of Musical Appreciation." *Behavioural Processes* 60, no. 2 (2002), 133–55.

Parker, Holt N. "Sappho Schoolmistress." *Transactions of the American Philological Association* 123 (1993): 309–51.

Parsons, James, ed. *The Cambridge Companion to the Lied*. Cambridge: Cambridge University Press, 2004.

Payer, Pierre J. *Sex and the Penitentials*. Toronto: University of Toronto Press, 1984.

Peraino, Judith A. *Giving Voice to Love: Songs and Self-Expression from the Troubadours to Guillaume de Machaut.* New York: Oxford University Press, 2011.

Pirrotta, Nino. "Before the Madrigal." *Journal of Musicology* 12, no. 3 (1994): 237–52.

Pitts, Michael R., and Frank W. Hoffmann. *The Rise of the Crooners.* Lanham, MD: Scarecrow Press 2002.

Plummer, John F., ed. *Vox Feminae: Studies in Medieval Woman's Song.* Kalamazoo, MI: Medieval Institute, 1981.

Prentice, William K. "Sappho." *Classical Philology* 13, no. 4 (1918): 347–60.

Primack, Brian A., Melanie A. Gold, Eleanor B. Schwar, and Madeline A. Dalton. "Degrading and Non-Degrading Sex in Popular Music: A Content Analysis." *Public Health Reports* 123, no. 5 (2008): 593–600.

Prizer, William F. *Courtly Pastimes: The Frottole of Marchetto Cara.* Ann Arbor, MI: UMI Research Press, 1980.

Prizer, William F. "Games of Venus: Secular Vocal Music in the Late Quattrocento and Early Cinquecento." *Journal of Musicology* 9, no. 1 (1991): 3–56.

Propp, Vladimir. *Down along the Mother Volka: An Anthology of Russian Folk Lyrics.* Translated and edited by Roberta Reeder. Philadelphia: University of Pennsylvania Press, 1975.

Quasten, Johannes. *Music and Worship in Pagan and Christian Antiquity.* Translated by Boniface Ramsey. Washington, DC: National Association of Pastoral Musicians, 1983.

Radice, Betty, ed. and trans. *The Letters of Abelard and Heloise.* London: Penguin, 1974.

Rayor, Diane J. *Sappho: A New Translation of the Complete Works.* Cambridge: Cambridge University Press, 2014.

Rayor, Diane J. *Sappho's Lyre: Archaic Lyric and Women Poets of Ancient Greece.* Berkeley: University of California Press, 1991.

Reynolds, Margaret, ed. *The Sappho Companion.* New York: Palgrave, 2000.

Reynolds, Simon. *Rip It Up and Start Again: Postpunk 1978–1984.* London: Faber and Faber, 2005.

Ribera, Julian. *Music in Ancient Arabia and Spain.* Translated by Eleanor Hague and Marion Leffingwell. Stanford, CA: Stanford University Press, 1929.

Robinson, David M. *Sappho and Her Influence.* Boston: Marshall Jones, 1924.

Rosselli, John. "From Princely Service to the Open Market: Singers of Italian Opera and Their Patrons, 1600–1850." *Cambridge Opera Journal* 1, no. 1 (1989): 1–32.

Rousseau, Jean-Jacques, and Johann Gottfried Herder. *On the Origin of Language.* Translated by John H. Moran and Alexander Gode. Chicago: University of Chicago Press, 1966.

Rowson, Everett K. "The Effeminates of Early Medina." *Journal of the American Oriental Society* 11, no. 4 (1991): 671–93.

Rubin, Ruth. *Voices of a People: The Story of Yiddish Folksong.* Urbana: University of Illinois Press, 2000.

Rubio, Gonzalo. "Inanna and Dumuzi: A Sumerian Love Story." *Journal of the American Oriental Society* 121, no. 2 (2001): 268–74.

Rubsamen, Walter H. *Literary Sources of Secular Music in Italy (ca. 1500).* New York: Da Capo, 1972.

Sanger, William W. *The History of Prostitution.* New York: Harper & Brothers, 1858.

Sasson, Jack M., ed. *Civilizations of the Ancient Near East.* Vol. 4. New York: Charles Scribner's Sons, 1995.

Saville, Jonathan. *The Medieval Erotic Alba: Structure as Meaning.* New York: Columbia University Press, 1972.

Schimmelpenninck, Antoinet. *Chinese Folk Songs and Folk Singers: Shan'ge Traditions in Southern Jiangsu.* Leiden: CHIME Foundation, 1997.

Scott, Derek B. *Sounds of the Metropolis.* New York: Oxford University Press, 2008.

Seagrave, Barbara Garvey, and Wesley Thomas. *The Songs of the Minnesingers.* Urbana: University of Illinois Press, 1966.

Sefati, Yitschak. *Love Songs in Sumerian Literature: Critical Edition of the Dumuzi-Inanna Songs.* Jerusalem: Bar-Ilan University Press, 1998.

Segel, Harold B. *Turn-of-the-Century Cabaret: Paris, Barcelona, Berlin, Munich, Vienna, Cracow, Moscow, St. Petersburg, Zurich.* New York: Columbia University Press, 1987.

Shapiro, Marianne. *De Vulgari Eloquentia: Dante's Book of Exile.* Lincoln: University of Nebraska Press, 1990.

Smith, Douglas G. "Male Singing Ability and Territory Integrity in Red-Winged Blackbirds (Agelaius Phoeniceus)." *Behaviour* 68, no. 3 (1979): 193–206.

Snowman, Daniel. *The Gilded Stage: A Social History of Opera.* London: Atlantic Books, 2009.

Spencer, Herbert. *Literary Style and Music.* Port Washington, NY: Kennikat Press, 1970.

Spitzer, Leo. "The Mozarabic Lyric and Theodor Frings' Theories." *Comparative Literature* 4, no. 1 (1952): 1–22.

Stehle, Eva. *Performance and Gender in Ancient Greece: Nondramatic Poetry in Its Setting.* Princeton, NJ: Princeton University Press, 1997.

Sternfeld, Frederick W. "Orpheus, Ovid and Opera." *Journal of the Royal Musical Association* 113, no. 2 (1988): 172–202.

Stevens, Denis, ed. *A History of Song.* London: Hutchinson, 1960.

Stonehouse, Bernard, and Christopher Perrins, eds. *Evolutionary Ecology.* London: Macmillan, 1977.

Strehlow, T. G. H. *Songs of Central Australia.* Sydney: Angus and Robertson, 1971.

Sullivan, J. P. "Two Problems in Roman Love Elegy." *Transactions and Proceedings of the American Philological Association* 92 (1961): 522–36.

Symonds, John Addington, ed. *Wine, Women, and Song: Medieval Latin Students' Songs.* London: Chatto & Windus, 1907.

Taft, Michael, ed. *Talkin' to Myself: Blues Lyrics, 1921–1942.* New York: Routledge, 2005.

Taruskin, Richard. *Oxford History of Western Music.* 6 vols. New York: Oxford University Press, 2005.

Tawa, Nicholas E. *Sweet Songs for Gentle Americans: The Parlor Song in America, 1790–1860.* Bowling Green, OH: Bowling Green University Popular Press, 1980.

Thorpe, W. H. *Bird-Song: The Biology of Vocal Communication and Expression in Birds.* Cambridge: Cambridge University Press, 1961.

Till, Nicholas, ed. *The Cambridge Companion to Opera Studies.* Cambridge: Cambridge University Press, 2012.

Tinney, Steve. "Notes on Sumerian Sexual Lyric." *Journal of Near Eastern Studies* 59, no. 1 (2000): 23–30.

Tomlinson, Gary, Leo Treitler, and Oliver Strunk, eds. *The Renaissance: Source Readings in Music History.* Vol. 3. New York: Norton, 1998.

Topsfield, L. T. *Troubadours and Love.* Cambridge: Cambridge University Press, 1975.

Touma, Habib Hassan. *The Music of the Arabs.* Portland, OR: Amadeus Press, 2003.

Trehub, Sandra. E. "Musical Predispositions in Infancy." *Annals of the New York Academy of Sciences* 930 (June 2001): 3–16.

Ukkola, Liisa T., Jaana Oikkonen, Päivi Onkamo, Kai Karma, Pirre Raijas, and Irma Järvelä. "Association of the Arginine Vasopressin Receptor 1A (AVPR1A) Haplotypes with Listening to Music." *Journal of Human Genetics* 56, no. 4 (2011): 324–29.

Ukkola, Liisa T., Päivi Onkamo, Pirre Raijas, Kai Karma, and Irma Järvelä. "Musical Aptitude Is Associated with AVPR1A-Haplotypes." *PLoS ONE* 4, no. 5 (2009): e5534. www.plosone.org.

Van Zoeren, Steven. *Poetry and Personality: Reading, Exegesis, and Hermeneutics in Traditional China.* Stanford, CA: Stanford University Press, 1991.

Vico, Giambattista. *The New Science of Giambattista Vico.* Translated by Thomas Goddard Bergin and Max Harold Fisch. Ithaca, NY: Cornell University Press, 1984.

Waddell, Helen. *The Wandering Scholars of the Middle Ages.* Mineola, NY: Dover, 2000.

Walker, Janet A. "Conventions of Love Poetry in Japan and the West." *Journal of the Association of Teachers of Japanese* 14, no. 1 (1979): 31–65.

Wallaschek, Richard. *Primitive Music: An Inquiry into the Origin and Development of Music, Songs, Instruments, Dances, and Pantomimes of Savage Races.* London: Longmans, Green, 1893.

Wallin, Nils L. *Biomusicology: Neurophysiological, Neuropsychological, and Evolutionary Perspectives on the Origins and Purposes of Music*. Stuyvesant, NY: Pendragon, 1991.

Wallin, Nils L., Björn Merker, and Steven Brown, eds. *The Origins of Music*. Cambridge, MA: MIT Press, 2000.

Walsh, P. G., ed. and trans. *Love Lyrics from the Carmina Burana*. Chapel Hill: University of North Carolina Press, 1993.

Wang, C. H. *The Bell and the Drum: Shih Ching as Formulaic Poetry in an Oral Tradition*. Berkeley: University of California Press, 1974.

Watt, Ian. *The Rise of the Novel: Studies in Defoe, Richardson and Fielding*. Berkeley: University of California Press, 1962.

Watt, Tessa. *Cheap Print and Popular Piety, 1550–1640*. Cambridge: Cambridge University Press, 1991.

Watt, W. Montgomery. *The Influence of Islam on Medieval Europe*. Edinburgh: Edinburgh University Press, 1972.

Weinstein, Roni. *Marriage Rituals Italian Style: A Historical Anthropological Perspective on Early Modern Italian Jews*. Leiden: Brill, 2004.

Weiss, Piero. *Opera: A History in Documents*. New York: Oxford University Press, 2002.

Weiss, Piero, and Richard Taruskin, eds. *Music in the Western World: A History in Documents*. 2nd edition. Belmont, CA: Thompson-Schirmer, 2007.

West, Martin L. *Studies in Greek Elegy and Iambus*. Berlin: Walter de Gruyter, 1974.

Whicher, George F. *The Goliard Poets: Medieval Latin Songs and Satires*. New York: New Directions, 1965.

Wickler, Wolfgang. "Duetting Songs in Birds: Biological Significance of Stationary and Non-stationary Processes." *Journal of Theoretical Biology* 60, no. 2 (1976): 493–97.

Wilkins, Nigel. *Music in the Age of Chaucer*. Woodbridge, Suffolk, UK: D. S. Brewer, 1999.

Williams, Craig A. *Roman Homosexuality*. 2nd edition. New York: Oxford University Press, 2010.

Williams, Leonard. *The Dancing Chimpanzee: A Study of the Origins of Primitive Music*. London: Allison & Busby, 1980.

Wilson, Edward O. *Sociobiology: The New Synthesis*. Cambridge, MA: Belknap Press, 1975.

Wong, Siu-Kit, and Kar Shui Lee. "Poems of Depravity: A Twelfth Century Dispute on the Moral Character of 'Book of Songs.'" *T'oung Pao* 75, no. 4–5 (1989): 209–25.

Yalom, Marilyn. *How the French Invented Love*. New York: Harper Perennial, 2012.

Yasushi, Ōki, and Paolo Santangelo. *Shan'ge, the "Mountain Songs": Love Songs in Ming China*. Leiden: Brill, 2011.

Zwartjes, Otto. *Love Songs from Al-Andalus: History, Structure and Meaning of the Kharja*. Leiden: Brill, 1997.

INDEX